Pushing Past the Human
in Latin American Cinema

SUNY series in Latin American Cinema
―――――――
Ignacio M. Sánchez Prado and Leslie L. Marsh, editors

Pushing Past the Human
in Latin American Cinema

Edited by
CAROLYN FORNOFF AND GISELA HEFFES

Cover image: Still from Bendito Machine V, "Pull the Trigger," created by Jossie Malis. Reprinted with permission.

Published by State University of New York Press, Albany

© 2021 State University of New York

All rights reserved

Printed in the United States of America

No part of this book may be used or reproduced in any manner whatsoever without written permission. No part of this book may be stored in a retrieval system or transmitted in any form or by any means including electronic, electrostatic, magnetic tape, mechanical, photocopying, recording, or otherwise without the prior permission in writing of the publisher.

For information, contact State University of New York Press, Albany, NY
www.sunypress.edu

Library of Congress Cataloging-in-Publication Data

Names: Fornoff, Carolyn, editor. | Heffes, Gisela, 1971– editor.
Title: Pushing past the human in Latin American cinema / edited by Carolyn Fornoff and Gisela Heffes.
Description: Albany : State University of New York Press, 2021. | Series: SUNY series in Latin American cinema | Includes bibliographical references and index.
Identifiers: LCCN 2020058285 | ISBN 9781438484037 (hardcover : alk. paper) | ISBN 9781438484044 (pbk. : alk. paper) | ISBN 9781438484051 (ebook)
Subjects: LCSH: Motion pictures—Latin America—History and criticism. | Climatic changes in motion pictures. | Ecology in motion pictures.
Classification: LCC PN1993.5.L3 P87 2021 | DDC 791.43098—dc23
LC record available at https://lccn.loc.gov/2020058285

10 9 8 7 6 5 4 3 2 1

Dedicated to our families, our friends, and the worlds that sustain us.

Contents

List of Illustrations ... xi

Acknowledgments ... xiii

Introduction: Latin American Cinema Beyond the Human ... 1
Carolyn Fornoff and Gisela Heffes

GENRE BEYOND THE HUMAN

1. Movies on the Move: Filming the Amazon Rainforest ... 25
   Patrícia Vieira

2. Visualizing the Geosphere: The 1985 Earthquake in Mexican Cinema ... 47
   Carolyn Fornoff

3. Revisiting Nature and Documenting the Americas: From Alexander von Humboldt to the Contemporary Latin American Documentary ... 69
   Juana New

4. Slow Violence in the Slow Cinema of Lisandro Alonso ... 89
   Amanda Eaton McMenamin

ENCOUNTERING DIFFERENCE

5. Humanimal Assemblages: Slaughters in Latin American Left-Wing Cinema   111
   Moira Fradinger

6. Reordering Material Hierarchies in Jossie Malis Álvarez's Animated Series, *Bendito Machine*   139
   Katherine Bundy

7. Mapping Queer Natures in Papu Curotto's *Esteros*   161
   Vinodh Venkatesh

8. Counterflows: Hydraulic Order and Residual Ecologies in Caribbean Fantasy Landscapes   181
   Lisa Blackmore

9. Differential Viscosities: The Material Hermeneutics of Blood, Oil, and Water in *Crude* and *The Blood of Kouan Kouan*   205
   Mark Anderson

SCREENING THE PLURIVERSE

10. Human Rights at the End of the World: Patricio Guzmán and the "Imperative to Reimagine the Planet"   231
    Fernando J. Rosenberg

11. Sea Turtles and Seascapes: Representing Human-Nature Relations in the Central American Caribbean   255
    Mauricio Espinoza and Tomás Emilio Arce

12. Refracting Lenses on the Atlantic Coast of Nicaragua: Documenting Social Ecologies and Biospheres in *El ojo del tiburón* and *El canto de Bosawas*   281
    Julia M. Medina

13. The Sacred Space of Motoapohua: Intercorporeal Animality and National Subjectivities in Nicolás Echevarría's *Eco de la montaña*   305
    Iván Eusebio Aguirre Darancou

14. Undisciplined Knowledge: Indigenous Activism and Decapitation Resistance   327
    Gisela Heffes

Contributors   345

Index   349

Illustrations

Figure 3.1	Selk'nam man with ritual body paint, photographed by Martin Gusinde in the Catholic mission of Dawson Island (1918–1924). Patricio Guzmán, *El botón de nácar*, 2015, video still.	82
Figures 5.1 and 5.2	Sergei Eisenstein, *Strike*, 1924, USSR, video still.	119
Figure 5.3	Margot Benacerraf, *Araya*, 1959, Venezuela, video still.	123
Figures 5.4 and 5.5	Glauber Rocha, *Deus e o diabo na terra do sol*, 1964, Brazil, video still.	125
Figures 5.6 and 5.7	Fernando Solanas and Gustavo Getino, *La hora de los hornos*, 1968, Argentina, video still.	129
Figure 6.1	Jossie Malis Álvarez, *Bendito Machine*, "Obey His Commands," 2009, video still.	148
Figure 6.2	Jossie Malis Álvarez, *Bendito Machine*, "Fuel the Machines," 2012, video still.	151
Figure 6.3	Jossie Malis Álvarez, *Bendito Machine*, "Pull the Trigger," 2014, video still.	155
Figure 7.1	Haptic visuality and the aesthetics of New Maricón Cinema. Papu Curotto, *Esteros*, 2016, video still.	165
Figure 7.2	The geography of the natural in the title sequence. Papu Curotto, *Esteros*, 2016, video still.	167
Figure 7.3	Interstices of the aquatic and the erotic. Papu Curotto, *Esteros*, 2016, video still.	175

Figure 8.1	Johanné Gómez Terrero, *Caribbean Fantasy: Una historia del amor en el Río Ozama*, 2016, video still.	194
Figure 11.1	Esteban Ramírez, *Caribe*, 2004, video still.	264
Figure 11.2	Dania Torres, *Lih Wina*, 2012, video still.	267
Figure 12.1	Alejo Hoijman, *El ojo del tiburón*, 2012, video still.	286
Figure 12.2	"But here we do not want more harassment. We are not going to leave this place." Nirio Simion, chief of the Mayangna Sauni As territory. Brad Allgood and Camilo de Castro, *El canto de Bosawas*, 2014, video still.	296
Figure 13.1	The final shot reveals Santos de la Torre's mural in its totality. Nicolás Echevarría, *Eco de la montaña*, 2014, video still.	313
Figure 13.2	Close-up of Santos de la Torre's mural: humanimal and vegetal intersubjectivities. Nicolás Echevarría, *Eco de la montaña*, 2014, video still.	315
Figure 14.1	Close-up of a police officer during the repression of local villagers and activists. Stephanie Boyd, *Operación diablo*, 2010, video still.	333
Figure 14.2	Police ready themselves to violently repress protestors. Danielle Bernstein and Anne Slick, *When Clouds Clear*, 2008, video still.	333

Acknowledgments

The idea for this volume began with a panel on Contemporary Latin American Cinema Beyond the Human at the 2017 Society for Cinema and Media Studies Conference in Chicago. There, we came together with Iván Aguirre and Jorge Marcone to discuss the unprecedented boom in ecologically oriented films occurring throughout Latin America. We wanted to better understand what this greening meant for Latin American film studies, as well as what Latin American approaches to environmental issues brought to broader theories of ecocriticism. We are grateful to the panelists and conference attendees for the vibrant conversation that took place in that room four years ago, which provided us with the necessary push to bring this project to fruition. It has been a pleasure working and thinking with our contributors about Latin American cinema's engagement with the human and more-than-human world.

We are thankful to the University of Illinois at Urbana-Champaign and to Rice University for their generous patronage of this work. Thank you as well to Jossie Malis Álvarez for allowing us to reprint his striking work from *Bendito Machine* on the cover. Thank you to Andrew Ascherl for meticulously indexing this book. An earlier version of Lisa Blackmore's chapter was previously published in Spanish in *Revista Iberoamericana*.

Finally, we would like to extend a heartfelt thanks to the editorial team at SUNY. Our project was shepherded through the publication process by Rebecca Colesworthy, editor extraordinaire. James Peltz kindly stepped in to support us during Rebecca's maternity leave. Eileen Nizer guided us through production. The two anonymous external readers helped us identify the volume's blind spots and solidify its argument. We are grateful to Ignacio M. Sánchez Prado and Leslie L. Marsh for including this volume in their vibrant series on Latin American Cinema.

Introduction

Latin American Cinema Beyond the Human

CAROLYN FORNOFF AND GISELA HEFFES

After years of visiting zoos in Mexico City, Caracas, and New York—strolling and sketching animals, gathering ideas for poems—in 1938, the Mexican writer José Juan Tablada declared that zoos were, in fact, hellish. Contrary to expectation, he wrote in a *crónica* published in *Excélsior*, little could be learned from seeing animals in captivity because the "diabolical torment of claustrophobia" rendered them unnaturally sluggish.[1] If his readers actually wanted to learn about animals, Tablada suggested, they should watch the films by Martin and Osa Johnson, which "reveal the secrets of the jungle."[2] Naturalist explorers and documentary filmmakers from Kansas, the Johnsons pioneered the nature film genre with films like *Congorilla* (1932) and *Baboona* (1935). The first to film Mt. Kilimanjaro and Mt. Kenya by air, they inaugurated the now-iconic aerial shots of herds traversing the African plains. Their adventure-documentaries simulated the face-to-face encounter with wild animals and interpreted the behavior shown on-screen.[3]

Taken with these moving images, Tablada concluded that cinema was a better pedagogical tool than the zoo. Unlike the zoo, "a color and sound film," he wrote, "captures the marvelous colors of hides and plumages, the savage and mysterious polyphony of the virgin jungle."[4] Tablada proposed that film was the optimal medium, ethically and aesthetically, for experiencing nonhuman wildlife—better than seeing it in the flesh. Cinema was less interventionist; the camera observed without disrupting. The cinematic experience of the nonhuman, he wrote, had become all the more "accurate" because of advances in color and sound technologies, diminishing the incentive to see it firsthand. In turn, the close-up provided a more intimate encounter than that contrived by the zoo.

What Tablada did not note was that the seemingly organic encounters filmed by the Johnsons were in many cases simulated. The Johnsons of course did disrupt wildlife during filming—often provoking animals to charge directly at the camera to heighten the experience for viewers back home. Additionally, their turn to the nature genre was steeped in racialized dynamics. Their earlier work focused on the ethnographic study of the "savage" peoples of Africa and the Southwest Pacific, as captured in silent films like *Cannibals of the South Seas* (1918) and *Head Hunters of the South Seas* (1922).[5] Upon realizing that the public was more eager to see difference across, rather than within, species, the Johnsons shifted focus to animals.[6] Put simply, the nature documentary's ostensible objectivity and ethical virtue occluded its participation in uneven global dynamics and its perpetuation of the myth of unmediated wilderness.

Nearly one hundred years after Tablada wrote his defense of cinema's ability to unveil the secrets of the nonhuman, film continues to be a privileged medium through which to gain awareness of nature. Cinema provides access—a means of entry—to locations, scales, and temporalities that exceed the singular human perspective. Techniques like time-lapse photography and underwater videography stretch anthropocentric experiences of the world. Such strategies provide glimpses of alternative timescales that govern creaturely life; timescales that are shorter or longer than processes of human history, or cyclical and aimless rather than linear.

As a medium that mediates our perception of environmental space, cinema has also propagated essentializing and comforting fictions about the nonhuman world. Principal among them is its figuration of the environment as a reliably unchanging setting, an aesthetically pleasing and self-regulating backdrop against which human action unfolds. Flora, fauna, and landscape have been indispensable cinematic props that give texture to character, mood, and narrative. Likewise, as the Johnsons' transition to animal subjects suggests, the fascination with nonhuman difference has often coincided with a racialized fetishization of human difference, leading to the troubling collapse of aboriginal peoples within the paradigm of local color, as was the case in early Latin American ethnographic film.[7]

Since the mid-1990s, scholars have begun to examine how film negotiates our understanding of the nonhuman through approaches that range from ecocriticism to posthumanism. While it is tempting to frame these conversations as proper to the present, the question of nonhuman representation has long occupied thinkers in Latin America and around the globe. Nonetheless, it is only of late that scholars of Latin American cinema have started to seriously account for the ways in which Latin American films imagine the more-than-human. In an era in which human practices are recognizably inflicting permanent ecological consequences, the task of making these effects visible feels all the more urgent. Coincident with this need to highlight human impact is the seemingly opposing impulse to destabilize cinema's anthropocentric thrust. A difficult undertaking, because cinema is, after all, the human creation of a world on-screen, and yet its materialization and materiality are embedded in the extraction of natural resources, and extractive capital is its condition of possibility. Furthermore, because it emerges from the "estrangement and denaturalization" of hegemonic print environment, many cinematic projects are critical about the materiality of their objects and methods as well.[8] Bearing this in mind, is it possible for cinema to detach itself from its anthropocentric origins and its anthropogenic effects? Is it tenable to disassemble the human subject from its filmic protagonism? How can it account for or speak for the more-than-human while simultaneously addressing human concerns?

Pushing Past the Human in Latin American Cinema brings together fourteen scholars who wrestle with how Latin American cinema attempts to push beyond the human. Some question the very nature of this enterprise—whether cinema should or even could actualize such a maneuver. Others signal the ways in which the category of the "human" itself is interrogated by Latin American cinema, revealed to be a fiction that excludes more than it unifies. The aim of this volume is not to simply reflect upon the response of Latin American cinema to environmental degradation—although some chapters do—but also to interrogate how the moving image reinforces or questions the division between human and nonhuman, and the settler epistemic partition of culture and nature that is at the core of the climate crisis. As the first volume to specifically address how such questions are staged by Latin American cinema, this book brings together analysis of films that respond to environmental catastrophe, as well as those that articulate a posthumanist ethos that blurs the line between species without extracting nature from its material and historical instantiations.[9] By including chapters on the representation of animals and natural phenomena alongside those invested in the toll of environmental destruction on vulnerable communities, we echo the expansive range of nonhuman imaginaries staged by Latin American cinema.

Although it is dedicated to the intersection of Latin American cinema and ecocritical, materialist, and posthumanist approaches, this book does not aim to be comprehensive, but to foster dialogue among scholars invested in the nascent study of Latin American cinema beyond the human. Building upon the ever-growing corpus of Latin American ecocritical research, this book adds to and diverges from existing scholarship by narrowing the focus to Latin American cinema. In doing so, we advance a medium-specific argument that cinema is uniquely able to trouble anthropocentric accounts of the world through form, technique, and genre. Furthermore, we posit that the fusion of film studies and ecocriticism proffers the ideal lens through which to examine different ways of representing reality, as well as the processes of signification through which reality can be rethought and transformed. We see this work as an initial step that will forge greater connective pathways between scholars of Latin American ecocriticism and of film, as well as among scholars interested in Global South accounts of environmental collapse.

The Anthropocene and Latin America

As a species, humans have become "a major environmental force."[10] Human energy use, fossil fuel emissions, and extractive activities have changed the makeup of the lithosphere. The term Anthropocene, coined by biologist Eugene Stoermer and atmospheric chemist Paul Crutzen, describes the current geological epoch shaped by human activity. The term is also invoked in reference to the planetary consequences of human activity, like climate change and the sixth extinction. It serves as a framework for critiquing the human role in the ongoing degradation of the Earth, which has been put in motion by new forms of colonialism and extractive imperialism, as James Petras and Henry Veltmeyer have rightly demonstrated, a pursuit for accumulation that has paradoxically put human longevity into jeopardy.[11]

The framework of the Anthropocene has been rigorously and justifiably critiqued by many. The undetermined prefix *anthropo* suggests that this crisis has been collectively engendered by all humans—regardless of race, gender, class, or location—without accounting for the highly uneven way in which different groups have contributed to, or are affected by, these changes. The invocation of "a phantasmic figure called "human,"" Neel Ahuja observes, replicates the colonial erasure of Indigenous peoples, this time by equating the entire species with "settler ways of life" that lead to planetary destruction.[12]

Others have suggested that the term naturalizes the fatalist idea that human practices inevitably lead down this path. Instead, critics suggest, it is the pursuit of capital gains, dominance, and development, ideologies structural to colonialism and capitalism that have brought us here. For this reason, Jason Moore prefers the term "Capitalocene" to situate environmental harm as the result of capitalist reliance on cheap nature.[13] Alternatively, Nicholas Mirzoeff suggests the "White Supremacy Scene" as a substitute that underscores the crisis's origin in racist practices like colonialism and slavery.[14] The link between colonialism and the Anthropcene has been accentuated by scientific documentation of the Orbis spike. The spike, which dates back to 1610, records a sharp drop in atmospheric carbon dioxide caused by the mass extermination of Amerindian peoples after the arrival of Europeans to the Americas. The climactic effects of this genocide, and the resulting decline in farming and regrowth of forests, is visible in Antarctic ice core records.[15] This geological record of European brutality echoes Aimé Cesaire's memorable equation, "colonization = thingification," the violent objectification of human and nonhuman bodies.[16] In contemporary resource extraction, this legacy of colonial land use has been thought about through the rubric of the Plantationocene. This term accounts, as Donna Haraway claims, for the devastating transformation of different kinds of "human-tended farms, pastures, and forests into extractive and enclosed plantations, relying on slave labor and other forms of exploited, alienated, and usually spatially transported labor."[17]

The task is a tricky one. It requires that we think about the entwined history of the species and the planet at the same time that we do not abandon critical theories of race, gender, sexuality, colonialism, imperialism, and so on—the analytical tools that have vigilantly identified the mechanisms of power that have enabled the systematic exploitation of life. As a field of critical inquiry, Latin American cultural studies has by-and-large obviated this elision. Ecocritical and posthumanist approaches to Latin American culture acknowledge the centrality of coloniality, imperialism, and capitalism to the perpetuation of a singular, linear, utilitarian approach to nature. They recognize that the contemporary crisis is the result of entrenched ways of being, a civilizational paradigm rooted in violent histories of colonization, patriarchy, and capitalist development. This "civilizational crisis," as Mexican environmental sociologist Enrique Leff described it in *Ecología y capital* in 1986, puts into doubt dominant epistemological paradigms.[18] It requires new methodologies that integrate human and ecological relations, a "new episteme" that combines "novel paradigms of criticism" with new strategies for survival.[19] As cultural scholars, we might add that these urgent questions necessitate new modes of narrating and visualizing: modes that help viewers stretch beyond themselves—beyond the partial human perspective—and toward other forms of life, human and more-than-human alike.

We agree with Arturo Escobar that the only solution to such structural ills is blanket change, and not just a departure from capitalism. It requires the utter transformation of "an entire way of life and a whole style of worldmaking."[20] This desire for total change—the revamping of ontologies, epistemologies, and praxis—has turned the attention of scholars and artists to groups that have long been marginalized from mainstream modes of thought and practice. The turn to Indigenous and Afro-descendent cosmologies is in part an effort to trouble the hegemony of Western thought, whose universalization, Walter Mignolo argues, "was part of its imperial project."[21] The drive to document different cosmologies reframes the world not as a unified totality, but as a pluriverse, a world that contains many worlds—"where many worlds might fit," as the Zapatistas put it in the *Cuarta Declaración de la Selva Lacandona*.[22] For many Latin American filmmakers, the commitment to place is equivalent to the valuation of other ways of being grounded in relation to those spaces. Indeed, many of the chapters included in this volume signal the inextricability of environmental preoccupation with that of the human cultures that inhabit those endangered spaces, themselves at risk.

Brazilian anthropologists Déborah Danowski and Eduardo Viveiros de Castro argue in *The Ends of the World* that as we contemplate the decisive catastrophe of climate change, which will effectively end the world as we know it, we should seek guidance from Indigenous peoples. Amerindian groups that survived colonialization effectively experienced the end of the world, but nonetheless persisted, and "carried on in another world."[23] Through documentary and fiction, Latin American filmmakers see in Indigenous cosmologies the possibility to reimagine the human, or, at the very least, to bring to Western publics an awareness of different ways of living in the world, and how the world we have created reflects our practices of being.

Renewed attention to Indigenous cosmovisions requires navigating stereotypes that have long dogged these groups. This includes the ghost of the good savage, or what Marisol de la Cadena identifies as the temptation to represent aboriginal groups as homogenous or innately good.[24] The depiction of Indigenous groups in harmony with nature and in diametric opposition to capitalism—rather than actively negotiating with ongoing processes of extraction, ecotourism, and development—can reinforce the nostalgic image of Indigenous peoples trapped in a precapitalist past. Several contributors explore films that focus on characters that are both complicit with and victimized by extractive economies, including Lisandro Alonso's *La libertad* (*Freedom*) and coastal Central American documentaries, *El ojo del tiburón* (*The Shark's Eye*, Alejo Hoijman) and *Lih Wina* (Dania Torres).

The chapters of this volume are indebted to the burgeoning field of ecocritism (attention to the nonhuman environment), new materialism (the agency of matter), and posthumanism (the deconstruction of human exemplarity) in Latin American cultural studies. The scholars who have laid the groundwork for the field include Jens Andermann, Mark Anderson, Laura Barbas-Rhoden, Jennifer French, Roberto Forns-Broggi, Gisela Heffes, Jorge Marcone, and Lúcia Sá.[25] In conceptualizing this volume, we decided not to compartmentalize these methodologies, but rather to allow their resonances to commingle. In other words, we are not interested in parsing the distinctions between these approaches (or between terms such as environment, nature, and nonhuman), but in fostering dialogue between film scholars circling around similar concerns. Together the contributors signal different modes of entry by which Latin American cinema produces and negotiates our understanding of human and nonhuman life, destabilizes (Western) human-centered ontologies, or transgresses the usual subject/object binary.

Cinema of Nature, the Nature of Cinema

We have produced our environment; there is no nature outside of the human. The desire to mold the world as we see fit is mirrored by many modes of aesthetic practice. The human aspiration to manipulate life, create artificial worlds, and simulate the weather is particularly evident in cinema. Cinema is a cultural practice of world-production that Adrian Ivakhiv terms "cosmomorphic" because it "makes, or takes the shape of, a world, a cosmos of subjects and objects, actors and situations, figures moving and the grounds they move upon."[26] Film is a medium through which humans can act out the fantasy of exerting control over time and space by physically reproducing the world and reenacting the weather. In this way, Jennifer Fay proposes, cinema can be considered "the aesthetic practice of the Anthropocene," or at the very least, a technology that "helps us to see and experience the Anthropocene as an aesthetic practice."[27]

Although cinema is the human mediation of worlds on-screen, it is also innately material. Itself a product of the human manipulation of the environment, filmmaking relies on organic materials farmed from the earth.

More so than any other cultural art form (like the book or photograph), the production, distribution, and reception of cinema requires a large amount of energy and generates copious electronic waste.[28] The recent move to the digitization of film and streaming platforms might appear to be less tangibly reliant on matter, but it too engages loops of extraction, energy, and discard.[29]

In Latin America, the fate of the film industry has risen and fallen alongside that of extractive economies. For instance, historians of Venezuelan cinema note that the birth of the nation's film industry coincided with an oil boom in the mid-seventies, which enabled President Carlos Andrés Pérez to pass legislation that promoted state funding of feature films.[30] Oil is not only a theme in Venezuelan cinema, but also structural to its vigor and decadence.[31] Thinking about cinema through a new materialist lens encourages us to attend to on-screen representations of the nonhuman, but also to acknowledge that media itself is material and begins with the geophysical.[32] As Anat Pick and Guinevere Narraway observe, this revelation means that the environment underlies "every aspect of the study and understanding of film."[33]

So, for a medium that is produced by and for humans, can there be a cinema "beyond the human"? Cinema is an anthropocentric exercise and an anthropogenic activity; its narratives largely center human protagonists who ground the emotional and narrative stakes. Even when the camera gaze adopts a nonhuman "view from nowhere," or a disembodied and objective perspective, it is important to be skeptical of this "god trick of seeing everything from nowhere," which Haraway warns obscures "the particularity and embodiment of all vision."[34] The seeming objectivity of the technological eye simply shrouds the filmmaker's partial way of seeing. In the same way that it is impossible to ever fully position oneself from the viewpoint of a subjective "other," it is likewise impossible to wholly adopt a more-than-human perspective. This dilemma can lead to a standstill. To counteract this paralysis, it is important to recognize, as the contributors to this book demonstrate, that Latin American cinema has been, and continues to be, a rich space for questioning the seeming universality of the cinematic view, particularly in its heteronormative, male, colonial iteration. The push beyond the universal "human" point of view affirms the value of situated knowledge.

Cinematic visualizations can encourage viewers to see the world otherwise, from perspectives that are diffracted or submerged, rather than from an all-knowing eye. Macarena Gómez-Barris advances the submerged perspective as decolonial methodology in *The Extractive Zone*, writing that it shifts how we sense the world "by reckoning with the thick opacity of what lies below the water's surface."³⁵ As portable cinematic technologies and computer-based editing have become more affordable, submerged perspectives that have been sidelined by dominant visualizations have proliferated. In the twenty-first century, access to filmmaking has become more democratic because of better handheld technologies and decreased costs, especially in documentary filmmaking—a privileged mode of ecocinema.³⁶ Regions and populations that were previously priced out of such practices are now enfolded into global festival networks where demand is high for "diverse" perspectives, funding the boom in Latin American environmental cinema, Central American cinema, and Indigenous documentary filmmaking, to name just a few.

Cinema can also contextualize, narrate, and make visible ongoing ecological transformations that are normally hidden. Representational practices have become increasingly important given that environmental damage unfolds over long, drawn-out timelines, or in locations marginalized from mass media visibility.³⁷ Because humans are ocular-centric creatures, when these crises are out of sight, they are also out of mind. Cinema offers a way to appreciate these alterations. It can narrate and contextualize environmental harm or tell stories that reorient our understanding of the relationship between human and nonhuman. These imaginings can be geared to different effects, as a means of compelling ethical response or simply induce enchantment: a new appreciation of the nonhuman prompted by affective and aesthetic engagement. Cinema can prompt what Jens Andermann calls a state of trance, in which viewers suspend their technocognitive judgment and give in to sensorial pleasure.³⁸

Greening Latin American Cinema

Latin American ecocinema, defined broadly as cinema concerned with environmental issues, has experienced an extraordinary boom since 2010. This boom, of course, is not without precedent. The environment has long been a privileged trope in Latin American cinema, whether out of fascination with the landscape's unique aesthetic possibilities, as in *Limite* (*Limit*, Mário Peixoto, 1931), or as a means of enacting social critique through allegorical images, like that performed in *La hora de los hornos* (*The Hour of the Furnaces*, Fernando Solanas and Octavio Getino, 1968). The medium's enthrallment with environmental phenomena can be traced back even earlier, to the very first silent films, like the actuality *Huracán en las playas de Veracruz*, filmed by

Gabriel Veyre of Societé Lumiere in 1897. *Revista de Mérida* praised Veyre's footage of the hurricane for capturing "the most handsome views" of tempestuous environmental drama.[39] The moving image translated the spectacle of atmospheric disruption to the delight of viewers safely removed from the event. Since its very beginnings, cinema has engaged viewers' ecological fascination by inducing the experience of remote geographies or environmental disturbances, communicating its beauty without the bodily peril.

Fast-forwarding to the twenty-first century, interest in environmentalist topics—writ large, as the entanglement of human life with our surrounding habitat—in cinema exploded, reflecting the widespread acknowledgment of climate change as an alarming reality. As of 2010, this thematization has intensified.[40] This boom can be attributed to the decreased cost of filmmaking, the greening of the zeitgeist, and the explosion of film festivals dedicated to environmental issues. The proliferation of art-house festivals like the San Sebastián Film Festival, Toulouse Latin American Film Festival, and Guadalajara Film Festival provide Latin American filmmakers with platforms to gain international visibility and funding opportunities for script development, editing, and postproduction. On a more specialized level, niche festivals dedicated to environmental issues help Latin American ecocinema circulate and recoup funds. Festivals like the United States' Environmental Film Festival in the Nation's Capital (established in 1993), Spain's International Environmental Film Festival (FICMA, since 1993), and Portugal's Cine Eco (since 1995) connect environmentally attuned international audiences with Global South filmmakers, revealing the increasingly decentralized and networked nature of activism and cultural consumption in the twenty-first century.

Scholars have signaled that while film festivals are invaluable sources of funding and distribution for Latin American cinema, they also tend to incentivize reductive tropes. Miriam Ross has argued that the "uneven benefactor-beneficiary relationship" between Global North funders and Global South filmmakers perpetuates certain representational norms, namely the foregrounding of the national setting, poverty, and marginalized subgroups.[41] While the films produced with the help of transnational sources are far from homogenous, Ross signals that it is important to recognize that filmmakers participating in these circuits are aware of the international audience's expectations and desire for "authentic" depictions of the developing world.[42] Tamara Falicov has furthered that these unequal transnational collaborations have created a globalized art-house formula that is local in mise-en-scène, but universalizable in theme.[43] All of this is to say that while many of the films analyzed within this volume focus on national or hyperlocal concerns, given current structures of funding, production, and circulation, they are also inevitably interwoven into transnational dynamics that may or may not affect the environmental imaginaries produced by Latin American cinema.

Yet it would be a mistake to assert that these films are not deeply engaged with local publics and national conversations about place-specific futures. The surge in specialized film festivals in Latin America dedicated to environmentalist cinema attests to growing regional demand for these conversations. Green film festivals in Brazil were the earliest on the scene: Festival Internacional de Cinema e Video Ambiental (FICA, since 1999), Festcineamazônia (since 2003), and FILMAMBIENTE International Environmental Film Festival (since 2010). Since 2009, Mexico has hosted the long-standing festival Cinema Planeta (FICMA MX, a spin-off of Spain's FICMA), which is funded jointly by the state and the United Nation's Environment Program. Mexico is also the host since 2011 of the ECOFILM Festival Internacional de Cortometrajes Ambientales, which focuses on short films.

Most Latin American environmental film festivals are not for profit and receive funding from a mix of government sources, arts councils, volunteer labor, and corporate sponsors. They often last a weekend or a week; attendance is inexpensive, as is the cost for submitting a film for consideration. This encourages participation and makes these generative spaces for face-to-face interaction between filmmakers and the public. Other ecofestivals in Latin American include Peru's Festival Sembrando Cine (2009–), Argentina's Festival Internacional de Cine Ambiental (FINCA, 2010–) and Patagonia Eco Film Fest (PEFF, 2016–), Bolivia's Festival Internacional de Cine Verde (2011–), Colombia's Festiver Festival de Cine Verde de Barichara (2011–), Dominican Republic's Muestra de Cine Medioambiental Dominicana (DREFF, 2011–), Venezuela's Festival Internacional de Cine y Video Verde de Venezuela (FESTIVERD, 2013–), and Ecuador's ECOador International Film Festival (2016–). These smaller-scale, regional film festivals generate local communities coalesced around shared concerns.[44] Increased festivalgoer interest in environmental films is perhaps due to the relative absence of these topics in the mainstream media, as issues of environmental degradation are often displaced by more outwardly pressing political concerns.[45]

Low-budget, small-scale Latin American ecofilms often find afterlives online. This is the case for many of the films included in this volume, which are available for international audiences on streaming sites like Netflix, HBO, Kanopy, or platforms like YouTube or Vimeo, where they circulate freely. To give one brief example, after select theater screenings, the low-budget

Guatemalan documentary about genetically modified seeds *Morir sembrando vida* (Matias Quinzio and Marcos Mendivil, 2015) found a robust viewership online on sites such as YouTube, Films for Action, and Cine Vivo. As of this writing in 2020, *Morir sembrando vida* had more than 250,000 views on YouTube, and comments from viewers across the globe, from Colombia to Vietnam, who noted similar varietal losses. These online platforms allow hyperlocalized, low-budget films to find an audience even in the absence of national exhibition infrastructures.

Chapter Outlines

This volume appraises Latin American cinema's depiction of the more-than-human planet. As the fourteen chapters indicate, engagement with the nonhuman in Latin American cinema is manifold and can be read in radically different ways. It is actualized through a multiplicity of strategies that alternatively foreground nonhuman bodies, criticize extractivist development, or document marginalized cosmologies. We have grouped the chapters in three thematic sections, which respectively attend to genre, bodily difference, and indigeneity. As these chapters attest, Latin American cinema frequently resists the imperative to move fully beyond the human, instead dramatizing the inextricability of planetary care and social justice. In productive tension with the volume's title, its chapters warn against losing sight of the human altogether.

The first section, *Genre Beyond the Human*, probes the role of the nonhuman in four distinct film genres. Through the repetition of images and narratives, genre establishes patterns that become recognizable and expected by audiences. It formulates a system of signification and a mode of approaching the world. The genres under consideration here—the road movie, the disaster film, the documentary, and slow cinema—invoke the nonhuman to different ends, giving shape to the cultural and symbolic meanings affixed to the natural world.

In the first chapter, Patrícia Vieira unpacks the centrality of traveling in films that take place in the Amazon. Vieira hypothesizes that because "nature itself is permanently on the move" in Amazonia, the momentum of constant growth, reproduction, and flow finds its mirror image in the traveling bodies of explorers and the moving images of cinema. Accordingly, the visual exploration of Amazonian plants, rivers, and landscapes has adopted the conventions of the road movie. The road movie genre, Vieira argues, is uniquely equipped to render visible the damage wrought by extractivist policies and to give screen time to the region's inhabitants that persist in the face of this violence.

Unlike the road movie's focus on lively ecologies, the natural disaster genre foregrounds the unsettling agency of seemingly exanimate forces, like the atmosphere or the geosphere. Through a reading of the cinematic representations of the 1985 earthquake that devastated Mexico City, Carolyn Fornoff argues that the earthquake is a visual interruption of geological agency and deep time into human history. The natural disaster film is a genre of the Anthropocene in that it dramatizes the collision of human and nonhuman forces, which compound to devastating effect. Fornoff furthers that in spite of generic convention, recent interventions like Jorge Michel Grau's thriller *7:19* (2016) disclose that the natural disaster is not wholly natural, or fully beyond the human.

Turning her attention to the documentary, Juana New traces the origin of the genre in Latin America back to an unlikely source: Alexander von Humboldt. According to New, Humboldt's blend of the sensorial, aesthetic experience of nature with scientific inquiry anticipates contemporary approaches to documentary cinema. Two recent documentaries, *Farmacopea* by Beatriz Santiago Muñoz (2013) and *El botón de nácar* (*The Pearl Button*, 2015) by Patricio Guzmán, particularly resonate with Humboldt's nonrational approach. By foregrounding the sensorial, these films articulate other ways of being in the world that no longer marginalize non-Western cosmologies and representational modes.

In the section's final chapter, Amanda McMenamin draws parallels between the genre of slow cinema and the representational dilemma of environmental slow violence. In her analysis of Lisandro Alonso's *La libertad* (2001), McMenamin writes that long, observational takes materialize the drawn-out temporalities of gradual, often invisible environmental attrition. The contemplative praxis of slow cinema compels the audience to experience the time that it takes a tree to be felled and to witness the reduction of a vegetal life to an object. Alonso's experimentation with camera angles and extended takes, McMenamin posits, prompts viewers to reflect upon the pace of deforestation and the exploitation of human labor.

The second section of the volume, *Encountering Difference*, brings together chapters that stage cinematic encounters with the nonhuman. The forms of difference engaged in this section are disparate, including animals, technologies, and bodies of water. Collectively, these imaginings foreground Latin America as a multispecies habitat where human and nonhuman (including discarded objects) jumble together. These encounters are performed through modes that range from the archival capture of the documentary to the speculative animacy of animated film. Cinematic encounters with the nonhuman can be used to different ends—as pedagogy, allegory, or sensual texture—to heighten a film's political or aesthetic interpretation of the human experience.

Moira Fradinger discusses the long-standing use of the nonhuman animal body as a prop in Latin American left-wing cinema. Fradinger argues that the contiguity between victimized nonhuman and human bodies allegorizes the violence of capitalist exploitation. On-screen animal slaughter stands in for violence against humans, blurring the distinction between species. Yet at the same time, this "pedagogy of slaughter" reinforces humanist narratives that confirm the dignity of human life and the disposability of nonhuman animals. One line of flight from this anthropocentric paradigm, Fradinger suggests, is the close-up of the bloodied eye, which becomes deterritorialized from any one species.

The life-giving aesthetics of animation, Katherine Bundy argues, is another sort of pedagogy: one that teaches viewers to perceive the nonhuman anew. Through animation, seemingly inert, inorganic objects like technology and trash can be imbued with agency, movement, and emotion. Bundy describes how the animated short series *Bendito Machine* (2006–2017) by Peruvian-Chilean animator Jossie Malis Álvarez deploys animation to critique extraction and accumulation. The series, with its chorus of animated subjects, furthers a nonhierarchical—albeit nonsymmetrical—redistribution of agency among human, nonhuman, and posthuman subjects.

Vinodh Venkatesh describes how Papu Curotto's film *Esteros* (2016) fleshes out queer desire through the erotics of the rural landscape. *Esteros*'s privileging of the natural, rural setting, Venkatesh explains, reflects the trend away from urban spaces in contemporary Argentine cinema. Instead, desire is linked with the rural landscape, an association that is crystallized through haptic, tactile images of water. Through the positioning of the camera and the sonic evocation of the aqueous, *Esteros* dwells in queer bodily pleasures, enmeshing ethics and erotics.

Cinematic techniques can also be used to obscure difference and perpetuate a selective view of place. Lisa Blackmore explains that recent visualizations of the Dominican Republic have done just that by presenting the island as a tourist Caribbean fantasy. This fantasy is sustained by tricks of montage that cut out undesired images that do not align with the island's brand, like poverty, trash, and pollution. In contrast with the capitalist "hydraulic order," Blackmore is interested in films that detect its counterflows: the residual and contaminated spaces that are typically excluded from national marketing. The documentary *Caribbean Fantasy* (Johanné Gómez Terrero, 2016) opens a portal to one such counterflow. It redirects viewers away from the Dominican Republic's endless beaches and toward the contaminated River Ozama and the locals who reside along its banks.

Continuing with the idea of flow, Mark Anderson probes how viscosity and toxicity are represented in two documentaries that record oil spills in the Ecuadorian Amazon: *Crude: The Real Price of Oil* (Joe Berlinger, 2009) and *The Blood of Kouan Kouan* (Yorgos Avgeropolous, 2009). In their accounts of the "material logic of toxicity," these films underscore the porosity of human and nonhuman bodies, challenging ideas of bodily integrity vis-à-vis the environment. Anderson posits that film breaks down the myth of self-containment by affectively transmitting to the viewer the bodily sensation of toxicity, thus "leading to a form of ethical engagement that arises from the materiality of encounter rather than any ideological predisposition."

The final section, *Screening the Pluriverse*, brings together chapters that signal the inextricability of environmental and social justice. The consequences of environmental harm are unevenly distributed and disproportionately affect those already in a vulnerable social position. The cinematic impulse to document previously marginalized cosmologies troubles the supposed universality of Western humanism as well as the simplistic notion that an ahistorical, universal human is behind climate change. By tracing other ontologies and epistemologies, the films analyzed in this section seek to reframe the world not as a unified totality, but as a pluriverse, a world that contains many worlds.

While the compounding precarization of specific human communities due to environmental degradation might seem to suggest the renewed importance of human rights, Fernando J. Rosenberg delineates the limitations of this discourse. Rosenberg argues that Patricio Guzmán's documentaries *Nostalgia de la luz* (*Nostalgia for the Light*, 2010) and *El botón de nácar* (*The Pearl Button*, 2015) evidence the Chilean director's shift beyond the anthropocentric, nationalist discourse of human rights. These documentaries map new ways of thinking about the value of life after human rights by interweaving intimate human histories with exceedingly vast nonhuman life spans. Focalizing the spaces of the desert and the ocean, Guzmán takes viewers to the threshold where life and death intermingle in an effort to reimagine a planetary ethics of care.

Echoing Blackmore's critique of the tourist fantasy of idealized landscapes, Mauricio Espinoza and Tomás Emilio Arce discuss the representational imagery that characterizes the Central American Caribbean coast. Dominant, picture-perfect depictions of the region visualize it as an exotic, multicultural, and ecological paradise. The slickly produced Costa Rican feature *Caribe* (Esteban Ramírez, 2004) sells one such idyll to transnational viewers, sanitizing the region's socioeconomic realities. By contrast, the Nicaraguan documentary short *Lih Wina* (Dania Torres, 2012) questions the tensions that arise between top-down conservationist policies and local traditions, such as the customary consumption of turtle meat. Espinoza and Arce warn that concepts such as "fragility" and "endangerment" should not be exclusively applied to nonhuman nature, nor should environmentalist policies be put in place that compound the adversity faced by ethnic communities that have long cohabitated those spaces.

Julia M. Medina also focuses on Nicaragua's Caribbean coast. Through a close reading of two documentaries, *El ojo del tiburón* (Alejo Hoijman, 2012) and *El canto de Bosawas* (Camilo Castro and Brad Allgood, 2014), Medina interrogates their "(neo)imperial gaze," which perpetuates a certain othering of the subjects they document. The former film follows two boys coming of age along the San Juan River who must choose between traditional shark hunting and the drug trade. The latter documentary follows a film crew's efforts to record Mayangana music. The uneven power dynamics between filmmakers and subjects is charged with tension. Nonetheless, Medina argues, it can be read as "a contemporary rendition of testimonial narrative in the form of audiovisual recording" that expresses Mayangana relationship to space.

Similarly concerned with the dynamic of othering perpetuated by documentary film, Iván Eusebio Aguirre Darancou proposes that Mexican director Nicolás Echevarría's documentary *Eco de la montaña* (*Echo of the Mountain*, 2014) centers the Wixáritari peoples without exoticizing them. Aguirre unpacks the presentation of Wixáritari humanimal intersubjectivities, or the notion that the individual exists only in relation to others. Particularly resonant for Aguirre's analysis is a pair of eyes at the center of a mural woven by the film's subject, Santos de la Torre. The documentary resists overt explanation of Wixáritari cosmology and instead urges viewers to decipher, gaze at, and be gazed at by the mural. Aguirre argues that the mural's protagonism evidences Echevarría's political goal: the recognition of Wixáritari subjectivity as part of the national body.

In the final chapter, Gisela Heffes examines the role of activist documentaries in contesting extractivist policies in South America. The three films analyzed by Heffes—*Cielo abierto* (Carlos Ruiz, 2007), *When Clouds Clear* (Danielle Bernstein and Anne Slick, 2008), and *Operación diablo*

(Stephanie Boyd, 2010)—trace different case studies of mining. Together they articulate what Heffes terms "decapitation resistance," a political and aesthetic strategy that gathers alternative forms of knowledge to dispute the official rhetoric and homogenizing epistemological claims of modern extractive projects. The "undisciplined knowledge" of decapitation resistance recuperates threatened landscapes through collective action motored by hybrid modes of world making. These documentaries mobilize decapitation as a threat not only to the landscape, but also to the health and livelihoods of local populations.

As the first book-length work to seriously account for the representation of the nonhuman in Latin American cinema, the chapters in this volume collectively consider how filmmaking can operate as a generative posthumanist or environmentalist practice that imagines alternative ways of sensing the world while at the same time examining the cinematic mechanisms that allow for this to happen visually and materially. The corpus considered in these chapters covers different national contexts and genres to give readers a sense of how these questions play out across different frameworks. While the majority of the chapters are concerned with contemporary production, we also include chapters that analyze films from the twentieth century to combat the sense that these issues are new. Although filmmaking is an inherently human practice, meant for human consumption, the works considered here renew our perception of difference, both external and internal to the humans who make and consume them. Latin American cinema that pushes past the human activates our capacity to see beyond the human-nonhuman divide. These chapters mark the first incursion into this area of inquiry. Much remains to be done.

Notes

1. José Juan Tablada, "El infierno zoológico," in *Una antología general* (México: Fondo de Cultura Económica, 2007), 393. All translations are our own.
2. Tablada, "El infierno zoológico," 393.
3. Kelly Enright, *The Maximum of Wilderness: The Jungle in the American Imagination* (Charlottesville: University of Virginia Press, 2012).
4. Tablada, "El infierno zoológico," 394.
5. Lamont Lindstrom, "Shooting Melanesians: Martin Johnson and Edward Salisbury in the Southwest Pacific," *Visual Anthropology* 29, no. 4/5 (2016): 360–81.
6. Kelly Enright, *Osa and Martin: For the Love of Adventure* (Guilford: Lyons, 2011), 64.

7. See Christian Leon's discussion of Swedish filmmaker Rolf Blomberg's ethnographic documentaries in Ecuador. Christian León, *Reinventando al otro. El documental indigenista en el Ecuador* (Quito: La Caracola, 2010).

8. See Michael Ziser's discussion on how "ecological media" defies "traditional single-medium environmental disciplines." "Ecomedia," in *Keywords for Environmental Studies*, ed. Joni Adamson et al. (New York: New York University Press, 2016), 75–76.

9. Allison Carruth, "Ecological Media Studies and the Matter of Digital Technologies." *PMLA* 131, no. 2 (2016): 364–72.

10. Paul J. Crutzen, "Geology of Mankind," *Nature* 415 (2002): 23.

11. James Petras and Henry Veltmeyer, "Agro-Extractivism: The Agrarian Question of the 21st Century," in *Extractive Imperialism in the Americas* (Leiden: Brill, 2014): 62–100.

12. Neel Ahuja, "Posthuman New York: Ground Zero of the Anthropocene," in *Animalities: Literary and Cultural Studies Beyond the Human*, ed. Michael Lundblad (Edinburgh: Edinburgh University Press, 2017), 49.

13. Jason Moore, *Capitalism in the Web of Life: Ecology and the Accumulation of Capital* (New York: Verso, 2015).

14. Nicholas Mirzoeff, "It's Not the Anthropocene, It's the White Supremacy Scene," in *After Extinction*, ed. Richard Grusin (Minneapolis: Minnesota University Press, 2018), 123–50.

15. Simon L. Lewis and Mark A. Maslin, "Defining the Anthropocene," *Nature* 519 (2015): 171–80.

16. Aimé Césaire, *Discourse on Colonialism*, trans. Joan Pinkham (New York: Monthly Review Press, 2000), 42.

17. Donna Haraway, "Anthropocene, Capitalocene, Plantationocene, Chthulucene: Making Kin," *Environmental Humanities* 6 (2015), 162.

18. Enrique Leff, *Ecología y capital: racionalidad ambiental, democracia participativa y desarrollo sustentable* (México: Siglo XXI, 2005), 68.

19. Gisela Heffes, *Políticas de la destrucción/poéticas de la preservación: apuntes para una lectura ecocrítica del medio ambiente en América Latina* (Buenos Aires: Beatriz Viterbo, 2013), 24, 27.

20. Arturo Escobar, *Designs for the Pluriverse: Radical Interdependence, Autonomy, and the Making of Worlds* (Durham: Duke University Press, 2018), x.

21. Walter Mignolo, "Foreword: On Pluriversality and Multipolarity," in *Pluriverse: The Geopolitics of Knowledge*, ed. Bernd Reiter (Durham: Duke University Press, 2018), x.

22. EZLN, "Cuarta Declaración de la Selva Lacandona," January 1, 1996.

23. Déborah Danowksi and Eduardo Viveiros de Castro, *The Ends of the World*, trans. Rodrigo Nunes (Cambridge: Polity Press, 2017), 107.

24. Marisol de la Cadena, "Indigenous Cosmopolitics in the Andes: Conceptual Reflections Beyond 'Politics,'" *Cultural Anthropology* 25, no. 2 (2010): 360.

25. Other scholars who have recently widened the scope of the field include Monique Allewaert, Lisa Blackmore, Lucy Bollington, Zelia Bora, Irene Depetris Chauvin, Elizabeth DeLoughrey, Scott DeVries, Liliana Gómez, Macarena Gómez-Barris, Héctor Hoyos, Adrian Taylor Kane, Edward King, Ilka Kressner, Paul Merchant, Ana María Mutis, Joanna Page, Elizabeth Pettinaroli, Rachel Price, Charlotte Rogers, Victoria Saramago, and Macarena Urzúa Opazo, among many others.

26. Adrian J. Ivakhiv, *Ecologies of the Moving Image: Cinema, Affect, Nature* (Waterloo: Wilfrid Laurier University Press, 2013), 6.

27. Jennifer Fay, *Inhospitable World: Cinema in the Time of the Anthropocene* (New York: Oxford Press, 2018), 4.

28. Nadia Bozak, *The Cinematic Footprint: Lights, Camera, Natural Resources* (New Brunswick: Rutgers University Press, 2012).

29. While there are numerous attempts to "green" film productions, it is nonetheless anthropogenic. To mitigate its footprint, film productions should increase the use of LEDS, switch on-set heaters from propane to biodiesel made from reused cooking oil, as well as use 100-percent compostable materials or reusable plates and cutlery instead of plastic. Filmmaking also impacts local environments. It may disturb wildlife and the environment with sound and light pollution.

30. John King, *Magical Reels: A History of Cinema in Latin America* (London: Verso, 1990), 219.

31. For more on oil and Venezuelan cinema, see Rebecca Jarman, "Melodrama at the Margins: Poverty, Politics, and Profits in 'Golden Age' Venezuelan Cinema," *Modern Language Review* 112, no. 3 (2017): 645–65.

32. Jussi Parikka, *A Geology of Media* (Minneapolis: University of Minnesota Press, 2015), 6.

33. Anat Pick and Guinevere Narraway, "Introduction: Intersecting Ecology and Film," in *Screening Nature: Cinema beyond the Human* (New York: Berghahn, 2013), 1–2.

34. Donna Haraway, "Situated Knowledges: The Science Question in Feminism and the Privilege of Partial Perspective," *Feminist Studies* 14, no. 3 (1988): 581.

35. Macarena Gómez-Barris, *The Extractive Zone: Social Ecologies and Decolonial Perspectives* (Durham: Duke University Press, 2017), xiv.

36. María Guadalupe Arenillas and Michael J. Lazzara, "Introduction: Latin American Documentary Film in the New Millennium," in *Latin American Documentary Film in the New Millennium* (New York: Palgrave Macmillan, 2016), 1.

37. Rob Nixon, *Slow Violence and the Environmentalism of the Poor* (Cambridge: Harvard University Press, 2011).

38. Jens Andermann, *Tierras en trance: arte y naturaleza después del paisaje* (Santiago: Metales Pesados, 2018), 25.

39. Juan Felipe Leal, Eduardo Barraza, and Alejandra Jablonska, *Vistas que no se ven: filmografía mexicana, 1896–1910* (Mexico: Universidad Nacional Autónoma de México, 1993), 45.

40. Rocío González de Arce proposes that of the nearly 1,200 Mexican films with identifiably green characteristics (counted expansively: documentary and fiction, shorts and features, coproductions), a whopping 92 percent were produced in the last decade, between 2008 and 2018. Rocío Betzabeé González de Arce Arzave, "El viaje del cine mexicano de ficción hacia la conciencia ecológica: Imaginarios de la naturaleza, ecoutopías y ética ambiental en la pantalla," master's diss., Universidad Iberoamericana, 2019: 142.

41. Miriam Ross, "The Film Festival as Producer: Latin American Films and Rotterdam's Hubert Bals Fund," *Screen* 52, no. 2 (2011): 263.

42. Ross, "The Film Festival as Producer," 267.

43. Tamara L. Falicov, "'Cine en Construcción'/'Films in Progress': How Spanish and Latin American Filmmakers Negotiate the Construction of a Globalized Art-House Aesthetic," *Transnational Cinemas* 4, no. 2 (2013): 261.

44. Salma Monani, "Environmental Film Festivals: Beginning Explorations at the Intersections of Film Festival Studies and Ecocritical Studies," in *Ecocinema Theory and Practice*, ed. S. Rust, S. Monani, and S. Cubitt (New York: Routledge, 2013): 253–78.

45. Kay Armatage, "Planet in Focus: Environmental Film Festivals," in *Screening Nature: Cinema Beyond the Human*, ed. Anat Pick and Guinevere Narraway (New York: Berghahn, 2013), 264.

Works Cited

Ahuja, Neel. "Posthuman New York: Ground Zero of the Anthropocene." In *Animalities: Literary and Cultural Studies Beyond the Human*, edited by Michael Lundblad, 43–59. Edinburgh: Edinburgh University Press, 2017.

Andermann, Jens. *Tierras en trance: arte y naturaleza después del paisaje*. Santiago: Metales Pesados, 2018.

Arenillas, María Guadalupe, and Michael J. Lazzara. "Introduction: Latin American Documentary Film in the New Millennium." In *Latin American Documentary Film in the New Millennium*, edited by María Guadalupe Arenillas and Michael J. Lazzara, 1–19. New York: Palgrave Macmillan, 2016.

Armatage, Kay. "Planet in Focus: Environmental Film Festivals." In *Screening Nature: Cinema Beyond the Human*, edited by Anat Pick and Guinevere Narraway, 257–74. New York: Berghahn, 2013.

Bozak, Nadia. *The Cinematic Footprint: Lights, Camera, Natural Resources*. New Brunswick: Rutgers University Press, 2012.

Carruth, Allison. "Ecological Media Studies and the Matter of Digital Technologies." *PMLA* 131, no. 2 (2016): 364–72.

Césaire, Aimé. *Discourse on Colonialism*. Translated by Joan Pinkham. New York: Monthly Review Press, 2000.

Crutzen, Paul J. "Geology of Mankind." *Nature* 415 (2002): 23.
Danowksi, Déborah, and Eduardo Viveiros de Castro. *The Ends of the World*. Translated by Rodrigo Nunes. Cambridge: Polity Press, 2017.
de la Cadena, Marisol. "Indigenous Cosmopolitics in the Andes: Conceptual Reflections Beyond 'Politics.'" *Cultural Anthropology* 25, no. 2 (2010): 334–70.
Enright, Kelly. *The Maximum of Wilderness: The Jungle in the American Imagination*. Charlottesville: University of Virginia Press, 2012.
EZLN. "Cuarta Declaración de la Selva Lacandona." January 1, 1996.
Falicov, Tamara L. "'Cine en Construcción'/'Films in Progress': How Spanish and Latin American Filmmakers Negotiate the Construction of a Globalized Art-House Aesthetic." *Transnational Cinemas* 4, no. 2 (2014): 253–71.
Fay, Jennifer. *Inhospitable World: Cinema in the Time of the Anthropocene*. New York: Oxford Press, 2018.
Gómez-Barris, Macarena. *The Extractive Zone: Social Ecologies and Decolonial Perspectives*. Durham: Duke University Press, 2017.
González de Arce Arzave, Rocío Betzabeé. "El viaje del cine mexicano de ficción hacia la conciencia ecológica: Imaginarios de la naturaleza, ecoutopías y ética ambiental en la pantalla." Master's diss., Universidad Iberoamericana, 2019.
Haraway, Donna. "Anthropocene, Capitalocene, Plantationocene, Chthulucene: Making Kin." *Environmental Humanities* 6 (2015) 159–65.
———. "Situated Knowledges: The Science Question in Feminism and the Privilege of Partial Perspective." *Feminist Studies* 14, no. 3 (1988): 575–99.
Heffes, Gisela. *Políticas de la destrucción/poéticas de la preservación: apuntes para una lectura ecocrítica del medio ambiente en América Latina*. Buenos Aires: Beatriz Viterbo, 2013.
Ivakhiv, Adrian J. *Ecologies of the Moving Image: Cinema, Affect, Nature*. Waterloo: Wilfrid Laurier University Press, 2013.
Jarman, Rebecca. "Melodrama at the Margins: Poverty, Politics, and Profits in 'Golden Age' Venezuelan Cinema." *The Modern Language Review* 112, no. 3 (2017): 645–65.
King, John. *Magical Reels: A History of Cinema in Latin America*. London: Verso, 1990.
Leal, Juan Felipe, Eduardo Barraza, and Alejandra Jablonska. *Vistas que no se ven: filmografía mexicana, 1896–1910*. Mexico: Universidad Nacional Autónoma de México, 1993.
León, Christian. *Reinventando al Otro. El documental indigenista en el Ecuador*. Quito: La Caracola, 2010.
Leff, Enrique. *Ecología y capital: racionalidad ambiental, democracia participativa y desarrollo sustentable*. 6th ed. México: Siglo XXI, 2005.
Lewis, Simon L., and Mark A. Maslin. "Defining the Anthropocene." *Nature* 519 (2015): 171–80.
Lindstrom, Lamont. "Shooting Melanesians: Martin Johnson and Edward Salisbury in the Southwest Pacific." *Visual Anthropology* 29, no. 4/5 (2016): 360–81.

Mignolo, Walter. "Foreword: On Pluriversality and Multipolarity." In *Pluriverse: The Geopolitics of Knowledge*, edited by Bernd Reiter, ix–xvi. Durham: Duke University Press, 2018.

Mirzoeff, Nicholas. "It's Not the Anthropocene, It's the White Supremacy Scene." In *After Extinction*, edited by Richard Grusin, 123–50. Minneapolis: Minnesota University Press, 2018.

Monani, Salma. "Environmental Film Festivals: Beginning Explorations at the Intersections of Film Festival Studies and Ecocritical Studies." In *Ecocinema Theory and Practice*, edited by S. Rust, S. Monani, and S. Cubitt, 253–78. New York: Routledge, 2013.

Moore, Jason. *Capitalism in the Web of Life: Ecology and the Accumulation of Capital*. New York: Verso, 2015.

Nixon, Rob. *Slow Violence and the Environmentalism of the Poor*. Cambridge: Harvard University Press, 2011.

Parikka, Jussi. *A Geology of Media*. Minneapolis: University of Minnesota Press, 2015.

Petras, James, and Henry Veltmeyer. "Agro-Extractivism: The Agrarian Question of the 21st Century." In *Extractive Imperialism in the Americas*, 62–100. Leiden: Brill, 2014.

Pick, Anat, and Guinevere Narraway. "Introduction: Intersecting Ecology and Film." In *Screening Nature: Cinema beyond the Human*, edited by Anat Pick and Guinevere Narraway, 1–18. New York: Berghahn, 2013.

Ross, Miriam. "The Film Festival as Producer: Latin American Films and Rotterdam's Hubert Bals Fund." *Screen* 52, no. 2 (2011): 261–67.

Tablada, José Juan. *Una antología general*. México: Fondo de Cultura Económica, 2007.

Ziser, Michael. "Ecomedia," In *Keywords for Environmental Studies*, edited by Joni Adamson, William A. Gleason, and David N. Pellow, 75–76. New York: New York University Press, 2016.

GENRE BEYOND THE HUMAN

1

Movies on the Move

Filming the Amazon Rainforest

PATRÍCIA VIEIRA

A large number of films set in the Amazon River Basin revolve around a voyage.[1] Movies from outside Latin America often portray the experience of foreigners who travel to the region, as in Harry Hoyt's *The Lost World* (1925), an adaptation of Conan Doyle's eponymous novel about a British scientist who journeys to Amazonia to find a plateau teeming with pre-historical animals. Later cinema follows this early pattern, with movies like *Creature from the Black Lagoon* (Jack Arnold, 1954), which portrays scientists on a research trip threatened by an amphibious being from the depths of an Amazonian lake, and Werner Herzog's *Aguirre, the Wrath of God* (1972) and *Fitzcarraldo* (1982), where the protagonists travel in the area only to see their designs to conquer and economically exploit it thwarted by the indomitable Amazonian nature, to name but a few well-known examples.

Films about Amazonia made by Latin American directors similarly resort to the trope of the journey as a key element of the plot. In Carlos Diegues's *Bye Bye Brasil* (*Bye Bye Brazil*, 1980), for instance, a troupe of vaudeville performers drives to the Amazonian city of Altamira in the hopes of finding a paying audience; in Luis Alberto Lamata's *Jericó* (*Jericho*, 1990), a Spanish priest travels to the Amazon to evangelize its Indigenous population and ends up acculturating into a tribe. Eschewing the more outlandish portrayals of the area as home to fantastic beasts and miraculous, disease-curing plants and animals, these and other Latin American directors, like their North American and European counterparts, depict the region as a space separated from the rest of the territory of Amazonian nations, a place one travels through, but rarely abides in.

Cinema inherited, in this respect, a literary tradition that dates back to the first texts about the Amazon by European chroniclers. In the mid-sixteenth century, Spanish Dominican Priest Gaspar de Carvajal penned an account of his trip with explorer Francisco de Orellana traversing the length of the Amazon from the Andes to the Atlantic Ocean in *Descubrimiento del río de las Amazonas* (*The Discovery of the Amazon*, ca. 1542), and Jesuit Priest Cristóbal de Acuña narrated his journey accompanying captain Pedro Teixeira in a return trip from Quito to Belém in *Nuevo descubrimiento del gran río de las Amazonas* (*New Discovery of the Great River of the Amazons*) from 1641. These and other early texts, usually by missionaries, were followed by a second wave of travel writings on the area by naturalists like Alexander von Humboldt (*Personal Narrative of Travels in Equinoctial Regions of America*, 1814), Alfred Russel Wallace (*A Narrative of Travels on the Amazon and Rio Negro*, 1853), Henry Walter Bates (*The Naturalist on the River Amazons*, 1863), and Louis Agassiz (*A Journey in Brazil*, 1868), who emphasized the scientific significance of the region. The so-called "jungle novel," which flourished during the first half of the twentieth century in the wake of the Amazonian rubber boom,[2] continued the tradition of narratives about journeys to the region in novels such as José Eustasio Rivera's *La vorágine* (*The Vortex*, 1924) and Ferreira de Castro's *A Selva* (*The Jungle*, 1930), about young men who journey to the area and witness the hardships endured by rubber tappers. Later texts continued to emphasize different aspects of traveling in the region in novels such as Alejo Carpentier's *Los pasos perdidos* (*The Lost Steps*, 1953), about a quest for a more authentic way of life by a city-weary man, and Márcio Souza's *Mad Maria* (1980), which revolves around the eventful construction of a railway line that cuts through the jungle.

The centrality of traveling in literature and then in cinema about the Amazon can partly be explained by regional specificities. The world's biggest river, in terms of the amount of water that runs from it into the sea (and, possibly, also in length[3]), the Amazon and its many tributaries drain an area that corresponds to roughly 7 percent of the surface of the planet. The Amazon rainforest accounts for more than 60 percent of the world's remaining rainforests, produces approximately 20 percent of its oxygen,[4] and is home to the planet's most important ecosystem, containing about half of all the earth's species of plants and animals. Amazonia's size, remoteness, and biodiversity fueled the imagination of the reading public and, later, of moviegoers both in the metropolises of South America and abroad. Regarded by outsiders as an almost empty space—the area was dubbed "terra sem gente" ("a land without people")[5] by the Brazilian government as late as the 1960s and 1970s—the Amazon was easily exoticized and portrayed as a space where anything could happen.[6]

Travel literature and cinema about Amazonia capitalized on this fascination with the unknown. In the case of early cinema, the travelogue, which revealed hitherto unseen areas to avid viewers around the world, became a popular genre to depict the region in the first decades of the twentieth century. Movies such as Hamilton Rice's *Explorations in the Amazon Basin* (1930), which narrated his expedition to the Rio Branco, and those by the Marquis of Wavrin about his travels in the area from 1913 to 1937, including *Au Pays du Scalp* (*In the Land of the Scalp*, 1931), were widely viewed travelogues that included footage and information about the Amazon and, often, the enactment of scenes (dance or other rituals) by the local population. Travel fiction films, for their part, tended to focus on journeys of (self-)discovery to faraway parts of the rainforest, in which the protagonists contended with potentially life-threatening flora, fauna, and Indigenous populations. In movies such as *At Play in the Fields of the Lord* (Hector Babenco, 1991), *Medicine Man* (John McTiernan, 1992), and *The Lost City of Z* (James Gray, 2016), the region beckoned with the allure of El Dorado in its various instantiations: hidden treasures, scientific breakthroughs, and personal enlightenment all promised to reward the intrepid explorers who ventured into the forest.

But there is a deeper reason behind the centrality of traveling in cinema about the Amazon than the didactic impulse of early travelogues and later documentaries—such as those by National Geographic, for example—and the wish to capitalize on the exoticism of a fairly far-flung location. In Amazonia, nature itself is permanently on the move, and therefore it invites the movement of explorers. Brazilian writer Euclides da Cunha, who himself journeyed to the Amazon in 1904–1905,[7] commented in his writings about his trip that the local nature is "incomplete" and marked by "volubility."[8] The numerous rivers constantly reshape the land, changing their banks and sometimes even their course, and seasonal floods drastically alter the landscape. Cunha speculates that the Amazon river puts South American land itself in motion in that it carries it deep into the Atlantic Ocean. He accuses the Amazon of defying "our patriotic lyricism" by being "the least Brazilian of rivers" because it robs the nation of its soil.[9] For Cunha, such movement passes on to humans, which is why, in his view, many Amazonians are nomads.[10]

The permanent movement of waters draining the Amazon river basin from the foothills of the Andes to the ocean is matched by the rapid growth of living matter in the rainforest. Staying with Cunha, we read in his Preface to a book of short stories about the region that "everything is life" in the Amazon, and life "reproduces itself easily, in the latent and unstoppable drive to always procreate."[11] Cunha's empirical observations are backed by scientific data, according to which the plant biomass and rate of growth in a tropical forest are five times those of a temperate one.[12] Living beings that constantly grow and reproduce in the Amazon, together with the flow of the rivers, create a natural environment that is perpetually changing.

A nature on the move finds its mirror image in the movement of adventurers and explorers traveling to the Amazon. Cinema, the art of the moving image, in turn, reflects these motions in its depiction of various journeys through the rainforest. In the rest of this chapter, I discuss the ways in which Latin American cinema has portrayed the Amazon river basin, its flora and fauna, in films about voyages. I start with a reflection on Amazonian travel cinema as a variation on the road movie genre and subsequently analyze three films about trips in the region that instantiate different stages in the cinematic representation of the Amazonian environment.

Amazonian Road Movies as Ecocinema

Films revolving around trips in the Amazon evoke the road movies that emerged in post–Second World War cinema. In his study about North American road movies, David Laderman identifies the "thrill of the unknown" as a core impulse of the genre,[13] together with a tension between rebellion and conformity and a focus on male protagonists.[14] Seen as inheritors of the American "frontier" ethos[15] and of the Western,[16] road movies frequently rely on an "open landscape bordered by seductive horizons" as a key part of their iconography and make extensive use of traveling shots from the point of view of the moving vehicle.[17]

For Laderman, the automobile is a key component of genre,[18] but recent scholarship on Latin American road movies has questioned the centrality of the car in the region's version of these films. As Nadia Lie points out, Latin American travelers often choose public transportation, including buses and trucks, bicycles, donkeys, boats, and canoes or simply travel by foot.[19] Verónica Garibotto and Jorge Pérez interpret these forms of transportation as a sign of a broader social critique that defines the region's road movies, which shed light on the "tense relationship of Latin American countries with modernity, as epitomized by precarious infrastructures and uneven access to motorized vehicles,"[20] an argument also espoused by Lie in her book about the genre. The use of nonprofessional actors, shooting on location, natural lighting, and neorealist and documentary-style techniques all contribute to highlight the harsh social realities of Latin America.[21]

Cinema about travel in the Amazon shares many of the features of the road movie genre, including, thematically, a fascination with an unknown, "frontier" location, into which male explorers venture, leaving the comfort of their routine existence behind, as well as, in technical terms, the preference for open vistas and traveling shots. Like many other Latin American road movies, Portuguese- and Spanish-speaking Amazonian travel films often entail a commentary on modernity and development in the area and frequently feature nonprofessional actors and shooting on location. In the majority of these movies, the car is replaced by the canoe or, more recently, by the motorboat, which remain important modes of transportation in Amazonia. Given that rivers have functioned, throughout the history of the Amazon, as its main connective paths, it makes sense to talk about *river* movies, as opposed to *road* movies, when discussing Amazonian travel cinema. If roads usually signal development and mastery over a given territory, the instability of rivers, with their waterfalls, rapids, and occasional flooding, place modernity and the domination of the Amazon under constant erasure and draw attention to the precarity and the challenges of traveling through it.

The emphasis on the river and not the road as the primary enabler of mobility and the main avenue for movement in the Amazon also points to the centrality of the natural world in the region's travel cinema. Road movies typically portray open spaces as the opposite of a stifling civilization, but they usually depict these as places one passes through while on the road, a natural scenario pretty much the same as any other: adorning the sides of the road, contemplated while the car is in motion. In classical road movies, then, nature tends to work as a setting and not a landscape, in the useful distinction of Martin Lefebvre. A cinematic setting, according to Lefebvre, is "the place where the action or events occur," a background to what is happening, while the landscape emerges when the setting is set free from the story.[22] In Amazonian river movies, the natural environment, including the river, plants, and animals, tends to function as an "autonomous landscape" that takes center stage as a protagonist.[23] The path runs *in* and *through* nature, which is therefore not an object contemplated by a detached observer but is itself a participant in the voyage.

Films about travel in the Amazon are, then, road movies with a twist. In this sense, they could be described as ecocinema, which, according to Scott MacDonald, who coined the term, hinges upon a retraining of perception.[24] By shifting the focus to the natural environment not merely as the surroundings of the road but as the road itself, Amazonian travel cinema makes for "new kinds of film experience." The attention to nature that is part and parcel of Amazonian cinematic journeys is reflected on traveling shots of the voyaging party on the river, close-ups of animals and plants, and point-of-view shots from the perspective of natural elements, all of which contribute to nurturing "a more environmentally progressive mindset," a hallmark of ecocinema, according to MacDonald.[25]

Other critics have focused primarily on thematic, rather than stylistic, choices as the defining feature of ecocinema. Paula Willoquet-Maricondi, for instance, distinguishes between movies that simply touch upon environmental issues without questioning the status quo and films that promote an ecological consciousness, the latter being the only ones that could be labeled "ecocinema."[26] While a large number of Amazonian "road" movies draw their viewers' attention to environmental destruction, I regard the term "ecocinema" to be more about the interpretative approach to a given film than about plot or cinematic technique. As Steven Rust and Salma Monani point out, "all films" subject to "productive ecocritical exploration and careful analysis can unearth engaging and intriguing perspectives on cinema's various relationships with the world around us."[27] In the rest of this chapter, I analyze three movies about trips in Amazonia through an ecocinematic lens: Silvino Santos's *No Paiz das Amazonas* (*In the Land of the Amazons*, 1922), Jorge Bodanzky and Orlando Senna's *Iracema: Uma Transa Amazônica* (*Iracema: An Amazonian Love Affair*, 1974), and Ciro Guerra's *El abrazo de la serpiente* (*The Embrace of the Serpent*, 2015). My goal is to reflect on both the evolution of Amazonian iconography and the different paradigms adopted to portray the environment of the Amazon in film.[28]

In the Land of the Amazons

A central impulse of cinematic travelogues about the Amazon was to show its landscape, fauna, and flora to viewers unacquainted with the region. Santos's *In the Land of the Amazons* appears, at first glance, to squarely fit into this mold. Produced under the patronage of Portuguese rubber baron J. G. Araújo to be shown at the International Exhibition in Rio de Janeiro in 1922 marking the centenary of Brazilian independence, the film aimed to make Amazonia known to the rest of Brazil and to the world.[29] Santos traveled more than 6,000 miles with his camera to offer viewers an encompassing portrayal of the region. The movie was awarded a Gold Medal at the exhibition and was released commercially in Brazil, Europe, and the United States to great critical acclaim and financial success.[30]

Still, the film differs in several ways from travelogues and other early documentaries about the Amazon river basin. For one, it was not made by a foreign explorer such as Hamilton Rice or the Marquis of Wavrin, who, even though they knew the territory well, could not help but adopt an outside perspective when filming it. Santos was born in Portugal but moved to the Amazon at an early age and therefore, in his movie, he was revealing his home region to outsiders. This is perhaps one of the reasons why, unlike other films from the same period, *In the Land of the Amazons* does not present the area as exotic. While Santos does strive to underline the specificities of Amazonia, he goes to great lengths to emphasize everyday activities that could have taken place anywhere: people working in factories, doing sports such as rowing or swimming, enjoying a day off with their children, and so on. The Amazon is not pictured as mysterious or outlandish but as a place like any other, whose inhabitants try to make the most of their lives. The movie begins in the city of Manaus, showing its modern harbor, paved roads, ample squares, and European-style architecture, together with cars, trams, and motorboats. A far cry from the fanciful images of impenetrable forests with menacing animals lurking in their shadows usually associated with the area, the initial impression viewers get of the land of the Amazons is that it boasts a thriving, modern city.[31]

Santos's efforts to demystify Amazonia, however, do not mean that he underestimates the centrality of the natural world. The very first image of the film is that of a sunrise over the river, and the first intertitles explain that the area is "almost a continent" with "countless rivers," a "very bountiful variety of fishes," "the most charming of birds," "opulent forests," and "other precious treasures of nature" that amount to an "incalculable wealth." The film falls back upon staples in the representation of Amazonian nature—its immensity, variety, and wealth—to introduce the area to its audience. Furthermore, the city of Manaus is first seen from the water, as though viewers were arriving to it by boat, a technique also used in later movies to stress the importance of the river in the lives of the local population.

The bulk of *In the Land of the Amazons* is organized around the various extractivist industries that make up the regional economy: fishing, rubber tapping, logging, cattle raising, and the harvesting and preparation of tobacco, Brazil nuts, and guarana for export. Again, Santos highlights the fertility of Amazonian nature while also showing its productive, modern side. In one memorable sequence, the director films female and male workers leaving a factory that processes Brazil nuts in a clear homage to the Lumière brothers' famous 1895 film. But the majority of the industries portrayed involve the gathering of the land's bountiful products. The capturing of manatees is a salient example of the area's rich natural environment. Now a protected species, manatees were so common at the time that they could easily be fished with simple canoes and harpoons. In a striking image, we see rows of recently caught manatees, some still moving, lined up on the ground, lying on their backs with their forefins crossed over their chests, as though they were human bodies.

The undertones of environmental critique were probably unintended in the case of the manatee hunting spree. In fact, the film depicts other scenes of fishing and hunting in a rather celebratory manner common in movies from the period.[32] Yet *In the Land of the Amazons* already displays an incipient environmental consciousness. Close to the end, the movie shows a flock of white herons taking flight, using several close-ups. These images are followed by an intertitle, where we read that "men and women, with the same inhuman instinct, persecute the defenseless birds to remove their rich and delicate plumage." After a few more shots of the birds flying and nesting, we again read in the intertitles that such a "war without truce, that makes millions of victims a year, is the result of fashion, and of ladies' vain caprice." The slaughter of the birds, who are seen as "victims," amounts to an ongoing war that, according to the movie, is all the crueler because it is groundless. The sequence ends with an opening iris that gradually reveals an adornment made of heron feathers and with a last shot of a heron taking flight. The ecological message of the film is clear. While activities deemed necessary for human sustenance are presented as morally justifiable and even laudable, the capture of animals for what are considered to be superfluous, futile reasons, such as the making of luxury items, is strongly condemned.

The ecological stance of *In the Land of Amazons* comes through at its most forceful in close-ups of plants and animals the filmmaker encounters in his journey: an orchid hanging from a tree, *Victoria amazonica* flowers on a lake, a grasshopper on a stick, a sloth slowly crossing a road and another one going up a tree, crocodiles waiting to feed on fish remains tossed by humans into the water, an otter with her young and another one feasting on a fish, a jaguar lazing on a tree branch; the list goes on. Most of these images are interspersed in the film without any commentary in the intertitles, and they usually are not related to the main plot. One of the goals of inserting these close-ups into the fabric of the movie was certainly to display the flora and fauna of the region to outsiders. But these images of animals and plants going about their business also create a compelling counterpoint to the human extractivist industries that structure the storyline.

This parallel is encouraged by the filmmaker, who, at one point, shows the same activity being performed by humans and nonhumans. A close-up of the machine used to peel Brazil nuts and of a woman's hands feeding the nuts into the machine—in a Chaplinesque moment *avant la lettre*[33]—is followed by intertitles explaining that "in the forest, Brazil nut peeling is more primitive." The next image is of a monkey banging a Brazil nut against a rock, which then cross-cuts with more images of the machine and the woman's hands, until we finally see the monkey eating the nut.[34] Rather than demeaning the woman's work or implying that the animal's way of doing things is inferior, the movie suggests that each uses the tools at his or her disposal to accomplish the same task. The film shows a continuum between the monkey's and the woman's activities and implies that both take advantage of the lavish products of the land to survive and thrive. These enterprises are justified as long as they directly contribute to human prosperity; Santos draws the line at the gratuitous killing of animals.

Amazonian extractivism has, since Santos's times, spun completely out of control, and contemporary viewers would probably decry the more brutal fishing and hunting scenes of the film, as well as, in hindsight, the wisdom of promoting logging and cattle raising in the region. Still, *In the Land of the Amazons*, with its care in depicting local plants and animals, highlighting of the ties that bind humans and nonhumans, and censoring of unwarranted violence toward nature, could be regarded as proto-ecological. Or, it could be interpreted, as we have attempted to do here, in an ecocinematic key that foregrounds its attunement to the natural world. An ecologically conscious approach to the Amazonian environment in cinema would only fully flourish in the wake of the postwar environmental movement, when the negative effects of decades of extractivism in the area became impossible to ignore.

Iracema: An Amazonian Love Affair

Santos's voyage through the Amazon was shot from boats, trains, and along roads, but the focus of his film was not on being on the road. The journey was a means to film the various aspects of the area, and the vagaries of traveling were featured only occasionally. Unlike Santos's film, the core of Jorge Bodanzky and Orlando Senna's *Iracema: An Amazonian Love Affair* is life on the road. And not just any road but the Trans-Amazonian Highway, a project of the Brazilian dictatorship government (1964–85) that aimed to build a 2,000-plus-mile-long highway connecting the country's Northeastern area with isolated parts of the Amazon, purportedly to bring economic progress to the region. The highway, whose construction began in 1969, was never finished, and its economic benefits were dubious. Nonetheless, it brought enormous ecological damage to vast stretches of the rainforest. *Iracema* shows the impact of the highway and, more broadly, of the government's developmental drive on Amazonian nature and the region's inhabitants.

Another difference between Santos's film and *Iracema* is that the former fit squarely within the documentary genre, while the latter is more ambiguous. In his "Notes for a Theory of the Road Movie," renowned Brazilian filmmaker Walter Salles names Bodanzky and Senna's film as a perfect example of the blurring of the boundaries between fact and fiction that he believes is a defining feature of road movies.[35] For Salles, road movies are fictional films that nevertheless tend to be "driven by a sense of immediacy that is not dissimilar from that of a documentary film."[36] While Salles regards *Iracema* as a road movie that incorporates documentary techniques, one might also interpret it as a documentary that makes use of elements from the road movie genre. Garibotto and Pérez coined the term "docu-road movie" to describe documentaries "enriched by incursions of visual techniques emblematic of fictional road movies," which is arguably the case with *Iracema*.[37]

Leaving matters of classification aside, the success of Bodanzky and Senna's film lies in adopting documentary-style techniques—handheld camera, shooting on location, use of non-actors and semiprofessional actors—to turn a trip on the Trans-Amazonian Highway into a powerful indictment of social inequality and environmental devastation.[38] The two main characters interact with people they meet on the road in unscripted dialogues that register the population's unfiltered opinion about the efforts to bring progress to the region. In *Era uma Vez Iracema* (*Once Upon a Time Iracema*, 2005), a documentary about the making of the 1974 movie, Bodanzky says that he filmed as inconspicuously as possible, without the use of a clapperboard, so that many of the locals did not even realize that a film crew was on site. The result is a raw portrait of life along the highway. A woman who came to the area with her family lured by the promise of a better life, for instance, complains that the Amazon is a land of misery and that people there are also miserable. Likewise, a client in a bar accuses the rich of stealing the land from the poor. The dire social situation of migrants who came to Amazonia from other parts of Brazil, encouraged by the government's promise of easy access to fertile agricultural land that, in many cases, never materialized, is mirrored by an ecological catastrophe that becomes more and more apparent as the film progresses. In a long traveling shot, the camera drives past a seemingly endless stretch of burning forest; another sequence shows chainsaws relentlessly cutting down trees; and aerial images reveal massive deforestation.[39]

The title of the film goes back to José de Alencar's eponymous novel from 1865 about the romantic relationship between Iracema, an Indigenous woman, and a Portuguese soldier in the early days of Brazilian colonization. In the text, Iracema—an anagram for America—is persistently linked to nature. She is described in comparison with plants and animals, and her tribal function was to prepare a sacred beverage made from a plant. Her death in the end of the novel signals the conquest of American land and the taming of its natural environment by European civilization. Similar to the protagonist of Alencar's text, in Bodanzky and Senna's film, Iracema (Edna de Cássia, a local girl chosen to play the part in her first and only cinematic performance)[40] is a young woman with marked Indigenous features[41] that contrast with the light-colored skin of Tião (Paulo César Peréio, an established, flamboyant Brazilian actor), a truck driver from the south of Brazil who transports legal and illegal Amazonian timber.[42] The asymmetries between the two retrace those between the Amazonian region and the Brazilian political and economic centers of power: Iracema is a young, vulnerable, and inexperienced girl, while Tião is a world-savvy, older man.

If, as Ismail Xavier has argued in his *Allegories of Underdevelopment*, many Brazilian "New Cinema" films from the 1960s and 1970s can be understood as allegories of national sociopolitical challenges, *Iracema* can also be productively interpreted in an allegorical key.[43] Tião, who calls himself Tião "Brazil Grande" ("Large Brazil"), is politically aligned with the ideals of the dictatorship. He adorns his truck with popular political slogans from the period, such as a sticker saying "Brazil, love it or leave it," an ominous statement in light on the many political refugees forced to leave the country for criticizing the regime. When a local man tells Tião that "nature is a mother" and that the Amazon is a "rich land" where "everything thrives," he replies that "nature is my truck, the road." He adds that everyone is "withered" in Amazonia, which will only become a wealthy land in the future, presumably when the government's developmental projects have been fully implemented. A little later in the dialogue, Tião drops the pretense of nationalism and confesses that he is "after the money, the dough" and that he chose the timber business because it is so profitable. Tião embodies the drive to dominate and exploit the Amazon for rapid economic gain, disguised under the cloak of nationalistic rhetoric. He identifies with his truck and the road, symbols of a modernity forcefully imposed upon the region, and his business selling timber denotes both the destruction of the rainforest and the draining of the area's resources. In the end of the movie, Tião starts to sell cattle instead. As logging cleared large swathes of forest, timber became less abundant, and cattle-raising farms occupied the newly deforested areas. Viewers are left to wonder what will become of the land when even pasture will no longer grow in the nutrient-poor soil of what was once a luxuriant rainforest.

The character of Iracema, like that of Tião, lends itself to an allegorical interpretation. We first encounter her on a boat coming to the town of Belém, and, during a break in the trip, she bathes in the river.[44] Her connection to a traditional Amazonian lifestyle that revolved around waterways is progressively lost as she becomes a sex worker in the city and especially once she accepts a ride on Tião's truck and joins him on his trip on the Trans-Amazonian highway. Halfway through the journey, Tião tells her that he no longer wishes to provide for her and unceremoniously leaves her at a roadside bar. From then on, her fortunes rapidly decline as she struggles to make ends meet. On a few occasions she is dragged off-screen by a man or a group of men, presumably to be raped. The movie's final sequence stages a last encounter between the couple. Iracema is sitting together with a group of other drunken women—according to Bodanzky in *Once Upon a Time Iracema*, the other women were real-life sex workers—trying to stop trucks and make a buck on the side of the road. She is now so disheveled, with her clothes torn and a tooth missing, that Tião fails to recognize her at first and, when he does, he tells her she looks very different and a lot uglier. The abuse endured by Iracema, manifest in her rapid physical decline, goes hand-in-hand with the destruction of Amazonia by outside forces of which Tião is an example. The film harks back to the age-old association of the female body with nature[45] to denounce both gender and ecological violence. It suggests that the root cause of both is a desire to ruthlessly take advantage of humans and nonhumans, no matter the cost.

Moving between allegory and raw snippets of reality, Bodanzky and Senna's journey through the Trans-Amazonian Highway is an unequivocal denunciation of the Brazilian dictatorship's policies in Amazonia. The film was produced with German funds, edited in Germany, and, because of its open criticism of the Brazilian government, at first released only abroad. It circulated underground, in private screenings, until 1980, when it was finally commercially released in Brazil.[46] An ecocinematic approach to the movie reveals that it brought the environmental cost of the drive for unbridled economic progress into sharp focus. In the film, the exploitation of nature and of the more vulnerable elements of society run parallel, thus establishing a link between the degradation of human and nonhuman lives in the Amazon.

Embrace of the Serpent

Similar to Santos and Bodanzky and Senna's films, *Embrace of the Serpent* begins on the water. But while in the other two movies we slowly make our way from the river into big cities—Manaus and Belém, respectively—Guerra's film remains mostly within a natural environment. The largest human communities depicted are an Indigenous village, a small Catholic mission, and a settlement populated by the last members of an Indigenous tribe. The effects of modernization are intuited, rather than shown, as they impact the life of one of *Embrace*'s protagonists, the Native Amazonian Karamakate (Nilbio Torres as the young Karamakate and Antonio Bolívar Salvador as the old Karamakate). Of the three movies discussed here, it is the only one in which an Indigenous person plays a central role.[47] Karamakate is one of the few survivors of his people who were decimated by the encroachment of settlers and rubber tappers into their land. The film revolves around his interaction with two foreign explorers: the German Theodor von Martius, or Theo (Jan Bijvoet), whom he meets in 1909, and the American Evan (Brionne Davis), who travels to the Amazon in 1940 in an attempt to retrace Theo's footsteps.

The movie skillfully interweaves historical fact with fiction. It portrays the horrifying working conditions of rubber tappers, who endured a slave-like existence at the mercy of rubber lords; the deleterious effects of Catholic missions that brainwashed Indigenous children into renouncing their native language, customs, and traditions in favor of a foreign culture; and the proliferation of violent cults that coalesced around self-styled Messiahs in the wake of widespread social upheaval.[48] The plot and the main characters, while fictional, are based on the journals and photographs of German ethnographer Theodor Koch-Grünberg and American ethnobotanist Richard Evan Schultes. The character of Theo fictionalizes the final days of Koch-Grünberg, as described in his journals, but his last name, "Martius," alludes to another Amazonian explorer, Karl Friedrich Philipp von Martius, who traveled in the area in 1817–20. Karamakate is also, according to Guerra, "a combination of many people [. . .] some of them appear in the journals. Some of them I met personally,"[49] and Karamakate's tribe is imagined as the amalgamation of a number of cultures.[50] Filmed in black and white, shot entirely on location, and spoken mostly in Indigenous languages, *Embrace* strives to re-create the ambiance of Colombian Amazonia in the first half of the twentieth century.[51]

Bringing information about pivotal moments in the history of the Amazon to a broad audience is certainly one of Guerra's goals. For the purposes of this chapter, however, it is more relevant to note that the two interwoven narratives revolve around the quest for a plant, the sacred yakruna, the knowledge of which was once guarded by Karamakate's tribe.[52] Theo, who is very sick, hopes that the plant will cure him and allow him to bring the information he gathered in his expedition back to Germany. Evan says at first that he is looking for the yakruna both for scientific reasons and for personal fulfillment. Later in the film, however, he confesses to being an envoy from his government, who wishes to identify a pure source of rubber as part of the American military efforts to win the Second World War. *Embrace* jumps between the two storylines and historical periods, underlining the long-lasting effects of economic exploitation in the region.

The movie emphasizes the connection between Native Amazonian populations and local plants and animals and shows how the destruction of Indigenous communities means a loss of knowledge about the natural world. Karamakate is depicted as the guardian of his tribe's wisdom about Amazonian fauna and flora. As Theo asks for his help to find the yakruna plant, he says that the jungle is fragile and that humans need to obey a number of rules to be in tune with nature. Later, when Evan introduces himself as someone who has devoted his life to plants, Karamakate replies that the statement is the wisest thing he has ever heard a white man say. To Evan's offer of money in exchange for assistance to get to the yakruna, Karamakate replies that, unlike ants, he does not like money because it does not taste good to him, clearly referencing the different values that guide Western and Amazonian cultures. When Theo, Manduca (Miguel Dionísio Ramos), and Karamakate visit a Catholic mission, the latter tells Indigenous children not to forget their heritage and teaches them about the medicinal properties of a plant. The young Karamakate epitomizes the symbiosis between local peoples and the environment, as when he is filmed from the back in a medium shot, surrounded by butterflies and looking at the river that viewers can also see from a vantage point behind his shoulder.

Despite Karamakate's efforts, local wisdom about nature is on the wane. His older self confesses to Evan that natural elements used to speak to him but that "stones, plants and animals have grown silent."[53] He has lost his memory and no longer even knows how to prepare the hallucinogenic beverage that used to be part of his tribe's sacred rituals. Theo and Evan's search for the yakruna is an attempt, however limited, to counter this loss and preserve some of the Indigenous knowledge. Theo's Native Amazonian helper Manduca understands this goal. When Karamakate accuses him of having forsaken his tribe to serve a white man, Manduca replies that Theo can explain the jungle to others and that if white people do not learn about the rainforest, it will be the end. In the final moments of the film, Karamakate also realizes that he can only keep the memory of his tribe alive by showing Evan the power of the yakruna. He says his function was not to teach his people, who are all gone, but to become a mediator between his culture and the outside by teaching Evan about the secrets of the sacred plant.

The ending of the movie is bittersweet. Theo's quest ends in disaster when Karamakate reaches the last survivors of his tribe, who now cultivate the yakruna to feed their drunken stupor. Karamakate feels the plant has been desecrated, burns down its bushes, and tells Theo he will not allow the soul of his people to be taken out of the Amazon. The Indigenous population scatters as the Colombian army enters the settlement, signaling that the remnants of the tribe will cease to exist. Evan's expedition does reach its destination when Karamakate leads him to the top of a mountain where the only remaining yakruna plant is still growing. Evan is allowed a glimpse into Indigenous culture by drinking a powerful drug made from the plant, but the last yakruna bush had to be destroyed for that purpose. The film suggests that Amazonian peoples' lived relationship with nature is slowly disappearing, as is their knowledge of local flora and fauna. What remains is a recollection of such a connection, which survives in travel writings and journals like those of Theo and Evan, and in films such as *Embrace*. The movie is dedicated to the "memory of the peoples whose songs we will never know," a tribute to the many stories about humans and nonhumans that will have disappeared with the decimation of Native Amazonian cultures.[54]

From an ecocinematic perspective, *Embrace* underscores the imbrication of people, plants, and animals. With the end of a human community and their cosmology, a certain view of nature also vanishes, which is tantamount to saying that a part of the natural world—the sacred yakruna in the film—dies along with the people who used to revere it. The movie is at once a sobering statement of what has already been lost in the Amazon and a hopeful reminder that the sharing of knowledge about the region may prevent further destruction. The film's nostalgic undertone, which hinges upon a sense of cultural loss, is countered by its critical and commercial success—it won an Art Cinema Award at Cannes and was shortlisted for the Best Foreign Language Film Academy Award, becoming the first Colombian movie to ever receive a nomination for an Oscar—that brought Amazonian culture, the recent history of the region and challenges it faces to a large international audience. *Embrace* is a call to action, so that the Amazonian natural world and its peoples will not become only a memory passed on through words and images.

Road movies are often as much about an inner, metaphorical journey as they are about a physical one. Amazonian cinema about travel, such as the movies discussed above, depict trips through the Amazon that are simultaneously a journey to the heart of our extractivist culture. The three films share the goal of making the region, its peoples, flora, and fauna known to those outside it. Depicting a natural world that is perpetually in motion, they portray Amazonia beyond the clichés of an exotic location brimming with natural treasures and focus instead on the social and ecological problems brought about by the unbridled economic exploitation of the area's natural environment. They show that the problems facing the Amazon are the result of the relentless resource extraction that has been the engine of economic growth in our societies in the past few centuries. Through camera work—close-ups of animals and plants, traveling shots of the forest, and tracking shots of boats on local rivers—these movies on the move reveal another Amazon that resists the logic of domination. The enduring legacy of these films is to have portrayed this other Amazon, with the humans and nonhumans who call it home.

Notes

1. The research for this article was funded by a Grant from the Portuguese Foundation for Science and Technology (FCT), Project IF/00606/2015.

2. The Amazon rubber boom took place in the last decades of the nineteenth and the beginning of the twentieth centuries, when the demand for latex, produced from the sap of the Amazonian *Hevea brasiliensis*, or rubber tree, for industrial purposes grew exponentially. This was a period of rapid economic development and social change in the region, with the migration of large numbers of people to the area to work as rubber tappers. The price of latex was so high that it was dubbed "white gold," and rubber barons quickly amassed prodigious fortunes. Once rubber tree plants started to be grown in Asia at a much lower cost, the Amazonian rubber trade entered a period of decline from which it never recovered.

3. There is some debate among experts about the length of the Amazon river; it is estimated to be somewhere between 4,000 and 4,300 miles long. If it is closer to 4,300 miles, then the Amazon is the world's longest river, surpassing the Nile.

4. The Amazon rainforest is often called the "lungs of the world" because it absorbs around 2 billion tons of carbon dioxide every year and produces 20 percent of the world's oxygen.

5. This and all other Portuguese and Spanish originals are rendered in my translations.

6. The Brazilian military dictatorship's slogan about the area was "a land without people for a people without land," which alluded to the government's plans to encourage the movement of migrants from the drought-ridden Northeastern region of the country to the Amazon, which was perceived to be a nearly empty territory.

7. Euclides da Cunha journeyed in the Amazon as head of the Brazilian team in the Brazilian-Peruvian Joint Commission to Map the High Purus (Comissão Mista Brasileiro-Peruana de Reconhecimento do Alto Purus), whose task was to define the Amazonian border between Brazil and Peru. His impressions about the region were collected in *Contrastes e Confrontos*, from 1907, and in *À Margem da História*, first published in 1909. All of his Amazonian texts were later published in *Um Paraíso Perdido* (1976).

8. Euclides da Cunha, *Um Paraíso Perdido. Ensaios Amazônicos* (Brasília: Senado Federal, 2000), 117, 126.

9. Ibid., 120.

10. Ibid., 126.

11. Euclides da Cunha, "Preâmbulo," in Alberto Rangel, *Inferno Verde. Cenas e Cenários do Amazonas* (Tours, France: Tipografia Arrault, 1927), 16.

12. John Hemming, *Tree of Rivers: The Story of the Amazon* (London: Thames & Hudson, 2008).

13. David Laderman, *Driving Lessons: Exploring the Road Movie* (Austin: University of Texas Press, 2002), 2.

14. Ibid., 20–21; Timothy Corrigan, *A Cinema without Walls: Movies and Culture after Vietnam* (New Brunswick: Rutgers University Press, 1991), 143.

15. Steven Cohan and Ina Era Hark, "Introduction," in *The Road Movie Book*, ed. Steven Cohan and Ina Era Hark (London and New York: Routledge, 1997), 1.

16. Laderman, 23.

17. Ibid., 14–15.

18. Ibid., 13.

19. Nadia Lie, *The Latin American (Counter-) Road Movie and Ambivalent Modernity* (New York: Palgrave MacMillan, 2017), 8.

20. Verónica Garibotto and Jorge Pérez, "Introduction. Reconfiguring Precarious Landscapes: The Road Movie in Latin America," in *The Latin American Road Movie*, ed. Verónica Garibotto and Jorge Pérez (New York: Palgrave MacMillan, 2016), 2.

21. Ibid., 16.

22. Martin Lefebvre, "Between Setting and Landscape in the Cinema," in *Landscape and Film*, ed. Martin Lefebvre (New York and London: Routledge, 2006), 21. Lefebvre argues that that there are two modes of spectatorial activity, a narrative and a spectacular mode. Landscapes come to the fore in the spectacular mode, when film foregrounds its natural or even social environments over plot development (29).

23. Ibid., 28.

24. The term "eco-cinema" was coined by MacDonald in a 2004 article published in *Interdisciplinary Studies of Literature and Environment*.

25. Scott MacDonald, "The Ecocinema Experience," in *Ecocinema Theory and Practice*, ed. Stephen Rust, Salma Monani, and Sean Cubitt (New York and London: Routledge, 2013), 20. For MacDonald, "the fundamental job of an ecocinema is not to produce pro-environmental narratives shot in a conventional Hollywood manner (that is, in a manner that implicitly promotes consumption) or even in a conventional documentary manner (although, of course, documentaries can alert us to environmental issues)" (20). He focuses on the use of avant-garde or experimental film techniques as a means to nudge viewers out of complacency and draw their attention to environmental problems.

26. Paula Willoquet-Maricondi, "Shifting Paradigms: From Environmentalist Film to Ecocinema," in *Framing the World: Explorations in Ecocriticism and Film*, ed. Paula Willoquet-Maricondi (Charlottesville and London: University of Virginia Press, 2010), 45.

27. Stephen Rust and Salma Monani, "Introduction—Cuts to Dissolves: Defining and Situating Ecocinema Studies," in *Ecocinema Theory and Practice*, ed. Stephen Rust, Salma Monani, and Sean Cubitt (New York and London: Routledge, 2013), 3.

28. While the three films, and especially *Embrace of the Serpent*, provide rich material for a discussion on the cinematic depiction of Indigenous peoples in the Amazon, this chapter focuses on the portrayal of the environment in the movies and mentions Native Amazonian cultures only in their relation to the representation of the natural world.

29. As Márcio Souza points out, J. G. Araújo's goal "was that of institutional propaganda, or, in other words, to register indelibly the company's name among the visitors of the Exposition of the Independence," Márcio Souza, *Silvino Santos: O Cineasta do Ciclo da Borracha* (Rio de Janeiro: FUNARTE, 1999), 229. The celebration of Brazilian independence was perhaps the reason why the film ends with a group of horse-riding cowboys "screaming patriotically: Long live Brazil!."

30. Luciana Martins, "Silvino Santos and the Mobile View: Documentary Geographies of Modern Brazil," in *The Brazilian Road Movie: Journeys of (Self) Discovery*, ed. Sara Brandellero (Cardiff: University of Wales Press, 2013), 4, 19. The film was produced by Santos and J. G. Araújo's son Agesilau de Araújo, who cowrote the intertitles with Alfredo da Matta.

31. Manaus contrasts with the Rio Branco area that, according to the intertitles, is "a very wild region of the Amazon, a 'Far West,' where the wealth is enormous. All kinds of minerals, gold, precious stones, rubber trees and bovine and equine cattle show how prodigious nature is over there." Unlike the image of an undifferentiated region covered in rainforest, the film portrays the Amazon as a space that has cities and wild, frontier spaces, much like the United States with its Far West and frontier areas in the nineteenth century.

32. Hunting scenes are also a staple of the film *River of Doubt* (Caroline Gentry, 1928) about American former president Theodor Roosevelt and Brazilian explorer Cândido Rondon's expedition into the Amazon in 1913–14.

33. *In the Land of the Amazons* preceded Charlie Chaplin's *Modern Times* by fourteen years.

34. Before this sequence, the film had already shown monkeys eating Brazilian nuts in the forest, preceded by the intertitle "In the forest, the Brazil nut also has its lovers."

35. Walter Salles, "Notes for a Theory of the Road Movie," in *The New York Times* (Nov. 11, 2007), 4.

36. Ibid., 3.

37. Garibotto and Pérez, "Introduction," 19.

38. Salles states that the success of *Iracema* lies precisely in mixing techniques from documentary and from fiction films: "Because of that ambiguity, *Iracema* is one of the most extraordinary cinematic experiences I have been fortunate enough to have." Salles, "Notes," 3.

39. In *Once upon a Time Iracema*, Bodanzky says that, when *Iracema* was being shot, it was so common to see large stretches of forest burning that the crew did not even bother filming that at first.

40. João Luiz Vieira states that Edna de Cássia was chosen to play the movie's main female role from among the audience of a local radio show that drew many teenage girls, João Luiz Vieira, "Women on the Road: Sexual Tourism and Beyond," in *The Brazilian Road Movie: Journeys of (Self) Discovery*, ed. Sara Brandellero (Cardiff: University of Wales Press, 2013), 204.

41. Iracema herself refuses to be associated with the Indigenous population of Brazil and gets upset when Tião tells her that she is "Indian," saying that the is the daughter of Brazilians. This rejection of Indigenous heritage points to the negative image that the Native Amazonian population has, even within the region.

42. When Tião is buying Amazonian timber, he asks the seller to place illegal timber at the bottom and legal timber at the top of his truck, which suggests that trade in illegal timber, probably from protected species of trees, was widespread in the region.

43. Ismail Xavier, *Allegories of Underdevelopment: Aesthetics and Politics in Modern Brazilian Cinema* (Minneapolis: University of Minnesota Press, 1997). Xavier reiterates this argument in his article, cowritten with Robert Stam, where they state that "any number of seventies and eighties films by Cinema Novo veterans [including *Iracema*] offer a globalizing vision of society expressed in allegories of underdevelopment and modernization," Robert Stam and Ismail Xavier, "Transformation of National Allegory: Brazilian Cinema from Dictatorship to Redemocratization," in *Resisting Images. Essays on Cinema and History*, ed. Robert Sklar and Charles Musser (Philadelphia: Temple University Press, 1990), 298.

44. The first image of the film is that of the dense Amazonian rainforest, but the first sounds are those of the engine of a boat while the credits are still being

shown. The sound of the engine continues as viewers look at the forest, and only after that do we see the boat transporting Iracema, which is the origin of the sound. The primacy of the sound of the engine, even over the images of the rainforest, suggests that modernity and technological development have arrived and taken over Amazonia.

45. See Carolyn Merchant, *The Death of Nature: Women, Ecology and the Scientific Revolution* (New York: HarperOne, 1989), xiii.

46. Jorge Bodanzky, dir., *Era uma Vez Iracema* (2005).

47. Santos's film includes a few sequences about daily life in Native Amazonian communities and, in *Iracema*, Indigenous peoples are mostly absent. In *Embrace of the Serpent*, conversely, the Indigenous population is central to the plot. According to the film's production notes, *Embrace* is "the first Colombian film to feature an Indigenous protagonist and to be told from his perspective" [Susannah Bragg McCullough, "Ask the Director. Interview with Ciro Guerra," in *ScreenPrism* (February 17, 2016)]. For an in-depth analysis of the representation of indigeneity in the film, see Maria Chiara D'Argenio, "Decolonial Encounters in Ciro Guerra's *El abrazo de la serpiente*: Indigeneity, Coevalness and Intercultural Dialogue," *Postcolonial Studies* 21, no. 2 (2018): 131–53.

48. According to Guerra, "only the weirdest parts of the story are the ones that are completely true." The filmmaker explains that the sequence of the Messiah, who persuades a group of Indigenous people to worship him as an incarnation of Christ, is based on a real man "who arrived in that quarter of Colombia and proceeded in the late 19th century to claim [he was] the living Messiah. He was way crazier than what you see in the film. [. . .] You cannot make this stuff up" (McCullough).

49. McCullough.

50. As Guerra's interviewer explains: "Using fiction, Guerra felt he could avoid co-opting the voice or compromising the sacred knowledge of any one tribe while expressing a general yet important point of view" (McCullough).

51. As Guerra points out, "[a]ll the cinematographic elements, we used them to create an altered perspective on life." The goal was to conjure up "another way of understanding the world. So you see a world that you can recognize, but everything is slightly off. Everything is slightly different. From the sound design to the black-and-white to . . . the way the film is told and structured, everything is taking you to a different logic. It's a way of bringing an audience into a different perspective on the world" (McCullough).

52. The yakruna is a fictional plant but it is based on real plants. As Guerra explains, "[t]he Indigenous people asked us to not use the name of real plants, real rituals, to modify them—it's not something that you can learn about just from watching a film" (McCullough).

53. Work in critical anthropology has developed the notion of the pluriverse to describe the close relationship that South American Indigenous peoples establish with nonhuman forms of existence. See Marisol de la Cadena, "Indigenous Cosmopolitics in the Andes: Conceptual Reflections beyond 'Politics,'" *Cultural Anthropology* 25, no. 2 (2010): 334–70) and Arturo Escobar, *Designs for the Pluriverse: Radical*

Interdependence, Autonomy and the Making of Worlds (Durham and London: Duke University Press, 2018).

54. Ana María Mutis argues that one of the aims of the movie is to "raise the public's awareness about the importance of preserving the Amazon and protecting its communities, reaffirming the film's ecological and postcolonial aims." Ana María Mutis, "*El abrazo de la serpiente* o la re-escritura del Amazonas dentro de una ética ecológica y poscolonial," *Hispanic Research Journal* 19, no. 1 (2018): 29–40.

Works Cited

Agassiz, Louis. *A Journey in Brazil*. Boston: Houghton Mifflin, 1909.
Arnold, Jack, dir. *Creature from the Black Lagoon*. 1954; Universal Pictures.
Babenco, Hector, dir. *At Play in the Fields of the Lord*. 1991; Universal Pictures.
Bates, Henry Walter. *The Naturalist on the River Amazons*. Cambridge: Cambridge University Press, 2009.
Bodanzky, Jorge, and Orlando Senna, dirs. *Iracema, uma Transa Amazônica*. 1975; Embrafilme.
Carpentier, Alejo. *Los pasos perdidos*. Madrid: Alfaguara, 1981
Carvajal, Gaspar de. *The Discovery of the Amazon, According to the Account of Friar Gaspar de Carvajal and Other Documents*, edited by H. C. Heaton and translated by Bertram E. Lee. New York: American Geographical Society, 1934.
Castro, Ferreira de. *A Selva*. Lisbon: Guimarães Editores, 2002.
Cohan, Steven and Ina Era Hark. Introduction to *The Road Movie Book*, 1–14. Edited by Steven Cohan and Ina Era Hark. London and New York: Routledge, 1997.
Corrigan, Timothy. *A Cinema without Walls: Movies and Culture after Vietnam*. New Brunswick: Rutgers University Press, 1991.
da Cunha, Euclides. *Um Paraíso Perdido. Ensaios Amazônicos*. Brasília: Senado Federal, 2000.
D'Argenio, Maria Chiara. "Decolonial Encounters in Ciro Guerra's *El abrazo de la serpiente*: Indigeneity, Coevalness and Intercultural Dialogue." *Postcolonial Studies* 21, no. 2 (2018): 131–153.
de la Cadena, Marisol. "Indigenous Cosmopolitics in the Andes: Conceptual Reflections beyond 'Politics,'" *Cultural Anthropology* 25, no. 2 (2010): 334–70.
Diegues, Carlos, dir. *Bye Bye Brasil*. 1980; Embrafilme.
Escobar, Arturo. *Designs for the Pluriverse: Radical Interdependence, Autonomy and the Making of Worlds*. Durham and London: Duke University Press, 2018.
Garibotto, Verónica and Jorge Pérez, Introduction to *The Latin American Road Movie*, 1–28. Edited by Verónica Garibotto and Jorge Pérez. New York: Palgrave MacMillan, 2016.
Gray, James, dir. *The Lost City of Z*. 2016; Amazon Studios.
Hemming, John. *Tree of Rivers: The Story of the Amazon*. London: Thames & Hudson, 2008.

Herzog, Werner, dir. *Aguirre: The Wrath of God*. 1972; Filmverlag der Autoren.
——. *Fitzcarraldo*. 1972; Filmverlag der Autoren.
Hoyt, Harry, dir. *The Lost World*. 1925; First National Pictures.
Laderman, David. *Driving Lessons: Exploring the Road Movie*. Austin: University of Texas Press, 2002.
Lefebvre, Martin. "Between Setting and Landscape in the Cinema." In *Landscape and Film*, edited by Martin Lefebvre, 19–60. New York and London: Routledge, 2006.
Lie, Nadia. *The Latin American (Counter-) Road Movie and Ambivalent Modernity*. New York: Palgrave MacMillan, 2017.
MacDonald, Scott. "The Ecocinema Experience." In *Ecocinema Theory and Practice*, edited by Stephen Rust, Salma Monani, and Sean Cubitt, 17–42. New York and London: Routledge, 2013.
Martins, Luciana. "Silvino Santos and the Mobile View: Documentary Geographies of Modern Brazil." In *The Brazilian Road Movie: Journeys of (Self) Discovery*, edited by Sara Brandellero, 3–25. Cardiff: University of Wales Press, 2013.
McCullough, Susannah Bragg. "Ask the Director. Interview with Ciro Guerra." *ScreenPrism*, February 17, 2016.
Merchant, Carolyn. *The Death of Nature: Women, Ecology and the Scientific Revolution*. New York: HarperOne, 1989.
Mutis, Ana María. "*El abrazo de la serpiente* o la re-escritura del Amazonas dentro de una ética ecológica y poscolonial." *Hispanic Research Journal* 19, no. 1 (2018): 29–40.
Rust, Stephen and Salma Monani, Introduction to *Ecocinema Theory and Practice*, 1–14. Edited by Stephen Rust, Salma Monani, and Sean Cubitt. New York and London: Routledge, 2013.
Salles, Walter. "Notes for a Theory of the Road Movie." *The New York Times*, Nov. 11, 2007.
Souza, Márcio, *Silvino Santos: O Cineasta do Ciclo da Borracha*. Rio de Janeiro: FUNARTE, 1999.
Stam, Robert and Ismail Xavier. "Transformation of National Allegory: Brazilian Cinema from Dictatorship to Redemocratization." In *Resisting Images. Essays on Cinema and History*, edited by Robert Sklar and Charles Musser, 279–307. Philadelphia: Temple University Press, 1990.
Vieira João Luiz. "Women on the Road: Sexual Tourism and Beyond." In *The Brazilian Road Movie: Journeys of (Self) Discovery*, edited by Sara Brandellero, 199–214. Cardiff: University of Wales Press, 2013.
Willoquet-Mariconovi, Paula. "Shifting Paradigms: From Environmentalist Film to Ecocinema." In *Framing the World: Explorations in Ecocriticism and Film*, edited by Paula Willoquet-Mariconovi, 43–61. Charlottesville and London: University of Virginia Press, 2010.
Xavier, Ismail. *Allegories of Underdevelopment: Aesthetics and Politics in Modern Brazilian Cinema*. Minneapolis: University of Minnesota Press, 1997.

2

Visualizing the Geosphere

The 1985 Earthquake in Mexican Cinema

CAROLYN FORNOFF

As a visual medium, cinema privileges what geochemists call the biosphere: the parts where life exists, the parts we can see and experience. What lies beneath the earth's surface typically remains shrouded. The geosphere's invisibility makes it tricky to grasp, even though it casts the landforms and processes that delimit our lives. Although the geological is not often visualized on-screen, geology is central to visualizing practices. As Jussi Parikka's work on the materiality of media has shown, "nature affords and bears the weight of media culture, from metals and minerals to its waste load."[1] Cinema requires natural resources to sustain it, materially and economically.[2] The extraction of forms of energy from the earth like coal, oil, and gas fueled industrialization processes as well as the development of visualizing technologies like photography and cinematography, leading André Bazin to write in 1945 that a photograph was akin to a natural phenomenon, "like a flower or a snowflake whose vegetable or earthly origins are an inseparable part of their beauty."[3] Even as cinema has moved from celluloid to digital, and exhibition practices from projection to streaming, geological materials extracted from the earth continue to be essential to the lives of visual technologies: from silica for optical fiber, to lithium for batteries.

This chapter does not explore cinema's materiality per se, but rather how the geosphere's dynamism has been visualized in Mexican cinema. I focus on a human encounter with geology that is not sought out (like oil exploration or mining), but unexpected and catastrophic: the earthquake. As a radical interruption of tectonic agency into the present, the earthquake makes geological energy palpable and thrusts deep planetary time into the shorter timescales of human history. When an earthquake coincides with human civilization, it has catastrophic consequences—the loss of life, habitat, and livelihood—leading it to be designated a "natural disaster." The devastating effects of natural disasters are not uniformly levied. They are most catastrophic to those who live in built environments shaped by uneven sociohistorical processes, which in turn produce vulnerability for some more than others. Yet the natural disaster nonetheless carries collective weight. Like other ecological crises, writes environmental sociologist Enrique Leff, the natural disaster "resignifies and reorients the course of history."[4] A disjunctive, trauma-inducing event, the earthquake leaves a long wake, even after its visible signs have been swept away.

Such is the case of the earthquake that rocked Mexico City the morning of September 19, 1985. The quake looms large in the national imaginary as Mexico's most catastrophic. Anywhere between 5,000 to 45,000 people died, and billions of dollars in damage were incurred. The enormity of this event, including the mass mobilization of Mexicans of all walks of life to contribute to relief efforts, as well as the government's inadequate and delayed response, transformed it into a cultural touchstone. For many it portended the collapse of Mexico's autocratic political party, the Partido Revolucionario Institucional (PRI), and the rise of civil society. The 1985 quake was as consequential to twentieth-century Mexican sociopolitical history as two other watershed events: the Revolution and the 1968 Tlatelolco massacre. And yet, as Ignacio Padilla notes in *Arte y olvido del terremoto*, while the Revolution and Tlatelolco became recurrent commonplaces in Mexican literature and visual arts, the 1985 earthquake did not.[5] This lacuna, Padilla speculates, can be attributed to the fact that the radical political transformation that the earthquake supposedly catalyzed so quickly faded. In response to this disappointment, it was preferable to frame the disaster as a wholly "natural" anomaly, rather than remember it as a failed attempt to demand state accountability and political change.

Although the 1985 earthquake has been less frequently visualized on-screen than comparably momentous sociopolitical events, it did produce a cinematic trail worth excavating. In the immediate years following the catastrophe, several films thematized the disaster as a devastating yet redemptive political turning point. Then, as hope soured to cynicism, films from the later 1980s deployed the disaster's rubble as a metaphor for the decay of Mexican society. Throughout the 1990s and early 2000s, the event receded from view. Decades later, in the 2010s, it surprisingly reemerged as a point of cinematic interest, even before the earthquake's eerie replication in 2017 on September 19, the very same date as its deadly predecessor. By looking at films that center the cataclysmic quake, we can get a sense of how the disaster is visualized, narrated, and framed as an event where human and nonhuman forces collide.[6]

This chapter focuses on three films that thematize the historic 8.0 magnitude seismic shock. First, two films produced in its immediate aftermath, albeit of distinct genres: *Trágico terremoto en México (Furia terrenal)* (*Tragic Earthquake in Mexico Earthly Fury*), a fictionalized melodrama about the collapse of a hospital directed by Francisco Guerrero in 1987, and Maricarmen de Lara's 1986 documentary *No les pedimos un viaje a la luna* (*We're Not Asking for the Moon*), which chronicles the fight for unionization by seamstresses whose factory collapsed.[7] While markedly different in style and ideology, both films craft uplifting messages of solidarity and resilience in the face of disaster. Second, I turn my attention to a recent film that revisits the catastrophic 1985 event, *7:19: La hora del temblor* (*7:19 AM: The Hour of the Quake*, 2016), directed by Jorge Michel Grau and written in collaboration with sci-fi author Alberto Chimal.[8] *7:19* diverges from the prior films' messages of solidarity and instead focuses on re-creating the claustrophobic experience of entrapment. Like de Lara's *No les pedimos un viaje a la luna*, *7:19* effectively communicates the tragedy of the lives lost in the sudden geological event, while also performing a strenuous critique of the uneven societal conditions it unearthed. Together, these cinematic portrayals articulate that natural disasters are never wholly beyond the human, but are complex collisions between the realms of the geological, the political, the economic, and the spiritual.

Mexico is a seismic region. Its southern shore is located on a subduction zone where the Cocos, Rivera, and North American tectonic plates meet. Tectonic plates float on top of a layer of the Earth's mantle known as the asthenosphere, where convection occurs. Unlike the dense igneous rock that composes the plates in the upper mantle, the asthenosphere is hot and viscous. Its rocks flow, break apart, and force their way to the Earth's surface as magma. As the plates jostle, they push and pull, stretch, and build up stress. When that stress becomes overwhelming, a plate might subduct, springing up and lifting the ocean floor, causing an earthquake. This seismic activity can be abrupt, producing a powerful earthquake, or slow and silent, generating weak tremors that humans do not even feel.

While an earthquake might seem to be an event that is totally independent from human intervention, scholarship has increasingly shown that human activity has exacerbated and even triggered seismic activity. Human-induced earthquakes are precipitated by three main practices: mining, dam building, and fracking. These anthropogenic activities cause geological instability by adding or removing mass from the earth, disrupting its distribution. It is difficult to determine with absolute certainty which earthquakes are accelerated by human activities and which are not. And to be sure, many occur in areas untouched by industry.[9] Nonetheless, the scientific consensus is that exploitation-induced stressors aggravate naturally occurring seismicity.[10] The impossibility of parsing human from nonhuman causation in this sort of event, as Nils Bubandt observes, is one of the defining characteristics of the new geological epoch that we inhabit, the Anthropocene, the era in which human practices have acquired geological force.[11]

The human role in compounding tectonic activity is absolutely the case for Mexico City, whose characteristic soft soils amplify seismic waves. Not only is the nation situated atop three large tectonic plates, but the capital was built on the drained lakebed of Lake Texcoco. After the conquest, Spanish settlers destroyed urban Tenochtitlan's unique hydraulic agricultural system so that the Valley of Mexico could be rebuilt in Spain's image.[12] This violent erasure of the Valley's natural properties was enacted in parallel with the genocidal obliteration of Indigenous peoples and ontologies. Today, the lacustrine clays and sediments left over from the city's days as a lakebed do not soften the blow of an earthquake, as was previously thought, but amplify its waves, causing the overlying buildings to shake "like jelly."[13] The exploitation of underlying aquifers has caused the subsoil to further consolidate, effectively sinking the city and destabilizing its infrastructure.[14] These human-induced transformations of the earth have been compounded by years of duplicitous engineering, bureaucratic chicanery, and unscrupulous oversight. As Padilla argues, in this sense the 1985 earthquake starkly illustrated the high price paid by citizens for decades of "corruption, bureaucratism, criminal real estate speculation, a total lack of urban planning, and open negligence by leaders of the institutionalized revolution who did not channel resources toward an effective disaster prevention system."[15]

Mexico City's vulnerability to tectonic forces is common knowledge, and the collective trauma suffered by Chilangos because of the 1985 earthquake lingers as a source of anxiety, as brilliantly parodied in Leonardo Teja's recent novel, *Esta noche el Gran Terremoto* (*Tonight, the Great Earthquake*, 2018). According to a 2014 study conducted by Jaime Santos-Reyes, Tatiana Gouzeva, and Galdino Santos-Reyes, the Mexican public considers seismic activity to be the greatest threat to daily life, outranking factors like crime or fire.¹⁶ These latent anxieties were brought vividly back to life by the 2017 Central Mexico earthquake, which struck on September 19, the 32nd anniversary of the 1985 catastrophe. The quake provoked the collapse of more than forty buildings, the injury of nearly 6,000 people, and 370 deaths. Somewhat surprisingly, it also brought renewed attention to cultural products produced in the wake of the 1985 disaster.¹⁷ The YouTube upload of the melodrama *Trágico terremoto en México* was peppered with commenters who flocked to the film after the most recent disaster. User "Andy" commented in September 2017: "Like si lo ves en 2017 después del terremoto CDMX" [Like if you are seeing this film in 2017 after the earthquake in Mexico City], and user "BH" wrote, "2017, se siguen construyendo edificios, segundos pisos A LO PENDEJO, LOS MEXICANOS NO ENTENDEMOS, CARAJO!!!" [2017, they keep IDIOTICALLY building buildings (with) second floors, WE MEXICANS DON'T UNDERSTAND, DAMN IT!!!]. These comments evidence the long afterlives of low-budget films from the 1980s as they circulate in venues like YouTube, allowing younger viewers to find them and enjoy them not just for their content, but also as a forum for catharsis and critique. The YouTube page for *Trágico terremoto* functioned as a virtual space to commune with others in the wake of the 2017 tragedy; it was a platform where users could vent their frustrations or share their shock at the eerie timing of the two disasters.

Trágico terremoto en México (Furia terrenal), directed by Francisco Guerrero, was the first fictionalized feature entirely structured around the 1985 earthquake. Released two years after the event in 1987, the film reconstructs how the disaster disrupted normalcy. Its narrative framework is neatly divided into two parts, the twenty-four hours before and after the quake. The first half introduces the quotidian concerns of the ensemble of characters who cohabit a working-class neighborhood. The second half depicts the quake and its aftermath, bringing the characters together around a fictionalized version of Hospital Juárez, where several are trapped and others work to free them. Like other affected hospitals in Mexico City, parts of the real-life Hospital Juárez collapsed, and extensive rescue efforts took place to save patients and workers. By referencing real locations and dramatizing ripped-from-the-headlines scenes like the miraculous recovery of newborns who survived up to a week of entombment, *Trágico terremoto* relies on "coded reality links" to enhance verisimilitude.¹⁸ While it doesn't shy away from depicting death and destruction, the film mitigates the disaster's tragedy with uplifting messages of solidarity and a focus on the positive results of rescue efforts, such as the rescue of infants.

The large ensemble of characters featured in *Trágico terremoto* mirrors the testimonial collage-style narrative technique established by key texts written in the disaster's aftermath. Mark Anderson has explained that Elena Poniatowska's *Nada, nadie: Las voces del temblor*, Enrique de la Garza Toledo's *Esto pasó en México*, and Marco Antonio Campos's *Hemos perdido el reino* all adopted the form of the collage to narrate the subsequent popular mobilization.[19] For these writers, the collective response to the disaster by individuals from all walks of life heralded the rise of civil society and the decline of the autocratic PRI. Formally, they sought to represent this surge of democratic plurality by bringing together a wide array of voices within the confines of one work. *Trágico terremoto* adapts this method with lackluster results. In the film's first half, the dizzying array of character vignettes feels cursory, seemingly slapped together for the purposes of future narrative payoff.

To maintain viewers' interest for the forty-five minutes leading up to the titular disaster, each character either embodies a trope of Mexican cinema—the worried mother, the comical wino, the friendly prostitute—or is entangled in a sensationalized drama—one woman wants an abortion against her boyfriend's wishes, a doctor plots to illicitly sell babies, a soon-to-be-father rejects paternal responsibility. Within this milieu, the story of the very pregnant Patricia (Diana Golden) and her deadbeat boyfriend Miguel (Miguel Ángel Rodríguez) takes center stage. Their story is not fleshed out, but bristles with melodramatic appendages: Miguel wants to give the child up for adoption, his mother is vehemently opposed, Patricia is entangled in a love triangle. The narrative focus on Patricia's imminent delivery injects suspense into a series of events that would have been largely predictable for the Mexican audience, including the quake's timing, because many had lived through the disaster just two years prior. After Patricia goes into labor in the hospital the night of September 18, viewers are led to worry about whether the baby's birth will coincide with the quake, to fear for their safety, and wonder if Miguel will get his act together in time to appreciate his nascent family.

In this sense, it can be deduced that the filmmakers were unsure of whether the earthquake in and of itself was emotionally fraught enough to hold viewers' interest. Its plot suggests that they decided that the spectacle of geological destruction needed to be supplemented by traditional melodramatic arcs. The narrative is propelled more by the drama of human agency and decision making—the "will he" or "won't he" of Miguel's paternal ambivalence—than by the disaster. The earthquake is, as the title declares, presented as a tragedy. It is framed as arbitrary and natural, and as such, infused with less emotional investment than Miguel's wishy-washy approach to fatherhood.

The quake does, however, augment this established melodramatic arc, operating as a plot device that spurs Miguel's character development by placing Patricia and their newborn into peril. Thanks to the geological injection of life-or-death stakes, Miguel is suddenly motivated to assume his paternal role. At the film's conclusion, he successfully saves his girlfriend and baby, emerging from the rubble a hero. In their final scene, he begs for Pati's forgiveness, which she grants him, solemnly declaring, "ahora solo existe el presente y el mañana" [all that matters is right now and tomorrow]. The natural disaster functions as a narrative mechanism that brings about moral clarity and erases the past. It is only through its destruction that the conservative values longed for by the female maternal characters (Patricia and Miguel's mother) can be reestablished. These conservative heteronormative values are articulated as the only horizon for present and future reconstitution of the fractured social foundation.

While Patricia and her child are saved from the collapsed hospital, others are not so lucky. The characters who meet their end within the wreckage include the prostitute, the young woman with a scheduled abortion, and the unscrupulous doctor who was going to sell her baby to foreigners. These didactic fatalities compound the film's conservative messaging, transforming the earthquake into an instrument of divine retribution. Because viewers are not set up to root for any of the characters who die inside the collapsed building, the immense loss of life is less emotionally fraught than other narrative threads like Miguel's paternal reluctance. The construction of characters as unlikeable within the film's orthodox worldview—for instance, the young woman seeking an abortion is abrasive and belittling—transforms these characters' deaths into more of a spectacle than a tragedy.

Trágico terremoto frames the earthquake as an organic event that only intersects with human civilization through its effects. Its causes remain mystified, and its interaction with specific human practices, like the use of subpar construction materials, goes unmentioned. Furthermore, in spite of the general furor around the deficient governmental response to the quake, political commentary is sidestepped. *Trágico terremoto* instead frames the catastrophic event as a wholly apolitical spectacle, a divine restoration of heteronormative family values, a disaster that made heroes out of lackluster men.

Whereas *Trágico terremoto* represents the earthquake as entirely disconnected from human forces, Mari Carmen de Lara's 1986 documentary, *No les pedimos un viaje a la luna,* decidedly points in another direction. While it too celebrates the collective nature of the rescue efforts and the subsequent campaigns for alternative forms of organized labor that were inspired by the quake, it also presents the disaster as unnatural: the result of tectonic forces compounded by human ones. De Lara's Ariel award-winning hour-long documentary follows the unionization efforts of seamstresses whose workplaces collapsed during the quake, killing their coworkers and causing them to lose their jobs. In total, more than 800 workshops were destroyed and 40,000 garment workers suddenly unemployed. Because the garment industry was the second-highest employer of female labor in Mexico at the time, the documentary focuses on women and has a feminist bent. De Lara was one of only a few female directors active in the Mexican film industry in the 1980s. She presents women as important historical actors and subjects deserving of representation.

Positioned within a tradition of documentary film that presents history from marginalized perspectives, *No les pedimos un viaje a la luna* is conducted in an expository/performative mode. De Lara eschews authoritative voice-over commentary in favor of an argument assembled through a chorus of testimonial interviews, another example of the collage format favored by contemporaneous earthquake culture. Individual stories are interwoven into a message of collective action, engendering an activist film that was used as an organizational tool in unionization efforts. It also puts forward a potent critique of the government's response to the disaster, drawn out through reflexive techniques. These include, as Diane Sippil observes, "cross-cutting official and unofficial reactions to the earthquake," a technique that stirs the viewer to recognize the gap between the state's words and its actions, the way things are and the way they should be.[20]

In a series of interviews conducted against the city's crumpled backdrop, workers who survived the collapse recount their employers' reprehensible behavior. The salvaging of safety-deposit boxes and machinery was prioritized over the rescue of women trapped inside; surviving workers were summarily fired without compensation. These shameful actions were aided and abetted by the government. Safeguarding the interests of factory owners, the army prevented residents and family members from helping with excavation efforts or accused them of looting. The seismic event became an unnatural disaster: its effects exacerbated and manufactured by human intervention. The unethical behavior of both the government and their employers led the women to question more quotidian aspects of their labor conditions, such as low wages and disproportionate punishment for tardiness.

The quake is thus explicitly presented by *No les pedimos un viaje a la luna* as the impetus for political mobilization and a catalyst for change. Its devastating consequences rip a tear in the *habitus*—what Pierre Bourdieu theorizes as generating "all the 'reasonable,' 'common-sense,' behaviors" that are encouraged by the logic immanent to social structures and reflexively reinforced through practice—unearthing troublesome conditions that were previously accepted as fixed.[21] One of the garment workers describes how the quake's physical and temporal disruption allowed her and her coworkers to see the conditions regulating their lives with fresh eyes:

> Este sismo vino a sacudir esas conciencias, y vino a sacudirnos a nosotros y abrirnos los ojos para valorar realmente lo que es el trabajo, lo que es un salario, lo que es la vida cotidiana. Realmente nadie valora su vida tal cual es, sino que seguimos creyendo que el recibir un salario es suficiente, lo que nos están pagando, sin tener conciencia clara de que es nuestra vida lo que vamos dejando ahí, nuestra juventud, nuestra fuerza, nuestra salud misma.

> [This earthquake came as a wake-up call, it came to shake us and open our eyes to reevaluate what work is, what a salary is, what daily life is. No one really values their life as it is, instead we keep thinking that the mere fact of receiving a salary is sufficient, that what they are paying us is enough, without having a clear awareness that it is our lives that we are leaving there (in the factory), our youth, our strength, even our health itself.]

The quake is destructive but also future making: it invites a reconsideration of the value of life, health, and labor. The new garment cooperative that the women form in the disaster's wake is centered around a "nosotras" rather than a "patrón," as one woman explains. The ingress of geological deep time into the historical present opens a portal from which to probe the status quo, reevaluate the self, and create new alliances—a stance not so different from that of *Trágico terremoto*, albeit to divergent ideological ends. This reframes our understanding of the geologic: from not only a force of the deep past that long ago structured our environment, but something with a hand in organizing the present and the future, economically and politically, through its corollaries of loss, reorganization, and creation. This idea that the quake signifies a schism with the past is shared by both films discussed so far—reflecting the contemporaneous sense that there was no going back to before the quake, that it had indelibly changed community, politics, and ideology.

While *No les pedimos un viaje a la luna* and *Trágico terremoto en México* are the two primary instances of contemporaneous cinematic production whose plot and content fully revolve around the 1985 quake, several other films shot during the 1980s also incorporate the event as setting or narrative device. In terms of set design, toppled buildings and debris were referenced or re-created on-screen to evoke this recognizable moment in the city's history as well as visually cue social and psychic turmoil. *Derrumbe (Esta historia no se olvida)* (*Collapse: This Story Will Not Be Forgotten*), directed by Eduardo Carrasco in 1986, opens with footage of a building collapsing and features protagonist Fabián (Eduardo Palomo) driving through a shattered Mexico City. Filmed shortly after the quake, Carrasco deploys the city's visible damage to allegorically magnify the film's themes of degradation, corruption, and ruination.

María Novaro's 1989 fictionalized feature *Lola* took a similar approach. While it does not dramatize the event itself, its plot unfolds against the backdrop of a Mexico City in ruins. Elissa Rashkin has written that omnipresent signs of the earthquake's damage "in the form of crumbling buildings" echo and heighten Lola's "crumbling emotional state."[22] In addition to reflecting the protagonist's internal malaise, the visual reminder of the wrecked metropolis performs an implicit criticism of the state's slow-moving efforts to rebuild poorer neighborhoods, such as Tlalpan, where the film takes place.[23] Novaro confirmed this interpretation in an interview with Isabel Arredondo, commenting that *Lola* manifests her disillusionment with the PRI.[24] Its backdrop of slumping buildings underscores the thematic critique of governmental neglect of the lower class, while also prompting viewers to think about the uneven societal impacts of disasters, which wreak the most damage on the most vulnerable sectors of society.

Other films, such as *El otro crimen* (*The Other Crime*, Carlos González Morantes, 1988), *El niño y el Papa* (*The Boy and the Pope,* Rodrigo Castaño, 1986), and *Ciudad de ciegos* (*City of the Blind,* Alberto Cortés, 1990), also include scenes or allusions to the disaster.[25] In some, the quake's destructive aftermath merely sets the mood, while in others the event occupies a pivotal plot point. In *El niño y el Papa*, it sets the film's events in motion by killing a boy's mother and prompting him to search for her. Inversely, in the detective thriller *El otro crimen*, it provides convenient closure by killing off the protagonist in the film's climax.

After the small flurry of films that thematized the 1985 quake through the decade's close, by the 1990s, the historic catastrophe largely receded from the national visual imaginary, just as it did from other modes of cultural production. While the Revolution or the Tlatelolco massacre continued to accrue artistic attention years after the fact, the 1985 earthquake did not. Rather, a sort of cultural amnesia set in, which Padilla posits resulted from the generalized malaise produced by the realization that the solidarity and political change that seemed imminent in the quake's wake had evaporated into thin air.[26] While the earthquake had been interpreted by so many as a definitive schism with the past—an unearthing of societal ills that could not be reinterred—it had no such watershed effect. While more stringent regulations were put in place and new popular movements formed, there was no justice for the victims, and the PRI held on to power for fifteen more years by co-opting the discourse of solidarity and successfully wooing the leaders of newly mobilized groups.[27] Consequently, the 1985 earthquake was more comfortably forgotten.

Perhaps unsure about how to revisit the traumatic event without transforming it into a spectacle of destruction or a deceptive promise of political transformation, artists chose not to represent it at all. This absence was also a form of self-protection, an assurance that the geotectonic catastrophe was a natural aberrance and not something that might be repeated and therefore helpful to keep alive in the cultural memory. It wasn't until recently, leading up to its thirtieth anniversary, that the 1985 disaster regained visibility within Mexican cultural production. Revitalized interest came from several cultural modalities: the aforementioned 2010 essayistic book by Padilla, Teja's sardonic 2018 novel, as well as several commemorative museum exhibits in 2015 at the Museo de la Ciudad de México and the Museo Nacional de la Estampa.[28]

Similarly, director Jorge Michel Grau hoped to time the premiere of his planned feature, *7:19 La hora del temblor*, so that it would coincide with the event's thirtieth anniversary in 2015. Because of financing setbacks, production was delayed, and *7:19* ultimately debuted in 2016.[29] Grau has mentioned in interviews that he was drawn to the topic because his father was an architect who was involved in the evaluative work that took place in the quake's aftermath. He could not shake the memory of his father crying because he was shocked to discover that "the government used really bad materials" to construct several of the collapsed buildings.[30]

Written by Grau in collaboration with novelist Alberto Chimal, *7:19* re-creates the terrifying experience of those victimized on September 19, 1985, commemorating the tragedy of the lives lost while also critiquing the inequity and corruption that compounded the geological event. Grau is best known for his debut feature *Somos lo que hay* (*We Are What We Are*) (2010), a horror cum drama about a family of cannibals. *7:19* is another genre-bending film: a claustrophobic thriller meets based-on-true-events period drama. Like *Trágico terremoto*, *7:19* can also be described as an example of the disaster genre, which Maurice Yacowar loosely defines as structured by "a situation of normalcy [that] erupts into a persuasive image of death."[31] For an art film meets thriller about a historical event, *7:19* was moderately successful at the box office, taking in 6.6 million pesos in revenue (about half that of contemporaneous thriller *Paraíso perdido*, a film about narco violence more preoccupied with plot than aesthetics).

7:19 takes place in the lobby of an office building on the morning of September 19, 1985. It opens minutes before the quake as a half-dozen office workers trickle in, chat, check their mail, and head upstairs. At 7:19 AM the tremor hits, and the seven-story building collapses. The boss, Licenciado Fernando Pellicer (Demián Bichir), and the security guard, Martín Soriano (Héctor Bonilla), are trapped together in the lobby's rubble: the Licenciado's legs pinned down by a beam, Martín stuck in a seated position at his desk. Both men are surrounded by debris but can see each other thanks to a flashlight. Several other office workers have also survived, but are buried elsewhere. The camera remains penned in with the two protagonists; the other survivors are never seen on-screen, present only as off-screen interlocutors. The rest of the film recounts small dramas of survival: attempts to glean information from the outside world, an effort to toss batteries from one character to the other, the decision to drink urine to stay hydrated, an aftershock that resettles the debris, and ultimately, an incautious rescue attempt conducted with heavy machinery that disrupts the wreckage and crushes both protagonists in the film's final minutes.

7:19 is innovative in its conceit. Other than the first five minutes, the entirety of the film involves only two on-screen characters, trapped in one space, who never move—except for one instance, when one character goes from sitting to lying down. This restricted space and cast give *7:19* a theatrical quality, supplemented by cinematographic techniques like the unorthodox tightening and widening of the screen aspect ratio to echo the survivors' cramped perspective and exceptional attention to mise-en-scène, like the use of only natural or diegetic light sources to enhance verisimilitude. The characters' limited mobility and the close proximity of the camera, which is confined within the rubble alongside the protagonists, places increased attention on the actors' emotive abilities. Rather than fill up each scene with dialogue, sound design builds texture through an unsettling cacophony of creaking materials, muffled screams, and indistinguishable whimpers. These elements give shape to a cinematic experience that places the viewer within the experience of the 1985 disaster, not gazing down at the rubble from the outside, but trapped within it—myopic and debilitated.

This focus on re-creating the sensations of claustrophobia and bodily vulnerability experienced by those hit hardest by the disaster differentiates *7:19* from previous films that dramatized the 1985 quake. This shift can be attributed to temporal distance, which allows Grau to dwell upon the event's horror without needing to sublimate it into healing affective modalities. Whereas *Trágico terremoto* and *No les pedimos un viaje a la luna* subsume trauma into restorative messages of solidarity, asking the audience to remember the disaster as a moment of collaboration, here the emphasis is on the traumatic experience and its numerous fatalities, deaths that the film argues should not be remembered as anything other than the appalling result of gross negligence. In this sense, Grau revisits the 1985 event in order to deflate the notion that it is a tragedy from which society has healed. *7:19* reopens that wound and dwells in it to suggest that the conditions that brought about the disaster have not really changed and thus is a horror that should be more present in the cultural imaginary, even three decades after the fact.

Because *7:19* uses a national tragedy as the basis for a thriller—one that ignites viewers' primal fascination with claustrophobic terror or unexpected catastrophe—it warrants asking whether this blending of disaster with entertainment is exploitative. Susan Sontag, writing about science fiction, famously explained that the appeal of disaster is that it allows viewers to vicariously live out their self-destructive desires and apocalyptic fantasies. She cautions that aestheticized disaster can be problematic; it can "normalize what is psychologically unbearable," "neutralize" real or anticipated terrors, or provide an easy out that magically erases a troublesome status quo.[32] Sontag condemns this "dispassionate, aesthetic view of destruction and violence" for being both moralizing and morally simplistic, stripped of social critique.[33]

Exemplary of what Sontag terms the "dispassionate, aesthetic view of destruction" is the classic footage circulated in the wake of an earthquake: a full shot of a building collapsing. It is normally taken from a nearby location, and captures within its frame the whole edifice, which seemingly comes to life, sways unnaturally, and crashes down like a wave, or buckles in from the middle, leaving only a billow of dust in its place. These sorts of images are riveting because they depict something that is presumably solid as suddenly in motion. The inanimate becomes animate; a looming presence is abruptly rendered powder. This spectacle of destruction also reenacts the Western archetypal dyad of human versus nature. A sign of human achievement, the building is easily crumpled by unseen environmental force. This external view obscures human causation. In fact, it obscures the human altogether, inuring the viewer to the violence of the collapse. We can watch this footage without feeling that we are experiencing death. We do not see the people inside the building; they are anonymous and invisible. The image is clean—there is no blood or suffering, only spectacular ruination.

Emblematic long shots of buildings collapsing like decks of cards are included in most films about earthquakes, including *No les pedimos un viaje a la luna* and *Derrumbe*, often as establishing shots. They also permeate the crowdsourced visual record of the 2017 earthquake in Mexico City, with smartphone footage of crumpling structures going instantly viral. This iconic visualization of the moment the earthquake hits, captured through a long shot of a collapsing building, is conspicuously missing from *7:19*. This absence could be chalked up to budgetary constraints, but other fiction films have skirted around similar limitations by including found footage to enhance verisimilitude through this visual trope.

The decision not to use this standard external visualization of the collapsing building in *7:19* avoids aestheticizing the disaster into an apocalyptic spectacle. By confining the camera alongside the trapped protagonists, the viewer cannot become a voyeur, nor the ruins a display. Instead, the use of the worm's-eye view localized within the rubble intensifies the identification between the viewer and the victim. Like the victim, the viewer's sight and mobility are limited because of the lack of traveling or external shots. This dampens the scopophilic power that is typically associated with the camera—in which the camera/audience occupies the viewpoint of the unharmed spectator who has freedom of movement, the optical power to peer down at victims or marvel at the reduction of an edifice to rubble. By narrowing the scope and only visualizing the disaster from within, *7:19* pushes back against the viewer's desire to derive pleasure from the moment of destruction or overly identify with the heroic rescuers, instead recentering the victims' trauma.

The experience of watching *7:19* is an exercise in endurance.[34] Its use of tight shots, a cramped set, and a limited number of on-screen actors enhances the sensation of claustrophobia experienced by the audience. In this sense, even though *7:19* forms part of the disaster film genre, the experience of watching it is not so distinct from that of slow cinema. It asks a lot of its viewers; it creates an uncomfortable viewing experience that requires the viewer's determination to continue watching.

7:19 also destabilizes the notion that natural disasters are democratic events that affect all people equally, regardless of class or race. This perception that a natural calamity's effects are borne evenly across society is often reinforced by disaster films, which tend to depict natural phenomena as uniformly injurious. Mexico's very first earthquake film, Sergei Eisenstein's groundbreaking documentary short, *Desastre en Oaxaca*, underscored the impartial wrath of Oaxaca's 1931 earthquake through a series of images that equated the destruction of rich and poor neighborhoods and the uniform harm of Indigenous, mestizo, and white victims.[35] This messaging of the earthquake's universal consequences served to drum up support for disaster relief from the elite Chilango audience that viewed the short in 1931 at a fundraising event at Teatro Iris, but it also reinforced the perception that natural disasters were wholly "natural" and entirely disconnected from existing social inequities.[36]

7:19 puts the naturalness of the 1985 disaster into question by writing culpability into the script. It is ultimately revealed that the Licenciado was involved in the subpar construction of the building that now entraps them, a corrupt scheme to skim money from the construction budget through bribery and the use of third-rate materials. Spurred by a hallucinated apparition of his young daughter urging him to "tell them," he confesses his crime to the other survivors, who angrily reject his guilt as of little use. He tries to justify his actions, sputtering that, compared to other politicians, his corruption was only a drop in the bucket.

This aspect of the plot underscores the anthropogenic nature of the disaster—and undermines the Licenciado's initial declaration that this is all just a terrible accident. As one of the off-screen characters sarcastically intones, how could they have known that Mexico City would experience such a tremendous earthquake, given that it merely sits atop three enormous tectonic plates? This narrative arc reframes the drama's premise to suggest that its horror is not just natural, but generated by all-too-human forces, situating the disaster at the interface of environment, politics, and capitalism. The dystopian scenario of being buried alive rehearsed in *7:19* is one that is triggered by tectonic force, but solidified by human hubris, greed, and wishful thinking.

Likewise, the dialectic drama between the Licenciado and Martín revises the fictive discourse of interclass solidarity emergent from the 1985 disaster, revealing that such solidarity is impossible when one class has systematically undermined the other. The evolution of the characters' rapport through the unfolding crisis morphs from one of mutual support to condemnation: bitter accusations fly of laziness and greed. While both men are caught in the same situation, only one of them has contributed to its creation. The film harnesses the audience's yearning for interclass solidarity to emerge from the rubble. But with the benefit of hindsight, Grau articulates the impossibility of this fantasy. This sentiment is crystalized visually in the final sequence before the protagonists are crushed. The two men are lying down, penned in by debris, hands outstretched to one another, but never reaching. The restrictive horizontal frame captures them as equals in desperation and death, helpless to overcome the weight of human history catalyzed by the earth.

Our remembrance of disasters is mediated and constructed by culture. Images of disasters allow us to affix meaning to destruction and give them emotional value.[37] The ways that we understand or recall a disaster shift over time, as is apparent in the disparate interpretations of the 1985 quake in Mexican cinema. These films reflect the concerns of the times, ranging from uplifting messages to strident critiques of the human role in perpetuating precarity. The chaos imparted on September 19 has been divergently encoded as cleansing societal decay in the conservative messaging of *Trágico terremoto*, or as a catalyst of political awakening in *No les pedimos un viaje a la luna*. In other films, like María Novaro's *Lola*, visual reminders of societal collapse are symbolic of political turpitude, but also its index—the physical evidence of venal cronyism. Thirty years after the fact, the event proves rich ground for the horror genre, evidenced by *7:19*'s profoundly pessimistic take that this dystopian nightmare is not necessarily confined to the past.

What unites these films is an interest in how the earthquake indexes the materiality of our world and the vulnerability of the spaces we inhabit. As a sudden interruption of the geosphere into the biosphere, the earthquake underscores the short temporal nature of humanity in comparison with the deeper history of the planet that we inhabit. Its cataclysmic effects are metonymic of the possible end of human history, illustrating humanity's precarious place on a planet that will long outlast us. Yet these films do more than just assert geological agency. Like other examples of the contemporary Latin American material turn analyzed by Héctor Hoyos, these films engage with the vibrant agency of the nonhuman world while never losing sight of "the human-centered methods of historical materialism": the entanglement of the nonhuman realm with politics, economics, and history.[38] The films that revisit the historic earthquake of 1985 reveal it to be a disaster that emerges from the intersecting forces of nature and human politics. They indicate that the natural disaster is never truly "natural" but bound up in questions of industry, politics, and corruption.

Notes

1. Jussi Parikka, *A Geology of Media* (Minneapolis: University of Minnesota Press, 2015), viii.

2. Carl Mora has observed for instance that the global collapse of oil prices in 1982 consolidated structural changes within the Mexican film industry, including its increased privatization. Carl Mora, *Mexican Cinema: Reflections of a Society, 1896–2004*, 3rd edition (Jefferson, NC: McFarland, 2005), 142.

3. André Bazin, "The Ontology of the Photographic Image," trans. Hugh Gray, *Film Quarterly* 13, no. 4 (1960), 7.

4. Mark Anderson, "Introduction: The Depths of Crisis," in *Ecological Crisis and Cultural Representation in Latin America: Ecocritical Perspectives on Art, Film, and Literature*, ed. Mark Anderson and Zélia M. Bora (Lanham, MA: Lexington Books, 2016), xiii.

5. Ignacio Padilla, *Arte y olvido del terremoto* (México: Almadía, 2010), 16.

6. Prior to the 1985 tremor, few Mexican films featured earthquakes. Sergei Eisenstein's short documentary *El desastre en Oaxaca* (*Disaster in Oaxaca*), filmed not long after the Russian filmmaker's arrival in Mexico, recorded the aftermath of a 1931 quake that devastated half of Oaxaca City. The footage was sold to international newsreels, and its positive portrayal of the government's response built goodwill between the foreign film crew and state officials. It also debuted several cinematic techniques that Eisenstein would later deploy in *Qué viva México!*, including low-angle shots of religious iconography, motionless Indigenous subjects, and an overall "pictorial" composition.

The first Mexican fiction feature to include an earthquake prominently in its plot was Fernando Méndez's 1959 melodrama *Señoritas* (*Young Ladies*), which concluded with a scene reenacting the earthquake that hit Mexico City on July 29, 1957. The 1978 feature *Terremoto en Guatemala* (*Earthquake in Guatemala*), a coproduction between Mexico and Guatemala directed by Rafael Lanuza, inspired by Hollywood disaster film *Earthquake* (Mark Robson 1974), crafted a thriller around newlyweds surviving the deadly quake that struck Guatemala City in 1976.

7. *Trágico terremoto en México*, directed by Francisco Guerrero (1987; México: Productora Metropolitana). *Trágico terremoto* was written by Reyes Bercini and based on a short story by Ignacio García Cardelle. It ran for two weeks in 1990 in

select Mexico City theaters. María Luisa Amador and Jorge Ayala Blanco, *Cartelera cinematográfica: 1980–1989* (México: UNAM, 2006), 494.

No les pedimos un viaje a la luna, directed by Mari Carmen de Lara (1987; New York: First Run/Icarus Films).

8. *7:19 La hora del temblor*, directed by Jorge Michel Grau (2016; Mexico: Almada Films).

9. Gillian R. Foulger, Miles P Wilson, Jon G Gluyas, Bruce R Julian, and Richard B Davies, "Global Review of Human-Induced Earthquakes," *Earth-Science Reviews* 178 (2018): 438–514.

10. Maria Kozlowska, Beata Orlecka-Sikora, Lukasz Rudzinski, Szymon Cielesta, and Grzegorz Mutke, "A Typical Evolution of Seismicity Patterns Resulting from the Coupled Natural, Human-Induced and Coseismic Stresses in a Long Wall Coal Mining Environment," *International Journal of Rock Mechanics and Mining Sciences* 86 (2016): 5–15.

11. Nils Bubandt, "Haunted Geologies: Spirits, Stones, and the Necropolitics of the Anthropocene," in *Arts of Living on a Damaged Planet: Ghosts of the Anthropocene*, ed. Anna Tsing, Heather Swanson, Elaine Gan, and Nils Bubandt (Minneapolis: University of Minnesota Press, 2017), G122.

12. Ivonne del Valle, "From José de Acosta to the Enlightenment: Barbarians, Climate Change, and (Colonial) Technology as the End of History," *Eighteenth Century* 54, no. 4 (2013): 435–59.

13. Seth Borenstein, "Soft Soil Makes Mexico City Shake Like It Was Built on Jelly," Associated Press, September 20, 2017.

14. Efraín Ovando-Shelley, Alexandra Ossa, and Enrique Santoyo, "Effects of Regional Subsidence and Earthquakes on Architectural Monuments in Mexico City," *Boletín de la Sociedad Geológica Mexicana* 65, no. 1 (2013): 157–67.

15. Ignacio Padilla, *Arte y olvido del terremoto* (México: Almadía, 2010), 12. All translations are mine.

16. Jaime Santos-Reyes, Tatiana Gouzeva, and Galdino Santos-Reyes, "Earthquake Risk Perception and Mexico City's Public Safety," *Procedia Engineering* 84 (2014): 662–71.

17. The 2017 disaster prompted director Kuno Becker, who was in the final stages of editing a film about the 1985 quake, to change both the film's title and conclusion so that it would be more sensitive to the recent tragedy. Becker altered the title from *El día del temblor* to *El día de la unión* and modified the conclusion to be "much more inspiring" than previously planned. This titular shift from presenting the tectonic event as a thrilling tragedy to a moment of solidarity reflects the malleable significance of the natural disaster, which shape-shifts depending on the temporal distance that separates viewers from the event. Diana García, "Kuno Becker sensibilizará al público con la cinta 'El día de la Unión,'" *La voz Arizona*, April 10, 2018.

18. David Wilt, "Based on a True Story: Reality-Based Exploitation Cinema in Mexico," in *Latsploitation, Exploitation Cinemas, and Latin America*, ed. Victoria Ruétalo and Dolores Tierney (New York: Routledge, 2009), 167.

19. Mark Anderson, *Disaster Writing: The Cultural Politics of Catastrophe in Latin America* (Charlottesville: University of Virginia Press, 2011), 178.

20. Diane Sippil, "*Al Cine de las Mexicanas: Lola* in the Limelight," in *Redirecting the Gaze: Gender, Theory, and Cinema in the Third World*, ed. Diana Maury Robin and Ira Jaffe (Albany: State University of New York Press, 1999), 38.

21. Pierre Bourdieu, *The Logic of Practice*, trans. Richard Nice (Palo Alto: Stanford University Press, 1990), 55.

22. Elissa J. Rashkin, *Women Filmmakers in Mexico: The Country of Which We Dream* (Austin: University of Texas Press, 2001), 190.

23. Traci Roberts-Camp, "Female Solidarity in the Films of María Novaro: *Aquí solo encontramos amigas*," *Chasqui* 41, no. 2 (2012): 55.

24. Isabel Arredondo, *Motherhood in Mexican Cinema, 1941–1991: The Transformation of Femininity on Screen* (Jefferson, NC: McFarland, 2014), 164.

25. These films are referenced by Wilt, "Based on a True Story," 169 n3.

26. Padilla, *Arte y olvido del terremoto*, 39.

27. Anderson, *Disaster Writing*, 186.

28. The exhibits commemorating the 1985 event included Museo de la Ciudad de México's "A 30 años del sismo: Emergencia, solidaridad y cultura política," "Réplicas: El imaginario colectivo del sismo 1985," and Museo Nacional de la Estampa's "Intemperie."

29. "Entrevista con Jorge Michel Grau, director de *7:19*," *Imcine*, September 23, 2016, https://www.imcine.gob.mx/comunicacion-social/comunicados-y-noticias/entrevista-con-jorge-michel-grau-director-de-7-19.

30. Jeremy Kay, "Ventana Sur: Jorge Michel Grau eyes next project," December 1, 2016, https://www.screendaily.com/news/ventana-sur-jorge-michel-grau-eyes-next-project/5111850.article.

31. Maurice Yacowar, "The Bug in the Rug: Notes on the Disaster Genre," in *Film Genre Reader II*, ed. Barry Keith Grant (University of Texas Press, 2003), 261.

32. Susan Sontag, "The Imagination of Disaster," *Commentary* 40 (October 1965): 45.

33. Ibid., 45.

34. My thanks to Olivia Cosentino for this insight and for her feedback on this chapter.

35. *Desastre en Oaxaca*, directed by Sergei M. Eisenstein (1931; Mexico: Mexican Film Trust).

36. Eduardo de la Vega Alfaro, "Visiones eisensteinianas de Oaxaca," in *Microhistorias del cine en México* (México: Universidad de Guadalajara/UNAM/Imcine/Cineteca Nacional, 2000), 355.

37. Gennifer S. Weisenfeld, *Imagining Disaster: Tokyo and the Visual Culture of Japan's Great Earthquake of 1923* (Berkeley: University of California Press, 2012), 1.

38. Héctor Hoyos, *Things with a History: Transcultural Materialism and the Literatures of Extraction in Contemporary Latin America* (New York: Columbia University Press, 2019), 28.

Works Cited

Amador, María Luisa, and Jorge Ayala Blanco. *Cartelera cinematográfica: 1980–1989*. México: UNAM, 2006.

Anderson, Mark. *Disaster Writing: The Cultural Politics of Catastrophe in Latin America*. Charlottesville, VA: University of Virginia Press, 2011.

———. "Introduction: The Depths of Crisis." In *Ecological Crisis and Cultural Representation in Latin America: Ecocritical Perspectives on Art, Film, and Literature,* edited by Mark Anderson and Zélia M. Bora, ix–xxxii. Lanham, MA: Lexington Books, 2016.

Arredondo, Isabel. *Motherhood in Mexican Cinema, 1941–1991: The Transformation of Femininity on Screen*. Jefferson, NC: McFarland, 2014.

Bazin, André. "The Ontology of the Photographic Image." Translated by Hugh Gray. *Film Quarterly* 13, no. 4 (1960): 4–9.

Borenstein, Seth. "Soft Soil Makes Mexico City Shake Like It Was Built on Jelly." *Associated Press*, September 20, 2017.

Bourdieu, Pierre. *The Logic of Practice*. Translated by Richard Nice. Stanford: Stanford University Press, 1990.

Bubandt, Nils. "Haunted Geologies: Spirits, Stones, and the Necropolitics of the Anthropocene." In *Arts of Living on a Damaged Planet: Ghosts of the Anthropocene,* edited by Anna Tsing, Heather Swanson, Elaine Gan, and Nils Bubandt, G121–G141. Minneapolis: University of Minnesota Press, 2017.

De Lara, Mari Carmen, dir. *No les pedimos un viaje a la luna*. 1987; New York: First Run/Icarus Films.

Del Valle, Ivonne. "From José de Acosta to the Enlightenment: Barbarians, Climate Change, and (Colonial) Technology as the End of History." *The Eighteenth Century* 54, no. 4 (2013): 435–59.

De la Vega Alfaro, Eduardo. "Visiones eisensteinianas de Oaxaca." In *Microhistorias del cine en México*, 337–65. México: Universidad de Guadalajara/UNAM/Imcine/Cineteca Nacional, 2000.

Eisenstein, Sergei M., dir. *Desastre en Oaxaca*, 1931; Mexico: Mexican Film Trust.

"Entrevista con Jorge Michel Grau, director de 7:19." *Imcine*. September 23, 2016. https://www.imcine.gob.mx/comunicacion-social/comunicados-y-noticias/entrevista-con-jorge-michel-grau-director-de-7-19.

Foulger, Gillian R., Miles P. Wilson, Jon G. Gluyas, Bruce R. Julian, and Richard B. Davies. "Global Review of Human-Induced Earthquakes." *Earth-Science Reviews* 178 (March 2018): 438–514.

Hoyos, Héctor. *Things with a History: Transcultural Materialism and the Literatures of Extraction in Contemporary Latin America.* New York: Columbia University Press, 2019.

García, Diana. "Kuno Becker sensibilizará al público con la cinta 'El día de la Unión.'" *La voz Arizona.* April 10, 2018. https://www.lavozarizona.com/story/entretenimiento/tvymas/2018/04/10/kuno-becker-cinta-el-dia-de-la-union/504472002/.

Grau, Jorge Michel, dir. *7:19 La hora del temblor.* 2016; Mexico: Almada Films.

Guerrero, Francisco, dir. *Trágico terremoto en México.* 1987; México: Productora Metropolitana.

Kay, Jeremy. "Ventana Sur: Jorge Michel Grau eyes next project." *Screen Daily*, December 1, 2016. https://www.screendaily.com/news/ventana-sur-jorge-michel-grau-eyes-next-project/5111850.article.

Kozlowska, Maria, Beata Orlecka-Sikora, Lukasz Rudzinski, Szymon Cielesta, and Grzegorz Mutke. "A Typical Evolution of Seismicity Patterns Resulting from the Coupled Natural, Human-Induced and Coseismic Stresses in a Long Wall Coal Mining Environment." *International Journal of Rock Mechanics and Mining Sciences* 86 (July 2016): 5–15.

Mora, Carl. *Mexican Cinema: Reflections of a Society, 1896–2004.* 3rd edition. Jefferson, NC: McFarland, 2005.

Ovando-Shelley, Efraín, Alexandra Ossa, and Enrique Santoyo. "Effects of Regional Subsidence and Earthquakes on Architectural Monuments in Mexico City." *Boletín de la Sociedad Geológica Mexicana* 65, no. 1 (2013): 157–67.

Padilla, Ignacio. *Arte y olvido del terremoto.* México: Almadía, 2010.

Parikka, Jussi. *A Geology of Media.* Minneapolis: University of Minnesota Press, 2015.

Rashkin, Elissa J. *Women Filmmakers in Mexico: The Country of Which We Dream.* Austin: University of Texas Press, 2001.

Roberts-Camp, Traci. "Female Solidarity in the Films of María Novaro: *Aquí solo encontramos amigas.*" *Chasqui* 41, no. 2 (November 2012): 51–62.

Santos-Reyes, Jaime, Tatiana Gouzeva, and Galdino Santos-Reyes. "Earthquake Risk Perception and Mexico City's Public Safety." *Procedia Engineering* 84 (2014): 662–71.

Sippl, Diane. "*Al cine de las mexicanas: Lola* in the Limelight." In *Redirecting the Gaze: Gender, Theory, and Cinema in the Third World*, edited by Diana Maury Robin and Ira Jaffe, 33–66. Albany: State University of New York University Press, 1999.

Sontag, Susan. "The Imagination of Disaster." *Commentary* 40. October 1, 1965, https://www.commentarymagazine.com/articles/susan-sontag/the-imagination-of-disaster/.

Weisenfeld, Gennifer S. *Imagining Disaster: Tokyo and the Visual Culture of Japan's Great Earthquake of 1923*. Berkeley: University of California Press, 2012.

Wilt, David. "Based on a True Story: Reality-Based Exploitation Cinema in Mexico." In *Latsploitation, Exploitation Cinemas, and Latin America*, edited by Victoria Ruétalo and Dolores Tierney, 158–70. New York: Routledge, 2009.

Yacowar, Maurice. "The Bug in the Rug: Notes on the Disaster Genre." In *Film Genre Reader II*, edited by Barry Keith Grant, 261–79. University of Texas Press, 2003.

3

Revisiting Nature and Documenting the Americas

From Alexander von Humboldt to the Contemporary Latin American Documentary

JUANA NEW

> Should we not learn the lesson that, for example, the woods, which poets praise as the human being's loveliest abode, is hardly grasped in its true meaning if we relate it only to ourselves?
>
> —Jakob Uexküll[1]

In his book *A Foray Into the Worlds of Animals and Humans* (1934), the German biologist Jakob Uexküll describes space as an effect of sensory perception that reveals the notion of the "one and only one world" to be nothing more than an illusion that validates human ascendancy over nature and alleviates our anxiety before the unknown.[2] The bodies of humans, animals, and plants appear in his work as essential dwelling-worlds that sustain existence by enabling, among other things, processes of signification that articulate our surroundings and living environments. For example, the elements in a plant's habitat become bearers of information causing purposeful plant behaviors that support and protect the life of the plant. Contrary to an abstract, disembodied geometry of space, Uexküll proposes a multiplicity of coexistent living environments engendered by sensory experience. He writes, "imagine all the animals that animate Nature around us . . . as having a soap bubble around them, closed on all sides, which closes off their visual space and in which everything visible for the subject is also enclosed."³ Visualizing his notion of the animal perceptual environment as an enclosed bubble, Uexküll extends his inquiry into the human world, asserting that "only when we can vividly imagine this fact will we recognize in our own world the bubble that encloses each and every one of us on all sides . . . There is no space independent of subjects."⁴

Following Uexküll's theorization of sensory perception as a process of signification that produces an existential territory, and contextualizing space as a sensory experience, I argue that documentary cinema is a form of geographical knowledge that incorporates subjectivity and personal experience as a legitimate means to see and represent the world. I examine Beatriz Santiago Muñoz's *Farmacopea* (Puerto Rico, 2013) and Patricio Guzmán's *El botón de nácar* (*The Pearl Button*, Chile, 2015), two documentary films that explore nature in an attempt to reimagine the landscape, the nation, and the planet, and reconfigure a sense of national identity and belonging. These films are models of a cartographic imaginary in contemporary Latin American cinema centered on experiences of environmental degradation, land struggles, displacement, and dislocation, intimately connected to the transformation of nature and to the disappearance of ecosystems and Indigenous worlds (such as Alejandro Fernández Mouján's *Damiana Kryygi*, 2015; and Vicente Carelli's *Martirio*, 2016). They articulate conflicting practices and notions of space that render visible Marisol de la Cadena's and Mario Blaser's notion of the pluriverse as "a multiplicity of worlds."⁵

While the myth of national identity relies on an abstract understanding of space that finds its most accomplished expression in the representational map, Uexküll's theorization of sensory perception can help us illuminate the embodied nature of space in documentary cinema and its significance for the preservation of marginal, nonhuman, and non-Western environments and worldviews. As abstract categories, space and nature are central articulations of a geoepistemology sustained by practices of economic extractivism that, as argued by Macarena Gómez-Barris in *The Extractive Zone*, have violently organized the region through physical and symbolic violence.⁶ In *Farmacopea* and *The Pearl Button*, space becomes visible and discernible through embodied notions of nature and territory, the planet and the cosmos. I contrast these films with the work of the German naturalist Alexander von Humboldt to demonstrate that the notion of space as a bodily and subjective experience is not foreign to the history of science. Restoring traumatic memories concealed from the national narrative and positioning nature as source of knowledge and aesthetic pleasure, *The Pearl Button* and *Farmacopea* reactivate practices of exploration and research that were developed by natural scientists in the late eighteenth and nineteenth centuries when travel writing, mapping, drawing, and the collection of vegetable, animal, and mineral specimens allowed the documentation and visualization of territories unknown to the European world. The reliance on skilled observation and on the image of nature as an endless source of knowledge and aesthetic pleasure situates these films within a larger documentary tradition as anticipated by Humboldt in his project for the popularization of science.

The notion of documentary cinema I advance in this chapter is built on Bill Nichols's theorization of evidence in "The Question of Evidence, the Power of Rhetoric and Documentary Film."[7] According to Nichols, it is evidence that places the documentary film among other discourses of sobriety that directly engage with the social world to promote knowledge and change.[8] For Nichols, in the documentary film, evidence has a double existence. It refers to verifiable and concrete facts in the external world and to the discursive frame that configures the film. Similarly, in the natural sciences, evidence animates the spectacular condition of physical reality while also serving an archival impulse essential to the naturalist's research. In Humboldt's work, evidence that is simultaneously scientific, aesthetic, and narrative transforms the archive into a vehicle of knowledge about the distant geography of the Americas, shaping a new image of the entire planet and the cosmos.

I use the term nature to recall Humboldt's notion of the unity of forces that rule the cosmos. Nature emerges in his work as a given order that preexists the human and that possesses aesthetic expression. It is for Humboldt the most important object of study and the greatest source of aesthetic pleasure. Nature, as an ambiguous domain, akin to but also different from the human, nurturing and hostile, occupies a central place in Latin American visual culture. It constitutes a key motif in the creation of what Walter Mignolo has called the idea of Latin America.[9] It became central to the projects of nation building across the region in the early nineteenth century. Likewise, through the exploration of nature, Guzmán's *The Pearl Button* and Santiago Muñoz's *Farmacopea* revisit the violent legacy of colonialism, bringing into consideration the permanence of extractivism in the region. The paradoxical status of nature in Humboldt as an endless source of desire and inquiry appears as unequivocal proof of the fallibility of scientific knowledge and the spirit of skepticism that guided his work. Likewise, the framing of rational and scientific knowledge as partial and limited is also essential to these two documentaries and to the precedence they give to subjective experience, affect, and sensory perception. Recording and manipulating the image of reality, these documentaries offer an embodied vision of nature.

Before the emergence of cinema and photography, the natural sciences played a central role in the production of images of the world. Alongside the methodical observation and classification of physical phenomena that characterized the project of the systematization of nature, in the early nineteenth century, sensory perception and emotion emerged as legitimate means for the advancement of scientific knowledge. Breaking with eighteenth-century botany, Humboldt emphasized in his work the pleasure and illuminating excitement that "merely looking at nature" produced and described the study of nature as an experience "essentially different from the impression given by studying the specific structure of an organized being."[10] Taking as an example fifteen groups of plants that would characterize his portrait of tropical nature, Humboldt explains in his first book, *Essay on the Geography of Plants* (1807), how his work diverges from traditional botany:

> These divisions based on physiognomy have almost nothing in common with those made by botanists who have hitherto classified them according to very different principles. Only the outlines characterizing the aspect of vegetation and the similarities of impressions are used by the person contemplating nature, whereas descriptive botany classifies plants according to the resemblance of their smallest but most essential parts, those relating to fructification. An artist of distinction would find it worthwhile to study, not in greenhouses or in botany books but in nature itself, the physiognomy of the plant groups that I have enumerated . . . The absolute beauty of these shapes, their harmony, and the contrast arising from their being together, all this makes what is called the character of nature in various regions.[11]

Proposing a divergence from plant physiology and describing nature through the larger framework of the geography of plants, Humboldt brings sensory perception to the foreground of his scientific research. This places him at odds with the historical turn toward the specialization of science that was taking place in the nineteenth century. His work ponders with skepticism the dissociation between science and art, reason and emotion, objectivity and subjectivity. Implying that images are not only sources of visual pleasure but also carriers of unknown truths, Humboldt anticipates the epistemic shift produced by the development of photography and cinema. This will be also articulated in the second volume of his book *Cosmos* (1847), where the German naturalist contemplates the construction across Europe of "panoramic buildings" where the public could enjoy "alternating pictures" of the "exalted grandeur" of distant geographies.[12] The image of tropical nature, exuberant and overabundant in his eyes, allowed him a sense of planetary unity.

Similarly, through nature, Guzmán and Santiago Muñoz's films discover the earth as a cosmic space. *The Pearl Button* opens with a piece of geological evidence evocative of the archives of science, a quartz crystal that contains a drop of water 3,000 years old. Isolated on a plain background for the examination of the spectator, this drop of water foreshadows countless interstellar journeys and the pulse of life in the universe. Water is described by Guzmán's voice-over as "Chile's longest border." It bonds Chile with the world and the universe. It ties together past, present, and future. In the film, water conceals and reveals life and death. It carries both the remains of thousands of people disappeared by the military dictatorship (1973–1990) and the memory of the Indigenous inhabitants of Tierra del Fuego, annihilated, displaced, and reduced to a Catholic mission on Dawson Island at the turn of the twentieth century when their territories were occupied by cattle breeders and farmers with the support of the Chilean and Argentinian governments. Guzman's voice-over situates the discovery of the quartz crystal in the Atacama Desert, where the radio telescopes of the ALMA project, an international astronomical partnership, search for water in the cosmos. Water in the film is a biological, geographical, and astronomical element. Examining the quartz and looking at the sky through telescopes, the film unfolds the mapping of the cosmos through two contrasting perspectives that become complementary in the process of spatial exploration.

While *The Pearl Button* develops a clear narrative structured by Guzman's exploration of water and nature as sources of memory, Santiago Muñoz's *Farmacopea* is an experimental film that submerges the spectator in an ambiguous temporal and spatial domain. The film opens with a long shot of the tropical rainforest and a superimposed text that reads "this is a film about a disappearing landscape." This text adds a nostalgic tone and produces an ambivalent relationship of loss and agency, proximity and distance between the documented world and the spectator. This effect is intensified by the lack of sound, a choice that further highlights the visual qualities of the images, exciting the senses and forcing the spectator into an increased state of alertness. The film follows a real character, a man called Pablo, through an unspecified area of the Puerto Rican rain forest where he has managed to build himself a house and cultivate the land for his survival. There are no staged scenes. Santiago Muñoz makes use of the interview as the main source of information, but its contents are only partially revealed with the aid of intertitles that merge the voice of an omniscient narrator with the voices of Pablo and other characters that remain otherwise absent in the film. First- and third-person narration as well as masculine and feminine identities blend. These voices can't be identified, much less restored to their original sources.

In his book *The Voice in Cinema*, Michel Chion describes the sound film as dualistic.[13] According to Chion, "the physical nature of film necessarily makes an incision or cut between the body and the voice. Then the cinema does its best to restitch the two together at the seam."[14] Chion builds his argument on the notion that the voice is an autonomous entity, separate from the body. In the sound film, the split between sound and image duplicates this opposition between voice and body. While reassembling voice and body, the sound film displays the suture between the two, an unnatural intervention, not "a seamless match."[15] Chion argues that silent cinema and the radio embody the unity of voice and body. In the radio, the voice becomes representative of the whole person. In the silent film, the body retains the integrity of the whole. The disembodied voices in *Farmacopea* translate for the spectator a fierce battle between human and nature, not just an opposition. They problematize the identity of the narrator. The film undermines the notion of nature as an autonomous, independent entity by severing the essential correspondence between the visible and the invisible, the forces of nature and their material manifestation. The absence of sound and the impossibility to reassemble the off-screen voices with their original sources reveal nature as a human fabrication. There are no bodies for the multiplicity of voices, no intelligible sources and locations for the forces that structure the apocalyptic narrative of Santiago Muñoz's film. The off-screen voices acquire a supernatural quality. Neither nature nor the human is a stable entity in this film. *Farmacopea* problematizes the notion of nature as an independent whole and as the ideal essence of being. At the same time, the thematic and formal exploration of nature places the film within the porous borders of documentary and fiction.

Farmacopea reconfigures the scientific tradition of the systematization of nature into an intimate discourse. Appropriating a basic practice of the natural sciences, the film develops a visual catalogue of botanical specimens from the Puerto Rican tropical forest. A handheld camera frames different plant species in a garden owned by Pablo, the only human character in the film. With the superimposition of text, the film provides their common names: *guayacán, maguey, tabaco*, etc. The use of these names, the freedom of the handheld camera submerged in the forest, and the presence of Pablo handling the plants and looking directly at the camera render an intimate relationship between spectator, filmmaker, and the documented world. While making reference to the study of medicinal plants, the title of the film ("pharmacopoeia" in English) evokes the efforts of Indigenous intellectuals to appropriate Western traditions that allowed them the means to preserve their own culture. Unwritten pharmacopoeias have been common across the Americas since colonial times. Martín de la Cruz's and Juan Badiano's *Libellus de medicinalibus indorum herbis*, also known as the *Codex Badianus* (1542), is the earliest written pharmacopoeia to register Indigenous knowledge about the therapeutic uses of plants in the Americas.[16] Illustrating 227 specimens, and using their Nahuatl names, the *Codex Badianus* embraces a European cultural artifact for the preservation and transmission of Indigenous knowledge. Like Santiago Muñoz's film, the *Codex Badianus* possesses a dual status as aesthetic and scientific instrument. It documents with images and words the natural world and cultural practices of sixteenth-century Spanish America.

Humboldt's work explored both the aesthetic power of nature's image and its documentary value. He believed that the image of tropical nature made possible the realization of the interconnection between all the elements and forces of the natural world. In her introduction to Humboldt's *Views of Nature* (1808), Dassow argues that Humboldt explored the "virtual grammar of plant forms, a visual language that we 'hear' through our eyes, the organ through which plants 'impress' us as if we were living wax and they the stylus that imprints us from childhood."[17] Similarly, in his introduction to *Essay on the Geography of Plants* (1807), Stephen T. Jackson explains that by studying the physiognomy of plants, Humboldt built the foundations of plant ecology.[18] These scholars underscore the meaning and significance of the image of nature in Humboldt's work. Here "plant form," "the physical structure of dominant plants," and "the visual grammar of plants" illustrate Humboldt's notion of the physiognomy of plants as a category that allows the visualization of the earth as a living organism. In fact, Humboldt's most creative and scientific relevant map, *The Geography of Equinoctial Regions* (1807), develops from his long journey across South America and his intimate experience of nature. It is a cross-section of Mount Chimborazo that illustrates plant distribution across the Andean mountain range. This is probably the first European artifact to map the Americas beyond the territorial order imposed by the colonial administration and its extractive economy. *The Geography of Equinoctial Regions* is an unconventional cartographic artifact where the contemplation of nature becomes a legitimate source of knowledge. In this map, experience as personal interaction with the environment uncovers aspects of space that had not been considered before in scientific discourse. Being in space is a subject of serious consideration. It entails different forms of looking, from detached and arguably objective observation, to the controlled practice of experiment and experience, to unrestrained and embedded forms of being in nature.

Like in Humboldt's *Geography of Equinoctial Plants*, in *The Pearl Button* and *Farmacopea* the larger image of nature allows the apprehension of space as a dwelling-world produced by sensory perception and personal experience. Exploring the universe from the ALMA station in the Atacama Desert, "the driest place on earth," according to the filmmaker's voice-over, Guzmán rediscovers water as a foundational element of Chile's national geography. But this geography is unfamiliar to the filmmaker and to his sense of national identity. Traveling across the estuary of Western Patagonia, described in the film as "a timeless place," Guzmán discovers Chile as an almost foreign territory. According to Guzmán, his country "denies the Pacific Ocean . . . It mistrusts its vastness." Trying to mitigate the sense of "spaceless, atopia, and atemporality" that, as argued by Tom Conley in his book *Self-Made Map*, "inaugurate an existential relation between subjectivity, writing, and cartography," Guzmán visualizes Chile through the image of a representational map made by the artist Emma Malig.[19] Guzmán tries to position the map as a mirror of nature but, contextualized in the film, the map seems to request completion, as water, nature, and the memory of the Indigenous inhabitants of Tierra del Fuego question the territory that this cartographical artifact describes. The film dismantles the notion of Chile as a coherent nation to show us the planet as a more intricate whole that belongs in the vastness of the cosmos. Chile here stands as a territory under interrogation.

Likewise, by suppressing the name of the country and by describing the loss of its disappearing landscapes, *Farmacopea* introduces the ambiguous political condition of Puerto Rico as part of the United States. This film depicts an existential territory severed from the nation and inadequate to fully situate the subject. Silence, ellipses, and the lack of a traditional narrative structure unsettle further the geography that the film describes. *Farmacopea* opens with no sound in a space that has no name, insinuating that Puerto Rico has somehow already disappeared. This sense of loss is emphasized by the fragile materiality of the celluloid film, revealed not only by the lack of soundtrack but also by the integration of overexposed material in multiple shots. Making evident the process of filmmaking and the precarious conditions of producing the film, *Farmacopea* suggests that, just like the natural landscape, images and memory also disappear. What remains of Guzman's Chile and Santiago Muñoz's Puerto Rico when these two films suggest that loss and the erasure of memory are the constitutive forces of Latin America? These documentaries are exercises in memory that find in the constant re-creation of Latin America the true identity of the region.

The notion of nature as a source of knowledge also nurtured Humboldt's journey to the Americas. In his work, nature serves as a vehicle to approximate the unknown. In *The Pearl Button* and *Farmacopea*, as in Humboldt's works, the unknown surfaces through nature and becomes familiar as sensory experience. Reimagining America through the vision of nature, Humboldt identifies what he believes to be the true face of the earth and the cosmos. The journey becomes a transcendental experience disrupting the opposition between reason and emotion:

> besides the pleasure derived from acquired knowledge, there lurks in the mind of man, and tinged with a shade of sadness, an unsatisfied longing for something beyond the present—a striving toward regions yet unknown and unopened. Such a sense of longing binds still faster the links which, in accordance with the supreme laws of our being, connect the material with the ideal world, and animates the mysterious relation existing between that which the mind receives from without, and that which it reflects from its own depths to the external world.[20]

The desire for knowledge stands at the source of Humboldt's experience of nature restoring the reciprocity between reason and emotion and remedying the divide between the naturalist and the physical world. Similarly, *The Pearl Button* and *Farmacopea* narrativize the journey as a sensory experience that excites the intimate reciprocity between human and nature opening a threshold for the acquisition of knowledge. However, while in *The Pearl Button* nature appears as the inexhaustible repository of cosmic memory and as a source of nourishment and refuge, in *Farmacopea* it has become inaccessible and hostile to humans. The main story that *Farmacopea* relates is the degradation and loss of the natural world destroyed by Pablo after he ingests a tea of *campana* flower. Under the hallucinatory powers of the *campana*, Pablo imagines himself at war with nature and cuts down every tree on his land: "The hallucination lasted for days. We were being attacked. And we fought back. In a few days we had cut down every tree on our land. And even some up in the hills." The film ends with these words on a black background that propounds an apocalyptic resolution to the ambivalent rapport between man and nature. It is as if the notion of a self-sufficient nature, severed from the human and animated with a life of its own, amounted to an intolerable offense to our sense of ascendancy in the order of things. Here the degradation of nature coexists with a sense of loss and with the frustrated expectation of reconfiguring the lost homeland. Time travel offers the discovery of a truth that nevertheless cannot be used to save the landscape. Nature becomes an inaccessible unearthly domain and our presence in the universe a futile interrogation.

Images of nature dominated the depiction of Latin America in foreign film travelogues and early documentaries like Burton Holmes's *Cataracts of Iguassu* (circa 1920) and Alexander Hamilton Rice's *Exploration of the Amazon's Basin* (1926). However, contrary to exploring nature, these films revamped iconic images of the naturalist collection, illustrating a cinematic cartography of tropical Latin America as a territory waiting for progress and civilization. This is the case of *The River of Doubt* (1928), a documentary film focused on Theodore Roosevelt's expedition in the Brazilian Amazon (1913–1914). Far from a return to nature, this film appears as a project of reconnaissance that allows for the surveillance of new territories and natural resources, turning Brazil into an object of study, a hostile territory to be mapped and controlled. As in *Farmacopea*, in *The River of Doubt* the exploration of nature turns into a war for human survival.

The journey as a structuring narrative device to visualize Chile as a nation finds a precedent in a 1947 travelogue produced by Hollywood Film Enterprises to be broadcast in American television titled *People of Chile* (Clifford Kamen, 1947). This film begins with an illustration of the map of Chile that is soon superimposed with a similar image of the map of the United States of America establishing a geographical comparison that renders the two countries allied nations. This is emphasized by a description of the population as predominantly white, built by European immigrants that have not "intermingled" with the native people. The image of the map naturalizes a political and economic project based on the idea of Chile as a homogenous and stable territory. This film not only traces a geographical itinerary, but it also builds a worldview. This geoepistemological operation is described by Tom Conley in *Cartographic Cinema*, where he argues that maps in fiction films produce an experience of spatial displacement and "beguile us into believing that we are naturally in the world."[21] For Conley, "ontology is a function of geography." Before describing Chile's natural resources and industrial development, *People of Chile* situates the spectator in the map. The map legitimizes the power of the state, projecting into the future the image of a stable nation, abundant in natural resources, and ready for foreign investment.

Taking advantage of digital technology, black and white images, and slow motion, *The Pearl Button* narrativizes water as the essential element for understanding Chile's geography and identity. The film embodies water: its sound, touch, taste, and sensation upon bodily immersion. It reframes water, and Chile, as unseen, unheard, unperceived. It pictures the immensity of the ocean but also its glittering surface, rain, and drops of water invisible to the unaided eye. Turning water into an abstract element, the film gives form to an intermediary space between the world and the cosmos. Water becomes evidence of the coexistence of a multiplicity of worlds. It allows the visualization and the mapping of Chile as a space of layered and interconnected cartographies: of the cosmos and the geological forces of the earth, of the people disappeared by the dictatorship, of the Indigenous inhabitants of Tierra del Fuego, and of Guzman's personal experience. Moreover, water stands as the bond between the human, the earth, and the vast space of the universe.

Predicting tendencies within Santiago Muñoz's and Guzmán's later documentary projects, Humboldt's work proposes an alternative geoepistemology by considering space as something more than an abstract representation.[22] Proof of this is found in Humboldt's *Geography of Equinoctial Plants*. Before its publication was completed, Humboldt shared a description of his botanical map with the poet Johann Wolfgang von Goethe. Goethe, who was fascinated by Humboldt's description and clearly eager to picture the totality of Humboldt's vision, drew his own image of Chimborazo for a botanical lecture in Jena.[23] The resulting image, *Sketch of the Principal Heights of Two Continents* (1804), dwells on the vastness of the American landscape, but remains visually foreign to the botanical richness of American nature and to Humboldt's notion of the unity of nature. America is just a mirror of the European landscape. While depicting the size of an overwhelming Mount Chimborazo (as rendered by Humboldt's account), Goethe misses the image of superabundant nature as well as the altitudinal progression of plant variation. In Goethe's picture, two geological formations face each other, representing the Old and the New Worlds. The American landscape, extending farther into the background of the picture, remains almost identical to the European. There are no traces of the untouched landscape of extreme fecundity that would soon characterize the image of tropical nature.

Only scarce palm trees at the foot of the Andean mountain range depict a substantive difference between the European and the American geographies, where nature indistinguishably appears as a domesticated human dominion. In contrast with Humboldt, Goethe's America remains an imaginary space, contained within the conventions of the European landscape. Nature is conceived as a garden designed for human habitation.

Humboldt's nature is not a European garden. On the contrary, conceiving America in opposition to the European landscape as an ordered segment of the larger planetary whole, Humboldt draws a new picture of nature as a nonhuman domain ruled by laws only discernible through the vision of tropical nature. Contrary to a fixed representation, his tableau, founded on direct observation and overflowing with interrelated data on plant, atmospheric, and geographical variation, demands that the viewer look again and reassess what has already been seen and taken as certain. Unlike Goethe's preconceived image of nature, Humboldt strives to retain nature's true physiognomy. His tableau operates as an aesthetic image, a map of plant geography, and an optical device. It exposes both his object of study and the grid he has used to examine it, displaying his entire scientific vision. Documenting with precision the sensory experience of physical reality, Humboldt's tableau turns into a frame to see and examine the world.

Every description of geography and vegetation and every argument Humboldt offers in his books foregrounds the aesthetic unity of nature, revealing the instrumentality of bodily perception in the development of his research. His work on plant geography results from the experience of the journey to South America and from climbing Mount Chimborazo, which at the time was believed to be the highest summit on earth. The tableau stands in for a scientific and transcendental experience. Humboldt comes back with a vision (almost a revelation) of not just the New World, but also the totality of the planet and the cosmos. His elevated vision anticipates elements of the aerial images of Tierra del Fuego in *The Pearl Button* and the technological developments that have expanded human perception. It encapsulates an experience beyond time and space.

Humboldt's totalizing vision has been largely associated with imperial power.[24] However, the impossible perspective and the unifying image of the planet that he proposes emerge from the experience of being in nature.[25] Considering the reduction of aerial vision to its dystopian associations with empire and military power, Paula Amad argues in her essay "From God's-eye to Camera-eye" that the premodern uses of the view from above also had strong ties with an "otherworldly, utopian context—its vantage point (especially the higher it got) designating the impossible no-place only literally inhabitable by a God-like presence."[26] Amad's understanding of aerial vision as a fluid figure with unsettled and paradoxical implications sheds light on Humboldt's totalizing vision by complicating interpretations that reduce his work to a project of European expansion. Humboldt's vision of America from the elevated perspective of Mount Chimborazo and his written description of the earth from outer space emerge from the practice of skilled scientific observation, aesthetic contemplation, and the experience of nature. Just like his image of the earth seen from above, Humboldt's tableau *Geography of Equinoctial Plants* embodies an otherworldly, utopian space that rests between the world and the heavens, sensory perception and reason, art and science.

Likewise, *The Pearl Button* starts by making sense of the cosmos from below. The film invites the spectator to visualize the cosmos from a drop of water trapped for thousands of years in a quartz crystal. Juxtaposing the view from above with the experience of being in the planet, the film expands the notion of a multiplicity of worlds and evokes an incommensurate image of the universe. Aerial images capture the vast landscape of Tierra del Fuego, the estuary of Western Patagonia, and erase all traces of human presence. The earth is revealed to be a living organism. The voice-over describes Tierra del Fuego as a landmass formed by geological events beyond description: "Here, the Cordillera of The Andes sinks into the water and reemerges as thousands of islands. It's a timeless place." The invocation of the Andes, a territory with a strong Indigenous presence, and the confluence of image and voice-over narration imbue the estuary with unknown mythical forces. The Tierra del Fuego archipelago turns into a place where Chilean identity and Western knowledge collapse, a place of hidden and unknown forces where a whole world sinks and reemerges from the water. This elevated view is followed by images of the heavens reflected on the water and by the inversion of sky and ocean in the vertical axis of the film screen. "When water moves," announces the voice-over, "the cosmos intervenes . . . Water is the intermediary organism between the stars and us."

The aerial view turns Tierra del Fuego into a transcendental geography, unknown to the filmmaker, who describes it as "a timeless place." The utopian and ecological overtones of this vision are corroborated by a second archaeological artifact juxtaposed with the image of the earth seen from outer space. It is a round stone carved by Indigenous hands. The juxtaposition of the two images and their similarity lead us to establish a parallel relationship between cinema and stone carving as related technologies that compel us to interrogate our presence in the cosmos. Here, the view from below, crafted through sensory perception and personal experience, is put forth as a legitimate means to visualize the planet and the universe, countering the totalizing vision of the view from above. Similarly, the film brings into consideration other elements of Indigenous life as evidence of the Indigenous people's knowledge of the cosmos. Guzmán incorporates images taken by the Austrian priest and ethnologist Martin Gusinde, who photographed Selk'nam, Yamana, and Kawésqar people in the nefarious Catholic mission of Dawson Island between 1918 and 1924. Gusinde's photographs show the bodies of Indigenous men and women covered with ritual paintings. Reframed by the film, these paintings reveal stars, constellations, and other images of the cosmos (figure 3.1). The photographic images and the carved stones rise above the film itself. They are no longer archival objects. The film identifies them through a connection with space that cannot be erased by contingency or dislocation. They are records of a special relationship between body and cosmos, signs that point to the presence of other worlds. Disrupting the binary that separates the Earth from the cosmos, the individual from the planet, and the subjective from the objective, in these images bodies and objects are imprinted by space, turned into surfaces for the transmission of knowledge. They carry the maps of the cosmos.

The film is also a map. It traces the cosmos for the spectator with the telescopes of the ALMA project and by re-creating the journey of the

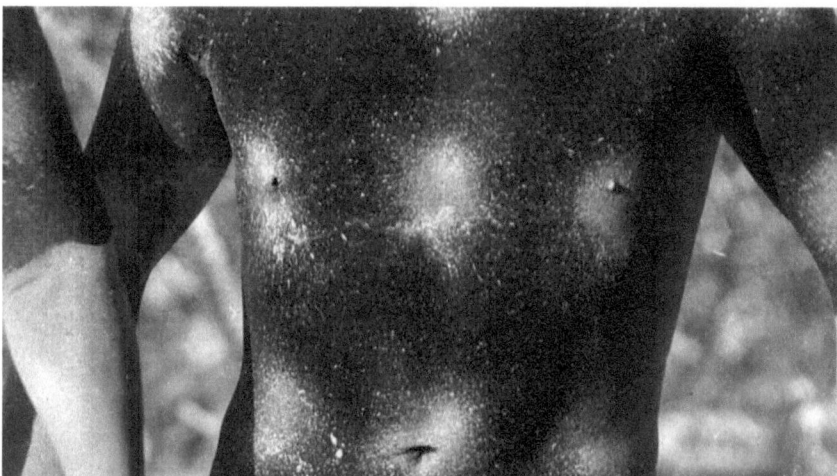

Figure 3.1. Selk'nam man with ritual body paint, photographed by Martin Gusinde in the Catholic mission of Dawson Island (1918–1924). Patricio Guzmán, *El botón de nácar*, 2015, video still.

Indigenous people across the fjords of Tierra del Fuego. Gabriela Paterito, an Indigenous woman who canoed a thousand kilometers across Tierra del Fuego at a very young age, doesn't feel Chilean but Kawésqar. According to Gabriela, "when you travel by canoe, you get to know the islands inside out." As the camera journeys through the estuary, Gabriela narrates in Kawésqar, narrativizing the landscape. Her testimony reanimates the world of her ancestors, crafting an existential and poetic spatiality, foreign to the epistemic authority of the representational map. Infused by her voice, the cinematic landscape reveals Gabriela's dwelling-world.

Holding evidence as central to the tension between the world and its representation and inscribing documentary cinema within the larger traditions of scientific exploration and travel writing, I have examined how nature emerges in two recent Latin American documentary films as sensory experience and as a means to see the world anew. In *The Pearl Button* and *Farmacopea*, nature appears connected to an otherworldly space and to the affirmation of planetary consciousness. The emergence of ecology and environmentalism in the Western world is intimately connected to the aesthetic perception of nature, to sight and images, and to sensory experience.

Humboldt's belief that the image of tropical nature would awaken the spirit of scientific inquiry and facilitate a higher understanding of the cosmos, his obsession with delivering to Europe the true image of America, his exploration of the media technologies of his time, and his understanding of knowledge as the sum of objective and subjective, sensory and abstract, aesthetic and scientific dimensions reveal him to be a key figure in the prehistory of the documentary tradition within cinema. In a way that anticipates the work of contemporary documentarians Patricio Guzmán and Beatriz Santiago Muñoz, Humboldt partakes in a tradition of reimagining America. I contend that his notion of the unity of nature and the central status of images and aesthetic pleasure in his work open the opportunity for an ethical interrogation into the production of scientific knowledge. This gesture, I argue, becomes essential to an environmental ethics within recent documentary trends in Latin America. In Humboldt, the sensory perception of nature is the best means to approximate the unknown. This sensory and aesthetic experience is articulated by Humboldt as essential to the development of knowledge and to the welfare of humanity. Without setting aside the paradoxical implications of his totalizing vision, in Humboldt the experience of nature is conceived as a subversive instrument that offers a possibility of reconciliation between Western and Indigenous worlds.

The Pearl Button recovers a knowledge about Chile, America, and the earth that can't be translated by representational cartography. It builds a reparative cartography of Chile that allows the emergence of traces of the Selk'nam, Yamana, and Kawésqar worlds. Re-creating space through the experience of water and drawing a close relationship with nature, the film renders visible the criminal and concealed landscapes of state violence and the ambivalence of the national map. Nature stands as documentary evidence. Likewise, *Farmacopea* develops an eco-apocalyptical narrative in which humans have surpassed the power of nature and become a major geological force. Reframing space through the sensuous and affective relationship with nature, these films enable the emergence of marginal identities and forms of belonging that have been concealed by the representational map. They raise questions about the failings of the democratic tradition across the Americas, such as the violation of Indigenous land rights and sovereignty, and reveal the need to find new ways of planetary integration beyond the colonial paradigm of extractivism. They reimagine nature and space as categories that attest to human experience and enable an alternative understanding of the world and our place in it.

Notes

1. Jakob von Uexküll, *A Foray Into the Worlds of Animal and Humans. With a Theory of Meaning* (Minneapolis: University of Minnesota Press, 2010), 142.
2. Ibid., 70.
3. Ibid., 69.
4. Ibid., 70.
5. See Marisol de La Cadena, *Earth Beings: Ecologies of Practice Across Andean Worlds* (Durham and London: Duke University Press, 2015); Marisol de La Cadena and Mario Blaser, eds., *A World of Many Worlds* (Durham and London: Duke University Press, 2018).
6. Macarena Gómez-Barris, *The Extractive Zone: Social Ecologies and Decolonial Perspectives* (Durham and London: Duke University Press, 2017).
7. Bill Nichols, "The Question of Evidence, The Power of Rhetoric and Documentary Film," in *The Documentary Book*, ed. Brian Winston (London: Palgrave Macmillan, 2013).
8. Ibid., 33.
9. Walter Mignolo, *The Idea of Latin America* (Malden: Blackwell Publishing, 2005), xv–xvi.

10. Alexander von Humboldt and Aimé Bonpland, *Essay on The Geography of Plants*, ed. Stephen T. Jackson, trans. Sylvie Romanowski (Chicago and London: The University of Chicago Press, 2009), 73.

11. Ibid., 74.

12. Alexander von Humboldt, *Cosmos: A Sketch of the Physical Description of the Universe. Vol. 1*, trans. E. C. Otté (Baltimore and London: The John Hopkins University Press, 1997), 98.

13. Michel Chion, *The Voice in Cinema* (New York: Columbia University Press, 1999).

14. Ibid., 125.

15. Ibid.

16. Daniela Bleichmar, *Visible Empire. Botanical Expeditions and Visual Culture in the Hispanic Enlightenment* (London and Chicago: University of Chicago Press, 2012), 35.

17. See Alexander von Humboldt, *Views of Nature*, ed. Stephen T. Jackson and Laura Dassow Walls, trans. Mark W. Person (Chicago and London: The University of Chicago Press, 2014), 8.

18. Alexander von Humboldt and Aimé Bonpland, *Essay on The Geography of Plants*, ed. Stephen T. Jackson, trans. Sylvie Romanowski (Chicago and London: The University of Chicago Press, 2009), 21–22.

19. Tom Conley, *Self-Made Map: Cartographic Writing in Early Modern France* (Minneapolis: University of Minnesota Press, 1996), 302.

20. Alexander von Humboldt, *Cosmos: A Sketch of The Physical Description of The Universe. Vol. 1*, trans. E. C. Otté (Baltimore and London: The John Hopkins University Press, 1997), 80.

21. Tom Conley, *Cartographic Cinema* (Minneapolis and London: University of Minnesota Press, 2007), 3.

22. See Arturo Escobar, *Designs for the Pluriverse: Radical Interdependence, Autonomy, and the Making of Worlds* (Durham and London: Duke University Press, 2018).

23. Andrea Wulf, *The Invention of Nature. Alexander von Humboldt's New Worlds* (New York: Alfred A. Knopf, 2015), 130.

24. See Mary Louis Pratt, *Imperial Eyes. Travel Writing and Transculturation* (New York and London: Routledge, 2008); and Nancy Leys Stepan, *Picturing Tropical Nature* (London: Reaktion Books Ltd., 2001).

25. Donna Haraway, "Situated Knowledges: The Science Question in Feminism and the Privilege of Partial Perspective," *Feminist Studies* 14, no. 3 (1988): 575–99.

26. Paula Amad, "From God's-eye to Camera-eye: Aerial Photography's Post-humanist and Neo-humanist Visions of the World," *History of Photography* 36, no. 1 (February 2012): 69.

Works Cited

Amad, Paula. "From God's-eye to Camera-eye: Aerial Photography's Post-humanist and Neo-humanist Visions of the World," *History of Photography* 36, no. 1 (2012): 66–86.
Bleichmar, Daniela. *Visible Empire. Botanical Expeditions and Visual Culture in the Hispanic Enlightenment.* London and Chicago: University of Chicago Press, 2012.
Bonnett, Alastair. *What Is Geography?* London: Sage, 2008.
Chion, Michel. *The Voice in Cinema.* New York: Columbia University Press, 1999.
Conley, Tom. *Cartographic Cinema.* Minneapolis and London: University of Minnesota Press, 2007.
———. *Self-Made Map: Cartographic Writing in Early Modern France.* Minneapolis: University of Minnesota Press, 1996.
de la Cadena, Marisol. *Earth Beings: Ecologies of Practice Across Andean Worlds.* Durham and London: Duke University Press, 2015.
de la Cadena, Marisol, and Mario Blaser, eds. *A World of Many Worlds.* Durham and London: Duke University Press, 2018.
Escobar, Arturo. *Designs for the Pluriverse: Radical Interdependence, Autonomy, and the Making of Worlds.* Durham and London: Duke University Press, 2018.
Gómez-Barris, Macarena. *The Extractive Zone: Social Ecologies and Decolonial Perspectives.* Durham and London: Duke University Press, 2017.
Guzmán, Patricio, dir. *The Pearl Button.* 2015; Chile: Atacama Producciones. Kino Lorber, 2016. DVD.
Haraway, Donna. "Situated Knowledges: The Science Question in Feminism and the Privilege of Partial Perspective." *Feminist Studies* 14, no. 3 (1988): 575–99.
Nichols, Bill. "The Question of Evidence, The Power of Rhetoric and Documentary Film." In *The Documentary Book,* edited by Brian Winston, 33–39. London: Palgrave Macmillan, 2013.
Pratt, Mary Louis. *Imperial Eyes. Travel Writing and Transculturation.* New York and London: Routledge, 2008.
Mignolo, Walter. *The Idea of Latin America.* Malden: Blackwell Publishing, 2005.
Santiago Muñoz, Beatriz, dir. *Farmacopea.* 2013; Vimeo. https://vimeo.com/86777237.
Leys Stepan, Nancy. *Picturing Tropical Nature.* London: Reaktion Books, 2001.
von Humboldt, Alexander. *Cosmos. A Sketch of The Physical Description of The Universe. Vol. 1.* 1845; repr., translated by E. C. Otté. Baltimore and London: The John Hopkins University Press, 1997.
———, *Views of Nature.* 1808; repr., edited by Stephen T. Jackson and Laura Dassow Walls, translated by Mark W. Person. Chicago and London: The University of Chicago Press, 2014.
von Humboldt, Alexander, and Aimé Bonpland. *Essay on The Geography of Plants.* 1807; repr., Edited by Stephen T. Jackson. Translated by Sylvie Romanowski. Chicago and London: The University of Chicago Press, 2009.

von Uexküll, Jakob. *A Foray Into the Worlds of Animal and Humans. With a Theory of Meaning.* Minneapolis: University of Minnesota Press, 2010.

Wulf, Andrea. *The Invention of Nature. Alexander von Humboldt's New Worlds.* New York: Alfred A. Knopf, 2015.

4

Slow Violence in the Slow Cinema of Lisandro Alonso

AMANDA EATON McMENAMIN

A man sits in front of a small cooking fire, cutting meat from bone and periodically scratching and swatting at his bare arms. Suddenly, a flash of lightning opens up the night sky, and our attention is drawn to the trees that it illuminates, surrounding the man. So begins—and concludes—Argentine cineaste Lisandro Alonso's opera prima *La libertad* (*Freedom*, 2001).[1] What occurs between these filmic bookends is minimal. The man, with Indigenous physiognomy, whom we learn is named Misael (Misael Saavedra), goes about his daily routine, which consists of cutting trees in the rural *pampa*, preparing meals, taking a *siesta*, and defecating. In fact, the film replicates much of Misael's real-life experience as an informal laborer from Chile in the *caldén* (*prosopis caldenia*) forests of Argentina, where he works clearing the native trees so that commercial agriculture and livestock can occupy the space, leading to ecological deterioration.[2] One excursion—to sell wood that he has cut and to restock some supplies, like gasoline and cigarettes—punctuates the midpoint of the film. This is where Alonso veers from Misael Saavedra's typical day, as he is actually a waged worker who does not need to sell the wood that he fells and as such does not participate in these transactions.[3] The filmic bookends, illuminating man and nature, with little drama in between and lacking the traditional diegetic thrust of narrative cinema, place Misael on equal footing with the nature that surrounds him, representing the film's overall ecocinematic drive.

Through composition steeped in the formal elements of slow cinema, including its hapticity, *La libertad* exposes the un-spectacular slow violence of environmental deterioration. It asks us to push past idealized portrayals of Nature with a capital "N," which Timothy Morton in *The Ecological Thought* describes as symptomatic of typical "ecological thinking" that "has set up 'Nature' as a reified thing in the distance, under the sidewalk, on the other side where the grass is always greener, preferably in the mountains, in the wild."[4] Instead, through its protagonization of nature, with a lowercase "n," *La libertad* asks us to consciously perseverate on the problematic relationship between modern centers and their ecological margins, which are not outside, over yonder, but rather are the constitutional boundaries delineating the resources that structure and uphold those centers. What is more, as is suggested by the equal focus on nature and human protagonist in the film, we are called to contemplate the subalterns of the neocolonial margins, who serve to maintain neoliberal modernity for the center by providing its necessary resources, while at the same time are devalued and considered no more than expendable resources themselves.

If the project of (neo)modernity/coloniality degrades both nature and subaltern subjects, Alonso seems to place the two in parallel not only to illuminate such degradation, but also to interrogate it. The film resounds with an ecological appeal to push past the Human—here, I would suggest, with a capital "H," invoking the ways in which the First-World inhabitants of modern centers are often delineated as full people, while marginalized subalterns are designated as less-than-Human.[5] Hence, as Morton incites and *La libertad* asks us to contemplate, "In an age of ecology without Nature, we would treat many more beings as people while deconstructing our ideas about what counts as people."[6] In other words, this gesture does not reify the superiority of the Human but rather elevates the status of subaltern people, as well as flora and fauna, rendering them equals. This call reflects what Gisela Heffes denominates "bioecocrítica," a more appropriate lens through which to analyze the cultural products of Latin America, which surpasses any sort of Nature-centered, shallow environmentalism that remains stridently sutured to Human concerns.[7]

To understand *La libertad*'s dual-pronged ecocinematic encounter with the violences perpetrated against nature and marginalized humans in the service of modern progress, it is first crucial to understand how the formal elements of slow cinema portray the sorts of slow violence that pervade ecological devastation. In his text *Slow Violence and the Environmentalism of the Poor*, Rob Nixon dubs this eponymous violence as "occur[ing] gradually and out of sight, a violence that is typically not viewed as violence at all."[8] Because it is incremental, such violence is difficult to perceive. It stands in direct contrast to the temporality of the neoliberal world order, or "turbo-capitalism," because of the latter's emphasis on the empty rush of techno-commercialism, in which "violence is customarily conceived as an event or action that is immediate in time, explosive and spectacular in space, and as erupting into instant sensational visibility."[9] For Nixon, then, the representational economy of slowly accruing ecoviolences becomes a question of how econarratives can be rendered forceful enough to ignite public interest and investment in the environmental depredation that they convey. He thus proposes narratives with "dramatic urgency" to match the spectacularization of violence typically accorded screen time under turbo-capitalism.[10]

La libertad, however, does not bring such dramatic urgency to the screen. Instead, its slow temporality mimics the slow violence that it depicts. The lethargic time of slow cinema might provide a more powerful tool in representing and understanding the temporality of ecological devastation. As Stephanie Lam recognizes, "[w]ithout the ability to experience environmental change as a temporal condition, and to recognize nature as concrete, present, and all around us, it will be difficult to find ways or reasons to step out of habitual modes of seeing the world at a remove."[11] In other words, we must learn to experience slow temporality before we are primed to perceive the monumentality of drawn-out, slowly unfolding ecoviolences. Lam's ideas are akin to the value that Scott MacDonald finds in contemplative nature cinema. He explains that these films offer us "perceptual retraining" in mindfulness, which counters time in overdrive under the neoliberal order, whose promotion of "hysterical consumption" has extraordinary environmental costs.[12] In this sense, *La libertad*, with its long takes and weak narrative drive, provides a temporal experience of slowness equivalent to the slow violence of ecological destruction. This visual experience of slowness is, in fact, jolting because of its deferral of the spectacular regime, which audiences have come to expect of the filmic medium under the auspices of turbo-capitalism and commercialized Hollywood.

What also becomes jarring in the film is its persistent questioning of the Human, typically the unequivocal focus of narrative cinema. *La libertad* accomplishes this through its focalization of Misael as marginal subaltern, as well as his equation in the visual register with the natural world that surrounds him. In Nixon's terms, Misael would belong to the "uninhabitants" of the "unimagined communities" interior to nation-states, whose precarious and liminal positionality nations must produce along the margins of their imagined communities, in order to undergird the (neo)modern narrative of national development.[13] While this certainly helps to explain how the Argentine center of Buenos Aires, particularly under the neoliberalization of Carlos Menem's government of 1989–1999, comes to rely on its rural, underdeveloped *pampa* to sustain that center, the relationship between neoliberal center and subaltern margin extends much further in geopolitical reach.[14] In *The Darker Side of Western Modernity*, decolonial Argentine thinker Walter Mignolo explains how the modern (Western) center erected itself as a nucleus by creating the concept of the "primitive"—the faraway in space and time—which became modernity's constitutive margins.[15] In this way, the West, through the regime of coloniality—that eponymous "darker side of western modernity"—has been able to delineate itself as "humanitas," or fully Human. Meanwhile, the subjects of coloniality have been designated as "anthropos," or less-than-Human.[16] The Western center establishes a relationship with Argentina as anthropos, or subaltern margin to its First-World order, signs of which also arise in the film.

When describing New Argentine Cinema, the generation to which Alonso pertains, Horacio Bernades, Diego Lerer, and Sergio Wolf aver that the new cinema subversively eschews the hyper-consumerism of Western humanitas centers.[17] Alonso himself has harsh words for the frenetic commercialism of mainstream film under the auspices of neoliberal modernity: "Todo eso genera un consumismo innecesario y tener que generar dinero para nada. Para vender más y más, y mucho del cine que se filma es una propaganda para vender cosas" [All that produces an unnecessary consumerism and the need to create more money for nothing. To sell more and more, and much of the movies that are made are advertising in order to sell stuff].[18] Nonetheless, there is no small irony that, following *La libertad*, which was subsidized by his family, Alonso must frequently turn to international funding sources such as the Hugo Bals Fund (Rotterdam Film Festival), the World Cinema Fund (Berlinale), and Programa Ibermedia.[19] Although allied with the art cinema circuit in lieu of mainstream Hollywood blockbusters, such foundations are still imbricated in uneven dynamics of production, which too often favor Western, neoliberal models that seek to forward particular—namely disenfranchising—narratives about poverty and marginality in the Global South.[20]

We must also be attentive to the ways in which slow cinema has frequently been aligned with the "high" culture of art cinema, removed as it is from public access and comprehension. After all, Alonso's films have habitually premiered at the Cannes film festival. Several have formed part of the *Un certain regard* section—perhaps the premier destination for the experimental aesthetics of art-house film, including slow cinema masterpieces—or have been nominated for the CICAE Award, an honor given by the *Confédération international des cinemas d'art et d'essai*, designed to promote art-house cinema internationally.[21] Thus, as David Ingram implores, deeming particular aesthetic techniques—such as the lingering, contemplative shots of slow cinema—as automatically equivalent to heightened environmental consciousness among the viewing public is deceptive. It relies on "unexamined assumptions about cinema spectatorship, particularly concerning audience predisposition and training."[22] The experimental filmic form, traditionally reserved for privileged circles of art-house consumers, does not necessarily resonate with the larger public. No one film style should be deemed the representative technique of ecocinema. Nonetheless, slow cinema does provide one venue for the articulation of ecoviolences, and Alonso himself tends toward this potentiality, stating of his "lonely men trilogy," which includes *La libertad*, *Los muertos* (2004), and *Liverpool* (2008): "These men live from the earth, but by what means do they do so? Without Pachamama [Mother Earth] there is no possible life."[23] Here the Argentine cineaste highlights an inherent, if underanalyzed, aspect of his oeuvre—its ecological focus on the slow violence of environmental destruction, pushing past bucolic versions of Nature as separate from modernity, while critiquing the exploitation of the uninhabitants of the anthropos margins, thus also pushing past the Human.

Pushing Past Nature, Protagonizing Nature: Slow Violence in Slow Cinema

Connections to the Western epicenters of art-house cinema aside, Alonso, a member of the rural landowning class and current resident of Buenos Aires, in many ways also forms part of the modern omphalos of Argentina. Why, then, this protagonization of nature that exposes exploitation along the margins? For one, as a result of the national economic crisis of 2001, itself imbricated in an intricate geopolitical web, including heightened neoliberalization under Menem, increased inflation, elevated foreign debt, and concomitant recession, new Argentine cineastes have faced "[c]onstant 'economic difficulties' [that] have led filmmakers to conceive of aesthetic solutions . . . turning the supposedly limited conditions into elements working in their favor."[24] For example, Alonso firmly believed that he could only make *La libertad* with modest investment from his own family; at the time, receiving other funding would have been nearly impossible.[25] Moreover, much of the "aesthetic solutions" that Alonso deploys in his opera prima are steeped in elements of slow cinema—little narrative, lack of spectacular effects, long takes, lingering shots, and a mobile camera entrenched in traveling shots, which produce an affective hapticity. I propose that these aesthetic devices, born of necessity and innovation, lead to the protagonization of nature, thus exposing the slow violence of environmental degradation and rooting Alonso's first feature in ecocinematic tendencies.

Long takes saturate *La libertad*, mimicking the temporality of slow violence, particularly vis à vis the typically short takes of narrative cinema, which replicate the visual regime of vapid rapidity endemic to commercial turbo-capitalism. As MacDonald suggests, requiring that we watch an image for longer than the typical seven-second shot asks us to think consciously about what we see and its importance.[26] This temporal differential is literally experienced, as well as allegorized, in several scenes. As Misael uses an axe to fell a tree, long takes pervade. For nine minutes that include only three cuts in the montage, we watch intently as Misael endeavors to bring the tree down, clear it of branches, and strip its bark. The limited cuts become highly symbolic. The second cut, for example, occurs after we have seen Misael digging out the space around the tree's trunk and beginning to chip away at its base, a long take that lasts a minute and twenty seconds. After the cut in montage, we see the trunk again, but it has dwindled in girth, and the hole surrounding its base has become significantly larger. The cut symbolically substitutes the many additional cuts, or chops, that Misael must make to fell the tree. This causes us to experience the monumental temporality of slow violence in at least three ways. First, we watch Misael's work for much longer than we normally would, which mimics the pace of slow violence. Second, the duration of the shot forces us to contemplate the action-deficient scene (typically left out of narrative cinema for its lack of spectacularity) as a form of violence against this living creature, the tree. It compels us to recognize violence itself, which, in relationship to ecological deterioration, is sluggishly accrued and typically fails to register as overt because of its slowness. Finally, the fact that the cut in montage relates to a significant jump in time, when Misael has whittled away the trunk, demonstrates the inability, even within slow cinema, to fully represent the intrinsic monumentality of environmental destruction.

As the nine-minute scene continues, we watch for almost two-and-a-half minutes as Misael finally fells the tree. He begins cleaning the tree of its branches with his axe, and suddenly there is another cut. The jump cut focalizes a chainsaw, leaning against another *caldén*. Misael picks it up and begins to quickly remove the rest of the fallen tree's branches. He then grabs his axe and uses it to strip the wood of its bark. We note the difference in time that it takes Misael to make quick work of the branches versus the slow process of stripping the bark. The speed with which the gas-powered chainsaw slices through the tree branches becomes stellar. It provides a clear reminder of how the mechanized tools of modernity can produce the rapidization of devastation, while at the same time ecological effects can take centuries to be fully felt.

This contrast is brought to the fore by the film's trailer, which presents the film—in its entirety—sped up to fewer than thirty seconds and ends with an almost fifteen-second, long take of Misael eating his armadillo meal, thus recapitulating the cinematic bookends. The disparity between the time spent on the entire diegesis—those twenty-five seconds of accelerated time that its uneventful action would typically be accorded by commercial cinema—and the slow temporality of the opening and closing scenes—which is conferred almost as much time—brings into focus the typical spectacularization of time in action-packed narrative cinema. The juxtaposition characterizes such time in overdrive as a violent discourse that conceals, or normally causes us to *not* notice, the slow violence of neoliberalism, including its environmental degradation.

Another tool of slow cinema that exposes the slow violence of ecological devastation is the lingering shot. Jens Andermann asserts that "a lingering of the camera beyond the length of a shot required by the diegesis" indicates one form of "'spectatorial' engagement with the landscape [that] can be actively encouraged by a film's framing and editing choices."[27] One scene opens only to focalize the dry, caked earth in an area that has already been cleared of trees. Abruptly, the camera starts to pan up, and Misael comes into focus. As he traverses the infertile land, he bends down to touch the arid ground. He looks pensive, as if he were contemplating its barrenness. He moves farther and farther away from the camera, examining the earth in different spots. He eventually exits the frame to the right. The camera, however, lingers with the sterile soil. The long take and focus on the dry earth cause the audience to pause and ponder with Misael the reasons this area has become a dead zone: desertification of the *pampa* caused by systematic deforestation of the native *caldén* trees.

The process of modernization in Argentina has been characterized by a 1990s neoliberal model of agricultural development that participates in deforestation in order to support the harvesting of transgenic crops like soy.[28]

Typically, the *caldén* trees contribute to the development and protection of the soil at the forest floor and regulate the hydrological cycle of the local and global climate.[29] Because neoliberal markets induce producers to underestimate the value of the ecosystem and overestimate the commercial goods it might produce, ecological destruction takes place. In response, Misael—who has himself felled the trees—deliberately contemplates the dry earth, pointing out its aridity to us (including its viewing public in modern, Western arthouse theaters and festivals), directing us to reflect on ecoviolences now and to come, as the effects of desertification accumulate gradually.

In complementary fashion, the fact that this long take begins and ends focalized on the ground alone, without Misael's presence, provides a moment in which nature is protagonized and speaks back at Nature. Visually rendered on equal footing with protagonist Misael, nature appears to call its own destruction into question.[30] This likewise occurs when the camera lingers on the dust trail that a truck kicks up, driving over the barren, scorched earth. By the end of the twenty-second shot, all we see is the dust trail, spanning the entire width of the screen, as the truck exits left. The dry earth speaks back through the cloud of dirt—nature fills the frame of its own accord and reminds us of the cumulative and accretive aspects of slow violence, lasting long after the initial moment of ecological desequilibration.

The friend's truck also provides a locus for another formal innovation in *La libertad* that bespeaks such slow violence—the literalization of the traveling shot. Unlike the tracking shot, typically captured via expensive dolly systems, Alonso deploys a mobile camera that rides along, or travels, with Misael as he journeys in his friend's vehicle. Traversing the uneven ground, the truck bounces around. Consequently, the camera jostles. We bounce too; the effect is destabilizing and dizzying. The images become haptic, inviting us to relate to the film spatially and experientially, not simply temporally and cognitively (in a narrativized sense). If ecological violence is often too slow to adequately represent on the visual register, the instigation of the other senses more readily convey a sense—an affective, embodied reaction—of urgency in relationship to environmental depredation.[31]

The film's hapticity, its heightened sensory awareness, takes on central significance when, in a traveling shot of a different sort, nature itself becomes embodied. This occurs in an oneiric sequence in which, as Misael takes his siesta, the camera leaves him and begins to float, as if it were the wind—circling, panning up and down, maneuvering through the forest of *caldenes*, becoming nature personified. The camera's movements are dizzying and disorienting; nature calls us back to our own corporeality. We *sense* nature's own embodiment as living creature and *feel* its affective effect on our very bodies, helping us to resist the anthropocentric abstraction of slow violence. Such affectivity is immanently bioecological, given that the Western centers of modernity, at least since the Enlightenment, have long privileged the mind and cognition over the corporeal and experiential, which they have ejected to the margins, the spaces in which both nature and the anthropos have been cloistered.

Pushing Past the Human, Protagonizing Humans: Uninhabitants of Ecological Margins

As the camera takes leave of Misael in the oneiric siesta sequence, it floats through a field of corn and eventually comes to a halt when it encounters a row of barbed-wire fencing, delineating crop from adjacent road. A careful viewing of the film finds that fences populate the visual register in excess. There are the fences used to maintain livestock and cash crops, demarcating the boundaries of domesticated Nature; the fences tightly woven around Misael's friend's domicile, delineating his private property; and even the tin-roof barrier that Misael sets up in the woods to provide protection for his encampment. The vast array of fences and barriers provide literal and metaphorical reminders of the ways that modern centers set themselves off from their constitutive margins, which are filled with the resources needed to sustain those centers, as well as the subalterns who produce them. The fact that these barriers overpopulate even the rural *pampa* bespeaks the all-pervasiveness of the reach of the project of modernity/coloniality, which infiltrates even the margins within the margins (i.e., Argentina to the Global North, rural Argentina to Buenos Aires, and enclaves of nature to privatized rural space). As Andermann avers, this helps to explain Misael's marginality, a space-time that is not outside global markets, but rather an indelible part of its constitutive margins.[32] The end result is the feigned separation of the Human of modern centers from what that nucleus deems the uninhabitant of coloniality.[33] In this sense, *La libertad* pushes past the Human as it accounts for the effects of slow violence. By exposing the equivalence between Misael and the nature that surrounds him, the film heeds Morton's call to count more beings as people, while also reconsidering what it means to be human (refusing to reify the Human).[34]

There are various instances of equation between the protagonist, Misael, and the nonhuman life with which he interacts. When we watch Misael eat his lunch, he moves very little, only enough to shovel stew into his mouth as he sits at his makeshift table. Meanwhile, the trees sway in the wind, moving just as much as he does, drawing our attention equally. There is an implied equivalence between the trees soaking up sunlight to produce energy through photosynthesis and Misael nourishing his body with food. Further, because Misael must cut down these trees to make a living and provide himself with sustenance, we come to understand that his production of resources for modernity becomes an act of self-violence, one that ultimately works against his own interests by increasing his precariousness as an uninhabitant of the ecological margins. This same critique is ironically inferred when we watch Misael kill the armadillo that he catches for dinner. Evoking an affective, visceral reaction, the camera focalizes the armadillo, upside down on its shell, writhing and twitching after Misael clobbers him. On Misael's small radio, we suddenly make out someone saying, "He cometido un crimen" [I have committed a crime]. Does the crime refer to Misael, who kills the animal for sustenance, or to his production of resources for modern centers of hyper-consumption, or to those consumptive centers themselves, given that this film will find its home on the elite art-house cinema circuit in the Global North? In one way or another, all involved are intrinsically imbricated in eco-crimes.

Like the trees converted into fence posts, and the armadillo cooked into consumable meat, Misael too becomes an *object* of modernity. As Andrew Hageman puts it, "ecology loses to economy and transforms people and the nonhuman world alike into readily interchangeable things."[35] Misael seems to intuitively recognize his objectification on the neoliberal market. After his journey into town, where he spends more than a third of his earnings in a matter of seconds on a bit of gas, food, and cigarettes—demonstrating the devaluation of his work *and* the trees that took so much time and effort to cut—he whistles a tune on his way back to his encampment in the wooded *pampa*. He sings: "Me dicen el paguandero de noche y de día trabajador, yo tomo por mi dinero, y en fin y así valgo yo . . ." [They call me payer by night and worker by day, I drink what my money allows, and in the end, that's what I'm worth . . .]. He understands that his value is interchangeable with the little capital that he earns turning natural resources into commercial goods.

As uninhabitant on the margins, Misael mediates Nature and modernity. It is his job to work the land to produce modernity for Western centers. Via the slow violence of neoliberalism, he is forced to disidentify with Nature/nature. He is at once required to identify with/as the primitive, the far off and back in time of Nature, as well as against nature, the ecology of the natural world that surrounds him and with which he could form a sustainable community.[36] It is out of necessity, not choice, that Misael must abandon a more sustainable lifestyle and participate in the neoliberal economy.[37] Throughout the film, then, Misael acts as the compulsory intermediary between nature and resource cum saleable good. This is overtly symbolized as he measures the trees that he intends to cut with the length of his axe, always already calculating their commercial value on the market, even as they stand living, roots plunging into the depths of the earth.

When Misael does venture out to sell these trees cum logs, the sawmill owner with whom he negotiates insists on calling them "postes," pointing to their symbolic function as the dead signifiers of live trees that will be used to erect barbed-wire barriers between modernity and its ecological margins, including its anthropos uninhabitants. He immediately sets to categorizing the logs, commenting, "Acá hay mucho poste y mucho medio poste. Esto hay que clasificarlo" [There's a lot of posts and half posts here. This, it must be sorted]. Three times he reemphasizes the need to "classify" the logs, now fence posts, and strategically asserts this process of cataloguing via market value in order to *de*value Misael's work. He objects to paying Misael the price that the woodcutter requests and instead asserts, "Y mirá, yo te pagaría uno con treinta esta madera, porque lo que pasa es que hay mucho medio, y yo el medio tengo que clasificarlo sí o sí, y es cambiar la plata nada más" [And look, I would pay you one and thirty for this wood, because what's going on is that there are lots of halves, and I, I *do* have to sort the halves, yes, and it's exchanging money nothing more]. Recalling that the only alteration that Alonso has imposed on Misael Saavedra's "real" life in the fiction-film *La libertad* is that, as a waged worker, he does not participate in the sale of the logs, the filmmaker's critique of the neoliberal economy is overt. This scene relays how the fastidious consumption of more and more resources subsequently converts nonhuman life into commodities, while also objectifying and devaluing those on the ecological margins that procure such resources.

While the transaction between Misael and the sawmill owner would seem to represent, on the national level, the contentious relationship between the modern centers of Argentina—those imagined communities of *civilización* delineated by the fence posts that Misael produces—and the unimagined communities of the *barbarie* ecomargins to which Misael belongs, another symbolic encounter demarcates these borders on a grander geopolitical scale. After selling his logs cum *postes*, Misael heads to the town gas mart. As the attendant pumps a small amount of petrol to power his chainsaw, the camera focalizes, in another long take, the motto inscribed on the pump: "Cómprele YPF al país" [Buy YPF from the patria]. Christian Gundermann was the first to label this scene an ironic commentary on the neoliberalization undertaken during the Menem years, in which the formerly nationalized oil company, YPF (*Yacimientos Petrolíferos Fiscales*), was privatized.[38] He explains that this image exposes the fact that with each purchase made, Argentina sells itself out, because the profits now benefit the transnational corporation, its headquarters in Spain. In other words, while Misael's transaction with the Argentine sawmill owner symbolically leads to the erection of fences that will further cut him off from modernity, with his gas purchase, he takes part in the transnational neoliberal economy that makes of Argentina the primitive margins of the modern, First-World order. The extended duration of the long take provokes reflection on the complex processes by which Misael becomes at once marginalized from, constitutive of, and mediator between turbo-capitalist modernity and its attendant ecomargins, as well as, perhaps, our own positionality in the circuit.

Conclusion: A Decolonial, Bioecological Option

As Alonso exposes how an anthropos uninhabitant like Misael is coerced to live on the ecomargins at the service of turbo-capitalism, churning Nature into objects for hyper-consumption, he equally asks us to ponder how Misael's ability to live in a self-sustaining community with other living creatures is truncated by neoliberal modernity. Mignolo refers to this calculatingly precluded "decolonial option" as the "communal," which he describes as the social order that was disrupted by European colonization, but which all the same has persisted in unexpected ways.[39] The communal fosters a non-neoliberal potentiality for society, distinct from the "common good" of liberal thought and the Marxist "common," which both are steeped in the *Zeitgeist* of modern centers.[40] Roberto Forns-Broggi denominates this potentiality *buen vivir*, which derives from Indigenous worldviews that seek communion between human and nonhuman life, in contrast with the modern objective of socioeconomic well-being.[41] Nonetheless, Western neoliberalism has endeavored to present itself as the only option. As Joanna Page explains, in the context of Menemist Argentina, neoliberalism was proposed to the populace as "the only possible choice, arising from economic necessity rather than a political decision."[42] Or, as Hageman puts it in terms of the problematic intersection of neoliberalism with Nature, "the current ideology of capital sets the limits of how we can think ecology, so we don't know what being ecological might be in a non-capital world."[43]

Yet, as Mignolo asserts, the decolonial option that the communal represents still subsists, even if it is intentionally overwritten at every turn. He sees it alive and well in Latin American Indigenous movements, which assert that "Pachamama (Mother Earth) has to be able to regenerate her bio capacity."[44] This idea of "regeneration" is key, as it supersedes recycling as a mode of reproduction, which abides by the principles of consumerist capitalism. We might equally assert that the communal is offered as an option by slow cinema. Tiago de Luca argues that its slow temporality is indivisible from "cooperation and mutuality."[45] Its sluggish pace, revelatory of slow violence, replaces the productive drive of spectacular consumerism with the unproductive time of contemplation, which allows the time and space to perseverate on previously unimagined ecoviolences, asking us to commune with the anthropos uninhabitant and to interrogate the Human. Likewise, its slow temporality also takes to task anthropocentric imaginings of Nature as bucolic, primitive space. Instead, it approximates us to nature through hapticity, which draws us closer to our bodies and to those of others. This recuperates lost sensory experiences that can sustain the communal—a bioecological option—in the face of modern, Western abstraction and its insistence on economic and epistemic productivity.

La libertad is emblematic of this sort of committed, communal option. Calling Misael his "alter ego," Alonso pushes past his privileged existence in the modern humanitas center of Buenos Aires in order to align with the rural anthropos, a positionality not completely unfamiliar to the director, since the nation of Argentina also finds itself on the ecomargins of the geopolitical order. This is crucial because, as Mignolo emphasizes, the humanitas must endeavor to think about (and sense) the world like the anthropos because decolonial thinking remains outside the realm of humanitas, and insisting on modern, Western ideals simply reengages the oppressive framework of coloniality and appropriates the margins for the center.[46] Alonso, aligning with decolonial thinking, comments of his cinematic oeuvre: "the final version stems directly from my conversations with the people who live in those places and *not* from my Buenos-Aires-based head, which maybe wants to change the world by showing all its misery."[47] When, in the denouement, Misael, still sitting by his campfire as lightning illuminates the darkness, looks directly into the camera for the first time, Alonso's alliance with the anthropos willfully extends one last time, and in its strongest manifestation yet, to the spectator. It is in this sense that the director asserts that "la película no habla de un hachero sino de un tipo que mira a ese hachero en el cine" [the film doesn't refer to a woodcutter, rather to a guy who watches that woodcutter at the movies].[48] *La libertad* calls us to push past the privileging of the humanitas as the only Humans (beings) to inhabit the planet. We are equally called to push past the depiction of Nature as ecological margin. In short, we are called to question what the world might look like—and *feel* like—if the eponymous freedom cited by the title were to be understood in bioecocritical perspective.

Notes

1. *La libertad*, in *100*, dir. Lisandro Alonso (2001; Barcelona, Spain: Intermedio, 2010), DVD.

2. See Diego Sebastián Tello, Jorge Dante de Prada, and Estela Raquel Cristeche, "Economic Valuation of the Calden (*Prosopis caldenia* Burkart) Forest in the South of Córdoba, Argentina," *Revista Chapingo Serie Ciencias Forestales y del Ambiente* 24, no. 3 (2018): 297–312. See also Mariano González-Roglich, Jennifer J. Swenson, Diego Villareal, Esteban G. Jobbágy, and Robert B. Jackson, "Woody Plant-Cover Dynamics in Argentine Savannas from the 1880s to 2000s: The Interplay of Encroachment and Agriculture Conversion at Varying Scales," *Ecosystems* 18 (2015): 481–92.

3. Quintín, "El misterio del leñador solitario," *El Amante* 111 (2001), sec. "Pero Misael no es un tipo cualquiera . . . ," http://no-reconciliados.blogspot.com/2012/08/el-misterio-del-lenador-solitario.html. Herein, Alonso explains, "La única diferencia en su trabajo cotidiano es que no vende la madera sino que trabaja por un sueldo" [The only difference in his daily work is that he doesn't sell the wood but rather works on salary].

4. Timothy Morton, *The Ecological Thought* (Cambridge, MA: Harvard University Press, 2010), 3.

5. In paying attention to the force of language in my contrast of Nature with nature and Human with human, I follow Latin American ecocritic José Manuel Marrero Henríquez when he asserts, in "Pertinencia de la ecocrítica" (*Revista de Crítica Literaria Latinoamericana* 40, no. 79 [2014]: 74): "El compromiso con la naturaleza será también compromiso con el lenguaje. El compromiso con el lenguaje será también compromiso con la ecología" [Commitment to the environment will also be commitment to language. Commitment to language will also be commitment to ecology].

6. Timothy Morton, *The Ecological Thought*, 8.

7. Gisela Heffes, "Introducción. Para una ecocrítica latinoamericana: Entre la postulación de un ecocentrismo crítico y la crítica a un antropocentrismo hegemónico," *Revista de Crítica Literaria Latinoamericana* 40, no. 79 (2014): 31–32.

8. Rob Nixon, *Slow Violence and the Environmentalism of the Poor* (Cambridge, MA: Harvard University Press, 2011), 2.

9. Ibid., 8.

10. Ibid., 10.

11. Stephanie Lam, "It's About Time: Slow Aesthetics in Experimental Ecocinema and Nature Cam Videos," in *Slow Cinema*, ed. Tiago de Luca and Jorge Nuno Barradas (Edinburgh, Scotland: Edinburgh University Press, 2016), 217.

12. Scott MacDonald, "The Ecocinema Experience," in *Ecocinema Theory and Practice*, ed. Stephen Rust, Salma Monani, and Sean Cubitt (New York, NY: Routledge, 2013), 20.

13. Nixon, *Slow Violence*, 150.

14. Laura Barbas-Rhoden, in "Hacia una ecocrítica transnacional: Aportes de la filosofía crítica cultural latinoamericanas a la práctica ecocrítica" (*Revista de Crítica Literaria Latinoamericana* 40, no. 79 [2014]: 81), calls for a similar transnational focus in Latin American ecocriticism, stating: "Una ecocrítica transnacional, que incluya el diálogo ambientalista de la filosofía y crítica cultural de diversas tradiciones culturales-lingüísticas, como la latinoamericana, puede reconfigurar la ecocrítica de las metrópolis coloniales y neocoloniales, y fomentar entre los investigadores ecocríticos, un desenvolvimiento intelectual más honesto e inclusivo" [A transnational ecocriticism, which includes the environmentalist dialogue of diverse cultural-linguistic traditions of philosophy and cultural theory, as in the Latin American tradition, can reconfigure the ecocriticism from colonial and neocolonial metropolises, and promote a more honest and inclusive intellectual development amongst ecocriticism scholars].

15. Walter D. Mignolo, *The Darker Side of Western Modernity: Global Futures, Decolonial Options* (Durham, NC: Duke University Press, 2011), 145.

16. Ibid., 85.

17. Horacio Bernades, Diego Lerer, and Sergio Wolf, Introduction to *New Argentine Cinema: Themes, Auteurs and Trends of Innovation*, ed. Bernades, Lerer, and Wolf (Provincia de Buenos Aires, Argentina: Ediciones Tatanka, 2002), 14.

18. Hector Bujía, "Entrevista: Lisandro Alonso también habla," *Cinémas d'Amérique Latine* 13 (2005): 95. All in-text English translations have been generated by the author of this chapter.

19. See *Los muertos*, in *100*, dir. Lisandro Alonso (2004; Barcelona, Spain: Intermedio, 2010), DVD; *Liverpool*, dir. Lisandro Alonso (2008; New York, NY: Kino International, 2010), DVD; *Jauja*, dir. Lisandro Alonso (2014; New York, NY: The Cinema Guild Inc., 2015), DVD. *Los muertos* and *Liverpool* received funding from the Humberto Bals fund; *Liverpool* and *Jauja* received funding from the World Cinema Fund; and *Liverpool* received funding from Programa Ibermedia.

20. See Tamara L. Falicov, "Film Funding Opportunities for Latin American Filmmakers: A Case for Further North-South Collaboration in Training and Film Festival Initiatives," in *A Companion to Latin American Cinema*, ed. Maria M. Delgado, Stephen M. Hart, and Randal Johnson (West Sussex, England: Wiley Blackwell, 2017), 85–98; Tamara L. Falicov, " 'Cine en construcción'/'Films in Progress': How Spanish and Latin American Filmmakers Negotiate the Construction of a Globalized Art-House Aesthetic," *Transnational Cinemas* 4, no. 2 (2013): 253–71; Tamara L. Falicov, "Programa Ibermedia: ¿Cine transnacional ibero-americano o relaciones públicas para España?," *Revista Reflexiones*, 91, no. 1 (2012): 299–312; and Miriam Ross, "The Film Festival as Producer: Latin American Films and Rotterdam's Hubert Bals Fund," *Screen* 52, no. 2 (July 2011): 261–67.

21. See Festival de Cannes, "71 Editions," https://www.festival-cannes.com/en/69-editions/retrospective/. *La libertad* premiered in May 2001 at Cannes in the *Un certain regard* section, where it was nominated for the Golden Camera. *Los muertos* initially premiered in Argentina at the Buenos Aires International Festival of Independent Cinema in April 2004, then at Cannes in May 2004 in the Director's Fortnight Section, where it was nominated for the CICAE Award. *Fantasma* likewise premiered at Cannes in May 2006. *Liverpool* premiered in the Director's Fortnight section of Cannes in May 2008 and was again nominated for the CICAE Award. *Jauja* premiered at Cannes in May 2014 in the *Un certain regard* section, where it won the FIPRESCI prize.

22. David Ingram, "The Aesthetics and Ethics of Eco-Film Criticism," in *Ecocinema Theory and Practice*, ed. Stephen Rust, Salma Monani, and Sean Cubitt (New York, NY: Routledge, 2013), 47.

23. Dennis West and Joan M. West, "Cinema Beyond Words: An Interview with Lisandro Alonso," *Cineaste* 36, no. 2 (2011): 37.

24. Bernades, Lerer, and Wolf, Introduction to *New Argentine Cinema*, 10.

25. Quintín, "El misterio del leñador solitario," sec. "¿Cómo llegaste a hacer *La libertad*?" Alonso explains, "Estuve hablando con mi viejo un año y medio para que me diera la plata. Era la única forma. Si iba al instituto o a ver un productor con las cinco páginas que tenía escritas no me iban a dar mucha bolilla" [I was talking to my dad for a year and a half so that he would give me the money. It was the only way. If I went to the institute (INCAA) or to see a producer with the five pages that I had written, they weren't going to play ball].

26. MacDonald, "The Ecocinema Experience," 26.

27. Jens Andermann, "The Politics of Landscape," in *A Companion to Latin American Cinema*, ed. Maria M. Delgado, Stephen M. Hart, and Randal Johnson (West Sussex, England: Wiley Blackwell, 2017), 134–36. Relying on Martin Lefebvre's division between "landscape," which disrupts narrative continuity, and "setting," which is aligned with the diegesis, Andermann argues that landscape, in contrast to setting, purposefully calls the spectator's attention, encouraging contemplative and critical viewing. Nonetheless, landscape for both Lefebvre and Andermann would

fall under the category of Nature (in the capital). In *La libertad*, by contrast, the lingering shots of the natural world seem to protagonize—on its own terms, as much as is possible in a human medium, nature (in the lower case)—the ecological margins of modern centers, which never cease to be in contact with the exploitative forces of modernity and form its constitutive borders.

28. See Laura M. Martins, "Desciudadanización: Trabajo, identidad y políticas neoliberales en Argentina (El cine de Lisandro Alonso)," in *New Readings in Latin American and Spanish Literary and Cultural Studies*, ed. Laura M. Martins (Newcastle upon Tyne, UK: Cambridge Scholars, 2014), 72.

29. Tello, de Prada, and Cristeche, "Economic Valuation of the Calden," 298.

30. For an alternate take on nature in *La libertad*, see Gonzalo Aguilar, *New Argentine Film: Other Worlds* (Basingstroke, England: Palgrave Macmillan, 2011), 64. For Aguilar, "nature is a refuge and a dwelling, a secure and inhabitable place. It is the withdrawing into a circular time that offers not so much positivity as the possibility of avoiding a world in which everything is quantifiable." Such a characterization immerses nature in Nature, that space that First-World centers seek to theorize as distinct from the spaces of modernity and progress.

31. For another take on affect in ecocinema, see David Ingram, "Emotion and Affect in Eco-films: Cognitive and Phenomenological Approaches," in *Moving Environments: Affect, Emotion, Ecology, and Film*, ed. Alexa Weik von Mossner (Ontario, Canada: Wilfrid Laurier University Press, 2014), 26. For an analysis deploying affective criticism in relationship to Alonso's cinema, see Laura M. Martins, "En contra de contar historias. Cuerpos e imágenes hápticas en el cine argentino (Lisandro Alonso y Lucrecia Martel)," *Revista de Crítica Literaria Latinoamericana* 37, no. 73 (2011): 409; Laura M. Martins, "Cine, política y (post) estado. *La libertad* de Lisandro Alonso," *Nuevo mundo mundos nuevos* 10 (2010): para 6, doi: 10.4000/nuevomundo.58374.

32. Jens Andermann, "La imagen limítrofe: Naturaleza, economía y política en dos filmes de Lisandro Alonso," *Estudios* 15, no. 30 (jul–dic 2007): 287.

33. For an alternate viewpoint, see Edgard Dieleke, "The Return of the Natural: Landscape, Nature and the Place of Fiction," in *New Argentine and Brazilian Cinema: Reality Effects*, ed. Jens Andermann and Horacio Bernades (New York, NY: Palgrave Macmillan, 2013), 66. Dieleke states that Alonso's solitary characters "inhabit a delimited refuge that we are not allowed to enter." This fails to recognize the constitutive relationship between ecomargins and modern centers.

34. Morton, *The Ecological Thought*, 8.

35. Andrew Hageman, "Ecocinema and Ideology: Do Ecocritics Dream of a Clockwork Green?," in *Ecocinema Theory and Practice*, ed. Stephen Rust, Salma Monani, and Sean Cubitt (New York, NY: Routledge, 2013), 72.

36. See also Gisela Heffes, *Políticas de la destrucción/Poéticas de la preservación: Apuntes para una lectura (eco)crítica del medio ambiente en América Latina* (Rosario, Argentina: Beatriz Viterbo Editora, 2013), 62.

37. Andermann, "La imagen limítrofe," 286.
38. Christian Gundermann, "*La libertad* entre los escombros de la globalización," *Ciberletras* 13 (2005).
39. Mignolo, *The Darker Side of Western Modernity*, 320.
40. Ibid., 311.
41. Roberto Forns-Broggi, "Ecocinema and 'Good Life' in Latin America," in *Transnational Ecocinema: Film Culture in an Era of Ecological Transformation*, ed. Pietari Kääpä and Tommy Gustafsson (Bristol, UK: Intellect, 2013), 86–88.
42. Joanna Page, *Crisis and Capitalism in Contemporary Argentine Cinema* (Durham, NC: Duke University Press, 2009), 195.
43. Hageman, "Ecocinema and Ideology," 65.
44. Mignolo, *The Darker Side of Western Modernity*, 311.
45. Tiago de Luca, "Slow Time, Visible Cinema: Duration, Experience, and Spectatorship," *Cinema Journal* 56, no. 1 (Fall 2016): 41.
46. Mignolo, *The Darker Side of Western Modernity*, 90.
47. West and West, "Cinema Beyond Words," 35. Note that while Alonso refers explicitly to *Los muertos* here, his thoughts are generalizable to his entire filmography.
48. Emilio Toibero, "En torno a *La libertad*," *Enfocarte.com: Revista de arte y cultura* 3, no. 20 (2003): para. 6, http://www.enfocarte.com/3.20/cine.html.

Works Cited

Aguilar, Gonzalo. *New Argentine Film: Other Worlds*. Basingstroke, England: Palgrave Macmillan, 2011.
Alonso, Lisandro. *La libertad*, in *100*. 2001; Barcelona, Spain: Intermedio, 2010, DVD.
———. *Los muertos*, in *100*. 2004; Barcelona, Spain: Intermedio, 2010, DVD.
———. *Liverpool*. 2008; New York, NY: Kino International, 2010, DVD.
———. *Jauja*. 2014; New York, NY: The Cinema Guild Inc., 2015.
Andermann, Jens. "The Politics of Landscape." In *A Companion to Latin American Cinema*, edited by Maria M. Delgado, Stephen M. Hart, and Randal Johnson, 133–49. West Sussex, England: Wiley Blackwell, 2017.
———. "La imagen limítrofe: Naturaleza, economía y política en dos filmes de Lisandro Alonso." *Estudios* 15, no. 30 (jul–dic 2007): 279–304.
Barbas-Rhoden, Laura. "Hacia una ecocrítica transnacional: Aportes de la filosofía crítica cultural latinoamericanas a la práctica ecocrítica." *Revista de Crítica Literaria Latinoamericana* 40, no. 79 (2014): 79–96.
Bernades, Horacio, Diego Lerer, and Sergio Wolf. Introduction to *New Argentine Cinema: Themes, Auteurs and Trends of Innovation*. Buenos Aires, Argentina: Ediciones Tatanka, 2002.
Bujía, Hector. "Entrevista: Lisandro Alonso también habla." *Cinémas d'Amérique Latine* 13 (2005).

de Luca, Tiago. "Slow Time, Visible Cinema: Duration, Experience, and Spectatorship." *Cinema Journal* 56, no. 1 (Fall 2016): 23–42.
Dieleke, Edgard. "The Return of the Natural: Landscape, Nature and the Place of Fiction." In *New Argentine and Brazilian Cinema: Reality Effects*, edited by Jens Andermann and Horacio Bernades, 59–71. New York: Palgrave Macmillan, 2013.
Falicov, Tamara L. "Film Funding Opportunities for Latin American Filmmakers: A Case for Further North-South Collaboration in Training and Film Festival Initiatives." In *A Companion to Latin American Cinema*, Edited by Maria M. Delgado, Stephen M. Hart, and Randal Johnson, 85–98. West Sussex, England: Wiley Blackwell, 2017.
———. "'Cine en construcción'/'Films in Progress': How Spanish and Latin American Filmmakers Negotiate the Construction of a Globalized Art-House Aesthetic." *Transnational Cinemas* 4, no. 2 (2013): 253–71.
———. "Programa Ibermedia: ¿Cine transnacional ibero-americano o relaciones públicas para España?" *Revista Reflexiones* 91, no. 1 (2012): 299–312.
Festival de Cannes. "71 Editions." https://www.festival-cannes.com/en/69-editions/retrospective/.
Forns-Broggi, Roberto. "Ecocinema and 'Good Life' in Latin America." In *Transnational Ecocinema: Film Culture in an Era of Ecological Transformation*, edited by Pietari Kääpä and Tommy Gustafsson, 86–88. Bristol, UK: Intellect, 2013.
González-Roglich, Mariano, Jennifer J. Swenson, Diego Villareal, Esteban G. Jobbágy, and Robert B. Jackson. "Woody Plant-Cover Dynamics in Argentine Savannas from the 1880s to 2000s: The Interplay of Encroachment and Agriculture Conversion at Varying Scales." *Ecosystems* 18 (2015): 481–92.
Gundermann, Christian. "*La libertad* entre los escombros de la globalización." *Ciberletras* 13 (2005).
Hageman, Andrew. "Ecocinema and Ideology: Do Ecocritics Dream of a Clockwork Green?" In *Ecocinema Theory and Practice*, edited by Stephen Rust, Salma Monani, and Sean Cubitt, 63–86. New York: Routledge, 2013.
Heffes, Gisela. "Introducción. Para una ecocrítica latinoamericana: Entre la postulación de un ecocentrismo crítico y la crítica a un antropocentrismo hegemónico." *Revista de Crítica Literaria Latinoamericana* 40, no. 79 (2014): 11–34.
———. *Políticas de la destrucción/Poéticas de la preservación: Apuntes para una lectura (eco)crítica del medio ambiente en América Latina*. Rosario, Argentina: Beatriz Viterbo Editora, 2013.
Ingram, David. "The Aesthetics and Ethics of Eco-Film Criticism." In *Ecocinema Theory and Practice*, edited by Stephen Rust, Salma Monani, and Sean Cubitt, 43–62. New York: Routledge, 2013.
———. "Emotion and Affect in Eco-films: Cognitive and Phenomenological Approaches." In *Moving Environments: Affect, Emotion, Ecology, and Film*, edited by Alexa Weik von Mossner, 23–40. Ontario, Canada: Wilfrid Laurier University Press, 2014.

Lam, Stephanie. "It's About Time: Slow Aesthetics in Experimental Ecocinema and Nature Cam Videos." In *Slow Cinema*, edited by Tiago de Luca and Jorge Nuno Barradas, 207–18. Edinburgh, Scotland: Edinburgh University Press, 2016.

MacDonald, Scott. "The Ecocinema Experience." In *Ecocinema Theory and Practice*, edited by Stephen Rust, Salma Monani, and Sean Cubitt, 17–42. New York: Routledge, 2013.

Marrero Henríquez, José Manuel. "Pertinencia de la ecocrítica." *Revista de Crítica Literaria Latinoamericana* 40, no. 79 (2014): 57–77.

Martins, Laura M. "Desciudadanización: Trabajo, identidad y políticas neoliberales en Argentina (El cine de Lisandro Alonso)." In *New Readings in Latin American and Spanish Literary and Cultural Studies*, edited by Laura M. Martins, 68–80. Newcastle upon Tyne, UK: Cambridge Scholars, 2014.

———. "En contra de contar historias. Cuerpos e imágenes hápticas en el cine argentino (Lisandro Alonso y Lucrecia Martel)." *Revista de Crítica Literaria Latinoamericana* 37, no. 73 (2011): 401–20.

———. "Cine, política y (post)estado. *La libertad* de Lisandro Alonso." *Nuevo mundo mundos nuevos* 10 (2010).

Mignolo, Walter D. *The Darker Side of Western Modernity: Global Futures, Decolonial Options*. Durham, NC: Duke University Press, 2011.

Morton, Timothy. *The Ecological Thought*. Cambridge, MA: Harvard University Press, 2010.

Nixon, Rob. *Slow Violence and the Environmentalism of the Poor*. Cambridge, MA: Harvard University Press, 2011.

Page, Joanna. *Crisis and Capitalism in Contemporary Argentine Cinema*. Durham, NC: Duke University Press, 2009.

Quintín. "El misterio del leñador solitario." *El Amante* 111 (2001). http://no-reconciliados.blogspot.com/2012/08/el-misterio-del-lenador-solitario.html.

Ross, Miriam. "The Film Festival as Producer: Latin American Films and Rotterdam's Hubert Bals Fund." *Screen* 52, no. 2 (July 2011): 261–67.

Tello, Diego Sebastián, Jorge Dante de Prada, and Estela Raquel Cristeche. "Economic Valuation of the Calden (*Prosopis caldenia* Burkart) Forest in the South of Córdoba, Argentina." *Revista Chapingo Serie Ciencias Forestales y del Ambiente* 24, no. 3 (2018): 297–312.

Toibero, Emilio, "En torno a *La libertad*." *Enfocarte.com* 3, no. 20 (2003): http://www.enfocarte.com/3.20/cine.html.

West, Dennis, and Joan M. West, "Cinema Beyond Words: An Interview with Lisandro Alonso." *Cineaste* 36, no. 2 (2011): 30–38.

ENCOUNTERING DIFFERENCE

5

Humanimal Assemblages

Slaughters in Latin American Left-Wing Cinema

MOIRA FRADINGER

To veil or unveil?: this is the gist of a visual dialectics around the slaughter or the death of human and nonhuman animals that shifted at the beginning of the trans-Atlantic nineteenth century with the onset of the Industrial Revolution and continues to this day. Left-wing cinema has intervened, since its inception during the Soviet 1920s, generating its own unveiling visual politics to combat industrial exploitation with intricate and unforgettable assemblages that I here call "humanimal." Humanimal assemblages are sequences or montages that associate human and nonhuman animals in subjugation, victimization, suffering, domination, death, or slaughter, such that each element of the compound can only be understood in relation to the others. They are not just scenes of precapitalist interspecies cohabitation: they are critiques of capitalism through montage or filmic narration. In fiction and documentary, left-wing visual politics unveil the slaughters that the industrial revolution veils. These cinematic humanimal assemblages humanize animals and animalize humans: their critique of industrial exploitation blurs the limits that would distinguish each category.

But seen from the point of view of our current "posthuman" imaginative horizon, the narratives in which left-wing cinema has embedded its humanimal assemblages as its critique of industrial exploitation take on a different urgency. Cary Wolfe suggests that as long as we deem it "all right to systematically exploit and kill nonhuman animals simply because of their species, then the humanist discourse of species will always be available for use by some humans against other humans."[1] The humanimal assemblages in left-wing cinema bear the question of whether they express a posthuman passion *avant la lettre*, or subscribe to the humanist discourse of the species, that is, the humanist penchant to employ the image of the dead (or vulnerable) nonhuman animal as a metaphor for a political change needed for human animals, but excluding nonhuman ones (as well as those humans who are politically rendered nonhuman). Are the nonhuman animals in these assemblages made *humanist pedagogues for man*—self-effacing pedagogues whose death may teach human animals to struggle against their exploitation, all the while allowing humans to remain mute as to the fate of nonhuman animals? Does the spectacle of killing animals as a stand-in for the killing of humans partake in the anthropocentric discourse of Western modernity? Is the distinction animal/human relevant or not in a visual regime that assigns both human and nonhuman animals the same kind of vulnerability to capitalist exploitation? The questions I pose to review filmic representations of nonhuman animals partake of the ecocritical efforts to "bring the animals back in" (per Lauren Derby's expression)[2] or to write the histories of human animals from the point of view of their relationality with nonhuman animals, unnoticed by the Western narrative that conceives of the nonhuman realm as "nature" (static, essentialist) and the human realm as "history" (in permanent change). In terms of a critique of capitalism, humanimal assemblages pose the question of whether liberation from capitalism can happen without the dismantlement of anthropocentrism.

For the limited scope of this chapter, I have chosen a sample of emblematic humanimal assemblages from the sixties wave of Latin American left-wing cinema to explore their ability to destabilize not only the capitalist narrative of exploitation but also its anthropocentric discourse. I have found in these examples some glimmering lines of flight, in the Deleuzian sense, out of the humanist discourse so characteristic of left-wing social movements at the time.[3] These glimmering moments bring the nonhuman animal back to our attention and generate reflection on how it has been used by the discourses of humanism. I use the term "left-wing cinema" to refer to the filmmaking practice that articulates aesthetics with politics, assigning to cinema a role in political projects for systemic change. This articulation between film and politics was theorized and explicitly put in practice first in the context of the 1917 Bolshevik Revolution, though it acquired a renewed impetus during the Latin American sixties—expanding later to Africa and Asia. Humanimal assemblages appear in almost every left-wing film in the Latin American corpus identified as "New Latin American

Cinema," or "Third Cinema," after Solanas and Getino's 1968 Manifesto titled "Toward a Third Cinema." The political film movement proposed an alternative to what the manifesto called "First Cinema" (Hollywood) and "Second Cinema" (independent European Art Cinema), strongly aligning its practice with the sixties anti-colonial movements. I focus here on scenes from a few predecessors of Third Cinema, Luis Buñuel's *Los olvidados* (*The Young and the Damned*, Mexico 1950), Margot Benacerraf's *Araya* (Venezuela 1959), Fernando Birri's *Tire dié* (*Throw Me a Dime*, Argentina 1958), and Humberto Ríos's *Faena* (Argentina 1960); from two classic examples of Brazilian "New Cinema" (Cinema Novo), Nelson Pereira dos Santos's *Vidas secas* (*Barren Lives*, Brazil 1963), and Glauber Rocha's *Deus e o diabo na terra do sol* (*Black God, White Devil*, Brazil, 1964); and from two Argentine Third Cinema examples, Fernando Solanas and Octavio Getino's *La hora de los hornos* (1966–68, hereafter *The Hour*) and Raymundo Gleyzer's *Swift* (1971). I end with two later shorts by Luis Ospina, *Cali: de película* (Colombia, 1971) and by Jorge Furtado, *Ilha das flores* (*Isle of Flowers*, Brazil 1989). These examples help me identify a left-wing filmic discourse that might apply to a larger sample of films from different regions and time periods.[4] Seen from today's point of view, it is a critical filmic discourse about interspecies relations. Along the lines of Few and Tortici's volume about "centering animals" in Latin American history, my exploration aims to put center stage human-animal relations to better understand the films that claim to be critical of the dominant order.[5]

My interpretation of Latin American examples is inflected by the dialectic between two types of humanimal assemblages established at the beginning of the left-wing tradition that filmed cattle slaughter and slaughterhouses: the now legendary 1924 Soviet pair, Eisenstein's *Strike* and Vertov's *Kino-Eye*. In these films, the humanimal assemblages orient us in opposite directions. *Strike* constructs the nonhuman animal as pedagogue of man. *Kino-Eye* offers a utopian vector that we may identify today as a posthumanist discourse *avant la lettre*.

The analysis of these two trends in a few iconic Latin American examples suggests that left-wing humanimal assemblages offer patterns that are worthy of a larger study. Consider, for instance, the repetition of the unforgettable image of the slaughtered bull's head in *Strike*. Shot from a high angle, during the bull's last throbs, a close-up of its open eye, as if it were looking up at the sky or the camera, makes us wonder if it had something to tell us from death. At the very least, it interrupts the diegesis. A similar dying cow's eye appears in Ríos's *Faena*. Solanas and Getino's *The Hour* cite it with an extreme close up of the eye "looking" at the camera while still twitching.

In 1970, Vladimir Carvalho filmed a high-angle close-up of a dying calf's head at the beginning of his *O País de São Saruê* (Brazil), though with the intention of showing the humanimal assemblage as a precapitalist cohabitation between peasants and their dying animals, tilting the camera below the half-shut eye down to the skin of the calf's muzzle, instead of glaring into it. In 2014, Göran Olsson began his film *Concerning Violence* (Sweden) with the moving image of a dying cow. The found footage sequence starts with a medium shot of a white cow gunned down on the green prairie by a soldier shooting from a helicopter in Cabinga, Angola. We see a close-up of its head with blood flowing out of its snout and around the semishut eye, out of which the cow "looks" up to the sky, as if in the direction of the soldier who fired his machine gun. With the exception of Carvalho's calf, in these cases, the fallen cow is a metaphor for the fallen human. And yet the eyes of these fallen cows seem to "look at us" with the question that we could extend to any image of a slaughtered animal: doesn't the shock of blood center on nonhuman animal suffering, rather than just instill its metaphorical value standing in for the human animal?

The inclusion of nonhuman animals in cinema is a borderline case for the critic's work of interpretation. Nonhuman animals are held dear by the documentary genre, insofar as it is a hybrid filmic form that aims at the "capturing of actuality" with minimal staging: a cow will be framed by the camera but it cannot "act," it cannot follow a script. This inclusion unveils the aspiration of left-wing documentaries to film "life caught unawares," to use Vertov's famous expression. In turn, the killing of nonhuman animals on-screen has been interpreted as metonymical to (or metaphorical of, depending on the *mise en scène*) human death: an ultimate confrontation with our finitude or our existential vulnerability—even our ontological one, insofar as we, as a species, are unable to witness our own death.[6] Animal killings on-screen can also be seen as allegorizations of film language itself—the chopping of nonhuman meat allegorizes the technique of montage.

But left-wing political films offer us different horizons for interpretation through their constructed assemblages, insofar as they are immersed in political denunciatory narratives of capitalism responding to the shift in visual politics in the wake of the industrial revolution that hid death and slaughter from the public sphere. That separation of the spectacle of death from the eyes of the public soon took legal and architectural expression in urban spaces: it meant the simultaneous creation of the first public cemeteries and abattoirs.[7] A "dissociative sentiment" grew along with the global mercantile bourgeoisie after the French and Atlantic Revolutions.[8]

The shift in the perception of animal slaughter coincided with a shift in the perception of human death. Human remains ceased to be buried exclusively in churchyards; they were sent to cemeteries in the outskirts. The slaughtering of animals previously carried out in farmyards or in city butcher shops was transferred to (industrial) isolated slaughterhouses outside the city. Thomas Laqueur and Philippe Ariès document how this geographic and cultural displacement of the sight of death has only deepened throughout the last two hundred years.[9] Amy Fitzgerald registers a similar process with animal killings.[10] In "Why Look at Animals," John Berger suggests that in capitalism, "the look between animal and man [. . .] with which all men had always lived until less than a century ago, has been extinguished."[11]

While the shift in visual politics resulted from economic conditions, it came with a humanist, speciesist narrative. The aftermath of the bourgeois revolutions witnessed the European dismantlement of powerful butchers' guilds and the emergence of individual rights to sell.[12] The rhetoric that legitimized the destruction of prerevolutionary guild privileges was more than legal parlance. Damien Baldin shows how in France, the passage from "tueries," where animals would be killed in the cities, to the abattoirs outside the city (walled up and encircled by water to disguise the sight of waste), was justified by appealing mostly to "*moral* hygiene [. . .]: the disappearance of the 'disgusting spectacle of blood' and of 'cruel scenes.'"[13]

A French anecdote just five years after the first garden cemetery, Père Lachaise, was built to the east of Paris in 1804, sheds light on the deployment of moral discourses for disassembling visual spectacle from animal slaughters, a political operation needed for industrial production. In 1809 Jacques Grammont justified his famous law for the creation of abattoirs outside Paris by citing an example that today could be part of a scientific experiment on the psychic effect of visual violence on human animals: a child, seeing a pig knifed on the streets, returned home to try it out—this time on his sister. Humanist discourse came in handy: Grammont's law to hide the abattoirs had the mission "not to teach by example." The concealment of animal killing was assigned a pedagogic role to protect human animals from their own violence. Sure enough, in 1845, the founders of the Society for the Protection of Animals used the same humanist logic. Like the father of the abattoir, they argued that seeing violence against animals would result in the violence of humans against humans.[14]

At the same time, industrial workers (human animals performing alienated work) started to be seen as nonhuman animals. The new industrial working class was disassembled (metaphorically) by industrial assembly lines as it also assembled itself by forming political associations and unions. By about 1891, strikes begin to happen every year (and more than once a year). Both for the right and the left, an animal imagination was at stake: the association between the exploited worker and the exploited horse or cow was readymade. Berger cites Taylor on the convenience of transforming the worker into an ox.[15] In 1913, Ford built the first automobile assembly line in Dearborn, Michigan, inspired by his visits to the slaughterhouses that had been in operation since 1850 in Chicago and Cincinnati. Nicole Shukin notes the similarities between the disassembly of animals and the assembly of automobiles thereafter: Ford's "automated lines sped the assembly of a machine body rather than the disassembly of an animal body. The auto assembly line, so often taken as paradigmatic of capitalist modernity, is thus mimetically premised on the ulterior logistics of animal disassembly that it technologically replicates and advantageously forgets in a telling moment of historical amnesia."[16]

To offer a radical alternative, the humanimal assemblages included in left-wing cinema in the early twentieth century would have to forego the moral pedagogy that legitimized the creation of the slaughterhouses (and zoos and cemeteries), and allow instead for a human identification with the exploited nonhuman animal. Otherwise they would merely repeat the capitalist discourse of extractivism, only with different politics: extract from "Nature" (capital N, essentialist and nonhistorical) but distribute among all. Off-screen, the creation of the slaughterhouse was supposed to prevent the spectacle of violence against animals from teaching human animals how to be violent. Yet in early Soviet left-wing cinema, the animal's pedagogical function reemerges, to teach what capitalism wants the viewer to forget. The question is whether some images or narratives may escape, or interrupt, the logic of this pedagogy.

The nonhuman animals that appear in the cinematic humanimal assemblages under study are recognizable in the wider (eco)system of global left-wing cinemas. A careful look at their specificity avoids the Western speciesist narrative whereby the distinction between animals and humans is insurmountable and decenters human animals from their history, as proposed by anthropologists who work with Indigenous ethnographies in Latin America (consider Eduardo Viveiros de Castro's understanding of the Indigenous worlds of the Amazon as "multinaturalism").[17] Herbivorous mammals (cows, sheep, bulls, horses), omnivores (pigs, rats), or omnivorous birds (chickens, crows, pelicans) are most often seen on-screen.[18] Neither primates nor domestic animals are seen being mistreated. The latter would invite spectators to identify with animal suffering too quickly. Reptiles and marine animals are not common on-screen either: alligators, iguanas, whales, or fish, with which identification would be too difficult. The humanimal assemblages are constructed with nonhuman animals that have long lived alongside human animals: used for meat, eggs, and food in general, leather and wool, transport and horsepower. This is why these nonhuman animals are easy prey for a humanist, speciesist narrative. They are instruments *for* human animals' survival. But they have also lived *with* human animals for millennia, making them candidates for the posthuman critique of speciesist discourses and granting them a role, identified by humans, in defining the human.

Because the humanimal assemblages are constructed with animals that have long cohabited with humans, they take on meaning in narratives that are in tension with, and can be unsettled by, violence. A shot of a dead or dying cow aspires to be a document: that kind of death cannot be staged, whereas a human death must—had better—be staged. If the image of a dead cow captures "the document," part of its pedagogical function is no doubt to show the ethical limits of the genre of documentary. In other words, slaughter points to what the documentary cannot document: the death of human animals must not be made visible.[19] The slaughterhouse stands in for human slaughter, as a transitional image, a bridge image between a pure document (inaccessible by definition) and the staged political narrative of the documentary. The slaughter is an image called to act as "reality" in the dialectics of montage and film narration in a documentary. As a document inserted in the discourse of documentary, it reveals a symptom: the anthropocentric regime of visibility must instrumentalize images of violence against nonhuman animals for pedagogic purposes. In the antihumanist tradition of the twentieth century, this image shows what every image shows: one of the paradoxes of representation *tout court*, where the impossibility of accessing reality makes any visual document an index, and at the same time a rhetoric of reality. The rhetoric of the slaughter image in humanimal assemblages shows animal slaughters as occluding human slaughters.

But in the tension between the "pure document" and the "political document," there may be lines of flight out of the humanistic narrative. Consider the dead cow, its twitching eye looking toward the camera. While it is not pure document, its power risks interrupting the film's narrative. Does the shock of this violence open a door to thinking about the nonhuman animal? Are the slaughterhouse spectacles for the consumption of violence (as pedagogy, as entertainment), or a chance to recognize our interaction with a sentient being, the chance for a left-wing nonanthropocentric narrative? These questions already emerge in Eisenstein and Vertov, who in my view set two parameters against which the critic can test for lines of flight in the 1960s Latin American left-wing film corpus. The slaughterhouse appears in both *Strike* and *Kino-Eye* as a document with a pedagogical aim, though offering opposite lessons. For Eisenstein, an unforgettable emotional shock: the animal pedagogue of man. For Vertov, an exercise in utopian imagination.

Eisenstein's montage at the end of *Strike* intercuts scenes of the slaughter of a bull with masses of workers escaping the repression of the Tsarist army. The montage unfolds across three intertitles. "Carnage" frames a sequence of long shots of workers running downhill under fire intercut with three close-ups of a bull's throat being slit at a slaughterhouse. "The Defeat" frames the juxtaposition of two shots of the bull's head and one of the bull's body in spasms intercut with workers running. After the last close-up of the bull's head, eyes wide as if looking to the sky, there is a cut to a long shot of a mass of workers dead on the steppe, many facing the sky.

The third intertitle comes right after a close-up of a worker's eyes (eyes that return from beyond the grave, because they belong to a worker who committed suicide near the beginning of the film): "Like the unforgettable bloody wounds on the proletariat's body, there lay the wounds of Lena, Talka, Zlataust, Yaroslavl, Tsaritsyn, Kostroma. Remember! Proletarians!"[20] We see close-ups of the butcher and the bull's passage from life to death, filmed from a slightly high angle (for shock effect). But we only see workers either in action or dead, filmed from a higher angle, in this case preventing us from focusing on any human face up close. For Eisenstein, at stake was showing real blood, so as to film without the mediation of acting and staging.

Eisenstein's humanimal assemblage imparts a lesson and a command to remember: proletarians are killed just as bulls are slaughtered. But where does this humanimal assemblage put the workers? Aside from the fact that the vanguard doubted the proletariat's mnemonic capacity, why was the bloodied bull necessary to jog the memories of the proletariat? Insofar as the filmmaker believes that the proletariat forgets, the latter is animalized: without training, workers lack a sense of present, past, and future. What is more, when spectators see the slaughter of the animal up close, they may not see the allegory but the blood. In other words, they may see the nonhuman animal at the center. The bull may be humanized when the horror of its death is captured as mostly that: horror. The key to the interruption in the

Figures 5.1 and 5.2. Sergei Eisenstein, *Strike*, 1924, USSR, video still.

humanist pedagogical narration about remembrance is that the association between killing animals and killing humans is a question of montage and not of narration.

In Vertov's take, slaughter is used to imagine a utopian assemblage that includes nonhuman animals in communion with human animals in a socialist world. Vertov's assemblage allows for spectator sensitivity to cruelty against nonhuman animals. While Vertov's film is a documentary, the image of the slaughterhouse is rendered malleable as an allegory for radical change. It acts as reality first and then is transformed into pure fiction. Paradoxically, the body of the animal that cannot act becomes its exact opposite: a locus to imagine it coming back to life after slaughter. Vertov's sequence aims to show the meat production process without the mediation of the private sector: direct and transparent, with no fragmentation of work, it is an allegory of communist society yet to come.[21] The first segment of the sequence is called "private sector": the mother realizes that she can't afford to buy what she needs in the market. The second segment, "the cooperative," films the mother in reverse, walking backward toward the entrance of the cooperative, "the first red supermarket." The next intertitle says: "Kino-eye moves time backwards." The third segment could be titled "communal utopia": here the slaughter is reversed, and we see the bull come back to life, be transported by truck to the fields, and walk free with other cows and a pioneer child. In three segments, "kino-eye" moves time backward so that the fragmented community of human and nonhuman animals reunites: an interspecies (proto) posthumanist communion.

Left-Wing Reports from Latin America

New Latin American cinema for the most part has been deemed complicit with speciesist, patriarchal, extractivist discourses prevalent on the left at the time. Capitalism was to blame for the violence transforming human animals into nonhuman animals on- and off-screen, but scarce film narratives explored the exploitation of nonhuman animals for the benefit of humans or interspecies relations. But human and nonhuman animals are often screened as sharing a common fate due to unnatural poverty: human animals are not owners of the means of production; nonhuman animals are owned either by humans without other means of subsistence or subjected to the same catastrophic conditions that capitalism creates for human animals. As Eisenstein's shock value reemerges as a strategy, in some cases, the equalizing of animals and human animals produces assemblages that the critic can see retrospectively, against the grain, as a nonspeciesist narrative. Vertov's question is still valid: if capitalism ended and socialism began, would nonhuman animals and human animals alike be freed from violence? Would their relations change?

It would be difficult to consider New Latin American Cinema assemblages without the inspiration of Buñuel's *Los olvidados*. The fiction presents itself as "wholly based on real events and authentic characters" in the credits, and is embedded in a humanistic narrative. Throughout his films, Buñuel's humanimal assemblages are mostly ironic.[22] But *Los olvidados* is almost entirely structured by an allegorical humanimal assemblage that encodes a particular humanist lesson: the violent encounter between a bull-boy and a bullfighter-boy in a slum. Buñuel's is a story about humans in poverty: when there is hunger, human animals become prey to humans just as if they were nonhuman animals.

The tone is set from the start when human animals role-play as nonhuman animals: two marginal youths in a decayed plaza act out the bullfighting game. A close-up shows a young boy who smiles with few teeth looking at the camera, playing bull as he walks toward the camera and then toward a taller boy-fighter who uses his shirt to perform a taunting "veronica." The camera's low angle makes the taller boy appear more menacing than the bull-boy. This visual hierarchy is the matrix for the film: the youngest, dirtiest, and poorest among the poor will fall prey to the taller, older, and stronger.

Allegorized by the first scene of "bull" and "bullfighter," the subsequent humanimal assemblages show a batterer, invariably filmed from a low angle, smashing to death a weaker boy or nonhuman animal with a stick. In one scene, the tall young Jaibo, the film's "bullfighter" par excellence, beats the shorter young Julián to death. Jaibo is filmed from a low angle, lifting his right arm repeatedly to plunge a wooden stick into his victim. In twenty-minute intervals, the killing scene repeats, changing characters but maintaining the batterer's gesture: arms held high and holding an instrument. In a later scene, Pedro hits a rooster in the same way to defend a chicken: if we are tempted here to see Pedro's feeling for the chicken, we may forget that Pedro is reliving the trauma of having seen Jaibo hitting Julián. Immediately after, Pedro's mother kills a rooster with a stick; later, Pedro beats chickens to death at the reformatory school; finally, Jaibo beats Pedro to death in the chicken yard. The assemblage of bullfighter and bull comes full circle: Jaibo, the bullfighter, has killed Pedro, the bull. For all the usual irony of Buñuel's films, here the humanimal assemblages serve a humanistic lesson: after seeing Pedro kill the chicken, the director of the reformatory school hopes to lock up poverty instead of kids.

But Buñuel's humanistic line was soon translated into filmic narratives beyond humanism. In some pioneer films of the time, the interchangeability between animals and humans is seen in assemblages that submit everyone to the political violence of poverty, though rarely is this violence visualized as an act of a human animal toward a nonhuman animal that would stand in for a human. Violence is seen in its effects (death on-screen), and assemblages portray communion among humans and animals facing the same violence. They share a history. The first short documentary to diverge from Buñuel's pedagogy was *Tire Dié* (Birri, 1958), which shows a humanimal assemblage of communal eating at the dining table of poverty in a slum. The camera first shoots pigs plunging their snouts into the garbage and then cuts to children extending their hands into the same pile. To represent systemic violence, the film does not portray humans killing animals, but everyone living in conditions of vulnerability. In some scenes, humans feed animals with what little they have. Nonhuman animals do not necessarily function as stand-ins for human animals. This alternative narrative is seen more clearly in contemporary films that engage images of drought as the equalizer between human and nonhuman animals. These films offer lines of flight toward what Ximena Briceño calls "an interspecies politics of survival."[23]

The Aesthetics of Drought: Benacerraf, Pereira dos Santos, Rocha

By imagining interspeciality in its capitalist form through an aesthetic of drought, some early third cinema films place nonhuman animals alongside human animals and beyond their mere instrumentalization as left-wing pedagogues. In 1959, Margot Benacerraf structured her pioneer poetic documentary *Araya* with humanimal assemblages in which *every* member shares a vulnerable fate. Benacerraf adds a nonanimal element to the assemblages: the tropical inclemency of the desert and its scorching midday sun. In Araya, all matter is eventually subjected to the sunburn of the salt-mining peninsula. The first montage shows images of desert shores and a squabble of seagulls flying over the sea as the voice-over says that this is a place "where everything is wind and desolation [. . .] where there are neither trees nor water fountains, nor rain, where nothing grows." Throughout the film, we hear repeatedly that "the sun hits stronger and stronger in Araya" along with a narration that associates life on the peninsula with 500 years of capitalist exploitation. A shot of the colonial fortress built to protect Araya is accompanied by a voice-over observation: who knows "how many men died in the enterprise." Diegetically the sun has replaced the colonial forces: it is narratively and visually the violent protagonist beating to death the (stylized) sea, shore, and all living creatures. It is the sun of oblivion and underdevelopment, as the peninsula is stuck in time.

Araya creates an aesthetics of drought, a precursor of Glauber Rocha's aesthetics of hunger.[24] Humanimals join together under the fiery sun. In one scene, an assemblage of women, children, dogs and crows meet together at dawn on the shore, waiting for the fish to arrive, under the first rays of the sun. The voice-over confirms their intimate communion: "the sea has been generous that day and all benefit." Humans, pelicans, and crows all gather at the fish feast. Women disentangle the fish from nets; pelicans fly over the seashore; crows come after humans start to leave. A girl stays longer and collects seashells to decorate the tomb of her dead.

The sun-machine operates as a metaphor for the industrial machine arriving to Araya in the final scenes: first, the colonial construction killed men, then underdevelopment left the peninsula under the whip of the sun, now the bulldozer will displace working hands forever. The fate of animals and humans is the same. The last shot is not the burning sun, but

Figure 5.3. Margot Benacerraf, *Araya*, 1959, Venezuela, video still.

the cloudy sky visually expressing the voice-over's doubt: "will the machine bring development with it?" The question sets the newly arrived form of extractivism against humanimal intimacies.

Araya's humanimal assemblages, plugged into the capitalist machine of the sun of underdevelopment, also appear in the pioneering films of Brazilian Cinema Novo, which have a utopian vector in their open ending. The blazing sun of the "sertão" northeast of Brazil is the setting in both Nelson Pereira dos Santos's *Barren Lives*, and Glauber Rocha's *Black God, White Devil*. *Barren Lives* makes human and nonhuman animals interchangeable under the common fate of the drought. There is only one scene of violence in which humans and animals are not exchangeable; the only three other scenes of violence represent humanimal assemblages that stage precapitalist interspecies cohabitation: Vittoria kills the parrot so that her family can eat and survive the desert; Fabiano tames a horse, and later kills the dog Baleia out of pity, because she is sick. Unsurprisingly, the scene of instrumental violence is the branding of a cow, evoking the scorching sun in a different way. The burn makes the cow private property, just as the burning drought (brought by underdevelopment) brands all humans and animals who are victims of *being*, rather than having, property.

A scene at the beginning of the film establishes the frame of interchangeability under drought. One of Fabiano's and Vittoria's sons faints of exhaustion; Fabiano whips him to make him stand up, but the child can't walk. Fabiano carries him the rest of the way. Halfway through the film, a cow falls agonizing under the sun. Fabiano whips her too, but he can't lift her himself. And the cow is not his. He gives up. Two close-ups show the cow's head: the first while it tries in agony to breathe before giving in to its imminent death, the second when it is already a skull abuzz with flies. The drought stands in for a capitalist machine, drying up the lives of the child and the cow, just like the sun dries up everyone in *Araya*.

A similar strategy of interchangeability frames the beginning of Rocha's iconic *Deus e o diabo na terra do sol*: a humanimal assemblage appears before the film's second minute. Gerardo del Rey meditates with a worried frown in medium shots and close-ups as the camera sees him looking at the horse (or cow) skull, now legendary. As Pereira dos Santos does in *Barren Lives*, Rocha's montage shows the animal's head twice: first from a high angle and freshly dead, and then with a close-up once it becomes a fly-covered skull.

A victim of drought, the nonhuman animal lies on the desert sand, filmed in almost the exact same position as Benacerraf's calf. Rocha's human animal, worried about the mammal victim of drought, weaves together

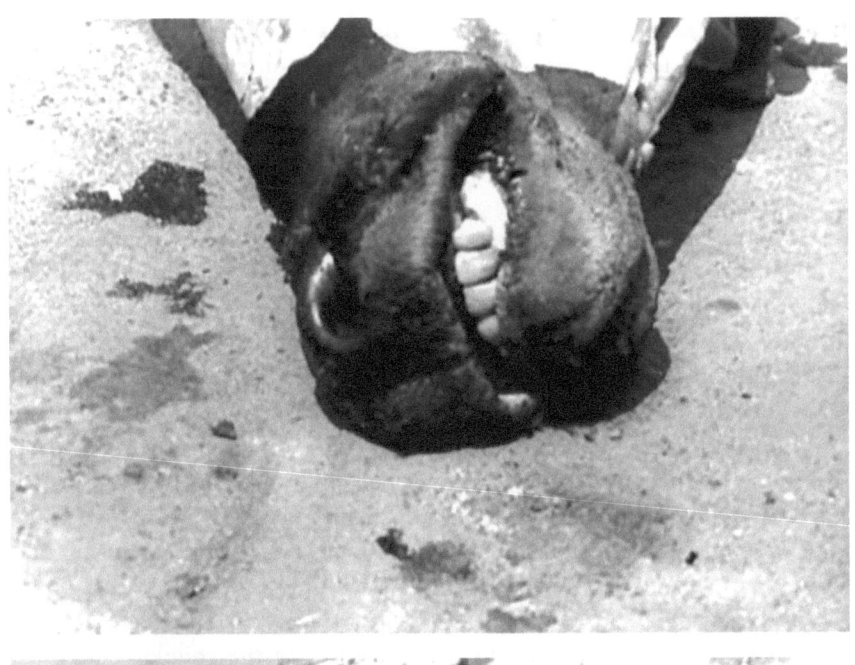

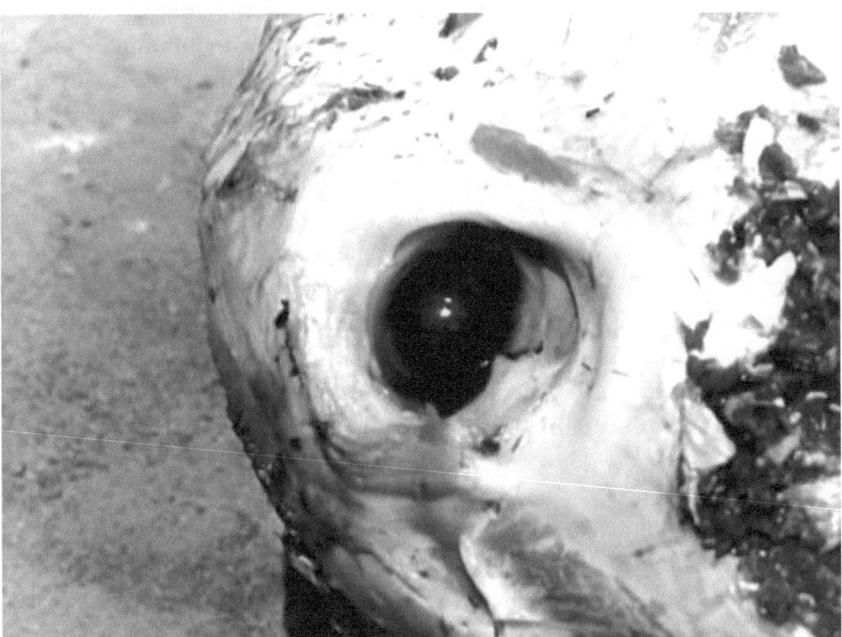

Figures 5.4 and 5.5. Glauber Rocha, *Deus e o diabo na terra do sol*, 1964, Brazil, video still.

Benacerraf's, Pereira dos Santos's, and Rocha's sun-machine as a killer of life and a stand-in for economic injustice. The human actor reproduces his apprehensive gesture, but this time he is looking at a human animal's skull, that of his mother, murdered ferociously by the landowner's assassins. Mother and horse, victims of the same "searing" system of land on the sertão.

Like Benacerraf, Pereira dos Santos and Rocha both end with a question. The spectator hears Vittoria asking Fabiano in despair: "can we continue living like animals?" She has wanted all along to live like those she regards as human animals, like those who own property. She has yearned for a bed made with nonhuman animal skin: a leather bed (*cama de couro*), the kind on which the owners of the land sleep. To be an owner is to own many nonhuman animals for different purposes—alive (branding them) or dead (using their skin). For Vittoria, a leather bed will make her *gente* (a person). Vittoria's angst is humanist, but the film denies her the chance to become *gente*. Would it be possible for all to be "owners" of nonhuman animals and of nature? The last image is a long shot of the desert horizon under the sweltering sun, a true line of flight in its polysemy: it is a horizon that seems not to lead anywhere other than desert. As the couple walks with their children in exodus, it may only take them to the unforgiving desert of slum urban life, where they will not be owners, but owned—just like nonhuman animals are owned. In its plea for agrarian reform in Brazil, *Barren Lives* renders some animals and humans exchangeable and equivalent to the privately owned land. Rocha's film also ends with an open question, along the lines of *Barren Lives*: will the desert become the sea? In the last shot, we see Gerardo del Rey run through the desert of the northeast toward the sea. But the filmmaker's cut to the image of the sea does not show any human animals in it. If the angst of the desert's drought is to become the plentiful sea of life, it will need a humanimal intimacy based on something other than ownership. As with Benacerraf, dos Santos and Rocha limit the pedagogical instrumentalization of humanimal assemblages.

Slaughterhouse Pedagogy: Ríos, Solanas, Getino, Gleyzer

The films I discussed above are structured around humanimal assemblages in allegorical capitalist machineries. In three iconic Third Cinema documentary films from Argentina—which cite each other—humanimals are placed in relation to the actual industrial machinery of the slaughterhouse, which stands in for capitalism: Ríos's *Faena* (1960), Solanas and Getino's *The Hour* (1966–68), and Raymundo Gleyzer's *Swift* (1971).²⁵ In *Faena* and *The Hour*, the Eisenstenian shock value of blood returns: the humanistic pedagogy assigned to the nonhuman animal there also produces the same line of flight as in *Strike*—the shocking sight of blood allows us to think through animal exploitation. In *Swift*, the Vertovian utopian vector reemerges, albeit limited to human animals.

The industrial assemblage of humanimals inside the slaughterhouse may be the most posthuman image of all: here everyone is equivalent to an iron link in the chains that move machinery. This is enhanced by the stark filmic contrast that establishes a humanist narrative for the city: shots from the city alternate with shots inside the slaughterhouses on the city's outskirts. The city is populated with humans (propertied), and the slaughterhouse (which reveals the city's truth) is populated by humanimals (cows and workers stand in continguity immersed in an intimate bloodbath). The three films visualize the human city differently: outside, in between, or inside the slaughterhouse. In *Faena*, the city is an actual montage of images of the urban space filmed before the camera enters its outskirts: there are only human animals in it. In *The Hour*, the city is visualized in a montage of its commercial advertisements for luxury products that interrupts the montage of images from the slaughterhouse. In *Swift*, the city is represented inside the slaughterhouse as the camera shows the workers as potential revolutionaries.

Although in the three films the slaughtered animal is the great humanist pedagogue of capitalist exploitation, the humanimal assemblages narrate the lesson differently. In *Faena*, the disparity between the shock of the bloody image on the one hand, and the music and poetic voice-over on the other, is so great that the excess of violence cannot be integrated into the narration. It may offer the viewer sympathy toward animal suffering. In *The Hour*, the voice-over narration is tight, the montage is fast paced, and the Kuleshov effect successful: there is less room for the question of the sentient animal to remain open, as the narration completely orients viewing. In *Swift*, we are spared most violence against nonhuman animals: the slaughterhouse teaches humans how workers' exploitation can become the opposite.

Ríos defamiliarizes the slaughterhouse by filming daily gruesome killing rituals to Shöenberg's background music and an existentialist narration. After vistas of the city and shots of bourgeois inhabitants entering cars, buses, cinemas, and cafés, Ríos cuts to the entrance of slaughter hell on the outskirts. The bellowing of animals and discordant music are the soundtrack for trucks heading toward the slaughterhouse and bulls entering the corrals.

The assemblage is sealed when the doors of the workers' elevators and the cows' corrals open. The camera shoots humans and nonhumans entering the space into which they will soon be locked. Inside, sequences of bloody manual labor alternate with images of the industrial iron hooks from which sheep and cows hang. The workers' labor is machine-like. Ríos does not spare the spectator any blood while showing the complete capitalist process from the disassembling of the cow to the assembly of the cans, mediated by workers whose alienation makes them look as listless as the dead cows. Eisenstein's 1924 effect—the image of the bull's dead head with its open eye looking up—is exploited by the middle of the film, when the camera zooms in an extreme close-up of a cow's dead head, falling after being hammered, so that we perceive the slight twitch of the cow's eye while listening to a heartbeat. Again, the spectator encounters the impossible gaze of an undead eye. A montage of still images of workers lifting hammers ready to strike animals or standing in the midst of hanging cows follows to the sound of the heartbeat. To the fragmentation of work produced by the assembly line, the camera adds the fragmentation of the body into organs: close-ups of guts, legs, heads, workers' hands, and iron tools. Organs stand in for the iron pieces that move the machinery. Metal noises and workers' automatisms complete the posthuman machine of the capitalist slaughterhouse.

The last scenes establish the humanist lesson: to the sound of industrial machinery, the voice-over tells us that we need to know who packs, labels, and transports the meat we eat. But the shock of blood throughout the film has been so brutal that the lesson may not reach the spectator, more aware perhaps of animal suffering in the end. Ríos himself ends by doubting the pedagogical import of his documentary: "Was it worth it to interrupt the assembly line [. . .] to throw [these] images [at the face of others]?"[26] The montage that follows is, once again, the shock of blood: the camera shows a herd of cattle (we hear roaring), the flayed skull of a cow hanging from a metal line (we hear a train whistle), and a worker's hand ready with its saw.[27]

The Hour cites slaughter images from *Faena*, but its blood lesson is a call to arms embedded in the narrative of national liberation. In the segment titled "Dependency" in the first part of the tripartite film, and to the angelical sound of J. S. Bach's *Concerto No. 5 in F minor* (largo) sung by the *Swinger Singers*, the spectator is shocked by a montage of slaughterhouse images and TV luxury commercials. The humanist lesson is clear: capitalist consumption depends on brutal violence. At the sound of a voice pronouncing the word "underdevelopment," a metal gate is lifted and slaughtered cows roll down the floor to be picked up by a metal hook. The following montage includes shots of the dead cow's eye (figures 5.6 and 5.7), bloody skulls, slit sheep

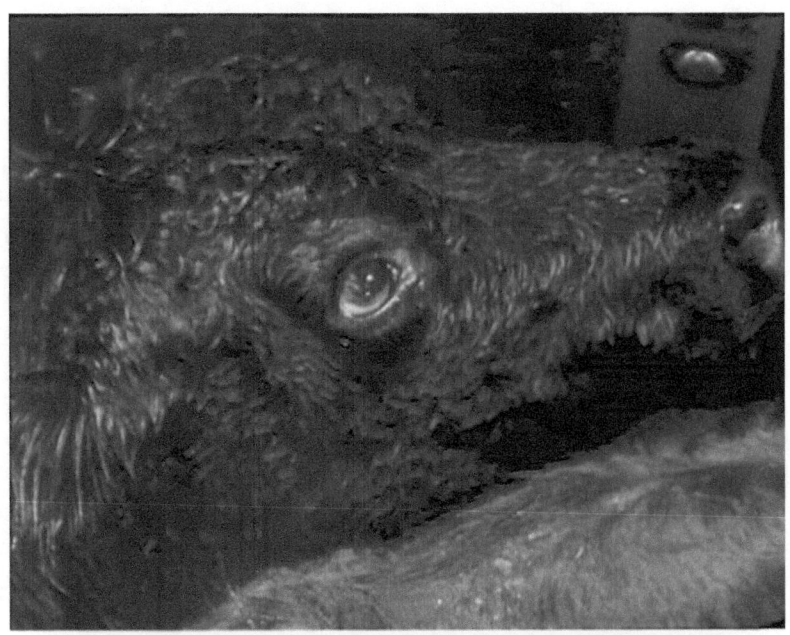

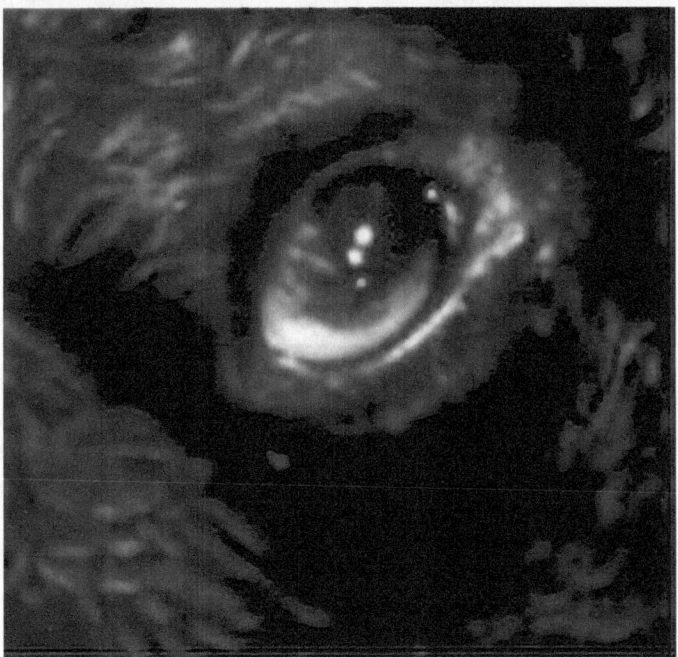

Figures 5.6 and 5.7. Fernando Solanas and Gustavo Getino, *La hora de los hornos*, 1968, Argentina, video still.

throats, workers bleeding cows to death, and commercial images of Coca-Cola, cigarettes, fancy cars, sexy women, champagne, and intertitles such as "every day we work more to be paid less." The cow's still blinking eye contrasts with preceding still photos of perfectly made-up female eyes. The last image of a flayed cow skull (almost the last also in *Faena*), shown for ten silent seconds, is followed by the final dictum: "today foreign monopolies and their local allies control practically the totality of national economy." The humanimal assemblage at the slaughterhouse shows how a dependent economy works: raw materials (humanimal assemblages) are sold in exchange for foreign products (Coca-Cola and cosmetics). The shock value of the dead cow's eyes lies in the rapid contrast of montage. And though its meaning is tightly controlled by the humanist narration of poverty, there is still the risk that its "look" at the camera breaks the narration for the spectator who will not get past the slaughterhouse brutality.

Gleyzer's *Swift* also cites images from *Faena*. But they are carefully woven within a voice-over narration about the worker's potential for struggle. The eleven-minute-long "urgent montage" is a "comunicado" from the Luis N. Blanco commando of the ERP (People's Revolutionary Army).[28] It announces the kidnapping and popular trial of Stanley Sylvester, then manager of the meat-freezing company Swift in Rosario, and British Consul. A montage of images of cattle and workers entering the slaughterhouse, citations from *Faena*, explains to the spectator how workers are exploited. The humanimal assemblage of the meatpacking industry has been established.

But the assemblage is sternly anchored in the humanist narration describing the workers' labor conditions and the planned guerrilla action of the ERP commando. Our attention is focused on this action and its results; the slaughterhouse as a gathering space, not the slaughter, is a pedagogical tool for armed struggle. We see contemporary newsreels, still images, locations, and citations from *Faena* while the voice-over explains the demands of the ERP for the liberation of the Consul. The documentary footage shows success: images of the distribution of food and blankets and the rehiring of laid-off workers.[29] The goal of the film is a pedagogy of action: the voice-over demands each citizen become a combatant. The filmed action aims to elicit spectator awareness of "the need to take with violence what the monopolies have taken with violence from the people." When we next see the slaughterhouse by the end of the film, it is through a utopian image: humans are liberated from the humanimal assemblage, and the meaning of the slaughterhouse as a space of oppression is overturned. In the montage of still and moving images of riots, Gleyzer inserts a panning shot of the group of workers inside the slaughterhouse sitting together at the lunch table, their backs to the camera.

We can see clearly what distinguishes these workers: they are all already armed. The medium shot shows us the *facón*—the local thick butcher knife—placed exactly in the same position on each and every worker's wide belt. What better place than a slaughterhouse to think of the people armed for the struggle? It is a space where they all have been trained to kill. They just need to know they are the human animals who can kill, not the nonhuman animals to be killed. Whether there is room for nonhuman animals in this dream of liberation remains a question: certainly armed struggle at the time was embedded in a thoroughly speciesist discourse.

By Way of Conclusion: Nonhuman Animal Lines of Flight

Except for the glimmering moments in the examples above, few films in the corpus of the New Latin American Cinemas of the sixties and seventies included assemblages opting out of the narrative: "animal, pedagogue of man." Films that engage more explicitly humanimal assemblages that resignify relations between human and nonhuman animals, as well as their role in a critique of capitalism, start appearing in the seventies. I end this chapter considering two shorts that have garnered little attention.

In 1973, Colombian Luis Ospina filmed the short *Cali: de película* with an almost Vertovian utopian line of flight in the form of nonhuman revenge. Ospina uses brutal footage of Spanish bullfighting, or "corrida," set to the soundtrack of Spanish music. The bull, almost dead, is pulled out of the plaza to have its throat slit; the horse that the bull has ripped apart endures the same fate. But the vision of the final killing has a different soundtrack: the Spanish music alternates with the growls of the bull and the horse yelling as if from beyond the grave. Like Vertov, Ospina makes the dead animal come alive—at least via the voice. Like Eisenstein's and Ríos's, Ospina's nonhuman animals speak after death. Ríos's recording of the seemingly ticking heartbeat of the slaughtered cow places the latter in a twilight space between life and death, but the sound may still be heard as a biological reflex. Ospina produces the same effect, though with a "response" from the slaughtered animals to the world that they endured. Here nonhumans utter sounds of complaint to humans about their fate. It may be the case that Ospina's bull, compared with the industrial slaughtered cow, recalls precapitalist interspecies cohabitation. And this may explain why Ospina's critique stabs the fabric of the anthropocentric relation with nonhuman animals that constitutes human masculinity (precapitalist in itself) rather than the identity of an exploited worker. This humanimal assemblage of horses, bulls, and men establishes masculinity as a deadly anthropocentric passion that celebrates hierarchies (and the actual taming) of both nonhuman and human animals—a bravado that shows an association whose only purpose is the spectacle of domination. Time for nonhumans to rebel, says the film.

In 1983, Brazilian Jorge Furtado decided on a humanimal assemblage that could teach human animals the lesson of capitalism by creating a category of human animals even more vulnerable than nonhuman animals. In his twelve-minute-long film *Isle of Flowers*, presented as "not a fiction," Furtado builds capitalist hierarchies so that some "human beings" (as the voice-over says) have less than some mammals, such as pigs, who at least are fed by their owners. Dialectical as it is, the discourse of the film implies that pigs will be fed so that their meat can then be sold for the dinner savored by those who own houses with kitchens. While pigs and some humans will be well fed while alive, other humans will simply die of starvation.

The film is structured around the itinerary of a nonanimal form of life—a tomato—through the flows of capitalist market economy. According to the credits, this is an "island that exists." Next we read: "God does not exist." The ironic tone and the intended audience indicate this is a lesson for those who may understand God. The collage of images and scientific discourse mocks a science film explaining how a tomato goes from a plantation to a garbage pile where nonhuman animals can eat it (pigs, in this case). Human beings are described as mammal animals, who, compared to other "mammals, like whales" or other "bipeds, like chickens," have a "highly developed brain and opposing thumbs." All those beings are, in turn, different from a tomato, which is described as a vegetable, whose principal utility is to "become food for human beings." But as it turns out, in some places—such as the "Island of Flowers"—there are nonhuman animals (pigs) who are transformed into human beings in that they enjoy tomatoes, meant to feed human beings, before any impoverished human being can do the same. As examples of human beings, we see a Japanese man who produces tomatoes: he is shot standing in a plantation, followed by mug shots, and a pseudoscientific explanation of what differentiates him from other human beings. We see Annette, for instance: a "biped Roman Catholic mammal." She buys tomatoes at the supermarket with the money she earns selling perfumes. In her kitchen, she throws an ugly tomato into the garbage because it does not look good enough for the sauce on the pork she will serve at lunch.

The twelve minutes are a string of ironies as to what these "highly developed brains and opposing thumbs" of human animals can do in the market economy for which every form of life is valued to the dollar. Against an animated collage of ancient architecture and works of art, we hear the voice-over: "they can do wonderful things, among them. . . ." A cut to an image of the atomic bomb matches a split second of silence. Another cut to an image of a tomato follows. The speech scripted after "among them" now continues: "among them [silent second; image of the bomb] the growing of tomatoes." The tomato goes from the plantation to the market to the supermarket to the kitchen to a garbage can to a privately owned garbage pile—in the Island of Flowers. Here it is selected by human animals to feed pigs. The owner of the garbage dump allows dispossessed human beings to search for food in the garbage only after his employees have extracted all that looks good for their nonhuman animals.

In this capitalist chain, if human beings are not owners and have no money, they end up below nonhuman animals. Unlike pigs, the wretched of the earth are forced to look for food in the garbage. Here the pig may be a pedagogue but of a different lesson. The poor are described as different from pigs: they may have developed brains and opposing thumbs, but they do not have money, and, what is more important, "they are free" (as the voice-over says). The final irony is that the free market of capitalism produces un-free human beings: under capitalism, nonhuman animals can eat more and live better than free humans. Being free, or having a developed brain, qualities our Western archive associates with human animals, does not guarantee any superiority with respect to nonhuman animals. The voice-over ends with "Freedom is something nobody can explain but everyone understands." Just as inexplicable is the word that the Western archive associates with "developed brains and opposing thumbs": superiority—a quality that the film's posthuman narrative blows to pieces.

Humanimal assemblages appear often in the left-wing filmic archive of the twentieth century as pedagogical tools to unveil capitalist violence. In the case of the New Latin American Cinema, humanimal assemblages appear prominently in films with an aesthetics of drought (and by extension, aesthetics of hunger) and in slaughterhouse pedagogies. In most cases, nonhuman animals are just instrumental teachers: they are pedagogues of man, an added task to their provisions of raw materials to be consumed by propertied human animals. For the most part, the slaughter of nonhuman animals on-screen shows the regime of visibility that allows these slaughters to stand in for human slaughters. The death of nonhuman animals should make us aware of the violence that the system imposes on us as humans.

But the violence of nonhuman animal suffering and slaughter images also offers lines of flight out of the humanist narration, seen in the repeated close-ups on the dead eyes of nonhuman animals, in humanimal intimacies under drought, in flickers of rebellion of nonhuman animals. Looking at us, these dead-alive images may result in the spectator's shame of being caught in the recognition that dismantling systems of capitalist exploitation means undoing their anthropocentric worldview.

Notes

1. Cary Wolfe, *Animal Rites: American Culture, the Discourse of Species, and Posthumanist Theory* (Chicago: University of Chicago Press, 2003): 8.

2. Lauren Derby, "Bringing the Animals Back In: Writing Quadrupeds into the Environmental History of Latin America and the Caribbean," *History Compass* 9, no. 8 (2011): 602–21.

3. Gilles Deleuze and Félix Guattari, *A Thousand Plateaus: Capitalism and Schizophrenia*, trans. Brian Massumi (Minneapolis: University of Minnesota Press, 1987).

4. To name a few: Luis Buñuel's 1933 *Las urdes* (Spain); George Franju's 1949 *Le Sang des bêtes* (France); Jorge Sanjinés's *1966 Ukamau* (Bolivia); Diop Mambéty's 1973 *Touki bouti* (Senegal); Frederic Wiseman's 1976 *Meat* (USA); Paul Leduc's 1977 *Etnocidio* (Mexico); Vladimir Carvalho's 1970 *O País de São Saruê* (Brazil); Charles Burnett's 1977 *Killer of Sheep* (USA); Gerardo Vallejo's 1978 *Reflexiones de un salvaje* (Argentina); Chick Strand's 1979 *Loose Ends* (USA); Chris Marker's 1983 *Sans Soleil* (France); Gaspar Noé's *1991 Carne* (Argentina-France); Richard Linklater's 2006 *Fast Food Nation* (USA).

5. Martha Few and Zeb Tortici, eds., *Centering Animals in Latin American History* (Durham: Duke University Press, 2013).

6. See Sara O'Brien, "Why Look at Dead Animals?," *Framework* 57, no. 1 (2016): 32–57; Vivian Sobchack, "The Violent Dance: A Personal Memoir of Death in the Movies," *Journal of Popular Film* 3, no. 1 (1974): 2–15. See also André Bazin, "Death Every Afternoon," in *Rites of Realism: Essay on Corporeal Cinema*, ed. Ivone Margulies (Durham: Duke University Press, 2003): 27–32; and Serge Daney, "The Screen of Fantasy (Bazin and Animals)," in *Rites of Realism: Essay on Corporeal Cinema*, ed. Ivone Margulies (Durham: Duke University Press, 2003): 32–41; Akira Mizuta Lippit, "The Death of an Animal," *Film Quarterly* 56, no. 1 (2002): 9–22.

7. John Berger, in *About Looking* (New York: Vintage International, 1991): 2–30, adds the enclosure of animals in zoos: the Jardin des Plantes in Paris was constructed in 1793. Norbert Elias argued in *The Civilizing Process* (1939) that an increasing concern with "civility" and the spectacle of violence started early on with the fall of the Middle Ages.

8. The case of slaughterhouses in South America follows the pattern established in Europe after the Enlightenment: the killing of animals is located farther and farther away from the city as the nineteenth century advances. For a case study of Buenos Aires, see José Martini, "Los antiguos mataderos de Buenos Aires," *Ciencia Hoy* 137 (2014), http://cienciahoy.org.ar/2014/04/los-antiguos-mataderos-de-buenos-aires/.

9. Philippe Ariès, *Western Attitudes Toward Death: From the Middle Ages to the Present* (Baltimore: Johns Hopkins University Press, 1974); Thomas Laqueur, *The Work of the Dead: A Cultural History of Mortal Remains* (Princeton: Princeton University Press, 2015).

10. Amy Fitzgerald, "A Social History of the Slaughterhouse: From Inception to Contemporary Implications," *Human Ecology Review* 17, no. 1 (2010): 58–68.

11. John Berger, *About Looking* (New York: Vintage International: 1991), 28.

12. See the excellent collection edited by Paula Young Lee, *Meat, Modernity and the Rise of the Slaughterhouse* (New Hampshire: University Press of New England, 2008).

13. My translation. Damien Baldin, "De l'horreur du sang à l'insoutenable souffrance animale. Élaboration sociale des régimes de sensibilité à la mise à mort des animaux (19ᵉ–20ᵉ siècles)," *Vingtième Siècle. Revue d'histoire* 3, no. 123 (2014): 62.

14. Jean Pierre Marguénaud, "L'animal en droit français," *Derecho animal* 4, no. 2 (2013).

15. Berger, *About Looking*, 13.

16. Nicole Shukin, *Animal Capital. Rendering Life in Biopolitical Times* (Minneapolis: University of Minnesota, 2009), 87. Within the field of Critical Animal Studies, Jason Hribal has argued that nonhuman animals are part of the exploited working class in capitalism, see *Fear of the Animal Planet: The Hidden History of Animal Resistance* (Chico: AK Press/CounterPunch Books, 2010).

17. Eduardo Viveiros de Castro, *A inconstância da alma selvagem e outros ensaios de antropologia* (São Paulo: Cosac and Naify, 2002).

18. Horses appear prominently in humanimal assemblages but almost always associated with humans who control humans. Santiago Álvarez chose a giant tarantula for his "¿Cómo, por qué y para qué se asesina a un general? . . ." (Cuba 1971) in order to associate it with the CIA and the killers of General Schneider in Allende's Chile in 1970.

19. Within the corpus of Third Cinema, two examples comes to mind: Argentine journalist Leonardo Henrichsen, filming his own death as he is shot by the Chilean military in Patricio Guzmán's *The Battle of Chile* (1973), and Santiago Álvarez's inclusion of found footage of US soldiers killing a Vietnamese man in *79 Springs* (Cuba 1969).

20. These are names of places where famous strikes took place before the Russian Revolution.

21. See John MacKay's analysis of this sequence as the difference between agitprop and propaganda: *Dziga Vertov: Life and Work. Volume 1: 1896–1921* (Boston: Academic Studies Press, 2018), 60. According to MacKay, in his childhood Vertov

was so impacted by seeing a cow being slaughtered that he wrote a humanitarian poem in its honor.

22. Jo Evans, "Luis Buñuel's Missing Dog and Other Animals: *Un Chien andalou* (1929), *L'Age d'or* (1930) and *Las hurdes: tierra sin pan* (1933)," *Bulletin of Spanish Visual Studies* 1, no. 1 (2017): 117–37.

23. Ximena Briceño, "*Vidas Secas* or Canine Melancholia: Reflections on Living Capital," *Journal of Latin American Cultural Studies* 26, no. 2 (2019): 299–319.

24. Karen Schwartzman, "An Interview with Margot Benacerraf: *Reverón*, *Araya*, and the Institutionalization of Cinema in Venezuela," *Journal of Film and Video* 44, no. 3/4 (Fall 1992 and Winter 1993): 51–75.

25. Georges Franju's 1948 *Le sang des bêtes* (France) is a precedent worth considering for comparison but outside the scope of this paper.

26. In the Spanish version we hear: "¿valía la pena meter la mano en el engranaje? ¿creer que uno la estaba metiendo, ¿valía la pena arrojar algunas imágenes al paso rápido de los otros?"

27. Slaughterhouses are foundational images in Argentine culture, given the country's cattle-raising economy. For an ecocritical analysis of twentieth-century slaughterhouse novels, see Isabel Quintana, "De mataderos, desiertos, éxodos y fronteras," in *Más allá de la naturaleza: Prácticas y configuraciones espaciales en la cultura latinoamericana contemporánea*, ed. Irene Depetris Chauvin and Macarena Urzúa Opazo (Santiago: Ediciones Universidad Alberto Hurtado, 2019): 155–82. In the texts Quintana studies, cows rebel and even commit suicide, exhibiting a different line of flight from the one identified in the films in this chapter.

28. A "comunicado" is a public announcement or statement. The word is commonly used for guerrilla announcements but also for official ones.

29. The kidnapping was so successful that it was used in Cuba for training purposes. It was considered an example of bloodless revolutionary action. In January 1971, the ERP kidnapped a Swift truck full of meat to distribute it among the poor of Saladillo. When they kidnapped Sylvester, they demanded the reentry of 800 workers who had been laid off and the payment of their salaries. They also demanded that bosses cease policing workers and distribute 25 million pesos in food, blankets, and school supplies. In the film, we see documentary footage of the distribution of food and blankets as well as the workers' return to the factory.

Works Cited

Ariès, Philippe. *Western Attitudes Toward Death: from the Middle Ages to the Present.* Baltimore: Johns Hopkins University Press, 1974.

Baldin, Damien, "De l'horreur du sang à l'insoutenable souffrance animale. Élaboration sociale des régimes de sensibilité à la mise à mort des animaux (19e–20e siècles)." *Vingtième Siècle. Revue d' histoire* 3, no. 123 (2014): 52–68.

Bazin, André. "Death Every Afternoon." In *Rites of Realism: Essay on Corporeal Cinema*, edited by Ivone Margulies, 27–32. Durham, NC: Duke University Press, 2003.
Berger, John. *About Looking*. New York: Vintage International, 1991.
Briceño, Ximena. "*Vidas Secas* or Canine Melancholia: Reflections on Living Capital." *Journal of Latin American Cultural Studies* 26, no. 2 (2019): 299–319.
Daney, Serge. "The Screen of Fantasy (Bazin and Animals)." In *Rites of Realism: Essay on Corporeal Cinema*, edited by Ivone Margulies, 32–41. Durham: Duke University Press, 2003.
Deleuze, Gilles, and Félix Guattari. *A Thousand Plateaus: Capitalism and Schizophrenia*. Translated by Brian Massumi. Minneapolis: University of Minnesota Press, 1987.
Derby, Lauren. "Bringing the Animals Back In: Writing Quadrupeds into the Environmental History of Latin America and the Caribbean." *History Compass* 9, no. 8 (2011): 602–21.
Evans, Jo. "Luis Buñuel's Missing Dog and Other Animals: *Un Chien andalou* (1929), *L'Age d'or* (1930) and *Las hurdes: tierra sin pan* (1933)." *Bulletin of Spanish Visual Studies* 1, no. 1 (2017): 117–37.
Few, Martha, and Zeb Tortici, eds. *Centering Animals in Latin American History*. Durham: Duke University Press, 2013.
Fitzgerald, Amy. "A Social History of the Slaughterhouse: From Inception to Contemporary Implications." *Human Ecology Review* 17, no. 1 (2010): 58–68.
Hribal, Jason. *Fear of the Animal Planet: The Hidden History of Animal Resistance*. Chico: AK Press/CounterPunch Books, 2010.
Laqueur, Thomas. *The Work of the Dead: A Cultural History of Mortal Remains*. Princeton, NJ: Princeton University Press, 2015.
Lippit, Akira Mizuta. "The Death of an Animal." *Film Quarterly* 56, no. 1 (2002): 9–22.
MacKay, John. *Dziga Vertov: Life and Work. Volume 1: 1896–1921*. Boston: Academic Studies Press, 2018.
Marguénaud, Jean Pierre. "L'animal en droit français." *Derecho animal* 4, no. 2 (2013): 1–29.
O'Brien, Sara. "Why Look at Dead Animals?" *Framework* 57, no. 1 (Spring 2016): 32–57.
Quintana, Isabel. "De mataderos, desiertos, éxodos y fronteras." In *Más allá de la naturaleza: Prácticas y configuraciones espaciales en la literatura latinoamericana contemporánea*, edited by Depetris Chauvín and Urzúa Opazo, 155–82. Santiago: Ediciones Universidad Alberto Hurtado, 2019.
Shukin, Nicole. *Animal Capital. Rendering Life in Biopolitical Times*. Minneapolis: University of Minnesota Press, 2009.
Sobchack, Vivian. "The Violent Dance: A Personal Memoir of Death in the Movies." *Journal of Popular Film* 3, no. 1 (1974): 2–15.

Viveiros de Castro, Eduardo. *A inconstância da alma selvagem e outros ensaios de antropologia*. São Paulo: Cosac and Naify, 2002.
Wolfe, Cary. *Animal Rites: American Culture, the Discourse of Species, and Posthumanist Theory*. Chicago: University of Chicago Press, 2003.
Young Lee, Paula, ed. *Meat, Modernity and the Rise of the Slaughterhouse*. New Hampshire: University Press of New England, 2008.

6

Reordering Material Hierarchies in Jossie Malis Álvarez's Animated Short Film Series, *Bendito Machine*

KATHERINE BUNDY

At the very root of animated cinema is the viewer's temporary amnesia that inordinate and nonliving objects cannot act, move, decide, show emotion, or possess agency. In fact, the etymology of the term "animation" derives from the Latin word *animare*, which means to "give breath to," and the nominative, *animationem*, translates to "the action of imparting life."[1] While live-action films often reenact the audiovisual ordering of the human spectator, animated films have the potential to rearrange audiovisual hierarchies of subjectivity in order to offer aesthetic alternatives to anthropocentric materialities. In this sense, the life-giving aesthetics of animation can act as an ecological process that can simulate a fluidity of existence, change, and agency that is not readily presented in live-action cinema. In the spirit of pushing past the human in Latin American cinema, this exploration of the animated short film series *Bendito Machine* by Peruvian-Chilean animator Jossie Malis Álvarez will connect ecocriticsm to the cartoony worlds in which objects, humans, and nonhumans interact with varying degrees of agency. The long-standing traditions of Latin American visual representations of humans, machines, nature, and spiritual iconography situate how the aesthetics of *Bendito Machine* condense and remix time and embodiment to eventually direct the viewer to an ecological warning of the "worst case scenario" of an anthropocentric power struggle in which humans will eventually lose. Along with comments taken from my interview with Jossie Malis Álvarez, creator of *Bendito Machine*, Ursula Heise's and Elizabeth Swanstrom's theorizations of digital aesthetics and object-oriented ontologies (OOO) facilitate critiques of human-centered worldviews by examining how animation reorders hierarchies to emphasize agency in nonhumans and posthumans.

Environmental Animation

One does not have to stretch to think of commercially successful animated films that directly engage with environmental and ecological themes, such as *Avatar* (2009), *Wall-E* (2007), *Happy Feet* (2007), *The Bee Movie* (2007), and *Ferngully: The Last Rainforest* (1992), along with Studio Ghibli's animated classics, such as *Spirited Away* (2001), *Princess Mononoke* (1997), and *Nausicaä of the Valley of the Wind* (1984). Referred to as enviro-toons or environmental animation, these films treat the environment as a central subject in need of preservation, activism, and/or awareness.[2] Nicole Starosielski defines environmental animation as "a genre of environmental media that uses animated form (and its strengths of abstraction and simplification) to deliberately construct knowledge about the social and ecological processes that affect us and/or the characters and therefore assist in the creation of environmental subjectivities."[3] The three short films examined in this chapter from Jossie Malis Álvarez's online animated series *Bendito Machine* are examples of enviro-toons because they directly engage with the destructive effects of anthropocentric practices of pollution, extraction, colonization, and development by using digital animation techniques to vivify objects, humans, and nonhumans.

Bendito Machine is an online-published series of six animated short films that is free and available for viewing on Malis's website, BenditoMachine.com. Started in 2006, the crowd-funded short films span over nearly fifteen years since the last and final short was published in spring 2020, and they steadily grew in popularity and production quality as visibility and funding increased. On the official website, Malis Álvarez introduces the series to viewers in the following summary available in Spanish and English:

> 6 short tales about charming vertebrate creatures and their holy machines. *Bendito Machine* is a series of simple-minded organisms and their dazed relation with machines. Gentle creatures that survive in a state of perpetual dependence, where artifacts

mark the passage of a glorious future. Everything you need is the spark of life, obey his commands, fuel the machines and pull the trigger . . .⁴

The description above is a singular piece of paratext for the website user and viewer given that the films themselves have no language-based dialogue. Even the descriptors within the paratext hint at the shifts in agency between "simple-minded" and "gentle" vertebrate creatures (the figures most resembling humans) and their "dependence" and "dazed relation" with "holy machines." In this sense, the god complex of anthropocentric humans is turned on its head, and the Savior of humans is hosted within the machines they worship. In this same spirit, the plots of each film follow a similar arc: first, the seemingly peaceful and anthropocentric coexistence of nonhumans, objects, posthumans, and human-like bodies; then an idea or a development that spirals out of control; and finally the backfiring of objects or nonhumans against the human-shaped protagonists. In theme and tone, the *Bendito Machine* series is hardly comical but rather deeply cynical because the destructive greed displayed in each short film leads to large-scale disaster born from disparaging human habits such as media obsession, exploitative capitalist practices, armed conflict, and even global extermination.

The globalized production of Malis's animation career (between Chile, New York City, Barcelona, and Mallorca) also informs its thematic content, which is as ambiguously local as it is global. When asked about the target audience of *Bendito Machine*, Malis replied that he hoped for a universal message for human viewers to reflect on their environmental impact whether they were watching "from a place like Perú or China."⁵ This ambiguous posture of place and cultural setting frames the general theme of *Bendito Machine*, which he describes as "an acute commentary on humans and their weaknesses, their machines, their dreams, and the mysteries of the universe."⁶ Such is the thematic panorama of *Bendito Machine*, which is absent of dialogue yet full of gags that poke fun at the simple-mindedness of the human-shaped characters who are desperately trying to domesticate otherworldly machines and creatures. Aside from the director's upbringing in Peru and Chile, the *Bendito Machine* films themselves are tricky to qualify as strictly Latin American, which is another point of contention with labeling, identification, and the infinite possibilities of web-produced animation to reflect real place and time. The title of the film series is a hint at its willingness to remix and condense the archaic and the futuristic, because "bendito" in Spanish translates to "blessed," which then modifies "machine," a term that has been tied into questions of humanity, labor, cognition, and agency for centuries. The choice to blend Spanish and English seems deliberate, especially because Spanish has been chosen to express devotion and belief, whereas the word that signifies progress and technological advancement is Anglophone. Nearly 500 years after colonial contact, the ecological concerns spanning the Americas continue to battle neocolonial and neoliberal practices in the name of global development and consumption. Contemporary cultural products like the short films in *Bendito Machine* speak to a multilevel understanding of the global colonialism and modernity across time while also keeping a more nuanced focus on the slow violence and their ecological consequences across Latin American history.[7]

One needs to look no further than the Latin American vanguard to exemplify fascinations with pre-Columbian civilizations as well as technological futurisms that were sweeping the globe in the 1920s and 1930s. Vanguard artists such as Xul Solar (Argentina, 1887–1963) portrayed utopian futures by painting urban landscapes that harmonized the global "best of" by remixing ancient iconography, national flags, and flying machines in surrealistic landscapes.[8] Meanwhile, Estridentismo in Mexico celebrated the mechanization of the human and a disruption of classical cultural production as Manuel Maples Arce declared, "¡Chopin, a la silla eléctrica!" [Chopin, to the electric chair!][9] Also, within the Mexican avant-garde, Diego Rivera's massive murals captured the Latin American circularity of historical struggle, oppression, and coexistence of humans, machines, nature, and spiritual idols.[10] Within the vanguard zeitgeist in Latin America and in Europe during the 1920s and 1930s, visual art and cinema were challenging the status quo of hierarchical structures, and artists aimed to break the representation of the real by consolidating space, time, and dimensions of thought. The evolution of animation techniques and cartoon industries around the world were also in full swing during those decades and were redefining the possibilities of how to mechanize and exaggerate bodies for an effect on the viewer that was larger than life. Around the mid-twentieth century, the graphic novel genre in Latin America began to surface and provided ample atmosphere for experimentations of reimagining the human body and its relation to nonhumans. Often dystopian and science fictional, posthuman representations in Latin American graphic novels spanning from Hector G. Oesterheld's *El Eternauta* series from Argentina (1957–59 and 1976–77) to more recent works like Edgar Clement's *Perros Salvajes* (2012) from Mexico combine allegorical reflections on political oppression as well as "their typically critical and parodic engagements with hegemonic (and humanist) European discourses of modernity and progress."¹¹ The prevalence of posthuman perspectives in Latin American visual narratives emphasizes how contradiction and chronology in modernist terms convert to hybridity and circularity in non-Western aesthetics. Jossie Malis Álvarez's *Bendito Machine* is another example of experimental animated short film that speaks to the long-standing cultural debates of Latin American cosmopolitanism, and reflects how nostalgia and futurism tell the ecological tales of development, disaster, and reinvention from the times of colonialism, modernity, neocolonialism, and neoliberalism.

Latin American Animation and *Bendito Machine*

Animation has strong roots in Latin America, including Argentina's claim to the world's first animated feature films (ca. 1917) by animator and cartoonist Quirino Cristiano. Presently, the epicenters of Latin American animation are housed in Argentina, Chile, Brazil, and Mexico, where the live-action film industry is also traditionally the strongest, yet in recent years there has been a growing animation presence in Peru and Ecuador, whose projects have been making the rounds in festival circuits regionally and around the world. Argentina's Ventana Sur Film Festival (c. 2009) houses a subsection called *Animation!*, which showcases the region's animation projects to foster work and alliances between commercial studios in Latin America. In 2018, the first Ibero-American animation awards event bearing Quirino's namesake, Premios Quirino, debuted in Tenerife of The Canary Islands. Another growing collection worth noting is the archive of Latin American and Spanish experimental animated shorts of Moebius Animación that showcases techniques and narrative ventures by animators across the region. In a global sense, Latin American animation is increasingly visible at international film circuits including two feature films in the world-renowned Annecy animation festival in 2017 as well as the region's first Oscar in 2017 for Chilean director Gabriel Osorio's animated short *Historia de un oso* (*The Bear Story*).¹²

While creative and innovative potential in Latin American animation is plentiful, the financial architecture has traditionally been difficult for Latin American filmmakers and animators. During my interview with Malis Álvarez in 2018, he responded to my question about the origins of *Bendito Machine* in 2006, as I was curious about the increasingly globalized nature in production and distribution online for a series that began around the time of YouTube's debut on the Internet. He initially worked on *Bendito*

Machine as a solo and improvised venture without any financial or distribution support, but then began to discover funding opportunities online through global distribution in addition to festivals and other traditional channels of distribution.[13] One of the online avenues that Malis Álvarez used to fund his short films was Kickstarter—an online crowd-sourcing platform. In exchange for financial backing, the Kickstarter campaign gifts posters, flip books, and posts of behind-the-scenes updates. Since the appearance of the first short film of the series in 2006, the completed short films have won more than eighty awards in film festivals worldwide. With the sixth short film only recently posted in April 2020, the *Bendito Machine* series is a testimony to the shifting industrial landscape for talented animators to patchwork financial support and transnational collaboration with the help of online platforms and programming.

Aesthetically, the silhouette-style animation of *Bendito Machine* revives early twentieth-century styles of animation such as "The Adventures of Prince Ahmed" (1926) by German animator Lotte Reiniger, as well as the cutout style of Italian-Argentine animator Quirino Cristiani's short film "El Apóstol" (1917). The animation style of *Bendito Machine* features digitally simulated silhouette cutouts, simplistic yet colorful landscapes that contrast with the detailed black shapes, and cartoony details that personify the silhouettes and their gestures, such as expressive eyes and mannerisms. Far from the physical rigor and tediousness of cutting and pinning figures from the old days, the fluidity of the digital-born silhouettes of humans, machines, nature, architectures, nonhumans, and posthumans pack the audiovisual landscapes with satirical content concerning colonialism, industrialization, and capitalization of natural landscapes, as well as violence and the betrayal between humans, nonhumans, and posthuman[14] bodies. *Bendito Machine* as a series not only touches upon ecocritical themes within the narratives of each episode, but the animation aesthetics destabilize the dominance of humans by redistributing affect among nonhumans and posthumans even though the human figures are the ones who are repeatedly creating environmental disasters in each short film. The pessimistic tone of the three environ-toons analyzed, namely "Obey his Commands," "Fuel the Machines," and "Pull the Trigger," present a didactic message for viewers to reflect on global environmental catastrophes within a digitally animated space. As environmental animation, *Bendito Machine* invites the viewer to reflect and speculate within a different sphere of agency and possibility how nonhumans, posthumans, and objects can quickly turn on the gullible humans who believe themselves to be the masters of their environments.

OOO and Environmental Animation

While animated films and cartoons are frequently infantilized and dismissed as childlike, the range of ecological themes from several award-winning films are a testimony to how animation can engage with the material realities of viewers. Embedded in many dialogues about animation is the concern of an increasing dynamism and agency of technologies as the human body is more susceptible to automation. Vivian Sobchack describes this anxiety in the twenty-first century: "We now live in a culture pervaded by perceptive and cognitive computational machines (perhaps better called 'entities') . . . In contrast, we also now live in a culture in which our 'humanity' is increasingly (to use a phrase familiar to animators) 'squashed and stretched' by forces beyond our control."[15] By foregrounding technophobia and anthropocentric anxieties brought forth by animation aesthetics, Sobchack's ecocritical approach is a posthuman one that merges criticism and cultural production in the digital age. The ability for animation to awaken subjectivities among humans, nonhumans, and posthumans as a digital and ecological process echoes Norman Klein's declaration that "cartoons [are] ever the barometer of changes in entertainment."[16] Therefore, engaging animated films with an ecocritical approach is more prevalent as cultural criticism continues to question the human stronghold as the ideological center of nature, technology, being, and development. Especially in this critical moment of development of animation techniques such as augmented reality (AR), virtual reality (VR), innovative immersion, and narrative in video games and mobile applications, careful reflections are needed for imagining how animation will become more intertwined with material space and landscapes, and how humans will manage this responsibility among nonhuman actors.

Cultural and media theorists Elizabeth Swanstrom and Ursula Heise examine how animated media presents alternative perspectives to objecthood by the very process of "imparting life" into nonhuman and posthuman figures. Swanstrom and Heise's work is part of a larger shift in ecocritical studies that includes the reification of nonhumans, posthumans, and objects in new media. In her text *Animal, Vegetable, Digital: Experiments in New Media Aesthetics and Environmental Poetics*, Swanstrom uses the framework of object-oriented ontology (OOO), which she defines as "a philosophical framework that includes, in the arena of being, objects of every kind, flattening categorical distinctions between animal, vegetable, mineral (and digital) entities."[17] Alternatively referred to as new materialism or speculative realism, OOO emphasizes the fluid relationship between the ecological, digital, and material, and does not leave out humans but rather recognizes them as only one of the many diverse agents that comprise a natural space. Ursula Heise's article points to the basic techniques of animation as engaged with the natural by portraying nonhuman actors and fluid bodies because "speaking and acting animals, plants, and objects invite the viewer to see humans as only one of the many manifestations of liveliness, intentionality, and agency in which human interests and endeavors are often pitted against those of animals, machines, or objects."[18] Both Heise's and Swanstrom's theorizing of nonhumans and objects as digital continuations of ecological poetics signals back to how the genre of animation presents new ways of perceiving the movement and liveliness of nonhumans and objects.

Swanstrom uses OOO to analyze different forms of media including video games, flash animated simulations, and music videos by envisioning environmental poetics and digital aesthetics as compatible platforms. She asserts that "ecocriticism and digital studies both question the disembodied model of subjectivity—that is, the Cartesian model—that was taken as a given in the understanding of both the natural world and the virtual one(s)."[19] Heise's ecocritical approach is more cautious of OOO because she sees animation as always having been a proponent of new materialisms. Heise goes on to argue that animation "should be understood as the principal aesthetic genre that engages with the reification of nature and its possible alternatives in modern society."[20] Both Heise and Swanstrom see the overlap between digital simulations of objects and ecological poetics through reviving the inanimate as an alternative cosmology to live-action re-creations of human-centered approaches to environmental topics.[21]

Jane Bennett's neomaterialist text *Vibrant Matter* takes up the possibility of vital and agent-bearing objects by proposing a peculiar question to traditional visions of environmentalism as human-activist-centered: "How would political responses to public problems change were we to take seriously the vitality of (nonhuman) bodies?"[22] While reimagining the agency and liveliness of the nonhuman and the inanimate requires a total rework of anthropocentric worldviews, an animation of those objects can create intra-action between agents rather than the human-centered one that is usually perpetuated in live-action films. Heise echoes Bennett's question in her claim that animated film has been exploring nonhuman agency in a playful manner since long before the surge of new materialist theories.[23] The 2D animation techniques in *Bendito Machine* indeed achieve a playfully sarcastic re-creation of the pitfalls of humans and their missteps with exploitative environmental practices. While the human figures in the episodes might represent human greed and ignorance at its worst, an alternative awareness of ecological orders is proposed in the series that simulates a direct animation of objects, nonhumans, and speculative posthumans that enact revenge on those that traditionally claim themselves the liveliest: humans.

Malis Álvarez also perceives the potential for animation to provide visible and tangible interaction between shapes that signal playful liveliness. Curious about the hybrid shapes of his characters, I inquired about how animation facilitates the interaction and comingling of humans, machines, nature, nonhumans, and posthumans in *Bendito Machine*. Malis Álvarez responded that the concept of (re)mixing, transforming, and fusing different elements to make a unique character is part of the passion of this project. By working with animation in cutout digital 2D, without volume and in dichromatism, the silhouetted characters allow him to play freely with the creation of a flat universe that maintains richness of details and shapes. Animation theory dating back to Sergei Eisenstein's series of notes about Disney's animation from the 1930s and 1940s describes an ever-changing form defined by movement itself as *plasmaticness*.[24] However, if animation is defined as the antithesis of static form, then it once again leans into oppositional semiotics that define object versus human and Science versus myth. While the mechanization of fluid movement does come into play when designing an animation atmosphere from scratch, Ryan Pierson's understanding of animation falls more in line with Swanstrom and Heise's ecocritical approach of OOO to digital and animated media. Pierson insists on notions from the Gestalt school of thinking, which, when applied to animation aesthetics, sees movement as a matter of coordination and relationality: "A figure is not exhaustively definable as fixed, closed shape . . . it is the result of the forces that scaffold it . . . Thus, we can note that movements bear formal specificities without ossifying them into fixed shapes. Movement is not the end of the analysis; it is the beginning."[25] This relational approach to movement, perception, and animation reflects that of ecological and cybernetic networks that destabilize hierarchies and shift into object-oriented ontologies that use affect to mold, coordinate, and narrate shifts in agency. In *Bendito Machine*, the design and craft of animation support the liveliness of all objects, humans, animals, and posthuman figures as well as comment on the clash of ecological worldviews at the center of many Latin American cultural debates. By analyzing three of the six short films that make up the *Bendito Machine* series, OOO facilitates critiques of human-centered worldviews by examining how animation can thematically and aesthetically reorder hierarchies to demonstrate agency in nonhumans and posthumans.

Bendito Machine: "Obey His Commands," "Fuel the Machine," "Pull the Trigger"

All six of the completed short films in the *Bendito Machine* series display a cover image bearing provocative titles, a still image from the film, and two definitions that explain the bifurcated pun of the title interpretation. In viewing all six of the shorts' titles in a row in ascending chronological order, a thought is strung together that suggests a series of commands from the God-like Machine to the "simple-minded" humans: "Everything You Need"; "The Spark of Life"; "Obey his Commands"; "Fuel the Machines"; "Pull the Trigger"; and "Carry On." Along with Malis's signature silhouette style with differentiated colored backgrounds for each episode, all six shorts feature the increasing speed of montage rhythm that condenses a chronology of human colonization over nonhumans, objects, and other humans. Malis's treatment of ecological themes as a Latin American animator demonstrates how OOO and animated media mutually construct an alternative cinematic order in which hierarchies between animated humans, nonhumans, and posthumans are flattened and reordered to underscore the mistakes of humans when they assume center stage.

In the third film in the *Bendito Machine* series, "Obey his Commands," the title presents the mandate as if it were a divine order from a (masculine) savior sent from the heavens. On the cover image of the film, human-shaped

Figure 6.1. Jossie Malis Álvarez, *Bendito Machine*, "Obey His Commands," 2009, video still.

figures on a grassy knoll look up in awe at a large mechanical apparatus that produces the only color differentiation in the frame. The visual dominance of the nonhuman machine over the awe-stricken human figures in the cover image sets the tone for "Obey his Commands" because the narrative comments on cultural anxiety when a lively machine colonizes human attention and devotion. In the film, a holy man performs a ritual on a hilltop, and a machine is subsequently dropped from the sky. He brings the color television down from the hilltop and quickly replaces a radio (shaped like the iconic Spanish bull silhouette) on the altar above the human-shaped disciples. Now the television is the source of divine worship after the radio is quickly thrown off a cliff and into a trash heap. The humans simultaneously worship and fear the television that can run, jump, and flip through its own channels. A quickening montage initiates as the scene transitions, mimicking channel flipping in a meta-nod to the viewers who are also worshipping their own machines while watching. During the climax of the episode, the television flickers through scenes of war and human destruction as the viewers begin to ceremonially bow while wearing gas masks. A human-shaped figure runs from the scene and up the hillside only to return riding a large machine that instantly destroys the television and launches its own screen that resembles an Internet video-streaming site. The machine barely lasts a few seconds before it collapses and breaks down, showing a blue screen, presumably the infamous "blue screen of death." Another massive machine shaped like a satellite with a phone dial (satellite cellphone service) drops from the sky and crushes humans and machines alike. The last scene shows the television still flickering in the dump, accompanied by other fragments of trash, and vultures that scavenge the remains.

This cynical approach to human worship of technology and entertainment as a habit of self-destruction and excessive material waste is central to "Obey his Commands." In the episode, the transmission of religious obedience to the divine perpetuates a magical causality in which sentient machines fall from the sky and grace the humans with a temporary savior figure, echoing Karl Marx's well-known declaration that "Religion is the opium of the people"[26] while also recalling Donna Haraway's assertion from her "Cyborg Manifesto" that "our machines are disturbingly lively while we, ourselves, are inert."[27] With each upgrade, the divine machines grow in size and posthuman quality, becoming more mechanically dominated and less associated with animal and human silhouettes. The final machine is massive and architectural, combining the sharp edges of gears and the geometric designs of pre-Columbian civilizations. Visually, the hybridization of machinery and Indigenous design creates a brand of Latin American steampunk that merges the embodiment of colonial conquest with that of a futuristic alien invasion. The circularity of futurist and precolonial aesthetics set the stage for animation to simulate how the magical powers of new technologies can seduce humans into a self-serving cycle of labor and destruction, denying their connections to other entities and objects around them. When the final machine suddenly drops from the sky, the comedic timing is reminiscent of the gags from Warner Brothers cartoons that might have a piano or an Acme weight fall from above and obliterate the characters underneath. Like this trope, there seems to be no explanation other than the divine punishment of justice served. In the case of "Obey his Commands," the humans are the gullible and blind worshippers of untrustworthy machines that are on a rapid path to self-destruction.

Malis Álvarez's cynicism toward humans in "Obey his Commands" serves as a warning about the idolization of ceremony and spectacle. He explained in our interview that the principle theme of *Bendito Machine* is the human conflict between machines, instincts, and fears. He went on to explain that the media worship of "Obey his Commands" reflects how humans are transfixed and inundated with global conflicts, mediated through screens as if they were in a constant state of emergency. The agency and mobility of the machines in this episode propose an alternative vision through 2D animation of the dangers of technology dependence over time.

Stemming from this critical theme of machine and media dependency is the erratic plot structure that emphasizes the ever-increasing speed of technology and the replacement culture that inevitably accompanies the continuous disposal of older devices. In the wasteland of the dump where the older machine-saviors are discarded, including the radio and the television, the viewer is confronted with the graveyard of objects that forms an alternative ecosystem of decay and discard that exists despite the absence of humans. In "Obey his Commands," the only surviving sentient material at the end of the episode are the fragments of garbage in the dump as the television flickers through channels on its color screen. The tremors and ticks of the nonhuman objects in the trash heap simulate a vitality that outlasts human distraction and submission to their technological deities. The relics of replacement culture in the dump remind the viewer of the collective interaction of discarded material as technological upgrades continue in the other sequences. The agency of machines as saviors, destroyers, material wastes, and conscious survivors exposes the vulnerability of humans as simultaneous worshipers and victims.

The fourth film in *Bendito Machine*, titled "Fuel the Machines," takes on the ecological consequences of human transportation across land, water, air, and even space travel. While the plot is centered on a human's journey from his quaint abode to a rocket launch to mine another planet for fuel, the viewer is presented with a world that is littered from the exploitation of natural resources, nonhumans, humans, and sentient machines. The cover image for the episode defines the term *fuel* in two senses: "1) Matter that can be burned to create heat or power, and 2) Something that maintains, encourages, or stimulates." These two definitions propel the narrative, which shows an evolution of transportation from the least polluting to the most contaminating in the search for fuel resources on another planet. At the heart of the film is the expectation of endless and infinite growth in capitalist extraction practices, which is visually expressed in a nonstop movement of modernity whose demand and pollution outgrow the planet itself.

Most of the film re-creates a cynical perspective of human selfishness and myopia with their ecosystems, especially during the sequence in which the protagonist rides a ferry over waters polluted with plastic bottles, trash, sick fish, and an oil spill (figure 6.2). The ferryman whips the seahorse to

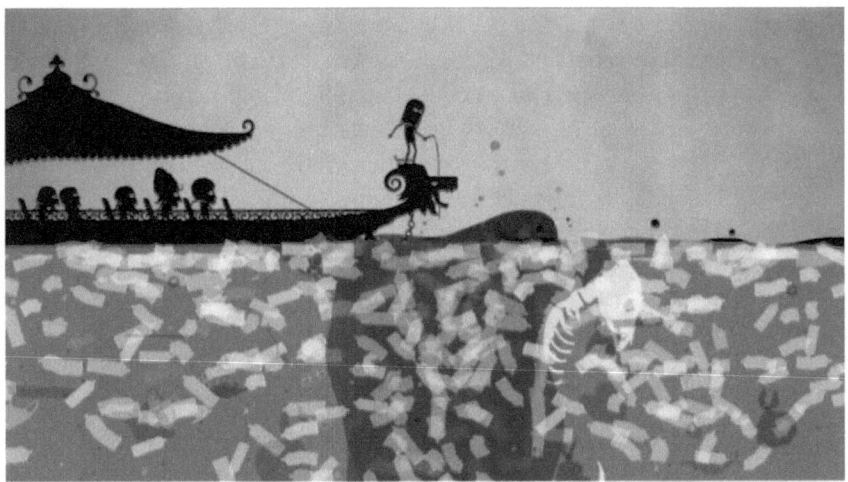

Figure 6.2. Jossie Malis Álvarez, *Bendito Machine*, "Fuel the Machines," 2012, video still.

pass through the oil spill and briefly mourns the death of his animal fuel before turning around to whip the passengers until they take out oars and row the ferry themselves. Panning out, the viewer now sees that the ferry is approaching the shore of a massive factory bearing the trademark icon for the Shell Oil corporation. The animation demonstrates the visual cacophony of water pollution under the ferry in contrast with the opaque surfaces of water in live-action films. Another evident contrast is that of the opaque silhouettes of the human figures against the transparency of the polluted objects and the aqueous fluid. The image depicts the extractive process as an expression of modernist hierarchies of human domination over nature and therefore positions humans as the manipulators of ecological disasters. Not unlike the mining and extractive practices that are well known in Latin America as (neo)colonial practices that exploit human and nonhuman bodies, the tale of capitalist fuel extraction in "Fuel the Machines" depicts how nonhuman bodies and landscapes are passive rather than agent-bearing entities. It is only when the human leaves his planet and changes atmosphere that the agency shifts from a human-centered to a posthuman cosmology in which humans are treated as decentered entities and exterminable invaders.

In the final sequence of "Fuel the Machines," the fuel-seeking astronaut lands on the foreign planet, and the space vessel begins to extract fuel from its surface. Suddenly, the human is poked, prodded, and crushed by an object off-screen as the frame reveals an enormous silhouette of a child with a red eye holding a stick, referencing René Laloux's *Fantastic Planet* (1973). The reference is appropriate, as the plot of *Fantastic Planet* allegorizes humans living on a strange planet populated by giant humanoid aliens who consider the humans to be animals and pets, thus reordering the hierarchy of agency by sheer size and alienation. The violent and sudden end to the human's life in "Fuel the Machines" is followed by a scene where the giant child rides a bicycle to the abode of his family, which mirrors the beginning when the human leaves his abode and rides his bicycle down the hill, initiating the journey of transportation, fuel, dependence, contamination, and exploitation.

The ecological message in "Fuel the Machines" suggests that the colonial quest for resources and dominance clings to the stability of anthropocentric orders to support extraction and systematic exploitation. In an alternative worldview (that of the foreign planet), human ingenuity is quickly displaced and destroyed by a childish curiosity. The decentering of the human reimagines this ecological point by politicizing nonhuman affect upon the perception of the foreign invader, which might be perceived as an animal, a spirit, or a mineral to be exterminated. "Fuel the Machines" is a condensed and satirical replication of human impact in shared spaces when the insistence of hierarchical dualisms asserts the human as protagonist of the ecosystem and therefore the mediator of civilization, extraction, disaster, and conquest.

Animation aesthetics create quick shifts in perspectivism by simulating OOO from nonhumans and posthumans who have suffered under the domination of human figures and their exploitative practices. By condensing the evolution of transportation, extraction technologies, and colonial aspirations in thirteen minutes, a "worst-case scenario" simulation is played out as single-use plastic bottles and bags plague the waters, and oil executives attempt to colonize the sky in search for more terrain. Far from the Anthropocene, humans are scaled as ants compared to the giant alien-child who squashes the tiny human without a second thought. While the atmosphere of the new planet resembles a tribal and communal atmosphere (much like Laloux's *Fantastic Planet*), the hierarchical structure that supports the foreign civilization suggests that anthropocentric dominance is destined to repeat itself through the highest bidder, whether they be humans, nonhumans, posthumans, or otherwise.

The fifth film of *Bendito Machine*, aptly named "Pull the Trigger," demonstrates the persistence of nonhumans (birds, rats, cats, dogs, insects, machines, and organic growth) as both witnesses and agents in the cyclical self-destruction of humans. The title image provides a paratext to the otherwise bleak prediction of apocalypse when it provides the three definitions of the word, "trigger" as "1. A small tongue in a gun that, when pressed by the finger, fires the gun; 2. A device pulled or pressed to release something; and 3. Anything that causes a reaction: *A trigger for the holy cause.*" In the film, the idea of the trigger is closely tied to these definitions in both content and aesthetics because an outside visitor (or space invader) bears witness to centuries of human power relations and conflict on Earth. Even the pace of the short film mimics the slow tension of the pull, the speed of release, and finally the aftermath of wounds and destruction. The third definition of "trigger" from the title image confronts an ontological defining of agency because the episode blurs boundaries of machines, animals, humans, and historical moments that reconfigured those boundaries as technology progressed. Swanstrom defines "agency" as denoting "the ability to act" and then clarifies that animals, humans, and objects have a varying degree of volition and agency within a given network rather than a completely flattened ontology of equally distributed agency.[28] Intervening in this paradigm is the animated aesthetic. In the case of the animation in

Bendito Machine, the nonsymmetrical distribution of agency is precisely the tension between what humans *do* and *what happens to humans* in the film.

The short film moves from an alien arrival to a natural space (presumably on Earth), and then to a medieval battle scene in which the alien is crushed under a mound of dead bodies in the castle's moat. As the castle is seized and occupied by the winning clan under a new banner, a plague wipes out the population of humans, leaving the remains to decompose and move back into the ground where the alien still lies. While the gaze of the "camera" stays fixed, the pace of montage suddenly increases as if an invisible hand were pulling its own trigger and observing a speeding bullet. Scenes flicker across the screen that signal key moments of development, struggle, and violence in human history, including the modernization of transportation (from carriage to the modern automobile), the first World War, the evolution of cinema, racist lynchings, refugee resettlement movements, and other references of exploitation and disaster in previous *Bendito Machine* episodes. As the scenes flash at an increasing speed, the shadowy landscape in the background becomes less tree lined and more industrial in silhouette. Finally, the speed slows down and halts to a present-day reality in which a man runs with his small dog on a street with a surveillance camera pointed downward. The dog digs curiously until the buried alien is revealed and photographed by the press but is interrupted by the sounds of military planes, tanks, and bombs. The alien is buried once again under the rubble of a post-nuclear blast, and a new time-lapse montage commences that shows the resilience of nature as the remains of human infrastructure decomposes into the landscape, and grassy shadows begin to build up under a hazy, nuclear sky.

The recurrence of apocalypse from premodern to modern to postmodern in "Pull the Trigger" does not always position humans as the founders of destruction but as the principal causers of a destructive reaction (referencing the title image's third definition). The plot sequences sadistically play with causality because humans are as much the victims of plague as they are the plague themselves. The configuration of the plague as an agent-bearing assemblage has strong implications for how humans position themselves as dominators of nature through the advancement of weaponry when it is the nonhuman natural processes that stand to outlive humans themselves. For example, the plague after the initial battle scene is a viral one (referencing the Bubonic Plague), depicting rats that attack and bite helpless victims followed by mass vomiting scenes, and a doctor (wearing the iconic beak mask) sifting through the rummage. This premodern plague emphasizes the agency of the invisible virus and the affect between contagions, nonhuman bodies, and human bodies. Following the viral plague, the montage of modernity depicts human development as a plague in itself that wipes out other humans as well as nonhuman subjectivities when the landscape changes from lush to sparse. During these sequences, the viewer is also aware of the alien that lies dormant under the Earth, and when it is excavated, a postmodern plague ensues of the nuclear annihilation of all life, except for the alien (figure 6.3). The semicomical persistence of the Other (the alien as an observer of the history of life on Earth) manages to frame the plague as a metaphor for the mass destruction perpetuated by humans when the agent pulls the trigger and causes a chain of reactions.

The conclusion of "Pull the Trigger" is consistent with the satirical tone of the other episodes in *Bendito Machine* when the alien emerges from the ground once again with a small mechanical companion. They activate their "phone home" button, and a massive spaceship arrives to collect them, but not before shots are fired and the camera pans out to reveal a war game of *Space Invaders* complete with the low-frequency beeps and buzzes of the classic videogame soundtrack. This sudden reframing of the episode through a video-game lens could suggest the simulacrum of human history as a game for outside players or as a cartoony gag that shifts the action away from Earth-bound destruction. Regardless, after briefly reveling in the winks and nods of this reference, the ship manages to escape and fly out of Earth's atmosphere and into space as enemy ships trail after them. Only at

Figure 6.3. Jossie Malis Álvarez, *Bendito Machine*, "Pull the Trigger," 2014, video still.

the end of the credits does the audience see a meteor approach Earth from off-screen, indicating another level of mass destruction. Again, this begs the ontological question: "Who pulled the trigger?"

Bendito Machine is the episodic and evolving narrative of the universal failings of the capitalist project at varying stages of contact between humans, nonhumans, and posthumans. Its films tackle environmental topics that re-create the violence and ignorance of colonial ventures that are globally relevant yet also specific to cosmologies and aesthetics of Latin America. Nearly each short film ends in the destruction and decentering of the overconfident humans seeking domination over the nonhuman. The catastrophe of this project depicted through animation aesthetics awakens other subjectivities besides those of humans yet, in the end, reinforces how humans are often the agent bearers of their own demolition scheme in a repeated Nature/Culture dualism. Even when the posthuman machines or aliens in "Obey his Commends," "Fuel the Machines," and "Pull the Trigger" manage to get the last laugh, their victory is a replica of colonization and exploitation that is simply reframed as invasion and extermination, signaling that even if material hierarchies are reordered, oppression and subjugation of others is the prevailing sentiment. While *Bendito Machine* is heavy-handed with irony and cynicism in its environmental themes, Malis's animation techniques shift and reorganize affect between humans, nonhumans, and posthumans. Thanks to the possibilities of animation to reimagine shape, movement, and timing outside live-action constraints, viewers perceive objects, humans, and posthumans in flattened hierarchies that evoke OOO frameworks even though the environmental content results in a violent and competitive attempt for subjectivities to survive and thrive at any cost.

Also at work in the *Bendito Machine* series is the suggestion of inevitable downfall and automation of humans as a result of their failed attempt at planetary domination. While this satirical notion seems comfortably positioned in animation, which is frequently regarded as a humoristic genre, the overall series of events has a tragic effect, and serves as a warning against the fixed categorizations of technology, nature, culture, and human. Moving forward from *Bendito Machine*, Malis Álvarez's newest short film project concerns the relationship between humans and the universe, because he maintains that social parody as narrative tool and the genre of science fiction is the realm in which he feels most comfortable. With the final episode of *Bendito Machine* released online in spring 2020, the fourteen-year-long project marks Jossie Malis Álvarez's signature use of animation to convey sharp critique of environmental exploitation, one that is as speculative as it is prescientific. Because Malis Álvarez's primary concerns are with humans themselves, his ecological message for humans watching the *Bendito Machine* films is the following: "If you're not part of the solution, you are part of the problem."[29]

Notes

1. "Animation," Online Etymology Dictionary, https://www.etymonline.com/word/animation.

2. Two well-known studies of mainstream US animation dedicated solely to ecocriticism include Murray and Heuman's anthology of ecological themes in twentieth-century Disney cartoons, *That's All Folks? Eco-Critical Readings of American Animated Features* (2011), as well as David Whitley's study of wild nature in cartoons in *The Idea of Nature in Disney Animation* (2008).

3. Nicole Starosielski, "'Movements That Are Drawn': A History of Environmental Animation from *The Lorax* to *FernGully* to *Avatar*," *The International Communication Gazette* 71, no. 1–2 (2011): 146.

4. "Bendito Machine," Bendito Machine, Safari, www.benditomachine.com.

5. Jossie Malis Álvarez, "A Decade of Holy Machines—Jossie Malis' Beloved "Bendito Machine" Series Heads to Its Grand Finale," interview by Mar Belle, *Animation*, Directors Notes, May 10, 2016, written, http://directorsnotes.com/2016/05/10/jossie-malis-bendito-machine.

6. "Biofilmography" Madrid En Corto: Selección de cortometrajes de Madrid, Safari, http://www.madridencorto.es/2012/sub.

7. See Ilka Kressner, Ana María Mutis, and Elizabeth Pettinaroli, *Ecofictions, Ecorealities and Slow Violence in Latin America and the Latinx World* (New York, NY: Routledge, 2020).

8. See Xul Solar, *Drago*, Watercolor painting (1927).

9. Manuel Maples Arce, *Actual Núm. 1*. 1921. Reproduced in Schneider, Luis Mario. 1985. *El Estridentismo: México, 1921–1927*. 1a ed. Monografías De Arte, 11 (México, D.F.: Instituto de Investigaciones Estéticas, Universidad Nacional Autónoma de México).

10. See Diego Rivera, *Man at the Crossroads / Man, Controller of the Universe*, Mural Painting (1933–1934). Palacio de Bellas Artes, Mexico City, Mexico.

11. Edward King and Joanna Page, *Posthumanism and the Graphic Novel in Latin America* (London: UCL Press, 2017): 3.

12. *Ana y Bruno* by Mexican animator Carlos Carrera, and *Pequenos héroes* by Venezuelan animator Juan Pablo Buscarini were shown at the Annecy Film Festival in 2017.

13. Jossie Malis Álvarez, "*Bendito Machine* Interview," interview by Katherine Bundy, April 2018. Unpublished.

14. Although the definition of the posthuman is not homogenous across critical theories, I borrow from Edward King and Joanna Page's definition as a critical perspective that "draws on a history of human-technological-animal entanglements

to interrogate the ways in which agency and production of knowledge have always been the emergent product of a distributed network of human and nonhuman agents." King and Page, *Posthumanism and the Graphic Novel in Latin America*, 4.

15. Vivian Sobchack, "Animation and Automation, or, the Incredible Effortfulness of Being," *Screen* 50, no. 4 (2009): 375.

16. Norman M. Klein, *Seven Minutes: The Life and Death of the American Animated Cartoon* (New York: Verso, 1993), 211.

17. Elizabeth Swanstrom, *Animal, Vegetable, Digital: Experiments in New Media Aesthetics and Environmental Poetics* (Tuscaloosa: University of Alabama Press, 2016): 12.

18. Ursula K. Heise, "Plasmatic Nature: Environmentalism and Animated Film," *Public Culture* 26, no. 2 (2014): 305.

19. Swanstrom, *Animal, Vegetable, Digital*, 54.

20. Heise, "Plasmatic Nature," 303.

21. Latin American studies reminds us that new materialism is not so "new." Brazilian anthropologist Eduardo Viveiros de Castro critiques new materialisms by arguing that Amerindians presupposed this fluidity of existence and subjectivity in perspectivism, which perceives only one innersubjectivity (a soul/spirit) with different natures. Eduardo Viveiros de Castro, *Cannibal Metaphysics: For a Post-Structural Anthropology*, trans. Peter Skafish (Minneapolis: Univocal, 2014).

22. Jane Bennett, *Vibrant Matter: A Political Ecology of Things* (Durham, NC: Duke University Press, 2010), 13.

23. Heise, "Plasmatic Nature," 308.

24. Heise, "Plasmatic Nature," 310.

25. Ryan Pierson, "Introduction: Perception and Metamorphosis," in *Figure and Force in Animation Aesthetics* (New York: Oxford University Press, 2019), 6.

26. Most often misquoted as "Religion is the opiate of the masses."

27. Donna Haraway, "A Cyborg Manifesto: Science, Technology, and Socialist-Feminism in the Late Twentieth Century," in *Simians, Cyborgs, and Women: The Reinvention of Nature* (New York: Routledge, 1991), 151.

28. Swanstrom, *Animal, Vegetable, Digital*, 89.

29. Jossie Malis Álvarez, "*Bendito Machine* Interview," interview by Katherine Bundy, April 2018. Unpublished.

Works Cited

Bennett, Jane. *Vibrant Matter: A Political Ecology of Things*. Durham, NC: Duke University Press, 2010.

Haraway, Donna. "A Cyborg Manifesto: Science, Technology, and Socialist-Feminism in the Late Twentieth Century." In *Simians, Cyborgs, and Women: The Reinvention of Nature*, by Donna Haraway, 149–81. New York: Routledge, 1991.

Heise, Ursula K. "Plasmatic Nature: Environmentalism and Animated Film." *Public Culture* 26, no. 2 (2014): 301–18.
Klein, Norman M. *Seven Minutes: The Life and Death of the American Animated Cartoon*. New York: Verso, 1993.
King, Edward, and Joanna Page. *Posthumanism and the Graphic Novel in Latin America*. London: UCL Press, 2017.
Kressner, Ilka, Ana María Mutis, and Elizabeth Pettinaroli. *Ecofictions, Ecorealities and Slow Violence in Latin America and the Latinx World*. New York: Routledge, 2020.
Malis Alvarez, Jossie. "A Decade of Holy Machines—Jossie Malis' Beloved "Bendito Machine" Series Heads to Its Grand Finale." Interview by Mar Belle. *Animation, Directors Notes*, May 10, 2016. http://directorsnotes.com/2016/05/10/jossie-malis-bendito-machine.
———. "Bendito Machine." Website. Benditomachine.com.
———. "Interview with Jossie Malis (*Bendito Machine*)." Interview by Andrew S. Allen. Interview. *Short of the Week*, June 29, 2012. https://www.shortoftheweek.com/news/interview-with-jossie-malis-bendito-machine.
———. "Interview with Jossie Malis Álvarez." Interview by Katherine Bundy. Written exchange, April 29, 2018.
Maples Arce, Manuel. *Actual Núm. 1*. 1921. Reproduced in Schneider, Luis Mario. 1985. *El Estridentismo:México, 1921–1927*. 1a ed. Monografías De Arte, 11. México, D.F.: Instituto de Investigaciones Estéticas, Universidad Nacional Autónoma de México.
Murray, Robin L., and Joseph K. Heuman, *That's All Folks? Ecocritical Readings of American Animated Features*. Lincoln: University of Nebraska Press, 2011.
Pierson, Ryan. *Figure and Force in Animation Aesthetics*. New York: Oxford University Press, 2019.
Rivera, Diego. *Man at the Crossroads/Man, Controller of the Universe*. Mural Painting (1933–1934). Palacio de Bellas Artes, Mexico City, Mexico.
Sobchack, Vivian. "Animation and Automation, or, the Incredible Effortfulness of Being." *Screen* 50, no. 4 (2009): 375–91.
Solar, Xul. *Drago*, Watercolor painting. 1927.
Starioselski, Nicole. "'Movements That Are Drawn': A History of Environmental Animation Form *The Lorax* to *FernGully* to *Avatar*." *The International Communication Gazette* 71, no. 1–2 (2011): 145–63.
Swanstrom, Elizabeth. *Animal, Vegetable, Digital: Experiments in New Media Aesthetics and Environmental Poetics*. Tuscaloosa: University of Alabama Press, 2016.
Viveiros de Castro, Eduardo. *Cannibal Metaphysics: For a Post-Structural Anthropology*. Translated by Peter Skafish. Minneapolis: Univocal, 2014.
Whitley, David. *The Idea of Nature in Disney Animation*. Burlington: Ashgate, 2008.

7

Mapping Queer Natures in Papu Curotto's *Esteros*

VINODH VENKATESH

Papu Curotto's debut feature-length film, *Esteros* (2016), can be included in what several critics such as Jorge Ruffinelli have identified as a boom in LGBTQ-themed cinema in Latin America in the twenty-first century. Tracing the presence of non-normative sexualities, Ruffinelli argues that at the turn of the twenty-first century, "como uno de los avatares del traspaso a otra época, el cine latinoamericano multiplicó sus referencias, personajes, temas de la diferencia sexual" [among the avatars of transition from one era to another, Latin American cinema multiplied its references, characters, and themes of sexual difference].[1] Curotto's film may be further subcategorized into a specifically Argentine boom, where directors such as Lucía Puenzo (*XXY*, *El niño pez* [*The Fish Child*]), Marco Berger (*Plan B*, *Hawaii*, *Ausente* [*Absent*]), and Julia Solomonoff (*El último verano de la Boyita* [*The Last Summer of La Boyita*]) have made critically praised films that address a wide array of LGBTQ issues. Aside from meditating on the thematics and ontology of gender and sexuality, these films also further an extant issue in contemporary Argentine cinema: the variable of spatiality and geography. This gesture is twofold, as on the one hand it examines the import of space in the social construction and performance of gender and the political regulation of sexuality. On the other, in a move that is derivative of the first, it presents the autochthonous and identitarian element of *civilización y barbarie* that has populated the national imaginary since its formation. Puenzo and Solomonoff, for example, use the trope of spatial displacement from a large city to the countryside as an organizing principle in developing their characters and plot lines; Berger, in turn, works across films to tease out how the dialectic of space may be concomitant with the discussion of sexuality. The dialectic in Argentine cultural production harbors several juxtapositions, including center and periphery, "the modern and the pre-modern, the developed and the underdeveloped, the city and the country."[2] I would add to Matthew Losada's listing the opposition between the human and the natural, as the former unit in each dyad is correlated to the exceptionalism of the human over nature and the natural. In this chapter, I examine the dyad of space in Curotto's film, paying particular attention to the relationship between the human and the natural, and how this conjugates issues of gender and sexuality. I then parlay this discussion into an examination of the narrative development of the characters and the techniques by which the director engenders a queer ethos through a strategy I term axioerotics.

The plot in *Esteros* is not overly complex or situated in the historicity or politics of allegory (which has come to characterize a wide swath of postdictatorship cinema). It is a quiet drama that, through two alternating timelines, unfolds the romantic and physical relationship between Matías and Jerónimo, two boys from the town of Paso de los Libres in the province of Corrientes. In the first chronotope, the two boys spend the summer in the farmhouse owned by Jero's family in the estuaries of the Uruguay River. They spend their days running around and exploring the countryside and river, engaging in playful teenage horseplay.[3] Their physical and emotional bond leads to one intimate encounter where the boys kiss and Jero manually pleasures Matías. Their budding connection is cut short when Matías's father accepts a lucrative job in Brazil and takes the family with him. The second chronotope, which appears in an alternating fashion with the first, brings Matías back to Paso de los Libres to celebrate Carnival, but this time accompanied by his Brazilian girlfriend, Rochi. She innocently arranges for a makeup artist, who serendipitously ends up being Jero, to paint their faces and bodies for the celebration. The plot thus plays out the familiar triangle of openly gay man, unsuspecting girlfriend, and sexually questioning boyfriend in a touching and beautifully filmed piece that favors a fluidity that encourages the audience to focus on the emotions and feelings of the characters over any explicit identitarian gesture. Commenting on the emotive nature of the film, Ezequiel Boetti argues that:

> *Esteros* es un film irregular, con algunas escenas algo obvias y otras en los que la cámara está atenta a los detalles de sus protagonistas. En esa capacidad de auscultarlos a través de sus gestos

y miradas anidan los momentos más auténticamente sensibles y memorables. Lo mejor de la ópera prima de Curotto sucede cuando ellos respiran y reconstruyen progresivamente su vínculo, y la cámara se pone al servicio de sus sentimientos contradictorios y de varios silencios que dicen más que muchas palabras.[4]

[*Esteros* is an uneven film, with a few somewhat obvious scenes and others in which the camera is attentive to its protagonists' particularities. In those astute examinations of gestures and looks dwell the most authentically sensual and memorable moments. The best parts of Curotto's directorial debut are the breathing room given to the progressive reconstruction of their connection, the way the camera is put at the service of their contradictory feelings, and the various silences that say more than many words.]

Boetti's signaling of emotion and the ways in which the film technically and formally elicits this reaction from the viewer evokes the presence and possibilities of affect as a register—alongside the visual and the sonic—in the confectioning of the moving image.

In fact, *Esteros* is an excellent example of what I have previously identified as a vein of contemporary Latin American film known as New Maricón Cinema, which includes works by the Argentine directors identified above in addition to contemporaries from across the continent such as Javier Fuentes-León (Peru), Diego Araujo (Ecuador), and Mariana Rondón (Venezuela). The movement coincides in large part with Ruffinelli's identification of a boom in LGBTQ-themed film and stands in opposition to what I term Maricón Cinema, or a scopic cinema that portrays what David William Foster calls queer issues, which do not necessarily engender a queer praxis or ethics.[5] Maricón films "foment an observational or commentarial position" and build no lasting affective ties between the image and the viewer.[6] They favor the visual register in telling a story, but do not encourage an affective transmission or empathic relationship with the viewer. Such classics as *Doña Herlinda y su hijo* (*Doña Herlinda and Her Son*, Jaime Humberto Hermosillo, 1985), *No se lo digas a nadie* (*Don't Tell Anyone*, Francisco Lombardi, 1998), and *Fresa y chocolate* (*Strawberry and Chocolate*, Tomás Gutiérrez Alea and Juan Carlos Tabío, 1993) and recent features like *Azul y no tan rosa* (*My Straight Son*, Miguel Ferrari, 2012) may be included in this genre.

New Maricón films, instead, favor the affective register over the purely visual, that is, they favor an aesthetics and a stylistics that provoke a polysensorial and haptic relationship between the viewer and the image. By favoring the affective register, "the viewer is no longer privy to the ethical comfort or distance afforded by the scopic but is instead oriented to and actively encouraged to feel (through the five senses) and partake in the exploration (sometimes lateral) of difference."[7] New Maricón films exhibit a qualitative focus on sex/gender difference and, most notably, an engineered hapticity to the viewing experience that foregrounds the generation, transmission, and circulation of affective intensities that kindle a relationship and experience of empathy in the viewer vis-à-vis the characters and desires of the moving image.[8] They resist the privilege of the visual and propose instead a destabilizing sensorial engagement with the image. This, to an extent, explains Boetti's approximation to the film and the sensorial language it engages in.

Yet also essential to New Maricón cinema are its spatial referents; a movement toward and representation of nonurban landscapes, metaphors, and spaces that untangle the subject from the systems of gendered hegemony in the city. These films run against the grain of conventional queer narratives that showcase the movement by the queer body to the city (and all the possibilities it opens up). In doing so, these films deterritorialize—and then reterritorialize—desire onto the second unit of the center-periphery dyad, from the city to the rural, the developed to the underdeveloped, and, I would further, the human to the natural. This epistemological shift is produced on the one hand through the use of natural landscapes and, on the other, the presence of the aqueous as a polystate substance, narrative component, and affective form. The aqueous both provokes a haptic image (enhancing the somatic resonance of the affective register) and collapses desire as a purely human category to reconfigure or deterritorialize it along the plane of the natural. Desire is thus brought into being, feeling, and representation through the aqueous, though the aquatic is conjured as a centrifugal component in the portrayal of the nonurban.

Curotto's appellation to the ethics and aesthetics of New Maricón Cinema are evident from the very beginning of the film. The black introductory credits include an audio prelap of the first scene where the two young boys are playing in a bathroom. We hear them laughing as the image cuts to a close-up of a sink covered in foam as the boys spray each other with shaving cream. Immediately following this close-up is a shot of the bathroom mirror that captures the naked torsos of the two boys in joyful play. Their bodies are covered in light foam, drawing the viewer's attention to them as a surface and skin; the presence of the foam and bubbles on their skin and hair (accompanied by the enhanced sound effects of its spray and lather) produces what Laura Marks calls a haptic visuality.[9] According to Marks, in haptic visuality "the eyes themselves function like organs of touch."[10] She furthers that a film may employ haptic images that "do not invite identification with a figure so much as they encourage a bodily relationship between the viewer and the image."[11] This relationship intrinsically provokes an affective transmission between the film and viewer, enhancing this register in our experience of the image.

The shift to an affective register can be witnessed in other facets of this scene. The mirrored surface, for example, is separated by hinges where a cabinet opens, the line of the hinge producing a doubling effect as one of the boys, Matías, is reflected twice on its surface. The double suggests that what is seen is not always what is really there, and that the visual cannot be entirely trusted as an epistemological basis. The director uses a slow-motion capture in this image, and the audio track reflects the pace of the action, as their laughter and voices are similarly refracted through a manipulation of time and space. Sound here and in the black credit frames is produced in a sort of echo chamber that amplifies its resonance, drawing the viewer's senses to its production and proliferation in the time-space of the image. The use of slow motion combined with this audio effect—when linked to the image of the boys in the mirror and the doubled reflection

Figure 7.1. Haptic visuality and the aesthetics of New Maricón Cinema. Papu Curotto, *Esteros*, 2016, video still.

of Matías—suggests a severing of the supremacy of the visual and sonic registers as an axiomatic truth, or point of entry into the narrative. Instead, the first images of *Esteros* provoke a multisensorial access to the film, where the image is no longer a surface of projection but rather a polyvalenced and pluridirectional experience.[12]

The spatial move from the periphery to the center similarly occurs early in the film, as an adult Matías returns to the town with Rochi. A setting shot has the two of them riding in a taxi as a close frame captures a pondering look on Matías's face. The image then cuts to him going out on the second-story balcony of their hotel room, where Rochi tells him that she has hired a makeup professional (Jero) to transform them into zombies for the Carnival celebrations. The taxi shot is short and unimportant in the narrative, but poses the notion of movement and travel from a there to a here. This "there" and "here" are hinted at in the balcony scene where the camera, in a medium shot, foregrounds the conversation between the two characters taking place in the "here" of Paso de los Libres. In the background and in the distance, however, the viewer is presented with the blurry outline of a tall and wide building. This building as part of the frame is intentionally blurred as the lens focuses on the couple kissing in the foreground. The blurred building is a city-image that is neither a real space nor topological reference, but an image of a virtual space that is relational but not ontological to the narrative.[13] Its presence evokes Jean-Clet Martin's notion of the city-image, as a virtuality that is

> neither the profile of a city, variable to infinity, nor the construction of a panoramic territory refers to a state of things. Rather, [the city-image] refer[s] to an errant line that runs through space as a scaffolding of relations, a maze of depths, relative to the more or less typical place that one occupies—which implies that every landscape is a virtual construction in relation to a memory able to stock piles of images in all their encroachments upon one another . . . which is nothing like an objectively realized solid.[14]

The city-image in this shot is the "there" from which the couple comes, the territory of the urban center that is now removed to the periphery of Corrientes, or the "here" that is underlined in the title of the film.[15]

I want to draw our attention to the title credit that appears after the film's first scene of the boys in the bathroom and their subsequent outing to the Carnival festivities. The loud percussive music cuts to an extreme long

Mapping Queer Natures in Papu Curotto's *Esteros*

Figure 7.2. The geography of the natural in the title sequence. Papu Curotto, *Esteros*, 2016, video still.

shot of the *esteros*. The wide frame is divided in two by the horizon line; above is a waning sky either at sunrise or sunset, and below is the reedy marshland of the shore in contact with the river. We must remember that estuaries are spaces in transition between river and maritime ecosystems, between freshwater and saltwater. The brackish quality of the estuary's water is fluid and resists the rigid duality of river and sea salinities. Therein lies the film's initial gesture toward a queer sexuality, as the ionic composition of the water is a metaphor for the decentering force that contests hetero and homo normativities.

This opening image of the landscape presents the viewer with a spatial and tropic map to read the development of the plot and its characters. As Tom Conley reminds us:

> It can be said that in its first shots a film establishes a geography with which every spectator is asked to contend. It may be in the logo, preceding the credits, that is often manufactured from cartographic elements (the globe in Universal Studios, the mountain of Paramount), or it may begin from an intertitle in the field of the image indicating the time and place of the story that will follow.[16]

The focused sound of flowing water and fauna makes way for the strumming of a guitar in an opening track that accompanies the forming of the title "*Esteros*" in a dissolve effect on the horizon line. The letters are not simply superimposed on the landscape but are molded to the contours of the flora—the lower sections of the first "S" and "T" are obstructed by a large bush. The film explicitly sutures the landscape (its sounds, sights, and affects) to the title (as symbol and signifier), thereby engendering the notion that what we have before us, and in the "here" of subsequent scenes, is a natural geography intimately linked to the queer trajectory of the narrative and its characters.

This space of the nonurban, the peripheral, and the natural, stands in contraposition to the city-image, the virtual "there" in the following scene of the couple on the balcony. The transition shot of the taxi ride adds to the assembly of this dialectic as a framing device in the setting of the plot. The camera located on the outside of the window centers on Matías looking outward at the landscape traversed by the car. Projected onto him (and Rochi, for that matter), by way of the reflection on the window, is a dense foliage not altogether different from the large bush partially obstructing the title in the previous setting shot. The continuity of the music adds to the linking between the setting long shot and this close image in the taxi. There is an interplay between the human and the natural in this image, as the latter is projected onto the former in a relationship that is ontoformative, in that the human body (as assemblage of discourses and desires) is screened through the lens of the natural.[17] The music comes to an end as Matías opens the sliding door of the balcony that permits a visioning of the urban "there" in the background. This short montage of three images (estuary, taxi, balcony) effectively maps out the "time and place of the story that will follow," and also maps out the cartographies of desire in this New Maricón film, as a fluid ebbing and flow of queer desires and bodies that come into being in the natural topography of the *esteros*.

The landscape of the estuaries—the natural in opposition to the virtual urban city—is primordial in understanding the ethos, trajectory, and erotics of the film and its characters.[18] Writing on the presence of rural landscapes in contemporary Argentine film, Jens Andermann notes that portrayals of the rural "are to an extent contested by an archival self-consciousness, that is, by the way in which they both call on and dismiss the repertoire of rurality proper to a previous, national cinematic modernity."[19] In contrast with third and new cinema that "once used to mobilize the landscape's political and mnemonic dimensions through a temporalization of the image that forced out the historicity of places beyond their diegetic function as settings of the action," recent movies posit the landscape not as a Deleuzian time-image (that, excised from the narrative proper, permitted a multivariate exploration of the excess of landscape) but to "the rhetorical, indeed conventional, nature of this kind of image."[20] For Andermann, landscape "becomes the measure here for the crisis of meaning that separates the present from the national-popular moment from which . . . 'new Latin American cinema' took [its] [cue]—a separation that, historically speaking, corresponds to the periods of dictatorship and of neoliberal dismantling of national economies and societies."[21] Recent films posit landscape and the natural as integral to the movement-image through the careful placement of characters within its space and the semantics of its representation; landscape is no longer delinked from the plot through the mechanism of the time-image that was characteristic of an earlier swath of films.[22] While this critical gesture may be true in Curotto's film, I believe *Esteros* also poses an altogether different quandary of the ontology of landscape, not as a measure "for the crisis of meaning" in the postdictatorship and neoliberal episteme, but rather as a reconsideration of the erotics of the image. The extreme long shots of the countryside bring us back full circle to the sounds, sights, and affects of the opening bathroom scene, where what is contested is the audience's means and mode of engaging the erotics of the moving image.

Central to this proposal and reading of the film is the notion of axioerotics, or a combination of Bill Nichols's notion of axiographics—from the study of documentary—and Ben Sifuentes-Jáuregui's epistemerotics—from literary analysis.[23] Axioerotics is the examination of how the ethical and erotic come into spatial being and dialogue in the moving image. The tool stresses the linkage between not only erotics and politics, but between the image and viewer, suggesting that the former creates ethical threads in the act of spectatorship that position the viewer's body (and drives, pulses, and affective intensities) with those on the screen. Axioerotic analysis deconstructs the autonomy of the viewer and image into something that better resembles a perpetual and multidirectional flow between the subject and the image. The extreme long shots of the estuaries are an axioerotic intervention, as they reorient desire away from the urban and onto the natural, away from the scopic and onto alternative ways and sites of knowing. They situate the viewer in direct relation to the ethics and erotics of the film.

This first takes place in the title credit of the film and then in later images is interspersed throughout the eighty-three-minute run time, including an early montage of the young boys riding in Jero's father's truck toward the farmhouse. The bucolic soundtrack accompanies them in a combination of medium shots (of the boys) and longs shots (of the scenery). They stand in the bed of the truck in a frontal shot, their outstretched arms resisting the wind, but also implicitly gesturing to the viewer that what is to be digested in the image is not their bodies or dialogue but rather the natural setting. This idea is strengthened in the following shot as Curotto splices in succession a low angle shot of trees (not entirely different from the reflection on the taxi window), a tracking shot of a bird in flight, and then an extreme long shot of the same bird now flying over the picturesque rice fields. This image cuts to a shot located from the back of the truck as the two boys open and close a gate leading to the house, metaphorically separating this natural space from the outside, creating a further iteration of the dialectic of there and here, accentuating the movement to the natural and the axioerotic implications that arise from it.[24]

In a later montage, albeit still early in the film, we see the two boys in an extreme long shot venture out of the house and into the countryside. They are minute specks walking from the left to the right of the image, as what is featured in the shot is the wide expanse of trees and grassland that the boys will now explore. This segues into a shot of them skipping rocks in a pond. An unsteady camera revolves around them as we hear the stones making contact with the rippling waves of the water. Matías abruptly informs Jero that he needs to urinate and unabashedly proceeds to do so. The audial gesture toward the aquatic (per the stones) is now enhanced by the stream of his urine, drawing our attention to the aqueous through the register of sound. The image then cuts to a crouched Jero rubbing his hands in the mud and then surprising his friend by slapping the wet substance on him. The two boys predictably engage in horseplay, in a similar image to that of the opening bathroom scene, drawing our attention to the hapticity of their bodies as production sites of affective intensities. This effect is carried out by a literal painting of their skin with the mud as a substance, texture, and signifier of the natural: their bodies are thus stitched to the geography of the landscape, tacitly linking in an inseparable bond the human and the natural.

They move into the water to rinse off and playfully remove their clothing.[25] This scene has no music track and instead highlights the sounds of the water, resonating the setting over the mood or tone that music would otherwise add as an element.[26] Emphasizing this reading is that the many droplets from the splashing and play now paint their bodies, and the camera is positioned in such a way that the audience is continually reminded of their location within the geography. The aqueous is the principle conjugation of the natural here, both in terms of what we see/hear/feel and in the erotics of how the two boys engage with each other. It is a vector of desire, signaling a thematic and ethical shift in the image and narrative.[27] It is elusive yet there, material yet ephemeral; its presence in the image resonates across visual, audio, and affective registers. Importantly, it functions as a vector of queer explorations, desires, and bodies. The aqueous is not simply part of the landscape—an excess of the setting, as Andermann would say—but rather ontoformative and integral to the hapticity of their bodies. In this scene, it points toward an awakening of sexuality (unsurprising given their age) and desires that are nonheteronormative, albeit camouflaged in play. The active vibrancy of this scene is contrasted with the following where the boys are shown floating in the water. A close side angle captures their faces above water while their bodies rest inanimate below. The lack of nondiegetic sound and the proximity to their faces serves to situate the viewer within the water, as we too are immersed in the eroticism of the aqueous. The aqueous is imperative in the production of a haptic image that permits a "dynamic subjectivity between looker and image" (Marks 3), posing an axioerotic intervention wherein the viewer is organically approximated to the flows and layers of the image before them. In posing a hapticity to the shot, the viewer (like the boys) is given permission to move from the rigid expectations and regulations of the center to explore the fluidity of desires and drives that are now reterritorialized in the natural. The aqueous is more than a metaphor here, serving as an epistemological disruption that collapses established identitarian positions (of both the boys and the viewer) in favor of a queer ethos.[28]

The shot is striking in its simplicity and disassociation from the narrative continuity of the previous images, as a time-image that refracts our notions of elapsed time. This is abruptly interrupted by an overhead shot of rain vigorously breaking the calm of the pond's surface and the two boys running toward the farmhouse. Curotto accentuates the presence of the aqueous (and its function as an erotic vector) by alternating between movement and serenity, culminating in the violence of the storm. The sequence of images—though unimportant in terms of dialogue and plot development—is an axioerotic gesture, as it provokes a spatial and relational exploration of the erotic by the viewer. Occurring early in *Esteros*, the sequence—which is very much a cognitive map—posits a structure for engaging the tripartite registers of the film and for reading the erotic evolution of its characters.

Their budding emotions and desires reach a climax when the two boys sleep over at the farmhouse one evening after a family dinner. Matías is cold and enters Jero's bed. The latter briskly and repeatedly rubs the former's back and blows hot air on his shoulder, signaling again to the viewer that the body is not a visual stencil but rather a haptic surface open to exploration (akin to earlier scenes of the application of makeup). Again, Curotto eschews the use of a musical track, preferring instead to accentuate the sounds of their bodily interaction. Matías turns to face him and the image captures a moment of intimacy between the two as they gaze into each other's eyes. Jero reaches down and begins to masturbate Matías, asking in the act if he is OK. The image cuts to a medium shot away from the bed and away from the intimacy of the previous close shot, giving the viewer some distance from what may be a very uncomfortable issue, that is, adolescent sex. We are, however, not completely disassociated from the bed, as we hear Matías groan in pleasure all while being physically placed (through sound) within the room.

The next scene takes off from the bedroom, as the camera portrays Matías slowly waking up and moving to an open window. Placed behind him in a medium shot, the camera frames him within the window frame, looking outward into the landscape. The audio register in the image is composed of the sounds of birds and other animals. The lens focuses on his back as he leans on the windowsill and peers to the side; the field and trees in front of him blur akin to the blurring of the urban in the earlier setting scene of Matías-adult returning to Corrientes. The natural we see in this frame is meant to be a virtual-image, that is, an image that collates multiple images, sounds, affects, and memories of the natural within a precise and discrete set, and not an actual or real scenery. Matías climbs out of the window and joins Jero on the outside. A side, close shot focuses their two faces looking toward the left, toward the natural. The image cuts to another behind-the-back shot of the seated boys looking at the landscape. Both shots lack dialogue and narrative importance and linger instead over the presence of the boys—their materiality—in relation to the natural. Andermann notes in his analysis of landscape in recent Latin American film that "the time-image is both being announced and being deferred by the presence of a "native character" who literally stands between the viewers and the landscape, thus denying us a view of the latter independent from the temporality of the character's actions" (51). This observation rings true in *Esteros*, as the landscape cannot be read as a narrative excess, but rather as a vector in relation to the characters in frame and their temporality within the plot. In this case, the natural is correlated to them having had their first (queer) sexual encounter with each other. The title of the film (and, by extension, the landscape onto which it is sutured), as the director explains in an interview, is not solely a reference to the filming location but also to the moment of sexual and libidinal desire.[29]

The narrative alternates to the adult plot line, to a scene where the two men drive to the farmhouse. The camera placed in the passenger-side window frame captures Matías looking outward with a faint smile forming on his face. Read against the previous scene, the smile may be a memory of the cold night and Jero's warm touch, as the image cuts to a point-of-view shot from the car window of the trees and landscape passing by. We are now privy to the landscape without a "native character" in our field of vision; instead, we occupy the character's point of view, situating us in the body, so to speak, of Matías as he returns to the *esteros*. The shot is haptic in two senses: first, the sight and sound of the wind rustling through the trees incites a tactility to the surface; second, by being in the skin of the character, the image evokes the feeling of the wind on our own skin through the open window. A montage of other natural images follows, leading to a shot of the car approaching the gate that the boys opened in the earlier scene. Matías opens the gate in a repetition of the axioerotic gesture of separating the here of the natural from the there of the urban; the gesture collapses the spatial markings of the diegesis with the libidinal interplay between the two characters, drawing the viewer closer into the intimate sensations, thoughts, and drives that guide their actions. The calqued sequence foreshadows the retaking of the erotics of the childhood scenes, melding together the two chronotopes along a common axis of desire.

In the following scene, the two men walk off into the woods looking for the estuaries from their childhood. Curotto uses this arrangement to situate both their bodies and the viewer in relation to the natural. The viewer is, after all, conditioned to make this link through the morning-after behind-the-back shot of the boys looking at the landscape. This axioerotic gesture is heightened when they reach its shores and get in a boat. Spliced in to this action are several images of the fauna and flora of the area, including a medium image of a capybara and a longer shot of a bird resting on a branch over water. This image cuts to a close shot of water lilies before transitioning to an image of Jero lighting a joint. The two water images introduce the aqueous as a vector of queerness, yet importantly also as an essential element of the natural in the landscape of the film. As in earlier montages of the natural, Curotto favors the sounds of birds, insects, and the water over a musical track. Jero's body is thus framed vis-à-vis a poly-facetic natural, its sounds and visual components becoming a compound vector of queerness in the estuaries.

The two characters take turns toking on the joint and engage in an ekphratic conversation outlining the different animals, birds, and plants surrounding them in a close shot that pans between them. Curotto then cuts to a long image of the boat as their conversation continues. The move to a wider angle explicitly situates their bodies within the geography of the *esteros* and in relation to the aqueous. This axioerotic cut and image, and the conversation that takes place between the two men, evoke what José Gil calls the "exfoliations of the space of the body."[30] Employing a Deleuzian paradigm and the natural as metaphor, Gil supposes that:

> If we are granted that the space of the body is composed of a multiplicity of exfoliations that compose volumes, polymorphous spaces, leaves, loops; and if, in addition, each of these leaves presupposes a set of relations to things, integrated relations, that is, ones that are decoded in and through the body, it follows from this that the unity of the multiplicity of spaces of the body must be defined by its activity as a decoder.[31]

The body as a whole decodes these individual exfoliations, or "the essential way the body 'turns onto' things, onto objective space, onto living things."[32] In this scene, their two bodies turn onto the natural and the aqueous through dialogue, position, and movement. The exfoliation is strengthened by their discussion of the spot where Jero has taken them. He says it is his secret, like the castle of sleeping beauty, and that "este refujio no se revela a cualquiera" [this refuge isn't revealed to just anyone]. Matías's reaction to this implicit declaration is to dip his hands in the water, exfoliating his body, desire, and their conversation onto the aqueous. He removes his shirt and wades into the wetland, physically and narratologically engaging the enigma of Jero's secret refuge.

This scene plays out in a parallel trajectory to the childhood sequence of them in the water: they engage in horseplay (which is anachronistic given their adult age) and then float face-up in the water, repeating the earlier image. They are not only visually subsumed by the water, but are ontologically and semantically interconnected to its queer nature. The aqueous is a key component of New Maricón cinema, and Curotto's film does not disappoint in following a blueprint established by its Argentine and Latin American antecedents in using the liquid as a narrative and affective turning point toward the queer. The image then cuts to a montage of close, medium, and long shots of the *esteros* and its animals and plants. Here the natural is excess—as the images do not add to the narrative or setting—yet an excess that portends specific affective and erotic transmissions.

Mapping Queer Natures in Papu Curotto's *Esteros*   175

Figure 7.3. Interstices of the aquatic and the erotic. Papu Curotto, *Esteros*, 2016, video still.

The parallel nature of this scene with the earlier sequence is inverted, however, in the subsequent shot, as a behind-the-back camera frames the seated men looking at the water. The shot does not come after an amorous moment, but rather precedes a discussion between the two. In what is the deepest and most honest interaction between the two, Jero affirms that "los esteros tiran" [the estuaries beckon] in response to Matías expressing his longing for the space. They proceed to argue, with Jero criticizing Matías for not being true to himself, and Matías critiquing the other's lack of ambition. The heightened tension is smoothed over by Jero smearing blue cheese on Matías, akin to the mud. The scene reverts to paralleling the adolescent sequence as a thunderstorm forces them to return from the water. This time, they are in no rush to get back. A low angle shot captures them looking up at the sky and at each other as the rain pelts their hair and skin. The image, like others featuring the aqueous, is vibrantly haptic, drawing our attention to their bodies. Metaphorically, the rain falling onto them signals an erotic shift in that Matías may now also smoothly flow into the queer desires permitted by the space.

Curotto effectively uses the parallel narratives to emphasize the impact of the spatial and haptic in confectioning the romantic and physical relationship between the characters. They hurry back to the house and, after a brief argument, kiss. It is telling that Matías now makes the moves on Jero and not the other way around, another inversion of the early narrative. The men wake up the next morning and are joined by Jero's parents. The two drive back after spending a pleasant day with them. On the way out, Matías tries to address what happened between them: "Jero, yo . . ." [Jero, I . . .].

The ellipses drag out and are only put to rest by Jero when he says that he understands that Matías has his girlfriend and work "allá" [over there], away from the *esteros* and the sexual fluidity it permits. In driving back, they are returning to the rigid matrices (of the city-image, the compound complexity of the urban as virtuality and lexeme and not an actual real space) of heteronormativity that Matías has so far successfully aligned himself with.

Once back in the city and away from the natural, he realizes that his relationship and life with Rochi is a farce, a mask worn as a signifier within the public theater of acceptability. In the concluding minutes of the film, Matías abruptly breaks up with her and tracks down Jero in a clothing store. Without saying a word, the two men engage in a passionate kiss, closing the erotic and narrative arc of the film. This scene is a tropic scene in recent LGBTQ-themed Latin American cinema in that it signals an outing of queer desires onto the public space, effectively outing non-heteronormative bodies and flows from the dark and stigmatized recesses of the abject. Other films such as Javier Fuentes-León's *Contracorriente* (*Undertow*, 2010) and Diego Araujo's *Feriado* (*Holiday*, 2014) end in a similar manner, where a character who once rejected his sexuality now openly manifests a same-sex desire irrespective of the consequences.

The final alignment with same-sex desire, however, is not an iteration of Anglo-identitarian notions of the closet and its leaving, as Matías never expresses that he is gay, but rather a distinctly queer gesture in that all that is portrayed (and needed) is a kiss between the two men. It is an open kiss and open ending, similar to the final scene of Berger's *Plan B*, leaving whatever comes next entirely up to the imagination of the viewer. Importantly, their tryst takes place within the sociocultural milieu of the urban, bringing a queer desire that was once only formulated in the natural space of the *esteros* into the recognizable spaces of the city. In a closing masterstroke, *Esteros* pushes queerness past the human and onto the natural, in specific spatial topographies and topologies that broaden the scope of sexuality and gender.

Notes

1. Jorge Ruffinelli, "Dime tu sexo y te diré quién eres: La diversidad sexual en el cine latinoamericano," *Cinémas d'Amérique Latine* 18 (2010): 67.

2. Matthew Losada, "Argentine Cinema and Rural Space," *Chasqui* 40, no. 2 (2011): 19.

3. The film is based on Curotto's earlier short that had the two boys witness a hate crime against a queer performer in the town's Carnival celebrations. This

scene does not make its way into *Esteros*, which avoids some of the more difficult and violent issues of LGBTQ life.

4. Ezequiel Boetti, "Critica de *Esteros*, de Papu Curotto," *Otros Cines* 22 (February 2017): n.p.

5. David William Foster, *Queer Issues in Contemporary Latin American Cinema* (Austin: University of Texas Press, 2003).

6. Vinodh Venkatesh, *New Maricón Cinema: Outing Latin American Film* (Austin: University of Texas Press, 2016), 23.

7. Ibid., 7.

8. Another central characteristic is the visual dismembering of the body through focused close shots that render the body not as a whole, but rather as fragmentary. This technique typically occurs in sex scenes, thus recalibrating the visual signs and identifications of desire as they are deployed in movement across the screen.

9. Laura Marks, *Touch: Sensuous Theory and Multisensory Media* (Minneapolis: University of Minnesota Press, 2002), 2.

10. Ibid., 2.

11. Ibid., 3.

12. This shift toward the affective can be seen in several scenes throughout the film, including the first interaction between an adult Matías and Jerónimo, when the latter applies sensual brushstrokes of makeup to the former, instructing him (and the viewer) to close his eyes.

13. This juxtaposition is evidenced in a later scene as Matías stands outside a club looking out on the river, the city blurred in the background in contrast to the aqueous closer to the camera.

14. Jean-Clet Martin, "Of Images and Worlds: Towards a Geology of the Cinema," in *The Brain Is the Screen. Deleuze and the Philosophy of Cinema*, ed. Gregory Flaxman (Minneapolis: University of Minnesota Press, 2000), 66.

15. Kristen Cochrane adds that "fluidity is not limited to linguistic and sexual formations [in the film]. It is telling that the film's setting is based in Corrientes province in northeastern Argentina, a province that borders southeastern Brazil. This in-between space, like many geographical spaces in which two nations share a border, is the boundary that separates the relationship between Matías and Jerónimo. It disturbs the idea of nationhood . . . The construction of nations through invisible lines is a parallel to the structural boundaries which constitute monosexuality" (47). Kristen Cochrane, *Queering the Rural in Contemporary Argentine Cinema:* Taekwondo, Esteros, *and* Como una novia sin sexo. MA Thesis. Queen's University, 2017.

16. Tom Conley, *Cartographic Cinema* (Minneapolis: University of Minnesota Press, 2007), 2.

17. In an interview with Manuel Betancourt, the screenwriter, Andi Nachon, discusses the importance of the film's rural setting: "For me the script was really about that. There were two strands here: there's the love story between two boys but it's key that it happens in this specific context. But when it comes to Argentinean films, I

think it's also crucial to move away from the urban world, exploring different areas outside of the city. And in that the landscape was very important—it's almost a part of the characters. It's a place that Matías longs for. It's a kind of lost paradise for him. And then these vistas are also breathtaking. The setting may seem rather plain but it's so vibrant and alive, and it's something I think the film conveys really well." Manuel Betancourt, "The Director and Writer of *Esteros* on Why Rural Argentina Was the Perfect Setting for Their LGBT Drama," *Remezcla*, October 19, 2016.

18. Landscape and setting are indeed two different ideas, as outlined by Jens Andermann, "Exhausted Landscapes: Reframing the Rural in Recent Argentine and Brazilian Films," *Cinema Journal* 53, no. 2 (2014): 52. The former is "the excess or remainder of this subordinate function of space," not to be confused with diegetic setting that is "entrusted various rhetorical functions of exposition, emphasis, or counterpoint in relation to the plot or to specific characters."

19. Ibid., 51.

20. Ibid., 51.

21. Ibid., 51.

22. We may very well conceptualize New Maricón films as a sort of "ecocine." Discussing this vein of cinema, and the need for more ecocritical studies within contemporary Latin American cinema criticism, Roberto Forns-Broggi, "Los retos del ecocine en nuestras américas: rastreos del *buen vivir* en tierra sublevada," *Revista de Crítica Literaria Latinoamericana*, 40.79 (2014), suggests that "ecocine" is any cinema that uses the medium to awake environmental consciousness.

23. I understand the former as an "attempt to explore the implantation of values in the configuration of space, in the constitution of a gaze, and in the relation of observer to observed," whereas the latter term is the collapsing of "epistemology and erotics—ways of knowing and practices of sexuality" in Bill Nichols, *Representing Reality: Issues and Concepts in Documentary* (Bloomington: Indiana University Press, 1991), 78; Ben Sifuentes-Jáuregui, *The Avowal of Difference: Queer Latino American Narratives* (Albany: State University of New York Press, 2014), 104.

24. The gate-closing scene is a repeated trope in New Maricón films, signaling a spatial separation between the center and periphery. This is seen clearly in Puenzo's *XXY*.

25. Curotto cautiously keeps their pubescent nudity underwater and never in full view.

26. Writing on sound in relation to space, James Lastra, *Sound Technology and the American Cinema: Perception, Representation, Modernity* (New York: Columbia University Press, 2000) furthers that there are two distinct models of cinematic sound reproduction: "representation-as-(legible)-inscription" and "representation-as-sensory-simulation" (126). The former forwards a "sonic space whose principal goal is the intelligibility of some sounds at the expense of others" (141), whereas the latter is "constructed in order to represent a particular real act of audition" (141), where the point of audition contours the sonar mapping of space.

27. I use the term vector following a Deleuzian understanding, which as Felicity Colman, *Deleuze and Cinema: The Film Concepts* (Oxford: Berg, 2011) summarizes, is a "concept for the consideration of the physical and sensory dimensions of screen spaces and situations created through those narrative, stylistic and technical processes of filmmaking that involves the *transformation of forms*" (128).

28. The very presence of adolescent bodies is a queer gesture as it ruptures the taboo of representing young sexuality, though this line of inquiry falls outside the scope of these pages.

29. Matías Ezequiel González, "Entrevista con Papu Curotto," *Escribiendocine*, February 22, 2017: n.p.

30. José Gil, *Metamorphoses of the Body* (Minneapolis: University of Minnesota Press, 1998), 127.

31. Ibid., 128.

32. Ibid., 127.

Works Cited

Andermann, Jens. "Exhausted Landscapes: Reframing the Rural in Recent Argentine and Brazilian Films." *Cinema Journal* 53, no. 2 (2014): 50–70.

Betancourt, Manuel. "The Director and Writer of *Esteros* on Why Rural Argentina Was the Perfect Setting for Their LGBT Drama." *Remezcla*. October 19, 2016.

Boetti, Ezequiel. "Critica de *Esteros*, de Papu Curotto." *Otros Cines* 22 (February 2017).

Cochrane, Kristen. *Queering the Rural in Contemporary Argentine Cinema:* Taekwondo, Esteros, *and* Como una novia sin sexo. MA Thesis. Queen's University, 2017.

Colman, Felicity. *Deleuze and Cinema: The Film Concepts*. Oxford: Berg, 2011.

Conley, Tom. *Cartographic Cinema*. Minneapolis: University of Minnesota Press, 2007.

Forns-Broggi, Roberto. "Los retos del ecocine en nuestras américas: rastreos del *buen vivir* en tierra sublevada." *Revista de Crítica Literaria Latinoamericana* 40, no. 79 (2014): 315–32.

Foster, David William. *Queer Issues in Contemporary Latin American Cinema*. Austin: University of Texas Press, 2003.

Gil, José. *Metamorphoses of the Body*. Minneapolis: University of Minnesota Press, 1998.

González, Matías Ezequiel. "Entrevista con Papu Curotto." *Escribiendocine*, February 22, 2017.

Lastra, James. *Sound Technology and the American Cinema: Perception, Representation, Modernity*. New York: Columbia University Press, 2000.

Losada, Matthew. "Argentine Cinema and Rural Space." *Chasqui* 40, no. 2 (2011): 18–32.

Marks, Laura. *Touch: Sensuous Theory and Multisensory Media*. Minneapolis: University of Minnesota Press, 2002.

Martin, Jean-Clet. "Of Images and Worlds: Towards a Geology of the Cinema." In *The Brain Is the Screen. Deleuze and the Philosophy of Cinema*, edited by Gregory Flaxman, 61–85. Minneapolis: University of Minnesota Press, 2000.

Nichols, Bill. *Representing Reality: Issues and Concepts in Documentary*. Bloomington: Indiana University Press, 1991.

Ruffinelli, Jorge. "Dime tu sexo y te diré quién eres: La diversidad sexual en el cine latinoamericano." *Cinémas d'Amérique Latine* 18 (2010): 58–71.

Sifuentes-Jáuregui, Ben. *The Avowal of Difference: Queer Latino American Narratives*. Albany: State University of New York Press, 2014.

Venkatesh, Vinodh. *New Maricón Cinema: Outing Latin American Film*. Austin: University of Texas Press, 2016.

8

Counterflows

Hydraulic Order and Residual Ecologies in
Caribbean Fantasy Landscapes

LISA BLACKMORE

In *A Thousand Plateaus*, Deleuze and Guattari identify in capitalism a hydraulic leitmotif, where "The flow of capital produces an immense channel," they write, "a quantification of power with immediate 'quanta,' where each person profits from the passage of the money flow in his or her own way (hence the reality-myth of the poor man who strikes it rich and then falls into poverty again)."[1] This hydraulic metaphor resonates with evocations of global capitalism and economic liberalization as drivers of frictionless flows of capital, commodities, people, and images, which in turn connote personal freedom and prosperity. In the dominant imaginary of globalization, finance flows figure as tractive forces that dissolve borders as they gather human and more-than-human bodies within the developmentalist horizon of the so-called "global village" via the circuitry of investment, trade, and mobility. In this economy of affect, capital propels humanity toward progress and well-being, with free flows, commodities, and capital accumulation channeling individuals and nations toward freedom. As one of the principal gatekeepers of this optimistic narrative, State power is articulated through the control of diverse flows via the "subordination of hydraulic force to conduits, pipes, embankments, which prevent turbulence, which constrain movement to go from one point to another, and space itself to be striated and measured, which makes the fluid depend on the solid, and flows proceed by parallel, laminar layers."[2] In material terms of development and trade policies, hydraulic power means building infrastructures (ports, customs, road networks, and free trade zones) to channel finance, human and commodity flows. The impacts of hydraulic power can be felt by both human and more-than-human bodies, shaping people's lives and the environment writ large.

The transnational tourist industry provides fertile grounds on which to examine the frontiers of capitalism's emplacement as a circuitry of frictionless flows and social mobility, articulated at the intersections of economic policies, infrastructural spaces, and liquid ecologies. Since the 1960s, international development agencies began to promote tourism as a model for Dominican development, advocating macroeconomic adjustments that would open the Caribbean island to transnational investment, tourists, and goods. This paradigm shift in economic policy had dramatic implications for the physical and symbolic dimensions of the landscape, and for its human and more-than-human constituents. Mass tourism replaced the infrastructure of the waning sugar industry with constructions tailored to a service-oriented economy. In this territorial overhaul, sea and airports control the flows of tourists and commodities, while gated enclaves provide visitors with regulated scenographies that befit the new nation brand. As the landscape became the nation's most strategic capital, this drove a rebranding of the Dominican Republic in the global visual economy as a Caribbean fantasy—an island of modern infrastructure and pristine landscapes where poverty, marginality, and pollution were excluded from view.

Drawing on the Caribbean poet Kamau Braithwaite's term, the literary scholar Elizabeth DeLoughrey argues human and more-than-human worlding in the region is not shaped by smooth flows but by a turbulent "tidalectics" where the liquid and the solid are constantly mingling. Bodies of water and their contiguous terrains exceed material and epistemological enclosures as passive and empty spaces of "*terra* and *acqua nullis*, which were used to justify territorial expansion" since colonial times.[3] In the modern unfolding of global capitalism, the Caribbean's marine environments, territories, and social bodies have also been harnessed by the logics of enclosure: carved up into poles of development, ports, and resorts where hydraulic order produces a visual economy of landscapes figured as frictionless flow. If the Caribbean fantasy landscape is the setting where hydraulic order's political-economic, sociospatial, and aesthetic dimensions intersect through the flows of capital, people, goods, and images, then it bears asking what happens when this order is subject to stoppages, contaminations, and overflows.

Rather than a circuitry of frictionless flows, my contention is that the hydraulic order articulated in the Dominican Republic manifests dramatically in its counterflows: human and more-than-human lifeforms whose entangled coexistence in precarious and contaminated ecologies radically undercut the dominant imaginary of Caribbean fantasy landscapes articulated through transparent waters and luxury enclaves. To explore this idea, in the pages to follow I expand briefly on the concept of flow before analyzing filmic constructions of the Dominican landscape in official nation-branding campaigns and in the documentary *Caribbean Fantasy* (2016) directed by Johanné Gómez Terrero. While the former focus on strategically composed idyllic scenes, the latter directs the gaze to the marginal communities and residual ecologies of the polluted River Ozama, Santo Domingo's tourist seaport. Through the counterpoint between these Caribbean fantasies, I propose that Gómez Terrero's film interrupts and contests dominant discourses and imaginaries that leverage frictionless flows as leitmotifs of development by revealing the marginal human lives and more-than-human matter that decompose normative landscapes, recomposing them instead as counterflows in hydraulic order. At stake in this chapter is the assertion that hydraulic order perpetuates long-standing colonial worldviews that reduce Latin America and the Caribbean to bioterritories of extractible resources repackaged as picturesque tourist destinations. By extension, as cultural production puts into circulation "submerged perspectives" that, as Macarena Gómez-Barris writes, show "emergent and heterogeneous forms of living that are not about destruction or mere survival within the extractive zone, but about the creation of emergent alternatives," these countervisualities can disrupt the flow systems of colonial seeing that persist in today's globalized world.[4]

Flows, Frictions, Leakages

In imaginaries and discourses of globalization, the promise of hydraulic order draws on the positive connotations of liquidity and fluidity, which are associated with efficient systems, uninhibited mobility, and the absence of traces and residues. These elements compose an optimistic meta-image of buoyancy and unrestricted circulation that is further buttressed by the rigor attached to the science of hydraulics, which asserts human capacity to capture, contain, and channel liquid flows. The semantics of flow find their sources deep in human history and political economy. Efficient water management has been a condition for human flourishing and for the centralization of political power for millennia. In the mid-twentieth century, the historian Karl Wittfogel argued that the centralized power of hydraulic civilizations, which he traced from Mesopotamia to Egypt through to India and pre-Columbian Mexico and Peru, was a result of effective irrigation and flood protection.[5] Understood as a long-standing yardstick of development, infrastructures of irrigation and dykes, dams and sewers, rivers and hydropower populate a hydraulic imaginary whose symbolic dimensions cultural geographers have recently identified as indices of "liquid power" and urban modernity.[6]

The visual economy of landscape representation has also been significantly shaped by the positive cultural meanings attached to the harnessing of liquid flows. Not only do actual water management infrastructures constitute poetic and aesthetic artefacts that serve as vehicles for political ideologies, but representations of controlled aquatic environments also have determined the development of the landscape genre in art.[7] The drainage of land in the Netherlands provided literal grounds for the emergence of landscape painting in the seventeenth century, while John Constable's later depictions of water mills and canals rendered hydraulic infrastructure a central focus of the English picturesque landscape, suggesting human capacity to tame nature at will. In nation-branding campaigns and political propaganda, the "industrialized nature" of megadams and manmade shipping canals have long been leveraged for their geopolitical capital, as shown by the enduring visibility of sites like the Hoover Dam or the Panama Canal.[8] In the Dominican Republic, dominant and normative representations of the landscape draw on a wellspring of images of pristine nature and biodiversity. At the same time, industrialized nature and hydraulic systems serve as powerful symbols of progress in the physical landscape and in political discourses about development, as is evinced by the recent expansion of Santo Domingo's tourist port and the $250 million construction of a huge seaport and free trade zone at the nearby San Andrés that investors claimed would make the country the "Taiwan of the Caribbean."[9] These infrastructures embody politicians' promise to transform the nation into the Caribbean's largest tourist economy and a circulatory node for foreign capital, tourists, and goods.

The optimistic imaginary of hydraulic order must be scrutinized alongside the deterritorializing impacts of economic liberalization and globalization that have been conceived as a more turbulent liquid ecology of concepts, whose counterimaginaries encompasses erosion, opacity, and friction rather than free flow. Even as Arjun Appadurai schematized globalization as a vast network of interconnected flows moving across *ethnoscapes*, *mediascapes*, *technoscapes*, *finanscapes*, and *ideoscapes*, his ideas were situated in a critical turn to the concept of flow that emerged in cultural anthropology from the end of the 1990s and undercut ideals of unfettered mobility and interconnectivity amid the "global village."[10] In "Disjuncture and Difference," Appadurai highlighted the erosion of local identities and ecological damage as negative impacts.[11] Other influential theoretical contributions that countered frictionless flows have included Zygmunt Bauman's theory of "liquid modernity," which stressed the dissolution of rootedness and local identities engendered by the global economy, and the notion of "friction" that the scholar Anna Tsing wields to redirect attention away from illusive fluidity toward the material impacts that globalization enacts on human and nonhuman bodies. In Latin America, Arturo Escobar argues that hegemonic paradigms of industrialization and globalization have not brought the *making* but the *unmaking* of the region, critiquing the advocacy of the free market that pictures the economy as a circular, self-regulating flow.[12] More recently, Gastón Gordillo has focused attention on rubble as a figure for understanding the many forms of material debris left in the wake of capitalist and imperialist projects—offering a means to think through infrastructural landscapes and places of ruination as spatial testimonies of the attempts to capitalize and dominate human bodies and more-than-human matter in Latin America.[13]

These thinkers, and many others, contest free flow by signaling the profound inequalities of global capitalism and economic liberalization. Such thinking does vital work in unveiling sociospatial asymmetries and generating critical spaces to consider the unsustainable modes of production and consumption that compromise planetary futures. The paradigm of economic development in the Caribbean is a phenomenon where this dilemma plays out all too vividly. While in the mid-twentieth century the modern tourist industry was cast as a flagship for development based on the promise of opening up Caribbean economies and territories to transnational investment and tourist flows, in the first quarter of the twenty-first century the prospects of social and ecological well-being have evaporated. In the Dominican Republic, mass tourism was definitively installed as the nation's main economic motor in the 1970s, when it was proffered as a "smokeless" substitute to the sugar industry that would generate employment, diversify the economy, and, in theory, put a premium on ecological integrity.[14] Following viability studies carried out by international development agencies in 1968, the Dominican state decreed tourism a sector of national interest and created in 1971 the Department for the Development of Tourist Infrastructure (INFRATUR). Financed by the World Bank, INFRATUR was tasked with stimulating foreign investment, promoting the construction of infrastructure, and cooperating with the Ministry of Tourism to found five Tourist Poles (*polos turísticos*) devised to spread the dividends of the industry nationwide.[15] These official policies birthed a new national narrative that presented tourism as an income stream that would channel the Dominican Republic toward ever greater well-being. The decade after 1960 saw an unprecedented rise in the construction of hotels, with the number of tourists rising from 69 to 160 million, tripling numbers from the two previous decades.[16] In the 1990s, this success story continued with the liberalization of interest rates and the de facto dollarization that freed up finance flows and fueled Dominican economic growth.[17] Even with the economic downturn that accompanied the new millennium, the proliferation of transnational chain resorts offering all-inclusive packages has continued to grow the sector, effectively making Dominican tourism the largest sector in the Caribbean.[18]

These promising data explain why tourism consistently figures in political discourse as the economic motor that will thrust the country from its "backward" state toward modernity and prosperity.[19] The presidential report that Danilo Medina presented to the National Assembly in 2017 confirmed this through a celebration of the record amount of income generated by tourism as well as the state-led construction of one hundred roads and bridges in tourist regions, which the president promised would "dynamize" the economy.[20] Medina's official website also ratifies the president's conviction in the strategic importance of the tourist industry, noting that his support for the sector is due to the fact that he is "thinking of the future, thinking big because I have wanted the country to grow in that way."[21] Thinking big—as insinuated by the photograph of a huge cruise ship anchored at a tourist resort published alongside the article—meant opening up the country's shores to situate it as a desirable destination for tourists and investors in the global village.

Not all appraisals of tourism are as positive, however. Ethnographic and economic studies reveal significant inequalities and leakage in this system of capital flows. For critics, tourism is a continuation of elite economics, which "represents today what sugar did a century ago: a monocrop controlled by foreigners and elites at the service of global capitalism's structures of accumulation."[22] Rather than an immense canal of wealth buoying the local economy, the tourist industry is associated with forms of "economic leakage" whereby profits flow overseas to transnational investors. The Central Bank only captures a small percentage of profits from tourism, and, rather than stimulating the production of local goods, the sector mainly consumes imported merchandise.[23] Similarly, the concentration of capital flows around enclaves and official beach areas has led to a significant "trickle-down" effect that would circulate benefits to nontourist sectors. Tourist hubs have produced precarious labor conditions that attract "floating populations" of workers who seek out sources of employment without any guarantee of stable contracts.[24] Perhaps the most compelling evidence of economic leakage is the stagnation of national poverty rates. While tourism is consistently billed as an economic driver, from 2000 to 2016 almost a third of Dominicans were living in poverty.[25]

Economic dependency on tourism and the unequal distribution of its dividends condition pragmatic and strategic approaches to the ordering of human flows in the Dominican landscape. As chief stakeholder in this economic motor, the state flexes its hydraulic power to avoid confluences of tourism and poverty that might jeopardize the Caribbean fantasy nation brand. The designation of "tourist poles" and the construction of air and seaport infrastructure as well as road networks and official tourist itineraries all exemplify the state exercising hydraulic power. These interventions are not without violence. The creation of the Samaná tourist area on the northeastern coast in 1975, for instance, led to the forced relocation of residents and the physical destruction of the town.[26] Gated resorts follow the exclusionary logic of other enclave architectures linked to capital accumulation and global trade, such as oil fields, ports, and free trade zones. Services and infrastructure *intramuros* bear no resemblance to the public conditions *extramuros*.[27] In the Dominican Republic, these disjunctives become evident in the landscape through the asymmetric supply of basic urban infrastructure such as electricity, water, and waste removal. While urban areas suffer frequent blackouts, water shortages and lack of trash collection, tourist areas are constantly connected to the circuitry that keeps the Caribbean fantasy landscape intact. Other modes of flow control in tourist areas manifest in the regulation of bodies circulating on beaches. The state created a specialist police corps to oversee tourist areas, to control access to beaches, and to restrict commerce, leading to the persecution of unregistered hawkers and the demolition of unsanctioned kiosks and restaurants.[28] Finally, although Dominican law dictates that coasts and bodies of water are a "strategic national patrimony" that "belong to the public domain and are free access," it also enshrines the "respect for private property" and empowers the state to regulate how they are enjoyed and managed.[29] In sum, physical access to the landscape is mediated directly by the hydraulic power and flow control exercised at the intersection of state institutions and transnational corporations.

Caribbean Fantasy as Nation Brand

The visual economy of landscape—its composition through aesthetic strategies and circulation in global circuits—is also the product of flow control, but this time of images. The nation-branding campaign the Dominican Ministry of Tourism has funded over the past decade under the slogan "Dominican Republic has it all" circulates a repertoire of normative landscapes whose central leitmotifs are transparent bodies of water, unspoiled beaches, smiling faces, and modern infrastructure. The imaginary is heir to a long-standing stock of maritime vistas and beach scenes sponsored by the Dominican state from the first half of the twentieth century. The photographic archive at the National General Archives makes explicit, or even tautological, the now familiar encodings of tropical landscapes of beaches and palm trees by stamping such scenes with the caption "paisaje tropical" (tropical landscape), thus establishing the metonymic relationship between tropic bounty and unpolluted nature that is also the bedrock of representations of Caribbean nature.

The three-minute spot that launched the nation-branding campaign in 2009 perpetuates this lush imaginary, cementing the filmic construction of the Caribbean fantasy in which a seamless flow of fast-paced shots accompanied by a consistently upbeat soundtrack leverages landscapes and bodies of water as commodities and presents the nation as a space of tourist-friendly mobility.[30] The short film begins with a shot of a woman walking into the transparent Caribbean Sea, then cuts to a rapid sequence of aerial shots that cut between coasts, resorts, marinas, and golf courses before shifting to close-up images that tap into the country's affective capital by presenting it as a stimulus for joy through shots of smiling faces that cut between Dominican women and tourists enjoying water sports. In the second half of the video, jauntily angled aerial shots pan quickly alongside a new train as it crosses a new bridge over the River Ozama, before cutting to a sequence of shots that present the picture postcard highlights of the capital city. The edited stream of shots of the Malecón coastal walkway, colonial buildings, and shopping centers construe Santo Domingo as a city of pure mobility and commerce where poverty, waste, and stasis are inexistent. The official website for the nation-branding campaign offers further conduits for this imaginary, providing a home for short promotional films and economic data that confirm the country's status as the top destination for foreign tourists and investors alike. This Caribbean fantasy-scape does not just flow through the global visual economy; it is also a firm fixture of visual culture in the Dominican Republic. Although the tourist landscape is shaped to fit the desires of potential visitors and the agendas of investors, the same imaginary of ecological integrity, enclave architecture, and smiling faces circulates locally. Audiovisual proof that the "Dominican Republic has it all" thus occupies strategic sites in media circuits at home and abroad. In *An Eye for the Tropics*, Krista Thompson asserts that there is a strategic purpose in this alignment of imaginaries, noting that as they permeate the local imaginary, they generate modes of performatic identity in which the elements of the nation brand are assimilated and played out.[31] Given the importance of tourism, having Dominicans identify with the prevailing nation brand through its filmic outputs could galvanize consensus around the industry and mitigate criticisms of its economic leakages.

This perhaps explains why important local corporations have funded their own audiovisual versions of the Caribbean fantasy landscape. *Imagen nacional* (*National Image*)—a trilogy of films produced in 2000 by the Grupo Jimenes León, one of the key commercial and cultural institutions in the country—exemplifies this tendency. While the narrator extols the "landscapes worthy of being painted onto countless canvases," the montage assembles aerial shots of unspoiled beaches, gushing waterfalls, and submarine corals, producing a cinematographic cipher of Dominican identity in the ecological integrity of its bodies of water. In a similar vein, *Así es la República Dominicana* (*This is the Dominican Republic*), a video cosponsored in 2002 by public institutions and private companies, describes the country as a "heaven on earth," repeating hyperbolic clichés from the promotional vernacular of nation branding to reinforce the Caribbean fantasy of "spectacular landscapes, history, joy, beautiful beaches, contagious rhythms, fantastic people." Such renderings of the landscape recall the "production fetishism" that Appadurai uncovers in globalization, whereby "spectacles" of local culture mask the predominance of transnational capital flows in national economies as they stimulate patriotism.[32] The Caribbean fantasies produced for home and foreign audiences thus do double duty: they enable the state and local elites to reclaim natural and human resources as the bedrock of a patriotic national identity, even as these are fetishized as commodities that serve to attract transnational investors and tourists.

Caribbean Fantasy Gone Adrift

Nation-branding films are expedient media to construct and circulate Caribbean fantasy landscapes that reinforce ideals of pure mobility, joyous emotions, and ecological integrity, precisely because the technology of cinematic montage means that desired scenes can be cut into an audiovisual flow, while bodies, affects, and matter that might undercut the hydraulic order of mass tourism can be left *hors scène*. It is this conspicuously edited Caribbean fantasy that the documentary *Caribbean Fantasy: Una historia del amor en el Río Ozama* (2016), directed by the Dominican filmmaker Johanné Gómez Terrero, sets about decomposing by centering on counterflows in the hydraulic order analyzed above. Departing from the aerial shots and fast-paced montage, Gómez Terrero's film grounds the gaze on the banks of the polluted River Ozama, taking the slow flow of water as the metronome for the film's sparse and slow-paced portrait of a community isolated from the infrastructure that stimulates tourism. The title is an ironic appropriation of a cruise liner that connects the port of Santo Domingo, where *Caribbean Fantasy* is mainly set, with Puerto Rico.[33] Depicting life on the margins of global flows of capital, goods, and people, the film takes as a central motif the manual labor of river taxis and the dismantling of haulage ships that provide employment for the Ozama's riverbank communities. In so doing, it demystifies the tropical landscapes that circulate in the local and global visual economies by showing the limits of trickle-down economics and the physical frontiers of transnational investment and state-led development.

The film's protagonists are Ruddy Camacho, a relatively young river taxi driver, with no identity papers and health problems, and his girlfriend, Altagracia "Morena" Disla Polanco, an ex-alcoholic and fervent evangelical Christian who divides her time between Ruddy's riverside hut and the house she shares with her husband and son. Over the course of fifty-three minutes, the camera recurrently tracks this dismantling of large ships, Ruddy's trajectories as he rows passengers from one bank of the river to the other and accompanies the couple in their social outings, domestic activities, and arguments. Following the dichotomous representation of the Caribbean fantasy love story alluded to in the title, the documentary does not have a happy ending but culminates with the end of Ruddy and Morena's relationship. The choice of location where this love story plays out is itself a suggestive one that enables the documentary to reach far beyond the romantic narrative announced in its title. The opening credits identify the location as the La Ciénaga de Los Guandules, a densely populated riverbank community of self-built huts that flank the River Ozama as it flows out to the Caribbean Sea, just meters upstream from Santo Domingo's international seaport adjacent to the city's colonial center. At the end of the 1980s, the Ozama's banks were home to some 286,000 people—about 22 percent of the capital's entire population. Today, more than 300,000 people live in this sector, making it the most concentrated area of poverty in the city.[34] The area is a hub for flows of waste matter that spill over from the insufficient infrastructural networks that make up the capital's sanitation system. The lack of sewerage in Santo Domingo means that the riverbank communities on the Ozama are immersed in a residual ecology: the river and the Caribbean Sea are the dumping ground for 15 percent of waste produced by the capital city's inhabitants.[35]

The banks and port of the River Ozama are long-standing laboratories of colonialism and today are a strategic element in the cultural capital on which the Dominican Republic has built its nation brand as a tourist destination. After abandoning La Isabela in search of a site with better access to the mines in San Cristóbal and maritime routes back to Europe, in 1496 Bartholomew Columbus founded on the banks of the Ozama the second Spanish settlement. Colonial chronicles note that the river was deemed an expedient site for global trade because its depth would allow for 300-ton ships to dock there. Broad and deep, the port on the Ozama became a nodal point linking the Old and New Worlds, a nexus of transoceanic and maritime flows that enabled the entry and exit of goods, people, and culture. Centuries later, it continued to play a vital role, undergoing renovation in the 1980s when it was expanded to provide entry to large cruise ships and fitted with new docks to give tourists direct access to the colonial city just up the hill. Today, as trade shipping has shifted along the coast to the new San Andrés megaport, the River Ozama continues to operate as the point of entry for tourists who take brief tours of Santo Domingo's "*primicias*"—its first cathedral, first university, and so on—before continuing their itineraries to beaches and other Caribbean islands.

Its immersion in the tourist economy does not isolate the Ozama from urban marginality. To the contrary, the director of *Caribbean Fantasy* describes the river as "an abyss that separates the rich from the poor."[36] The contiguity of the divergent realities of cruise liners and river taxis, of towering bridges and makeshift huts, is the film's main wager. The dialogue between the two enables Gómez Terrero to lay bare the flows and counterflows that structure the Dominican landscape, where tropical fantasies coexist with poverty. The river, in this sense, becomes a more-than-human protagonist in the film: a presence whose ecology and economy are central to issues that exceed the (relatively limited) diegetic action linked to the two main characters. If the port symbolizes the flows of trade and mass tourism where remote destinations connect via the river, Ruddy's journeys from one bank to the other reframe the riverscape as a realm of limited mobilities: a local environment where individual agency *takes* and *makes* place as it cuts across the body of water's inexorable flow out to sea. The river taxi moves transversally, turning its back to the sea and moving from one edgeland to the other as it navigates floating trash and docked ships awaiting demolition. Through head-on, long shots of Ruddy that track his laboring body, *Caribbean Fantasy* challenges the invisibility of urban poverty. The use of this framing device throughout the film foregrounds precisely the type of human and more-than-human bodies—the infirm, dark-skinned man and the polluted, fetid river—that are banished from the hydraulic imaginary of development and well-being. Instead of smiling faces and transparent waters, the frame is filled with human and nonhuman bodies whose lives are entangled with the detritus of global capitalism. On the banks of the Ozama, we see how the residues of deficient infrastructures of flow are metabolized, whether through the pollution that, the viewer imagines, has caused the lesions on Ruddy's skin or through the dismantling of the obsolete ships that have gone to ground on the river's shores.

Riverine shanties such as La Ciénaga de Los Guandules are dramatic features of the landscape, yet *Caribbean Fantasy* was made as a response to the "(collective) blindness" that Gómez Terrero asserts keeps them hidden in plain sight.[37] By training the camera and the viewer's gaze on these communities, she enacts a reorientation of the filmic encodings of the nation-branded landscape that work to render marginality invisible. Far from a metaphoric blind spot, the occlusion of marginality is a policy put into action through urban planning. In a recent plan for the reinvigoration of Santo Domingo's colonial city, riverine communities and the river itself were posited as forms of optical interference that disturbed the composition of the picturesque visual field:

> The Colonial City *looks onto the river* (*mira al río*), the original [colonial] settlement area that faces it on the other bank, but the natural elements, such as the river water, that should unite these two spaces in fact separates them because of the *overwhelming pollution that assaults the gaze/view* (*la contaminación que lo agobia agrediendo la vista*) and generally makes it unattractive.[38]

The physiological "assault" on the gaze/view implies a broader attack on the hydraulic order of the network of (visual) flows that should link up different parts of the landscape into a coherent picture. Simply looking at polluted matter seems to pose a physical threat to landscape composition and hydraulic order. The polluted river is a counterflow in picturesque composition. It does not provide a conduit for the gaze to move from bank to bank, but interrupts this transit, repulsing the eyes with the trash the river carries into the visual field on its current. The river separates instead of uniting the landscape, de-composing it. In so doing, the river as motif serves to make the point that only stringent filmic montage can compose the sort of hydraulic landscape of free flows that would befit the Dominican nation brand and the ideals of pure mobility and seamless prosperity that underpin global capitalism. It is important to recognize the pathological and violent terms used to describe the river to understand the critical gesture that drives *Caribbean Fantasy* as it keeps the viewer's gaze on "contaminating" scenes of human marginality and nonhuman, residual matter. Engaging critically with normative visual regimes, *Caribbean Fantasy* foregrounds the sorts of residual ecologies that trouble entrenched modes of order by constituting, to use Mary Douglas's terms, matter out of place.[39] The documentary is a stoppage in the normative flows of images that compose the nation brand because it focuses on those elements—poverty, fetid water, postindustrial trash—that are construed elsewhere as sources of dangerous contagion.

The presentation of transnational flows as motors for development befits the accelerated temporality of late capitalism, where newness is celebrated and obsolescence is stigmatized. This stigmatization is, as Tim Edensor points out, inherent in capitalist order, where trash is deemed irrelevant, filthy matter that must be expulsed through systems that channel liquid and solid waste. This explains the destabilizing presence of residual and contaminated matter:

> With the abundance of commodities, to avoid the endless piling up of previous artefacts from an increasingly recent past, an unwanted surplus must be discerned. Identified as waste or rubbish, it is irrelevant, dirty and disorderly and must be expelled and disposed of. Thus it is matter out of place, especially where it spills into and infects those proliferating spaces designed to disguise ambiguity, in which material elements (together with functions, social practices and forms of information) are discretely distributed and continuously regulated.[40]

Organic and inorganic matter are destabilizing agents within the (de) composition of the landscape because their physical presence permanently exceeds the hydraulic systems devised to regulate and remove marginality and waste in the material world and visual field. The documentary problematizes value judgements that associate purity with morality and poverty with obsolescence. In one such sequence, the background of a wide frame shot is occupied by a flow of trash carried along by the river, while in the foreground Morena sweeps the shoreline in front of Ruddy's home (Figure 8.1). As he rows his river taxi toward the shore, circumnavigating a large moored ship, Morena calls out happily: "I've cleaned the shore already. Look, it's all clean." The incongruence of the claim is evinced by the trash that lines the riverbank at Morena's feet. Matter thus ruptures semiotic order of the audiovisual frame: what we hear (the claim of cleanliness) is not what we see (the presence of rubbish). Yet the incongruence generates a moment of humor through which the film eschews victimizing or patronizing attitudes toward the lives of marginal communities. After all, Morena's pursuit of order participates in the same "utopia of an odorless city" that Iván Illich associates in *H20 and the Waters of Forgetting* with the symbolic dimension of hydraulic infrastructures emplaced in cityscapes to channel residual matter out of sight.[41] Rather than alienating poverty as radical difference, these intersecting references situate the protagonists as participants within broader urban cultures: the evocation of the long-standing associations of infrastructures of sewerage and waste removal with urban modernity ultimately reveal how socioeconomic hierarchies are perpetuated when certain communities are left out of the circuitry of such flows.

Figure 8.1. Johanné Gómez Terrero, *Caribbean Fantasy: Una historia del amor en el Río Ozama*, 2016, video still.

Caribbean Fantasy confronts disdain for poverty and its occlusion from the visual economy through its cinematographic strategies. Wide shots of the riverscape are used recurrently to expose the points of intersection between the flows of global capital (ships, cruise liners) and the counterflows of marginal communities (river taxis, residual matter). Other side shot scenes fulfill a similar role, situating modern bridges and highways that cross the river in the same field as the precarious shacks that Ruddy connects with his rowing boat. This compositional strategy enables the viewer to identify the urban infrastructures that reduce these shanty towns to blind spots or, at best, momentary blurs apprehended from fast-paced vehicles moving in and out of the city. In Dominican history, the bridges that overfly the River Ozama have been recurrently presented as indices of development that amount, in reductive framings of their cultural meaning, to routes to progress. This began with the first US military occupation (1916–1924) when the first iron bridge replaced rudimentary mechanisms that enabled flows of people from one bank to the other.[42] It continued under Rafael Trujillo's dictatorship, in the wake of the devastation wrecked by the San Zenón Hurricane in 1930, when the rebuilt bridge was presented alongside other restored buildings as "vigorous manifestations of progress."[43] More recently, a new viaduct over the Ozama was billed as a "megaproject" that indexed national development. Constant investment in flow-enabling infrastructure that connects the city to the international airport and to the eastern beaches amounts to a "strategy of *invisibilizing control* of the habitat of disadvantaged communities and their poverty."[44] In this sense, while infrastructure megaprojects divert the gaze from shanties that "assault" it, *Caribbean Fantasy* renders visible the precariousness of urban life and gives voice to experiences such as those lived by Ruddy's girlfriend, Morena, who, in one shot of the couple filmed inside the river taxi, points up to the towering bridge and remembers: "I actually lived under that bridge [. . .]. And when it rained, the water fell down on the zinc roof where I lived." Her testimony represents this infrastructure not as a system of flows but as a remote artifact that, when narrated from below, has very different cultural meanings from those posited by normative discourse.

Other modes of infrastructure also receive attention in the film as the camera records the alternate riverbank structures that the local communities improvise from obsolete materials to mitigate the lack of urban planning policies. Benches and steps made from discarded tires constitute counterflows in capitalism's relentless cycles of production and consumption: rather than trash withdrawn from view, here it is placed in the foreground as part of a tactile, lived environment where the obsolete gains a second life. The documentary also tracks related economic activities that make use of the Ozama's residual ecology and constant streams of trash. The camera dwells on the work of young boys who dive into the polluted water to retrieve plastic bottles that, presumably, will be amassed for a small profit when handed over for recycling. It is the progressive dismantling of a huge rusted ship, however, that provides the leitmotif for the residual ecology of the river's life. Filmed from the river taxi as it bobs from side to side on the river's current, the viewer watches the workers burn through the discarded vessel with blowtorches and witness a crane peeling away flanks of metal amid the creaking din of obsolete rubble. These vacillating shots of decomposition restore a phenomenological gaze to the landscape, one that situates the gaze amid the material remnants of transnational trade flows. This gesture not only challenges the abstract notions of unfettered flows that underpin hydraulic order and the macro-optics of globalization; it also raises questions about the ethics of the urban neglect of marginal communities who live off the residues of the global capitalist economy.

Conclusions

The Caribbean fantasy landscapes fabricated at the heart of mass tourism have emerged here as highly regulated phenomena. These are formed at the intersection of myriad forces that channel transnational flows, circulate pristine water as symbols of ecological integrity, and occlude marginal bodies and polluted bodies of water. Placed at the service of the Dominican Republic's economic development, the landscapes that feature in the official nation-branding films analyzed above utilize montage to fabricate highly edited landscapes where socioeconomic asymmetries and the abject manifestations of environmental decline are negated and erased. The nation brand of free-flowing infrastructures and pristine waters leverages filmic fantasy landscapes to feed tourists' desires to consume tropical nature and colonial heritage. At the same time, the circulation of similar filmic imaginaries among local audiences marks an attempt to shore up identification with these fabricated landscapes, even as lived experiences in real time—plagued as they are with blackouts, deficient infrastructure, and stagnating poverty—demonstrate that tourist landscapes are commodities that are only fully available to those who pay for them.

In *All That Is Solid Melts into Air*, Marshall Berman extracts from his reading of Goethe's *Faust* an axiom of developmentalism that resonates with the concept of hydraulic order and the residual ecologies that interrupt it. In "The Tragedy of Development," Berman describes how Faust is overwhelmed by the way that the sea's hydraulic energy constantly goes untapped so he responds by envisaging grand plans to nature's power to drive human civilization:

> He outlines great reclamation projects to harness the sea for human purposes: man-made harbors and canals that can move ships full of goods and men; dams for large-scale irrigation; green fields and forests, pastures and gardens, a vast and intensive agriculture; waterpower to attract and support emerging industries; thriving settlements, new towns and cities to come—and all this to be created out of a barren wasteland where human beings have never dared to live.[45]

Berman presents Faust's vision as constitutive of an inherent ambiguity in development whereby the dogged pursuit of well-being entails myriad forms of destruction. This quest to remake the world through a macro-system that controls diverse liquid flows is interrupted by the presence of Philemon and Baucis, an elderly couple who refuse to leave their shoreline home where they take in castaways. Faced with this counterflow, Faust reacts with blind violence, sending Mephistopheles to evict the couple. When Faust realizes that the couple has been killed, he refuses to take responsibility. Instead, he is buoyed up by his hubristic dream of "bringing the earth back to itself, / Setting the waves a boundary, / Putting a ring around the ocean"—simply put, by harnessing the power of flow.[46]

Faust's vision of a tractive system where ports, canals, and irrigation systems drive progress still resonates with the contemporary era, where transnational finance flows and global trade are presented as conditions for universal well-being. This similitude reinforces the relevance of hydraulic order as a concept that interrogates past and present paradigms of development. It also reiterates the importance of recognizing the critical potential of counterflows as interruptions of dominant paradigms and their forms of direct or indirect violence. Ruddy and Morena might thus be viewed as updated versions of Philemon and Baucis, representatives of the category of "obsolete persons" who, as Berman notes, are considered obstacles in the path of development.⁴⁷ In the contemporary global order, where capital flows are concentrated in an increasingly small number of hands, critical approaches to this notion of obsolescence garner more relevance than ever. This is particularly so given that the lethal end that Philemon and Baucis meet presages the ongoing deterritorialization and violence imposed on people considered to pose counterflows to hegemonic economic systems. Moreover, it is no challenge to connect Faust's hubristic dream of harnessing hydraulic force by "putting a ring around the ocean" and the ecological devastation wrought by the modes of ceaseless extraction, production, and consumption. The onslaught of manmade inorganic matter—like the myriad bottles floating on the River Ozama in *Caribbean Fantasy*—represents a novel category of obsolescence whose proliferation is encroaching on human metabolism as well as on the visual field. Overflowing anthropogenic waste is a further sign of the unsustainability of the social and ecological impacts of global capitalism. In the age of the Anthropocene, more-than-human bodies of matter constitute new stratigraphic records of obsolescence that cannot be ignored, not only because they form the environments amid which marginal communities, such as those of Ruddy and Morena, are forced to live, but also because they constitute the indissoluble residue of the long history of capitalist industrialization: counterflows to the promises of well-being underpinning hydraulic order even as it breaches the limits of sustainability.

The question, then, is one of optics. What does it take to counteract the blindness that continues to enable developmentalism at all costs? In the Dominican Republic, the nation brand of Caribbean fantasy perpetuates a vision of development that fetishizes transnational flow and transparent waters, even as the landscape is composed (or decomposed) by precariousness and pollution. Far from exceptions, the counterflows that shape its landscapes mirror patterns of contingency and vulnerability that characterize other geographies cast in the mold of profoundly unequal development. It is in this context that *Caribbean Fantasy*'s deeply local reframing of the landscape shows how cinematographic strategies can generate alternate visual economies that situate the gaze precisely among the "obsolete" human and more-than-human bodies that are rendered invisible by the flow-scapes of hydraulic order. Ultimately, to recognize counterflows in hydraulic order is to signal the profound socioeconomic asymmetries and environmental challenges produced at the intersections of historic and enduring forces that privilege some lifeforms at the cost of others. Making counterflows visible and audible to demystify the *utopia of the odorless landscape*, to adapt Ivan Illich's phrase, thus helps not only to de-compose the pristine imaginary of hydraulic order. When cultural production directs attention on residual ecologies of precarious lives and marginal spaces that play out on the frontiers of global capitalism, it contributes to broader debates about the need for alternate paradigms of development and coexistence where greater social equity and environmental awareness are placed center stage.

Notes

1. Gilles Deleuze and Felix Guattari, *A Thousand Plateaus* (London: Bloomsbury, 2013), 20.

2. Deleuze and Guattari, *A Thousand Plateaus*, 363.

3. Elizabeth DeLoughrey, "Tidalectics: Navigating Repeating Islands," *Routes and Roots: Navigating Caribbean and Pacific Island Literatures* (Honolulu: University of Hawai'i Press, 2007), 3.

4. Macarena Gómez-Barris, *The Extractive Zone: Social Ecologies and Decolonial Perspectives* (Durham and London: Duke University Press, 2017), 4.

5. Karl Wittfogel, *Oriental Despotism: A Comparative Study of Total Power* (New York: Random House, 1957).

6. For the links between hydraulic infrastructure and power, see Eric Swyngedouw, *Liquid Power: Contested Hydro-Modernities in Twentieth-Century Spain* (Cambridge, MA: MIT Press, 2014); and Matthew Gandy, *The Fabric of Space* (Cambridge MA: MIT Press, 2014).

7. Brian Larkin, "The Politics and Poetics of Infrastructure," *Annual Review of Anthropology* 42 (2013): 327–43.

8. Paul Josephson, *Industrialized Nature* (Washington, DC: Island Press, 2002).

9. The project was not without its detractors; see Steven Gregory, *The Devil Behind the Mirror* (Berkeley: University of California Press, 2014), 209–33.

10. See Ulf Hannerz, "Fluxos, fronteiras, híbridos: palabras-chave da antropología transnacional," *Mana* 3, no. 1 (1997): 7–29; and Stuart Rockefeller, "'Flow,'" *Current Anthropology* 52, no. 4 (2011): 557–78.

11. Arjun Appadurai, "Disjuncture and Difference in the Global Cultural Economy," *Theory, Culture, Society* 7 (1995): 295–310.

12. See Arturo Escobar, "Economics and the Space of Development: Tales of Growth and Capital," *Encountering Development: The Making and Unmaking of the Third World* (Princeton: Princeton University Press, 1995), 55–101.

13. Gastón Gordillo, *Rubble: Afterlives of Destruction* (Durham: Duke University Press, 2014).

14. Early infrastructure under the dictatorship of Rafael Leónidas Trujillo (1936–1961) included a national chain of hotels and the construction of Hotel Hamaca in Boca Chica, close to Ciudad Trujillo, as Santo Domingo was then called, after the dictator bought the US-owned sugar mill located there. In the capital city,

the state expanded the passenger port on the River Ozama, restored some of the colonial architectural heritage, and built the bar and bathing area at Güibia on the city's western beaches. By the 1950s, promotion of the country as a tourist destination consolidated with the establishment of an air link between Ciudad Trujillo and New York, the production of tourist guides in English, and the construction in 1955 of the Free World's Fair of Peace and Brotherhood, a new urban complex that hosted a year of celebrations to mark twenty-five years of the Era of Trujillo. Tourist development halted in the 1960s because of the political conflicts arising after Trujillo's assassination in 1961, the ousting of democratically elected president Juan Bosch in 1965, and the second US military occupation that ran from 1965 until 1966.

15. Richard Alan Sambrook, Brian Kermath, and Robert N. Thomas, "Tourism Growth Poles Revisited: A Strategy for Regional Development in the Dominican Republic," *Yearbook: Conference of Latin American Geographers* 20 (1994): 87–96, 89.

16. Sambrook et al., "Tourism Growth Poles Revisited," 89.

17. José R. Sánchez-Fung, "Exchange Rates, Monetary Policy, and Interest Rates in the Dominican Republic during the 1990s Boom and New Millennium Crisis," *Journal of Latin American Studies* 37, no. 4 (2005): 727–38, 728.

18. "International Tourism, Number of Arrivals" (2017), http://data.worldbank.org/indicator/ST.INT.ARVL?locations=DO.

19. See Gregory, "Structures of the Imagination," *The Devil Behind the Mirror*, 92–129; and "The Politics of Transnational Capital," *The Devil Behind the Mirror*, 209–33 for evidence of this official line and ways in which Dominicans contest and negotiate it.

20. Marcelo Ballester, "Presidente Danilo Medina ratificó al turismo como gran sostén de la economía dominicana," *Puntacana-bavaro.com*. February 27, 2017, http://puntacana-bavaro.com/2017/02/28/presidente-danilo-medina-ratifico-al-turismo-gran-sosten-la-economia-dominicana/#.WO5MbRhh2Rs.

21. "República Dominicana se consolida como principal destino del Caribe," http://danilomedina.do/canales/turismo/128/republica-dominicana-se-consolida-como-principal-destino-del-caribe. Translation here and all to follow are the author's own.

22. Amalia L. Cabezas, "Tropical Blues: Tourism and Social Exclusion in the Dominican Republic," *Latin American Perspectives* 35, no. 3 (2009): 21–36, 21.

23. Tilman Freitag, "Tourism and the Transformation of a Dominican Coastal Community," *Urban Anthropology and Studies of Cultural Systems and World Economic Development* 25, no. 3 (1996): 225–58, 227.

24. Gregory, *The Devil Behind the Mirror*, 11.

25. "Porcentaje de población en condiciones de pobreza general y extrema por zona de residencia. Datos semestrales, marzo y septiembre, 2000–2016," http://www.one.gob.do/Estadisticas/183/pobreza.

26. Richard Symanski and Nancy Burley, "Tourist Development in the Dominican Republic: An Overview and an Example," *Publication Series Conference of Latin American Geographers* 4 (1975): 20–27.

27. James Sidaway, "Enclave Space: A New Metageography of Development?," *Area* 39, no. 3 (2007): 331–39.

28. Gregory, *The Devil Behind the Mirror*, 32.

29. "De los Recursos Naturales," *Constitución de la República Dominicana*, 2015, http://www.poderjudicial.gob.do/documentos/PDF/constitucion/Constitucion.pdf.

30. The *spot* won awards at the EUROAL2009 tourism fair and can be watched on Vimeo at https://vimeo.com/60065859.

31. Krista A. Thompson, *An Eye for the Tropics: Tourism, Photography, and Framing the Caribbean Picturesque* (Durham and London: Duke University Press, 2006).

32. Appadurai, "Disjuncture and Difference," 306.

33. The ship was owned and run by American Cruise Ferries, transporting 100,000 people, vehicles, and goods per year between the neighboring islands, 6 times a week. Curiously, in August 2016 a fire led to the evacuation of the ship, and it was left adrift at sea. This generated speculation that it would be tugged back into the port and dismantled in precisely the location where *Caribbean Fantasy* was filmed.

34. Haroldo Dilla, *Ciudades en el Caribe: Un estudio comparativo de La Habana, San Juan, Santo Domingo y Miami* (Mexico City: Facultad Latinoamericana de Ciencias Sociales, 2014), 96.

35. Dilla, *Ciudades en el Caribe*, 102.

36. Johanné Gómez Terrero, Untitled Facebook post, January 27, 2016, https://www.facebook.com/CaribbeanFantasyDocumental/photos/a.166883439 6720177.1073741828.1625504997719784/1670306283239655/?type=3&theater.

37. Gómez, 2016.

38. Cited in Dilla, *Ciudades en el Caribe*, 105. Emphasis added.

39. Mary Douglas, *Purity and Danger: An Analysis of Concepts of Pollution and Taboo* (London: Routledge, 1966).

40. Tim Edensor, "Waste Matter: The Debris of Industrial Ruins and the Disordering of the Material World," *Journal of Material Culture* 10, no. 3 (2005): 311–32, 315.

41. Ivan Illich, *H20 and the Waters of Forgetfulness* (London: Mario Boyars, 1986), 48.

42. Dilla, *Ciudades en el Caribe*, 67.

43. *Álbum de Oro* (Santo Domingo: no publisher identified, 1936), n.p.

44. Maribel Villalona, "Santo Domingo: El estado manifesto de sus mundos paralelos," in *Ciudades fragmentadas: Las fronteras internas del Caribe*, ed. Haroldo Dilla and Maribel Villalona (Santo Domingo: Grupo de Estudios Multidisciplinarios Ciudades y Frontera, 2006), 64–65; emphasis added.

45. Marshall Berman, *All That Is Solid Melts into Air: The Experience of Modernity* (London: Penguin, 1988), 62.

46. Berman, *All That Is Solid*, 65.

47. Berman, *All That Is Solid*, 70.

Works Cited

Álbum de Oro. Santo Domingo: no publisher identified, 1936.
Appadurai, Arjun. "Disjuncture and Difference in the Global Cultural Economy." *Theory, Culture, Society* 7 (1995): 295–310.
Así es la República Dominicana. New York, 2002. 60 minutes. JVC Productions.
Báez, Fernando, dir. "República Dominicana: Sus playas." Vol. 3 of *Imagen Nacional*. Dominican Republic, 2000.
Ballester, Marcelo. "Presidente Danilo Medina ratificó al turismo como gran sostén de la economía dominicana." *Puntacana-bavaro.com*. February 27, 2017.
Bauman, Zygmunt. *Liquid Modernity*. Malden, MA: Blackwell, 2000.
Berman, Marshall. *All That Is Solid Melts into Air: The Experience of Modernity*. London: Penguin, 1988.
Bohn Gmelch, Sharon. *Tourists and Tourism: A Reader*. Long Grove: Waveland Press, 2010.
Cabezas, Amalia L. "Tropical Blues: Tourism and Social Exclusion in the Dominican Republic." *Latin American Perspectives* 35, no. 3 (2009): 21–36.
"De los Recursos Naturales." *Constitución de la República Dominicana*, 2015.
Deleuze, Gilles, and Félix Guattari. *A Thousand Plateaus: Capitalism and Schizophrenia*. London: Bloomsbury, 2013.
DeLoughrey, Elizabeth. *Routes and Roots: Navigating Caribbean and Pacific Island Literatures*. Honolulu: University of Hawai'i Press, 2007.
Dilla, Haroldo. *Ciudades en el Caribe: Un estudio comparativo de La Habana, San Juan, Santo Domingo y Miami*. Mexico City: Facultad Latinoamericana de Ciencias Sociales, 2014.
Douglas, Mary. *Purity and Danger: An Analysis of Concepts of Pollution and Taboo*. London: Routledge, 1966.
Edensor, Tim. "Waste Matter: The Debris of Industrial Ruins and the Disordering of the Material World." *Journal of Material Culture* 10, no. 3 (2005): 311–32.
Escobar, Arturo. *Encountering Development: The Making and Unmaking of the Third World*. Princeton: Princeton University Press, 1995.
Freitag, Tilman. "Tourism and the Transformation of a Dominican Coastal Community." *Urban Anthropology and Studies of Cultural Systems and World Economic Development* 25, no. 3 (1996): 225–58.
Gandy, Matthew. *The Fabric of Space: Water, Modernity, and the Urban Imagination*. Cambridge, MA: MIT Press, 2014.
Gómez-Barris, Macarena. *The Extractive Zone: Social Ecologies and Decolonial Perspectives*. Durham: Duke University Press, 2017.
Gómez Terrero, Johanné. *Untitled Facebook post*. January 27, 2016. https://www.facebook.com/CaribbeanFantasyDocumental/photos/a.1668834396720177.1073741828.1625504997719784/1670306283239655/?type=3&theater.

———, dir. *Caribbean Fantasy: Una historia del amor en el Río Ozama*. 2016; Dominican Republic: Makandal.

Gordillo, Gastón. *Rubble: Afterlives of Destruction*. Durham: Duke University Press, 2014.

Gregory, Steven. *The Devil Behind the Mirror: Globalization and Politics in the Dominican Republic*. Berkeley: University of California Press, 2014.

Hannerz, Ulf. "Fluxos, fronteiras, híbridos: palabras-chave da antropología transnacional." *Mana* 3, no. 1 (1997): 7–29.

Illich, Ivan. *H20 and the Waters of Forgetfulness*. London: Mario Boyars, 1986.

"International Tourism, number of arrivals" (2017). http://data.worldbank.org/indicator/ST.INT.ARVL?locations=DO.

"Inversiones extranjeras." http://www.godominicanrepublic.com/es/sobre-rd/inversiones-extranjeras.

"Investment Promotion Council of the Dominican Republic." *Dominican Republic: Investors Handbook and Business Guide*. Santo Domingo: ACCDR, 1986.

Josephson, Paul R. *Industrialized Nature: Brute Force Technology and the Transformation of the Natural World*. Washington DC: Island Press, 2002.

Larkin, Brian. "The Politics and Poetics of Infrastructure." *Annual Review of Anthropology* 42 (2013): 327–43.

Moreno, José. "Economic Crisis in the Caribbean: From Traditional to Modern Dependency: The Case of the Dominican Republic." *Contemporary Marxism* 14 (1986): 97–114.

"Porcentaje de población en condiciones de pobreza general y extrema por zona de residencia. Datos semestrales, marzo y septiembre, 2000–2016." http://www.one.gob.do/Estadisticas/183/pobreza.

República Dominicana . . . lo tiene todo. Dominican Republic: 2009. Director: unknown.

"República Dominicana lo tiene todo." http://godominicanrepublic.com.

"República Dominicana se consolida como principal destino del Caribe." http://danilomedina.do/canales/turismo/128/republica-dominicana-se-consolida-como-principal-destino-del-caribe.

Rockefeller, Stuart Alexander. "Flow." *Current Anthropology* 52, no. 4 (2011): 557–78.

Sambrook, Richard Alan, Brian Kermath, and Robert N. Thomas. "Tourism Growth Poles Revisited: A Strategy for Regional Development in the Dominican Republic." *Yearbook: Conference of Latin American Geographers* 20 (1994): 87–96.

Sánchez-Fung, José R. "Exchange Rates, Monetary Policy, and Interest Rates in the Dominican Republic during the 1990s Boom and New Millennium Crisis." *Journal of Latin American Studies* 37, no. 4 (2005): 727–38.

Sidaway, James. "Enclave Space: A New Metageography of Development?" *Area* 39, no. 3 (2007): 331–39.

Symanski, Richard, and Nancy Burley. "Tourist Development in the Dominican Republic: An Overview and an Example." *Publication Series Conference of Latin American Geographers* 4 (1975): 20–27.

Swyngedouw, Eric. *Liquid Power: Contested Hydro-Modernities in Twentieth-Century Spain.* Cambridge: MIT Press, 2014.

Thompson, Krista A. *An Eye for the Tropics: Tourism, Photography, and Framing the Caribbean Picturesque.* Durham: Duke University Press, 2006.

Tsing, Anna. *Friction: An Ethnography of Global Connection.* Princeton: Princeton University Press, 2005.

Villalona, Maribel. "Santo Domingo: El estado manifesto de sus mundos paralelos." In *Ciudades fragmentadas: Las fronteras internas del Caribe*, edited by Haroldo Dilla and Maribel Villalona, 43–69. Santo Domingo: Grupo de Estudios Multidisciplinarios Ciudades y Frontera, 2006.

Wittfogel, Karl. *Oriental Despotism: A Comparative Study of Total Power.* New York: Random House, 1957.

9

Differential Viscosities

The Material Hermeneutics of Blood, Oil, and Water in *Crude* and *The Blood of Kouan Kouan*

MARK ANDERSON

Oil on water has become the visual idiom of anthropogenic disaster, conveying in both a material and a symbolic sense the leakages within the material and conceptual enclosures by which petromodernity secures the culture/nature divide. If, as Stoekl, Barret, and Worden argue in *Oil Culture*, the materiality of oil is made culturally invisible through containment strategies such as storage tanks, pipelines, and, in the realm of public perception, massive propaganda campaigns, sheen is the indicator that those conceptual dykes have broken and that all that keeps bodies apart are the material differences in their densities and their flow rates, that is, their relative viscosities.[1] And yet the substances implicated in those differentials are also subject to chemical binding, osmosis, adhesion, and sedimentation processes, whereby the bodies implicated in the encounter alter each other in ways that are often irreversible.

Toxicity entails a form of violence that is often temporally displaced from the moment of encounter, a slow violence at which sheen hints in quasi-symbolic fashion—signifying what is to come—but whose cumulative effects will inevitably play out over decades, materializing and intensifying in bodies over time.[2] Bodies smeared with oil sheen but not yet fully immersed in its toxic effects configure the abject irony of the oncological subject of late modernity, who is well aware that despite its seeming self-containedness, its skin is porous and that these petrochemicals modify it at microscopic scales to which it is not privy as a subject. The full scale of toxicity can only be accessed indirectly through technological mediation such as blood analyses and through those toxins' deleterious effects on the subject's body over time.[3] In petromodernity, blood, oil, and water circulate through the world and through us.

This chapter examines representations of viscosity, porosity, and toxicity in two documentary films dealing with oil extraction and pollution in the Ecuadoran Amazon: *Crude: The Real Price of Oil* (dir. Joe Berlinger, Entendre Films, 2009) and *The Blood of Kouan Kouan* (dir. Yorgos Avgeropolous, Small Planet, 2009). I argue that viscosity functions within these films as a trope that disrupts static notions of the body, which rely on subject/object dualism, particularly in the relationships between human bodies, nonhuman bodies, and environments as a whole. This modern ideal of the self-contained, static subject and of the categorical apprehension of materials as passive objects of human instrumentality is further confounded by the experience of toxicity, which reveals the subject's porosity to material flows of different types and of the circulation within its body of "foreign" matter, some of which acts upon it in a perverse or toxic manner. Finally, I argue that the viscous materiality of the filmic medium creates effects by which the viewer is implicated in the bodily experience of toxicity, leading to a form of ethical engagement that arises from the materiality of encounter more than ideological predisposition.

I follow Nancy Tuana's theorization of "viscous porosity," which she frames as an "interactionist attention to the processes of becoming in which unity is dynamic and always interactive and agency is diffusely enacted in complex networks of relations."[4] Within this material logic of mutual affectivity, I engage the term "viscosity" in reference not only to the relative densities of the materials in question, which in a technical sense would be what produces the sheen that features so prominently in representations of anthropogenic disaster, but also to their flow rates. Like density, the temporal aspects of viscosity exist in a differential relationship, running through the short term of bodily encounter, the long durée of social history, and the geological timeframe of environmental history. Nonetheless, the concrete experience of viscosity disables these conceptual divisions because a high-density prehistoric fluid composed of the bodies of formerly living beings—petroleum—is made to flow into modernity through social labor carried out by materially constituted bodies. These bodies are dependent at a physiological level on flows of blood and water and at the mechanical level on electricity or gasoline, and they also flow in migrations fueled by the consumption of oil. In this sense, the work of oil extraction and the experience of oil spills alike reveal that there is no experience beyond the body, society, or the environment, all of which are constituted mutually and historically in material flows that, if not always converging fully or intersecting permanently, are nevertheless interactive in ways that modernity seeks to disavow through culturally determined symbolic and material enclosures.

As both of these documentaries were produced by outsiders who portray native Ecuadoran subjects as well as the Amazonian environment from specific ideological positions, I also scrutinize questions of re-representation and misrepresentation. Beyond acknowledging the filmic spectacle as an ideological representation that is superimposed over real events, ordering them according to its system of values, I argue that the documentaries' specularity, like sheen itself, is an effect produced by material interactions, in which the image is neither fully object nor fully representational in its relationship to either the bodies it features or those of its viewers. Despite the clichéd ideological misrepresentations that characterize both films, their portrayals of toxic porosity supersede the "secondary" ethics to which their ideologies appeal.[5] This is due to the material logic of toxicity, which is affective inasmuch as it is produced by and experienced within the body and its circulations. Nevertheless, these bodily "first ethics" and the secondary ethics promoted by the films' ideologies are compatible in a general sense, overcoming to a degree the problems posed by misrepresentation. In this way, I aim to show how a new materialist approach to the ethics that emerge in the affective encounter between human and nonhuman flows and their representations can reorient human rights discourse toward environmental ethics and what Isabelle Stengers has called cosmopolitics: the recognition that all political agency is ultimately constituted within fluid material meshworks (as Tim Ingold calls them) that implicate nonhuman as well as human actors.[6]

The Ethics of Misrepresentation

Comprising up to 40 percent of Ecuador's GDP, oil became the nation's single most important export in the years following the discovery of the Lago Agrio oilfield in the late 1960s and the completion of the Trans-Ecuadorian Oil Pipeline in 1972. Financed primarily by North American corporations Texaco and Gulf Oil, the intense development accompanying the Amazonian oil boom transformed the formerly remote region of Oriente, forcing its largely Indigenous inhabitants to adapt to the new economy and social organization and provoking a series of ongoing ecological and human health disasters arising from oil spills, dangerous working conditions, and the unsafe storage of hazardous materials in unlined, open pits. The severity and scope of these conditions have led some observers to refer to the area as the "Chernobyl of the Rainforest."[7] Local activists have worked with NGOs to hold the multinational corporations responsible for this situation accountable, orchestrating an international campaign aimed primarily at Chevron, which acquired Texaco in 2000. This loosely coordinated campaign involves litigation—a class action lawsuit was filed in New York on behalf of 30,000 affected people in 1993—as well as a high volume of cultural production, including public performance, websites, a substantial social media presence, videos, and film documentaries.[8]

The two documentaries I examine form part of this international outreach campaign. Both detail widespread oil pollution in Oriente, its effects for people and wildlife, and the region's high indexes of cancer and skin maladies, as well as the cultural impact of the oil industry and modernization in general on native Amazonians. From this initial expository mode, they transition toward a structure based on legal proceedings, in which contrasting arguments are presented alternately by the plaintiffs in the lawsuit, environmental lawyers, Indigenous rights activists, a variety of ecological and public health experts, and Chevron's corporate spokespersons and lawyers. Despite this strategy of mirroring legal proceedings, both films patently support the Indigenous and mixed-race plaintiffs in the lawsuit, usually by juxtaposing the oil companies' denials with footage showing contradictory material evidence.[9] A prime example of this form of visual irony is the inclusion in both films of images of discarded Texaco-branded oil barrels in a variety of settings, some smeared with oil on the edge of old retention ponds, others repurposed as trash containers or even cooking grills. These images confront statements by Chevron's spokespersons such as that featured in *Crude* of lawyer Adolfo Callejas downplaying Texaco's responsibility when faced with blatant evidence of improper remediation at a former Texaco pumping station: "everyone just assumed that material was oil and that it had the Texaco brand on it. I didn't see any logo."

In this sense, the films' structures display an ideological bias in favor of Indigenous rights and environmental justice. However, there are also somewhat more subtle ideological undercurrents at work within both films that reproduce to differing degrees North American and European misconceptions about Indigenous peoples, the Amazonian environment, Latin

America, and "underdeveloped" nations in general. In part, these stereotypical misrepresentations make the films more accessible to an international audience, simplifying a highly convoluted situation in the name of political expediency. However, they also elicit ethical quandaries that, at first glance at least, appear to undermine the films' political and juridical efficacy, thereby providing an opening for Chevron's lawyers as well as mass media apologists of neoliberal capitalism and multinational extractive industries.

Crude in particular reached a broad, international audience, appearing to critical acclaim in several prestigious film festivals. *Crude*'s critical success attracted several A-list Hollywood celebrities to its cause and spawned broad reporting on the situation in a variety of journalistic sources and pop culture magazines in 2009 and 2010. The negative portrayal of Chevron-Texaco's role in the ecological catastrophe resulted in a furious backlash from its corporate lawyers, who filed a countersuit against Steven Donzinger, the American lawyer who, together with Ecuadoran lawyer Pablo Fajardo, filed the lawsuit against the corporation. Chevron's lawyers subpoenaed Joe Berlinger, the director of *Crude*, claiming that he purposely suppressed evidence in the editing process and demanding access to 600 hours of uncut footage, which they were awarded by the US Second Circuit Court of Appeals in 2010. This implication of the documentary within the legal proceedings reveals the key roles that cultural production can play in litigation, even when it does not appear in the courtroom as evidence.

Although it was also shown at international festivals, *The Blood of Kouan Kouan* saw a much smaller distribution and critical reception, largely because it was produced by a Greek filmmaker with little prior documentary experience and distributed by the Greek independent film company Small Planet. Much of the film is narrated in Greek with English subtitles, which adds an intriguing twist to the already fraught politics of language and translation in these films, both of which open with speakers in A'ingae, the language spoken by the native Amazonian Cofán people, and feature Spanish interviews translated into English subtitles. More interesting aesthetically in some ways than the polished *Crude*, *Kouan Kouan* is patently low budget in comparison, rife with uneven technical expertise and stylistic inconsistencies (for instance, identifying some speakers at the beginning of their sequence, others in the middle, and many not at all). Intentional or not, these aesthetic inconsistencies raise several fundamental questions that not only draw attention to the film's own relationship to the conventions of documentary representation, but also bring into relief similar issues in *Crude* that are less salient because of the latter's polish.

Unlike *Crude*'s well-constructed argumentation, *Kouan Kouan* relies to a much greater degree on an aesthetics of dissonance that is generated through contrasting imagery and strident music, both of which provoke in the spectator a visceral sense of out-of-placeness that underpins its primary narrative about oil spills' toxic social and environmental effects. This aesthetics is evident from the outset, as the film opens with a close-up of an unidentified Cofán shaman chanting in A'ingae and gesturing with a branch in what appears to be a cleansing ceremony, immediately followed by footage of an oil pump head's rotation paralleling the shaman's circular movements, and then a ground-level first-person perspective sequence advancing through rainforest vegetation, first following a path and then veering directly into the undergrowth.[10] The soundtrack, composed by Yiannis Paxevanis, combines the shaman's chanting with a metallic beat that punctuates the visual dissonance. The following scene creates an effect of sudden calm within the intensifying rhythm of the images, as the soundtrack incorporates rainforest birdsong and the camera pans slowly on what appears to be a sunset reflected in a floodplain swamp, a quintessential feature in Amazonian amphibious environments. As the camera moves upward, oil machinery comes into view and one realizes that this is not a floodplain swamp at all, but an oil well retention pond. The reflection is produced not by water alone, but by chemical sheen speckled by bubbles of crude oil, and the "sunset" is actually the glow in the night from oil well flares. In this way, the film plays on the aesthetics of the nature documentaries that a Euro-American viewership has come to identify as the essential form of Amazonia, only to disrupt them by replacing the images of "pristine" natural features with toxic modern ones.

The next sequence begins with a series of takes filmed from a motorized canoe traveling up a river, a prototypical if clichéd Amazonian scene that captures the material otherness of an amphibious environment in which land travel is nearly impossible for much of the year. Overlaid text drives home the extent of the catastrophe: 18.5 billion gallons of oil spilled by Texaco and hundreds of other spills caused by PetroEcuador. The narrator recounts the history of oil discovery in the region and its disruption of uncontacted tribes living in harmony with nature as the camera pans on traditional Indigenous villages and children playing on the riverbank, cutting to images of monkeys playing in trees, back to oil well flares and swirling chemical sheen, children's faces, sedimented oil and contaminated soil, a cow carcass, a dead, oil-coated salamander, flames, pipelines, oil workers clearing the jungle, a dead bird, and discarded Texaco brand oil barrels.

The sequence ends abruptly with a young girl pulling congealed oil out of a stream with a stick, staining her hands.

In this interplay between the conventions of Amazonian nature imagery, anthropological documentary, and environmental disaster film, *The Blood of Kouan Kouan* sets the scene for a conflation of human rights abuses directed toward Indigenous Amazonians and ecological disaster. Indeed, the association of Indigenous genocide with ecocide is made explicit in the film's title and cover artwork. The Cofán shaman's monologue identifies the titular figure, *Kouan Kouan*, as a subterranean fertility deity, whose blood-oil is taken by oil companies in vampiric fashion, resulting in the death of the land and its Indigenous inhabitants. The cover art's text prefigures directly a reading of this bleeding of the inspired land as a form of Indigenous genocide: "Dedicated to the Tetetes and Sanshahuari people. Their voices were silenced forever at the dawn of the 21st century due to the oil activity in Ecuador's Amazonia." The reference to the twenty-first century is a key discursive marker, framing Amazonian oil extraction within the well-known history of colonial genocides of Indigenous peoples in the Americas, a history that is out of place in the present.

Crude begins in similar fashion. Following an introductory sequence that draws attention to North-South geopolitics as a map of Latin America is slowly doused from above in oil, the film features an elderly Cofán woman in traditional clothing singing a lamentation in A'ingae in which she describes the pollution of her riverine paradise by the oil industry and the subsequent deaths of family members. The refrain, translated in subtitles, repeats "I am the only survivor." In a figurative sense, the initial speakers in both films—the first human faces to appear—occupy the discursive position of the "last Cofán," whose solitude invokes the erasure of an entire ethnicity. The viewer is thus invited to make the comparison between solitude caused by traumatic loss and the invocation of a past of presumed cultural plenitude and harmonious or at least sustainable living within the Amazonian environment. This visual trope is reinforced with statistics: *Crude*'s narrator states that thirty years ago, there were more than 15,000 Cofán living in the region, a number that has been reduced to only a few hundred today. Likewise, *Kouan Kouan*'s narrator affirms that "the Cofán are one of the oldest tribes of the Amazonia. They live on the borders of Ecuador and Colombia. Today there are less than 1,000 left."[11] In this complementary visual and narrative idiom, ideologically oriented toward Indigenous rights, oil stands in symbolically for petromodernity and globalization's effects on

Indigenous lives and cultural identities. At the same time, the conjugation of Indigenous genocide with ecocide thrusts this ethical orientation beyond the terrain of liberal human rights (including Indigenous communal property rights to ancestral territories) into the muddied waters of the rights of nonhuman beings.

The problem of misrepresentation arises in these films not so much from what they show, but from what they don't show: from their use of reductive strategies such as stereotyping and overstatement for dramatic effect. This issue arises most transparently in *The Blood of Kouan Kouan*; the film's ideological frame clearly comes from an idealized European point of view that exoticizes the Amazonian inhabitants and erases their differences, transforming them into symbols of indigeneity—taken as the sign of a more authentic culture and harmonious coexistence with the environment that has largely been lost in Western and Westernized societies. This reification of the Cofán as stereotypical Indigenous figures becomes immediately apparent because the film neglects to name most of its Indigenous interviewees or to recognize the presence of political debate (and therefore of subjectivity and agency) within the Cofán community, some of whose members work in the oil industry and subscribe to the oil companies' and the Ecuadoran governments' arguments that oil extraction is necessary for social development and modernization.[12] In this sense, the film transparently falls into what environmental historian Shawn William Miller has called the "pristine myth" that concatenates indigeneity with the tenets of Western environmentalism.[13]

Framing oil as the blood of *Coancoan,* to use ethnologist Michael Cepek's Spanish-based transcription of the name, immediately elicits ethical problems. Not only does it thrust the viewer into the position of judging the validity of animistic belief systems featuring what Marisol de la Cadena calls *tirakuna*, or earth beings, with little context for comparison—thus making the film's argument rely exclusively on the tenuous and fraught discourse of cultural relativism and freedom of religion—but it also shows little sensitivity to the complexities of Cofán perceptions of this being.[14] In his critique of the film, Cepek points out that, according to his fieldwork at least, there is little consensus within the Cofán community as to who or what *Coancoan* is, never mind whether or not oil is his blood.[15] Within the context of the cultural hegemony of modern law and scientific discourse, romanticizing a somewhat unstable earth being may have the unintended effect of minimizing Indigenous political and cultural agency in real-life activism.[16]

Furthermore, framing oil extraction as a form of Indigenous genocide patently enters into contradiction with the bulk of the film's footage, which features a variety of ethnicities, few of whom ascribe to the traditional Indigenous worldview that opens the film. Most of the interviewees are mestizo Andean and/or Afro-Ecuadoran migrants to the region. The claims they make do not appeal to an infringement on a spiritual relationship with an earth being, or from a multicultural perspective, religious freedoms, but rather to what Guha and Martinez Alier famously called the "social ecology of the poor," that is, the environmental conditions that affect everyday life in impoverished "peripheral" zones of extraction and/or production.[17] The blood and bodies of all the inhabitants of the oil extraction zones of Oriente are portrayed as vulnerable to toxicity.

Crude is somewhat more effective in reconciling the Indigenous rights discourse that opens the film with the representation of the many non-Indigenous interviewees because it presents them within the framework of a multiethnic popular movement or alliance. Tellingly, it does not engage the figure of *Coancoan* at all, focusing instead on the juridical process, political activism, and effects of economic pressures on Indigenous cultural practices. A particularly powerful scene shows Cofán and Secoya people speaking at a 2006 Chevron shareholders' meeting in Houston, emphasizing Indigenous people's ability to challenge petromodernity on its own turf. Nevertheless, this scene also undermines its own premise to a degree, as the plaintiffs' testimony is carefully scripted and coached by their American lawyer, Stephen Donziger. The arguments Donziger presents defending this scripting are convincing, nonetheless, and while viewers may conceivably agree with Chevron's spokespersons that these Indigenous people are being used by their lawyers for their own financial gain, they are equally likely to recognize them as Indigenous people who have taken the initiative to be trained in modern legal practices, just as any modern subject must do to engage in litigation.[18] In this sense, *Crude* does not reproduce the stereotypical opposition between Indigenous identities and modernity that *The Blood of Kouan Kouan* makes; in *Crude*, Indigenous people engage Euro-American modernity on their own terms and put it to service in their struggle against Chevron through the use of public performance, mass media, and digital activism. Notwithstanding, in engaging the trope of Indigenous genocide, both films run up against the reality that the Cofán have not disappeared completely, but that many actually work in the oil industry, as well as failing to address internal debate within Indigenous cultures regarding the question of ethnic authenticity amid shifting cultural practices. In a general sense, the narrative appealing to Indigenous rights fails to account for the specificity and complexity of multiple ethnicities' experience of the disaster.

Misrepresentation weakens the ethics of ecological justice and long-term environmental and cultural sustainability that the films intend to promote. Nevertheless, another powerful ethics comes into play through the materiality of the filmic image, a "first ethics" that I argue, following Emmanuel Levinas, supersedes ideological values. Based on an experience in which he was treated with human dignity by a Nazi concentration camp guard who had in other instances systematically dehumanized his Jewish prisoners, Levinas argues that the face-to-face encounter with the other's extreme vulnerability provokes an ethical response that does not rely on either empathetic identification or a system of moral values.[19] For Levinas, the material encounter with the other's "naked" vulnerability places a demand for ethical treatment that supersedes any ideological predisposition, no matter how engrained it may be. This "first" ethics would necessarily be rooted in affective responses located in the body rather than symbolic mediation, although, as many scholars have pointed out, the symbolic always takes material form and therefore necessarily functions through the same affective pathways.[20] The bodily ethics of encounter does not necessarily replace an ideological stance, but it demands a response from that stance, either justifying it or placing it into a state of contradiction that must be addressed for the ideological position to retain its validity.

Two methodological problems immediately surface upon engaging Levinas's formulation of a first ethics for discussing these documentaries. First, Levinas's ethics is explicitly limited to the human face-to-face encounter, which could potentially work with the portrayal of human suffering in the films but would not address any ethical concerns arising within the ecocide narrative. As David Clark points out, despite raising the possibility of the animal demanding an ethical response from humans (specifically, a dog named Bobby that Levinas and his fellow prisoners encountered in the concentration camp), Levinas performs a series of rhetorical maneuvers to elide the potentiality of the human encounter with an animal face, never mind with faceless entities such as plants or bodies of water.[21] Second, Levinas's postulation of an ethics based on the affective encounter with the other relies explicitly on face to face interaction, whereas I am discussing two distinctly mediated encounters: the encounter of the camera with bodies affected by oil pollution and the encounter of the viewer with aestheticized, ideologically structured images. Nevertheless, I argue that these films place a Levinasian ethical demand on their viewers through three entwined affective pathways arising from specific forms of bodily encounter: the bodily memory of illness (particularly that related to toxicity), which works through mechanisms of abjection as much as symbolization; the daily material experience of viscosity as a state proper to fluids of all kinds; and the affective encounter with the image itself, particularly within its fluid-like, cinematic state as film. All three of these pathways involve encounters with an otherness that is not purely discursive (or categorical), but that emerges from a material differential between the relative viscosities of concrete, nonstatic, porous bodies.

Toxicity and the Porosity of Spectatorship

Illness can never be approached in purely symbolic fashion, whether through language or a specific visual idiom. In toxicity in particular, there may be few outward signs of the toxic effects that a person is experiencing internally. Even if external symptoms—skin lesions, rashes, abnormal coloration, sweating, and so on—may be said to communicate suffering through a form of symbolism, alluding indexically to internal distress, those symptoms could never be said to communicate the full bodily experience of illness. At most, they indicate the presence of a bodily disorder to which a healthy body has no access other than through the parallelism of its own past experiences of illness—whether that provoked by toxicity or others caused by biological agents such cancerous cells, bacteria, or viruses, since the body's immunological reactions to most illnesses are similar—and of the incommunicability of the bodily sensations it provokes when attempting to describe them to others. Ill bodies provoke a response that is akin to abjection (in the sense in which Julia Kristeva uses the term, as what must be abjected from the subject in order to preserve its integrity), but that is nevertheless transversal to the subject-object dichotomy that characterizes our conscious relationship to the relative opacity of our own bodies.[22] The encounter with others' illness makes us aware of the porosity of our own bodies and of our vulnerability to toxic agents that cannot be apprehended directly, only through the memory of our own past experiences in conjunction with the encounter in the present with the ill body of the other.

This question of the unrepresentability of illness is compounded in images of sickness, in which it can never be assumed that the symptomatic image closes the book on what the ill body is feeling or even displaying. This becomes quite clear in *Crude* and the *Blood of Kouan Kouan*. Both films feature the testimony of cancer patients, most of whom appear outwardly to be healthy. We only become aware of their illness through the descriptions of their symptoms, or in the case of one young, seemingly healthy woman in *Kouan Kouan*, through the skin lesions she displays to the camera, pulling aside her shirt. The image cannot foreclose in a symbolic sense the symptoms that it excludes in a fashion that is specific to the material form of the image as such; that is to say, the sounds (some of which may be captured on film, while others may not), odors, and textures of illness that cannot be represented directly in any medium, only experienced in person or secondhand through effects that elicit a parallel, if trace response. Furthermore, even though the cinematic image is able to capture the passage of time, its representation is always understood by the viewer as a cross-section of a particular moment or sequence of moments, never as an event in its entirety. There is always the supposition of both prequel and sequel. The viewer thus never has the luxury of taking cinematic images of illness as encapsulating their own meaning, that is, of making possible a cathartic, foreclosed, and therefore apolitical relationship to the suffering of an other. The symbolic insufficiency of the image is always readily apparent. In order for the representation of illness to convey any meaning, then, the viewer's body must step in to supplement the image, filling in its lacunae with its own experiences of illness, which itself is only partially able to articulate as subjectivity, as subjectivity is unable to deal with the abjection of its own body.

While the documentary image itself is representation, it evokes not only the very real suffering of the body that is represented but also the materiality of one's own past suffering, subordinated to the (symbolic) narrative of that experience during the healing process, which is essentially a restoration of the sovereignty of the healthy subject over its own body. As illness cannot be contained fully by representation, any memory of illness is necessarily the memory of an abjection, of what the healthy subject must repress in order to constitute itself as such. The encounter with an other's ill body thus opens the healthy subject to what it has repressed, provoking an affective response that cannot be fully accounted for through its own ideology, that is, its moral position regarding the origins, causes, and therapeutic methodologies relating to health, illness, and death. The affectivity of the image supplements the subject's memory through a material encounter by which that memory ceases to exist in purely symbolic terms and comes to life anew as an affective encounter with illness. In this manner, both *Crude* and *The Blood of Kouan Kouan* implicate the viewer in a material sense within the experience of toxicity of the people who have been affected by oil spills in the Ecuadoran Amazon.

In addition to drawing on the affective mechanisms within the viewer's own body to communicate the experience of toxicity itself, *Crude* and *The*

Blood of Kouan Kouan make extensive use of supplementary images to portray the latency of illness in the contaminated environment. These images can be grouped into four main categories, each of which plays a distinct role in communicating the porosity of human and nonhuman bodies to toxicity: images of oil on water; soil contaminated with oil sludge; people, often children, in contact with oil; and the dead bodies of oil-drenched animals and plants. These images are interspersed in collage fashion, thereby giving a global impression of an interconnected ecology of toxicity that, resisting containment, exists within a state of continual, viscous circulation between land, water, and human and animal bodies. Nevertheless, the sequencing of these images and the amount of space dedicated to each type at particular junctures generate a chronological narrative structured by the progression of the human experience of illness. This general progression begins with images of pristine Amazonian environments and the sustainable cultural practices of its Indigenous inhabits, then addresses the arrival of the oil companies, subsequent pollution, its effects on humans and animals, animal deaths (which stand in for and prefigure human deaths), and, finally, images of children touching oil, suggesting the ongoing cycle of toxic contamination and illness. The uniquely viscous quality of the filmic image—its ability to flow through time—produces an encounter with the chronology of illness that is not accessible in real life to either the people featured in the films or the viewer remembering past illnesses, since it places the viewer in the position of apprehending the full progression in a single sitting. Film allows us to experience the viscosity of the time of sickness, in which illness is not a state in which a body finds itself, but a process in which a nonhuman agent—in this case, a toxin—appropriates the human body in some way over time, demonstrating its porosity and its vulnerability.

The oil spill is the operative image within this processual chronology of toxic contamination. Initially, it appears as a catastrophic setting for the illnesses of the people featured in the film, thereby assuming a secondary, seemingly static position with respect to the film's public health disaster narrative. This sense of the spill as the setting for a plot centered on humans is quickly undermined by the fluidity of the substances themselves, as the viscosity of oil interrupts the staticity of containment systems such as tubing and tanks, but also the institution of the disaster area itself (as a technologically controlled zone of containment) and the idealization of the body as a self-contained, discrete entity. Indeed, both films feature key narratives on the pollution of drinking and bathing water that is supported by images of chemical sheen and oil spills in waterways in a region in which the majority of residents draw their water directly from wells and streams, thereby representing the uncontained circulation of viscous contaminants. In *Crude*, this water pollution narrative is linked to the cancer testimony told by local resident María Garofalo about her own illness and that of her eighteen-year old daughter, Silvia. Abject images of water contamination simultaneously disrupt the ecophiliac idealization of water in nature documentaries and earth art, in which it typically symbolizes ontonoetic freedom—that is, ontological freedom from biopolitical structures. As Irene Depetris Chauvin notes with respect to the work of Latin American visual artists Alejandro Argüelles, Cecilia Cavallieri, and Nuno Ramos, earth art depicting liquid ecologies often captures how the immutable natural forms of water are themselves endangered by anthropogenic environmental modifications.[23]

Animal suffering and death are used to make visible the most drastic effects of this pollution, thereby sidestepping the ethical pitfalls of appropriating through the image human others' mortal suffering. These ethical pitfalls can only be dispelled from images of animal death through the doctrine of human exceptionality, which relies on the instrumentalization of animal bodies and the assumption that their lives have value solely in relation to the human. However, this question is problematized in these films through the horizontality of toxic circulation, which affects all bodies irrespective of species. Tellingly, Garofalo's initial testimony is preceded by an image of a duck lying in a discarded tire shaking uncontrollably, suffering from an unspecified nervous disorder that she blames on its having drunk water from the stream below her property. As Garofalo narrates the suffering of her family and the financial difficulties she has encountered in paying for her daughter's cancer treatment in a center that is an eighteen-hour bus ride from their hometown of San Carlos, she recounts how the chicks she bought to raise in hopes of funding the treatment all died from drinking the toxic water in the same stream that her family used to bathe and drink. Her young son tosses the cadavers of two of these dead chickens into the underbrush, since they are unsafe for human consumption, as she summarizes with desperation: "There is no life here for animals, how much less so for humans."

Images of the deaths of domestic animals stand in for the toxic effects of oil pollution on humans, implying that María and her daughter may suffer the same fate. Despite this parallelism, the film carefully avoids animalizing the human victims of the oil pollution; the domesticity of the chickens—their auxiliary position with respect to their human owners—together with images of farmland pollution shortly after, place the blame squarely on Texaco for creating an uncontainable, toxic environment that is unable to support human or nonhuman life. In this way, the film turns the narrative away from Chevron's lawyers and environmental scientists' animalizing, racialized arguments that the affected people's substandard living conditions, unhygienic lifestyles, and even precocious sexual activity are responsible for their illnesses, framing it squarely as a question of environmental justice.

At the same time, the concatenation of the narratives of human suffering with images of animals in an abject state of absolute vulnerability—permeated by oil—blurs the boundaries between human and animal suffering; the doctrine of human exceptionality takes a back seat to the encounter with vulnerable bodies of any species. Devoid of human expression, the animals' bodies nevertheless convey their suffering in a way that cannot be rationalized as something that is proper to their status as domestic animals, that is, as instruments of human life. Confronting the viewer with its radically vulnerable body, the individual animal supersedes the animal category and species representativity—the notion that animals' individuality (their face or name) is always subordinated to their species. Through the viewer's encounter with their vulnerability, then, animal bodies exhibit a form of personhood that demands an ethical response that, despite their proximity to humans, is in no way dependent on the discourse of either human rights or property rights. The collage structure in these documentaries takes full advantage of what Leticia Gómez and Azucena Castro, citing Karen Barad, identify as film's potential for generating "diffraction" or "patterns of difference" that blur the human/animal divide.[24]

The sequestering logic of hygiene is further undermined in these films in their treatment of the problem of the seepage of oil through soil into water, driving home the reality that, like the cancerous human and animal bodies described above, the land itself is permeable and cannot serve as a barrier to toxicity. Both films feature extensive footage of soil samples being taken, often on areas near oil pump stations or supposedly remediated oil retention ponds, now covered with thin layers of soil and vegetation. These are complemented by sequences in which local people use machetes or shovels to dig into soil on their land and, especially, streambanks, revealing the presence of thick layers of oil sludge. The reiteration of soil sampling in different locales throughout the films generates a cartography of toxicity that captures the omnipresence of soil contamination. They demonstrate the fallacy of Chevron-Texaco's claims to have complied in full in 1996 with the environmental remediation plan stipulated by the Ecuadoran government, while also emphasizing the porosity of the human body to toxicity through the ingestion of contaminated food. The plaintiffs' lawyer, Pablo Fajardo, and several environmental experts discuss at length the problem of the seepage of these buried toxic materials into groundwater and nearby surface bodies of water. Through the parallelism of the physical process, the seepage of oil through soil into water suggests the porosity of the human skin: what appear in a superficial way to be discrete entities (soil, water, oil, the human body) are revealed to be open to each other, and the soil's unseen saturation with oil has its parallel in the microscopic toxins that are absorbed into human, animal, and plant bodies, circulating within them and sedimenting into vital organs.

The physical counterpart to oil's viscosity, which places it into circulation within the land, water, and bodies of all species, is sedimentation. Sedimentation is never portrayed as a discrete or static condition, as the end point of the oil spill, by which it may be removed and thereby remediated. What is sedimented instead serves as an indexical remnant of what has already seeped into other bodies and will continue to seep for the foreseeable future, which is again driven home in the continuity within the collage between sequences of children playing innocently with oil and the images of dead, oil-coated animal bodies.

Material Hermeneutics and the Cosmopolitics of the Viscous Image

In the filmic encounter with these dying human and nonhuman bodies, the viewer is also placed in proximity to oil. The viscous properties of the cinematic image—its ability to both flow across the eye and sediment in the viewer's memory—exceed the intentions or ideologically determined aesthetics of the filmmaker. There is no way for the auteur to ensure with complete certainty which properties within images or even which images themselves stick with the viewer and which flow by without attracting the viewer's focused attention. As Anthony Fredriksson argues, "the material traces—gestures, expressions, features—that end up on the record, with or without the intention of the author, are in no way neutral. They bear witness to a world outside the conceptions of the author. These traces are highly relevant, but their meaning is neither transparent nor fixed. They are emergent in the images, awaiting the attention of the viewer."[25] Roberto Forns Broggi notes that the collaborative form of the testimonial also exceeds authorial intention, as the real-life subjects of documentaries shape their narratives in ways that cannot be entirely controlled by the filmmaker, even through the editing process. Ontological differences seep through the porosity of the narrative's ideological superstructure.[26]

It is in this sense that Webb Keane refers to the inseparable "bundling" of properties within objects, even those represented in images; while a narrative may focus on only one or a select few of these aspects, other properties remain latent as a form of "futurity" or potential that may come to the forefront in the event of viewing, disrupting the narrative and forcing a reconfiguration of symbolic meaning.[27] As he writes, "we need to recognize how the materiality of signification is not just a factor for the sign *interpreter* but gives rise to and transforms modalities of action and subjectivity *regardless* of whether they are interpreted."[28] Fredriksson drives home, citing Bill Nichols, "a picture cannot carry with it a theory of how it is to be viewed, a concept cannot be illustrated."[29] In this sense, there is a fluidity within the image itself in relation to the act of perception and interpretation, one that rejects the staticity of ideology and renders it vulnerable. Viewers are opened to the affective potential of aspects that the film's narrative suppresses, and thereby experience the "opportunity to re-present themselves in light of a different ontological position."[30]

The Indigenous rights narratives in *Crude* and *The Blood of Kouan Kouan* rely primarily on an ethics derived from the liberal humanist tradition, which defines human rights in opposition to animals as the embodiment of nature. Nevertheless, I have shown how filmic images of the viscosity of oil and of the porosity of bodies of all kinds to oil's toxicity both complement and exceed the environmental justice narrative, implicating the viewer through affectivity in ways that disavow the perspective that this problem is limited to or contained within certain bodies or the disaster area. The experience of viewership replicates toxic contamination as disturbing images circulate within our own bodies, internalized within our memories. Representations of viscosity are not solely symbols of a physical process with the potential for toxic contamination, but in effect a reminder of the viscous fluids in our own bodies, of the flows that enter and leave our bodies on a daily basis, and of their abilities to transform us in both beneficial and toxic ways.

At the same time, the bodies in the films serve as proxies for the materiality of our own bodies through the affectivity of illness, stimulating physiological reactions that disrupt the distance of representation. This sense of presence—of implication within the materiality of the filmic image—is heightened through close-ups of spectators' reactions within the films, both of which prominently feature listeners and witnesses who respond to the encounter with the bodies before them, listening, smelling, and feeling for us. We read these internal spectator's expressions in a symbolic register, but they also elicit the traces of our own experiences, compelling us to relive and reconceive the sights, sounds, and smells of oil and other forms of viscous toxicity with which we come into contact. This materiality of comparison between nonstatic flows within bodies of all types within and outside the filmic medium does not function as a simple equivalence between two dissimilar symbols—a metaphor—but as a material differential between porous, mutually interacting bodies, those featured in the image, the image itself as a material form, and those viewing the image.

The visceral experience of viscosity disrupts the neoliberal conceptualizations of the oil industry, in which oil is presented as a static commodity that circulates as barrels on the global energy market, its liquidity measured in capital—its exchange value—not any material qualities in and of itself. In the process of viewing these films, an inversion occurs whereby oil becomes mobile and agentic through its ability to circulate throughout the environment and affect bodies toxically, while human and animal bodies are immobilized and deactivated in death, sedimenting into oil slicks.[31] Porosity—shared vulnerability to toxicity—levels the human-nature divide, placing humans, animals, and even plants within a shared personhood rooted in the affective encounter with the viewer and the horizontal loss of agency over their own bodies due to exposure to contaminants.

Despite the ultimate defeat of the effort to hold Chevron-Texaco accountable for the harm it caused bodies of all kinds in the Ecuadoran Amazon in a court of law, it was not a failure in a political sense: it led to a radical reformulation of liberal rights in the 2008 Ecuadoran constitution to include the rights of nature alongside human rights within a cosmopolitical framework. While this legislation has not always had the desired effect, largely because of the Ecuadoran state's reliance on natural resource extraction to fund its social programs, there have been several court cases in which the rights of nature have been upheld. The case of oil pollution in the Ecuadoran Amazon is by no means an isolated incident; it correlates directly with the global experience of toxicity arising from industrialized development in the neoliberal model, which has led to rising awareness worldwide of the fallacy of the notion that the modern subject can sequester itself from its socioecological environment. In portraying alliances between a broad range of multiethnic and multispecies political actors, *Crude* and *The Blood of Kouan Kouan* exemplify the kinds of cosmopolitical alliances that are becoming common worldwide, bringing together local popular movements, postcolonial Indigenous thought, Euro-American environmentalism, animal rights activism, public health advocacy, and feminist in a concerted effort to transform the hegemonic political ecology toward a livable future.

The material realities of porosity have been driven home by the COVID-19 pandemic in a way unmatched even by the widespread effects of chemical toxicity. The drastic bodily, social, economic, and political realities of nonhuman agencies have emerged into public view on a scale that cannot be assimilated convincingly by what Giorgio Agamben called the anthropological machine—the human—through technological and discursive mediation.[32] The violence the pandemic has exercised on the doctrine of human exceptionalism forces a reckoning with other, historically repressed ontologies that are better able to account for intra-active, cosmopolitical, material realities. And many of these other ontologies have emerged from communities that have been drastically, traumatically affected by viral pandemics even before experiencing the chemical toxicities associated with natural resource extraction.

In this sense, the narratives of toxicity in *Crude* and the *Blood of Kouan Kouan* are most powerful when viewed alongside Latin American films that feature cosmopolitical practices in more explicit terms. The humanist viewer cannot simply defer to the pathos of multicultural tolerance upon entering into contact with films that privilege relational ontologies—that is, worldviews that conceptualize subjectivity as intra-active becoming rather than a monadic, static position within rigid subject-object hierarchies. Such ontologies emerge full force in Latin American Indigenous filmmaking such as that studied by Freya Schiwy in *Indianizing Film* as well as collaborative ecofilms featuring Indigenous people speaking on their own behalf—for instance, Ursula Biemann and Paulo Tavares's multimedia installation on the Sarayaku Runa, *Forest Law*, and several of the documentaries analyzed by Forns-Broggi.[33] These films generate zones of equivocation—spaces in which difference is recognized as untranslatable, irreconcilable with any single narrative world—that place the viewer in the uncertain position of engaging in what Stengers calls ontological diplomacy.[34] This form of diplomacy emerges from the recognition of a common difference between Indigenous and Euro-American scientific perspectives—that the human-nature divide is purely ideological, with no incontrovertible basis in fact or experience.[35] And, as Biemann argues regarding her film, political acts of ontological diplomacy are precisely what is needed to create a common future capable of sustaining all species, in their differences.[36]

Notes

1. See Alan Stoekl's foreword to *Oil Culture,* ed. Ross Barret and Daniel Worden (Minneapolis: University of Minnesota Press, 2014), xiii; as well as Barret and Worden's introduction, xvii.

2. Regarding the concept of slow violence, see Rob Nixon, *Slow Violence and the Environmentalism of the Poor* (Cambridge, MA: Harvard University Press, 2011).

3. See the introduction to Stacy Alaimo's *Bodily Natures: Science, Environment, and the Material Self* (Bloomington: Indiana University Press, 2010).

4. Nancy Tuana, "Viscous Porosity: Witnessing Katrina," in *Material Feminisms,* ed. Stacy Alaimo and Susan J. Hekman (Bloomington: Indiana University Press, 2008), 188–89.

5. I use "secondary" in reference to Emmanuel Levinas's "first ethics," in which he describes an ethical response to the other that arises not from any cultural system of moral values, but from the direct encounter with the suffering "face" of the other. See Levinas, "Ethics as First Philosophy," in *The Levinas Reader,* ed. Seán Hand (Malden, MA: Blackwell, 1989), 75–87.

6. See Isabelle Stengers, *Cosmopolitics I,* trans. Robert Bononno (Minneapolis: University of Minnesota Press, 2010) and Tim Ingold, "Toward an Ecology of Materials," *Annual Review of Anthropology* 41 (2012): 427–42.

7. See, for instance, Chevron Tóxico's "A Rainforest Chernobyl" website.

8. Suraj Patel provides a concise history of this litigation up through 2012 in "Delayed Justice: A Case Study of Texaco and the Republic of Ecuador's Operations, Harms, and Possible Redress in the Ecuadoran Amazon," *Tulane Environmental Law Journal* 26, no. 71 (2012): 71–110. Up-to-date news can be found in a wide variety of highly polarized news sources on the internet.

9. Imre Szeman provides an admirably succinct summary of Chevron's lawyers' frequently contradictory arguments as they appear in *Crude,* noting that, "taken together, these points (and there are others in a similar vein) offer a confusing defense. Rather than building a coherent case, it is as if they are being thrown out in the hope that one or another will stick" ("Crude Aesthetics: The Politics of Oil Documentaries," in *Oil Culture,* ed. Ross Barret and Daniel Worden [Minneapolis: University of Minnesota Press, 2014], 356).

10. Michael Cepek identifies this shaman as Alejandro Criollo, an "informant" and friend with whom the ethnologist lived and worked closely. In the film, however,

he remains nameless. See Cepek's *Life in Oil: Cofán Survival in the Petroleum Fields of Amazonia* (Austin: University of Texas Press, 2018).

11. Both films fail to mention other, prior causes of this demographic decline, including enslavement during the rubber booms at the end of the nineteenth and mid-twentieth centuries (see Cepek's *Life in Oil*, 24), although it has clearly intensified with the arrival of the oil industry.

12. See Cepek's *Life in Oil* and "There Might Be Blood: Oil, Humility, and the Cosmopolitics of a Cofán Petro Being," *American Ethnologist* 43, no. 4 (2016): 623–35.

13. Shawn William Miller, *An Environmental History of Latin America* (Cambridge: Cambridge University Press, 2007), 10.

14. See Marisol de la Cadena, *Earth Beings: Ecologies of Practice Across Andean Worlds* (Durham, NC: Duke University Press, 2015).

15. See Cepek, "There Might Be Blood."

16. Ibid., 632–33.

17. Ramachandra Guha and Joan Martinez Alier, *Varieties of Environmentalism: North and South* (New York: Earthscan, 1997), 72.

18. Chevron's lawyers' arguments disparaging the authenticity of these Indigenous peoples' testimonies transparently constitute an attempt to silence Indigenous speech and political agency.

19. Levinas, "Ethics as First Philosophy," 83.

20. For example, see Mieke Bal, "Visual Essentialism and the Object of Visual Culture," *Journal of Visual Culture* 2, no. 1 (2003): 5–32; Karen Barad, "Posthumanist Performativity: Toward an Understanding of How Matter Comes to Matter," *Signs* 28, no. 3 (2003): 801–31; and Elizabeth Edwards, "Objects of Affect: Photography Beyond the Image," *Annual Review of Anthropology* 41 (2012): 221–34.

21. See David Clark, "On Being 'the Last Kantian in Nazi Germany': Dwelling with Animals after Levinas," in *Animal Acts: Configuring the Human in Western History*, ed. Jennifer Ham and Matthew Senior (New York: Routledge, 1997), 165–98.

22. See Julia Kristeva, *The Powers of Horror: An Essay on Abjection*, trans. Leon S. Roudiez (New York: Columbia University Press, 1982).

23. Irene Depetris Chauvin, "Ecologías líquidas: Geografías acuáticas en las artes audiovisuales de Brasil, Argentina y Chile," *452° F* 21 (2019): 133.

24. Leticia Gómez and Azucena Castro, "Shrieks from the Margins of the Human: Framing the Environmental Crisis in Two Contemporary Latin American Movies," *Ecozon@* 10, no. 1 (2019): 189.

25. Anthony Fredriksson, "Documentary Film Beyond Intention and Re-Presentation: Trinh T. Minh-ha and the Aesthetics of Materiality," *Journal of Information Ethics* 19, no. 2 (2010): 78.

26. See Roberto Forns-Broggi, "Los retos del ecocine en nuestras Américas: Rastreos del buen vivir en *Tierra sublevada*," *Revista de Crítica Literaria Latinoamericana* 40, no. 79 (2014): 322–23.

27. Webb Keane, "Signs Are Not the Garb of Meaning: On the Social Analysis of Material Things," in *Materiality*, ed. Daniel Miller (Durham, NC: Duke University Press, 2005), 188.

28. Ibid., 186.

29. Fredriksson, 182.

30. Joshua A. Bell, "Promiscuous Things: Perspectives on Cultural Property through Photographs in the Purari Delta of Papua New Guinea," *International Journal of Cultural Property* 15 (2008): 134.

31. As Stephanie LeMenager writes, "Oil challenges liveliness from another ontological perspective, as a substance that was, once, live matter and that acts with a force suggestive of a form of life" (*Living Oil: Petroleum Culture in the American Century* [Oxford: Oxford University Press, 2014], 6).

32. Giorgio Agamben, *The Open: Man and Animal*, trans. Kevin Attell (Stanford: Stanford University Press, 2004), 37.

33. See Freya Schiwy, *Indianizing Film: Decolonization, the Andes, and the Question of Technology* (New Brunswick: Rutgers University Press, 2009); Ursula Biemann, "The Cosmopolitical Forest: A Theoretical and Aesthetic Discussion of the Video *Forest Law*" (*Geohumanities* 1, no. 1 [2015]: 157–70); and Forns-Broggi, "Los retos del ecocine."

34. See Isabelle Stengers, "The Challenge of Ontological Politics," in *A World of Many Worlds*, ed. Marisol de la Cadena and Mario Blaser (Durham, NC: Duke University Press, 2018), 83–111.

35. Regarding equivocation as a methodology for addressing the untranslatable and the unassimilable, see Eduardo Viveiros de Castro, "Perspectival Anthropology and the Method of Controlled Equivocation," *Tipití* 2, no. 1 (2004): 3–20.

36. Biemann, "The Cosmopolitical Forest," 165–66.

Works Cited

Agamben, Giorgio. *The Open: Man and Animal*. Translated by Kevin Attell. Palo Alto: Stanford University Press, 2004.

Alaimo, Stacy. *Bodily Natures: Science, Environment, and the Material Self*. Bloomington: Indiana University Press, 2010.

Avgeropolous, Yorgos, dir. *The Blood of Kouan Kouan*. 2009; Small Planet. DVD.

Bal, Mieke. "Visual Essentialism and the Object of Visual Culture." *Journal of Visual Culture* 2, no. 1 (2003): 5–32.

Barad, Karen. "Posthumanist Performativity: Toward an Understanding of How Matter Comes to Matter." *Signs* 28, no. 3 (2003): 801–31.

Barret, Ross, and Daniel Worden, eds. *Oil Culture*. Minneapolis: University of Minnesota Press, 2014.

Bell, Joshua A. "Promiscuous Things: Perspectives on Cultural Property through Photographs in the Purari Delta of Papua New Guinea." *International Journal of Cultural Property* 15 (2008): 123–39.

Berlinger, Joe, dir. *Crude: The Real Price of Oil*. 2009; Entendre Films. DVD.

Biemann, Ursula. "The Cosmopolitical Forest: A Theoretical and Aesthetic Discussion of the Video *Forest Law*." *Geohumanities* 1, no. 1 (2015): 157–70.

Cadena, Marisol de la. *Earth Beings: Ecologies of Practice Across Andean Worlds*. Durham, NC: Duke University Press, 2015.

Cepek, Michael. *Life in Oil: Cofán Survival in the Petroleum Fields of Amazonia*. Austin: University of Texas Press, 2018.

———. "There Might Be Blood: Oil, Humility, and the Cosmopolitics of a Cofán Petro Being." *American Ethnologist* 43, no. 4 (2016): 623–35.

Clark, David. "On Being 'the Last Kantian in Nazi Germany': Dwelling with Animals after Levinas." In *Animal Acts: Configuring the Human in Western History*, edited by Jennifer Ham and Matthew Senior, 165–98. New York: Routledge, 1997.

Depetris Chauvin, Irene. "Ecologías líquidas: Geografías acuáticas en las artes audiovisuales de Brasil, Argentina y Chile." *452° F* 21 (2019): 127–50.

Edwards, Elizabeth. "Objects of Affect: Photography Beyond the Image." *Annual Review of Anthropology* 41 (2012): 221–34.

Forns-Broggi, Roberto. "Los retos del ecocine en nuestras Américas: Rastreos del buen vivir en *Tierra sublevada*." *Revista de Crítica Literaria Latinoamericana* 40, no. 79 (2014): 315–32.

Fredriksson, Antony. "Documentary Film Beyond Intention and Re-Presentation: Trinh T. Minh-ha and the Aesthetics of Materiality." *Journal of Information Ethics* 19, no. 2 (2010): 67–81.

Gómez, Leticia, and Azucena Castro. "Shrieks from the Margins of the Human: Framing the Environmental Crisis in Two Contemporary Latin American Movies." *Ecozon@* 10, no. 1 (2019): 177–95.

Guha, Ramachandra, and Joan Martinez Alier. *Varieties of Environmentalism: North and South*. New York: Earthscan, 1997.

Ingold, Tim. "Toward an Ecology of Materials." *Annual Review of Anthropology* 41 (2012): 427–42.

Keane, Webb. "Signs Are Not the Garb of Meaning: On the Social Analysis of Material Things." In *Materiality*, edited by Daniel Miller, 182–205. Durham, NC: Duke University Press, 2005.

Kristeva, Julia. *The Powers of Horror: An Essay on Abjection*. Translated by Leon S. Roudiez. New York: Columbia University Press, 1982.

LeMenager, Stephanie. *Living Oil: Petroleum Culture in the American Century*. Oxford: Oxford University Press, 2014.

Levinas, Emmanuel. "Ethics as First Philosophy." In *The Levinas Reader*, edited by Seán Hand, 75–87. Malden, MA: Blackwell, 1989.

Miller, Shawn William. *An Environmental History of Latin America*. Cambridge: Cambridge University Press, 2007.

Nixon, Rob. *Slow Violence and the Environmentalism of the Poor*. Cambridge: Harvard University Press, 2011.

Patel, Suraj. "Delayed Justice: A Case Study of Texaco and the Republic of Ecuador's Operations, Harms, and Possible Redress in the Ecuadoran Amazon." *Tulane Environmental Law Journal* 26, no. 71 (2012): 71–110.

Schiwy, Freya. *Indianizing Film: Decolonization, the Andes, and the Question of Technology*. New Brunswick: Rutgers University Press, 2009.

Stengers, Isabelle. *Cosmopolitics I*. Translated by Robert Bononno. Minneapolis: University of Minnesota Press, 2010.

———. "The Challenge of Ontological Politics." In *A World of Many Worlds*, edited by Marisol de la Cadena and Mario Blaser, 83–111. Durham, NC: Duke University Press, 2018.

Stoekl, Allan. "Foreward." In *Oil Culture*, edited by Ross Barret and Daniel Worden, xi–xiv. Minneapolis: University of Minnesota Press, 2014.

Szeman, Imre. "Crude Aesthetics: The Politics of Oil Documentaries." In *Oil Culture*, edited by Ross Barret and Daniel Worden, 350–65. Minneapolis: University of Minnesota Press, 2014.

Tuana, Nancy. "Viscous Porosity: Witnessing Katrina." In *Material Feminisms*, edited by Stacy Alaimo and Susan J. Hekman, 188–213. Bloomington: Indiana University Press, 2008.

Viveiros de Castro, Eduardo. "Perspectival Anthropology and the Method of Controlled Equivocation." *Tipití* 2, no. 1 (2004): 3–20.

SCREENING THE PLURIVERSE

10

Human Rights at the End of the World

Patricio Guzmán and the "Imperative to Re-imagine the Planet"

FERNANDO J. ROSENBERG

In his magnum opus *Altazor*, a narrative poem set mostly in the cosmos where the titular protagonist is swept up by the winds of history, Chilean poet Vicente Huidobro writes: "And I can feel a telescope pointed at me like a revolver."[1] Read as an impulse to map out emerging global trends in the fallout from World War I,[2] Huidobro seems to indicate with a sense of vanguardist urgency the need to supplement the celebrated surface of global flows with a sensibility to depths and heights where the war was also deployed. A telescope appears as a threat as long distances collapse too close to an objectified body that becomes petrified by a powerful technological gaze. Huidobro's verse rehearses the modern trope of the weaponized camera, as technologies of image capturing are often paired to those of distant killing, in a genealogy reaching a contemporary situation that documentarian Harun Farocki described as "cameras circling the world to make it superfluous"—telescopes fused with cameras now detached from the earthly ground, which rather than threatening individual bodies make whole worlds irrelevant.[3]

Following Hannah Arendt, the so-called "conquest of space" realizes the detachment from both human-centered viewpoints and humanistic concerns that is proper to twentieth-century science at least since Einstein.[4] This view from nowhere, the ideal observer "poised freely in space" very much like Huidobro's Altazor, is science's true "Archimedean point"; which "technicians," according to Arendt, are tasked with bringing "down to earth."[5] Farocki's insight regarding a present condition envelops filmmaking within technologies of global positioning and satellite imaging in a weaponized movement back to earth, which is clearly one possible development of modern science's break away from anthropocentric perspectives.[6] I show in this chapter a different possibility advanced by Chilean filmmaker Patricio Guzmán in the first two installments of his geographical trilogy, *Nostalgia de la luz* (*Nostalgia for the Light*, 2010) and *El botón de nácar* (*The Pearl Button*, 2015), which was followed by *La cordillera de los sueños* (*The Cordillera of Dreams*, 2019).[7] The first two films of the trilogy (on which I base my argument) trace a continuity from colonial management of space that entailed the displacement and extermination of Indigenous populations, to the disposal of the bodies deep in the Chilean desert of the Pacific Ocean by the Chilean state during Pinochet's dictatorship, in order to make them "disappear." The reiteration of founding violence rendered the world superfluous, as the crushing and flattening of worldviews and alternative economies in favor of the instrumentalization of space and life matter have been essential operations in the constitution of colonial and postcolonial modernity. But, contrary to Farocki's statement, Guzmán's documentaries engage technologies of image capturing, including satellite images, at the level of its visual presentation and narrative reflection, to compose pictures of the world that point to a continuum between organic and nonorganic matter, between the human and the nonhuman, thus decentering anthropocentric perspectives but in order to repair and reimagine life in the planet.[8]

By renewing a sensitivity to nonhuman worlds and incorporating non-Western epistemes and poetics that either defy logocentric perspectives or push them past their limitations, Guzmán's latest work responds to what I call, borrowing from cultural critic Gayatri Spivak, the "imperative to re-imagine the planet."[9] Although none of the variables associated with a planetary emergency (such as climate change, toxicity, ocean acidification, habitat loss and rapid extinction) is taken into explicit account, I submit that they respond to a paradigm change propelled by this emergency and haunted by its implications. Guzmán's trajectory, culminating in these films, turns from the human rights abuses of Pinochet's regime (the overriding concern of his previous films) to an attention to the environmental assumptions of modernity, to which both the notions of humanity and rights are foundational. I find Spivak's phrase compelling for conceptualizing these documentaries. An "imperative" speaks of a responsibility, but it also implies a mandate, and therefore an authority (also assumed in the legal construct of human rights). Second, the idea of reimagining highlights the role of an imagination that is both aesthetic and scientific, forging new ways to conceive human habitation. And third, as we will see, "the planet" suggests a level of estrangement from the more commonly conjured-up imagination of the world (of human habitation) and the globe ("globalization" glorifying the sphere of communication and exchange), thus taking, I would suggest, the universalistic appeal of human rights to a different level and imbuing it with a materialistic concern, with the matter of life. Engaging with the planet gestures toward matters that are simultaneously more alien and more intimate to the "universal human."[10]

Before I examine these documentaries, it is important to briefly introduce relevant aspects of Guzmán's trajectory. The 1973 military coup against democratically elected socialist president Salvador Allende occupies an inaugural place, as does his concern with the social process in the dictatorship's aftermath through the 1990s. His seminal film from the 1970s, *La Batalla de Chile* (*The Battle of Chile*, 1975), records with revolutionary urgency the popular support and violent opposition that Allende's government confronted in its attempt to create democratic socialism without dismantling traditional state institutions.[11] The first part of the film, titled the "La insurrección de la burguesía" ("Insurrection of the Bourgeoisie"), famously opens with footage of the end of this process: the government palace burning under air bombardment, marking the termination of the history in the making that the small film crew, guerrilla style, had set out to depict. It ends with footage recovered from the camera of a cameraman filmed as he was shot to death—the revelatory power of the camera defeated in its duel against the gun—by a military squad in the streets of Santiago, days before the air strike. What these two moving images incidentally depict is the closure, at the national level, of narrative strategies of an era of political films that relied on the power of denunciation, direct testimony, and witnessing. Guzmán's later films *Memoria obstinada* (*Obstinate Memory*, 1997)[12] and *El caso Pinochet* (*The Pinochet Case*, 2001)[13] reopened these possibilities, grounded now in the pivotal political strategies of human rights as a discourse that legitimized the transition to democratic governance. Testimony and witnessing are rearticulated in the project of collective memory and judicial prosecutions against former officials who committed human rights abuses. If these films signal the end of an era of political filmmaking of the 1960s and 1970s, they also accompany the rise of human rights activism, borrowing from judicial discourse its language, logic, and sense of process.[14]

Notions of rights, of the universal human, and of nature are inextricably enmeshed at the inception of the modern/colonial world.[15] When Brazilian avant-gardist cultural critic Oswald de Andrade famously affirmed in 1928 that "Without us, Europe wouldn't even have its meager declaration of the rights of man,"[16] he not only inverts the colonial mapping, but points to the extraction of labor and resources as the cornerstone of European worldmaking. Whereas the European idea of rights originated in the dissemination of entitlements beyond the noble class, the rights of Indigenous inhabitants of the Americas were conceptualized as "natural rights" endowed by God, warrantor of the order of an immutable Nature, to all humanity—thus sealing the right to conquest by rendering the whole world ecumenical. While traces of this "inalienable" human Nature are latent in the modern idea of "dignity" central to the human rights ethos, the "natural" condition of nonhuman nature has lost its immanence, its immutability, its eternal and transcendental status. Human rights partake of the modern ideal of the infinite expansive potential of humans realized in unbounded freedom—an ideal that is not only resource intensive but also has been historically tied to forms of coloniality or, more precisely, to destroying worlds for the extraction of value. The noble ideal that the 1948 Declaration articulates as "social progress and better standards of life in larger freedom"[17] might be inextricably indebted to the assumption of an "ever-expandable frontier of new land or resources . . . [an] assumption, long disguised by the free gift of fossil fuels," as Timothy Clark has expressed.[18] Needless to say, the transcendental assumption of a "free gift" for humanity occludes the fact that both human and environmental costs have been always unevenly distributed. Contemporary concern for the nonhuman as a supplement to the human rights narrative (e.g., animal rights, rights of natural entities) cannot leave the idea of humanity unchanged, as it registers our own dependence on the web of life that had been obscured by dreams of sovereign mastery of an externalized "nature," by the abstraction of universal humanism, and by the disembodied idealism of the cosmopolitan ethos.

Guzmán's documentaries reassert the imperative contained in human rights and social memory paradigms now articulated with the effort to re-imagine the planet. The dictatorship and its aftermath of confronting the trauma of the disappeared continue to be central to the trilogy, but testimony, mourning, and memory are now not only arranged into new ensembles, or called to perform a different task, but also disseminated through nonhuman worlds. These films are reflections on specific territories: the Atacama desert in *Nostalgia*, the ocean and the archipelagos of the southern Chilean coast in *Pearl Button*, and the Andean mountain range in the last installment of the trilogy *The Cordillera of Dreams*. While these geographies are integral parts of

Chilean national imaginary and have been spaces of colonial exploration and transnational capital since its inception,[19] they also have been, as Elizabeth DeLoughrey points out, "extraterritorial spaces that render an anticipation of the 'ends of earth.'"[20] These spaces have haunted the colonial imagination by challenging its ambition of dominance, as nature was conceived as both radically other and yet entirely at the colonizer's disposal. Following DeLoughrey, sea-level rise makes "the largest space on earth . . . suddenly not so external and alien to human experience," as the warming climate and deforestation bring the desert closer.[21] By introducing a reflective, meditative treatment of different elements of the Chilean landscape that suggest a sense of the "ends of earth" (spaces beyond human reach or mastery), Guzmán appeals to our collective experience of a crisis that pushes the human closer to the planetary. However, these films reframe this contemporary sensibility by aligning it with the threshold between life, survival, and death, common to both the first peoples of the Americas and the disappeared of the dictatorships (some of whose bodies were buried or sunk, discarded into the ocean or the desert), suggesting an intimate relation between the memory and vestiges of these experiences and the imperative to re-imagine the planet.

Nostalgia for the Light revolves around the unlikely convergence in the desert of a quasi-geological juxtaposition of temporal layers. A landscape dotted with astronomical radars coexists with well-preserved pre-Columbian inscriptions and mummies. Concentration camps for political prisoners recycle barracks built for miners and salt-field workers. The afterlife of this infrastructure left behind by Chile's main extractive commodities that officiated as points of entry into world capitalism also coexists with traces of mass graves for the dictatorship's disappeared (whose remains were later scattered in the desert to further erase any evidence). We are also introduced to female relatives of the disappeared, known as *las mujeres de Calama* (an enclave for the mining industry, the city of Calama neighbored a secret detention camp during the dictatorship), who have not relinquished the search for bone fragments in the open desert.[22] Whereas in *La batalla de Chile* Atacama had appeared as mere background, as a test ground for the struggling socialist project to win the support of miners (of Chuquicamata and El Teniente open pit mega mining operations, as essential for the economy and national imaginary as for the construction of a new working-class consciousness), no political or economic value is extracted in *Nostalgia*. Rather, the focus is on what survives or endures harsh desert conditions against all odds. The experience of observing the starry sky is a main narrative element—an activity not exclusive to astronomers, but taken up by political prisoners confined to the detention camp through makeshift telescopes, along with long-extinct Indigenous peoples with the naked eye, all encompassed in a long history of studying the cosmos. The stars, as an astronomer interviewed in the film asserts, share their chemical composition with bones, so the film establishes a parallel between astronomers and archeologists, political prisoners and relatives of the disappeared, all united in the search for material traces in the sky and in the soil. The camera eye focuses on the barren land, on the sky above, and on the astronomical observatory connecting both—intimately connecting the cosmos with bodily remains both human and nonhuman, distancing from the world to make it matter again, reverting Farocki's dictum.

Shifting focus from the desert's dry soil and atmosphere to water, from constellations to archipelagos, *The Pearl Button* suggests different but parallel intersections. The islands of the southern Pacific coast that remained largely unexplored and uncharted until the beginning of the nineteenth century were home to Indigenous peoples until they were brutally displaced, massacred, and hunted down by settler violence at the foundation of modern Chile.[23] The film includes archival photography and moving images of Indigenous people (Selk'nam and Kawésqar) taken by late nineteenth- and early twentieth-century travelers—when cameras arrived along with the guns that disseminated and exterminated them.[24] Guzmán interviews two Kawésqar descendants, a man and a woman currently inhabiting their ancestral land- and water-scape, who, while giving accounts of the extinct social world of their childhood, continue some of their practices and language. The film also narrates the story of an Indigenous person whom the Europeans christened Jimmy Button, as he was lured or perhaps exchanged for pearl buttons to cross the ocean to England—only to be brought back to his native islands years later, a person no longer belonging to any social world. The button is the magic token in an inaugural colonial encounter in which life and whole biomes are considered extractable and transportable,[25] while the violence of forced exchange is concealed behind the pure enchantment of the commodity.

While recalling the Indigenous experiences of the end of their world, the film recasts more recent chapters of social memory, as the Pacific Ocean was also a site of disappearance of bodies thrown either dead or unconscious from helicopters, wrapped with a piece of recycled rail track to prevent its resurfacing. The discarded iron rail track that had been forged for the advancement of the nation in neocolonial capitalism (based on the extraction of salt, nitrogen, and copper, mostly from mines and fields of the Atacama desert) was later repurposed by the dictatorship to this end.

Taking up a forensic narrative mode, the film examines one case of this sinister practice through a body that reached the shore years after it was disappeared—identified as the remains of Marta Ugarte—which opened an investigation into the state's criminal procedures during Pinochet's regime.

In 2004, a judicial process ordered that the remaining rail tracks be resurfaced as evidence, and the film displays this evidence on-screen. While a central purpose of recovering the remains for the human rights agenda is to achieve recognition of the crime and uncover the identity of the victim, Guzmán's voice-over, however, suggests a dissolution of the legal person into a different kind of material agency: "here are the secrets that the bodies left in the rails before they melted into water, taking up the shape of the ocean." These "secrets" are materialized in a white button, which is found inserted into the rusted rail track as the most improbable remainder of human existence, attached to a piece of wearable fabric and now to the rail. But unveiling this secret doesn't restitute the body or its name; rather, what appears is the inhuman becoming of the human (realized in death but anticipated by the body as its own ecosystem of which the human is estranged) that transcends the inhumanity of genocide and oblivion. Whereas the dictatorship repurposed material leftovers of former economic exploits—rail tracks and workers' barracks—as instruments of extermination, Guzmán highlights a different dynamic by which materials degrade and aggregate, guided by other principles and at a different pace, dislodging human agendas, albeit unleashing a vital cycle of regeneration.

The fortuitous encounter of this hybrid object—the corroded metal covered with organic sea matter and salt, a nacre button encrusted on the surface—does not recover meaning. The film's narrative doesn't comply with the imagination of a poetic justice, which, commanded by a providential force, would promise the restoration of human sovereignty and dignity. The dignified human of human rights presumably transcends matter and biology because there is always something "'proper to man' grounding human exceptionalism: "the species' precious private property . . . : language, labor, law, desire; time, world, death. Culture. History. Future."[26] But matter is of the essence here. Pearl buttons are technically made of nacre, the composite substance of organic origin from which the pearl is formed, hinting at a porous boundary between the organic and the inorganic, the biological and the mineral, life and nonlife.[27] If, as Guzmán's narration states, "both buttons tell the same story, a history of extermination," what this afterlife of material history encapsulates is the exhaustion of a particular imagination of the planet: that which figured the ocean and the desert as places outside history, places to be crossed and left behind, where history's leftovers and outcasts, its detritus, can be permanently cast away. As the camera fixates on this strange, unclassifiable compound, we are invited to broaden the significance of this piece of evidence beyond the judicial. A material witness to the disappearance during the dictatorship and to the genocide that pushed the Indigenous to annihilation, it also brings with it an alternative time and space, one that is neither outside history nor limited to its human scale: the depth of the sea, previously imagined as "nature"—forever neutral and unchanging, bottomless and mute, a place where remains could be safely expelled.

Rather than following a clear presentation of evidence and line of argumentation, these documentaries are composed as nonhierarchical aggregates of mutually determining, hybrid discourses and matter, inspired perhaps by the nonlinear, relational order of galaxies and archipelagos. Whereas the scale shifts from the infinite to the infinitesimal, from the telescopic to the microscopic, the camera fixates on hybrid objects and artifacts, presenting entities that sit at the border of the organic and the mineral, the biological and astrological, the technological and mythical. Complementarily, the order of discourse also moves between the forensic, the ethnographic, the historic, and the cosmological, inviting the viewer to a poetic reassemblage of discursive authorities. *The Pearl Button* opens with the image of a piece of quartz that, as Guzmán's voice-over explains, holds in its interior a drop of water—an image of interconnectivity in what is imagined as indistinct, continuous matter: a fertilization of the tectonic. The mineral world has served as a figuration of the inert, indistinct, eternal, indifferent, albeit foundational ground upon which civilization builds its transcendental spirit (from tools to architecture to energy) and seals its finality (ruins and tombs). "Stones are the partners with which we build the epistemological structures that may topple upon us," as Jeffrey Cohen suggests.[28] But this geological block doesn't lend itself easily to the classic allegory of history and its ruins; rather, it suggests an unaccustomed proximity between matter and bios, life and nonlife. The final image of *The Pearl Button* of a recently discovered quasar containing "one hundred and twenty times the quantity of water in our oceans" dissolves into the image of a paddle breaking the surface of water, propelling a canoe—the memory of Indigenous people who inhabited the archipelagos. This dissolution underscores the intimacy of the cosmic and the human, the cross-fertilization of organic and inorganic matter, the vast and the intimate. It encounters memory inscribed in both the resilience of the mineral and the fluidity of water, thus surviving against the will to forget and submerge it deep into a past immemorial.

To recapitulate, on one level these films move beyond the horizon of the forensic and memorialistic agenda of human rights in order to touch on the question of a postcolonial modernity by which the state is aligned with the colonial takeover of the Americas. In the expanded horizon of memory at which Guzmán hints, the category of the disappeared entails not only disposable life throughout colonial and postcolonial modernity, but also forms of inhabiting the world that have been actively disappeared. I am not speaking of a so-called worldview, which suggests a rather subjective, idiosyncratic "cultural" character independent of a perennial, immutable world outside, but of worlds themselves—economies of particular life-forms and experience—that have ended recurrently, as the imperial, globalist, capitalist forces were propelled by the idea of transportability of life-forms. The expanded horizon assumed by Guzmán's films corresponds to the increased visibility of Indigenous activism in Chile and elsewhere (not acknowledged by Guzmán explicitly) that has unleashed violent reactions from the state, along with the exhaustion of a purely oppositional and ultimately liberal notion of human rights (opposing totalitarianism, demanding civil freedoms) that guided transitions to democracy throughout the 1990s in various Latin American countries. A strong notion of rights (simultaneously cultural, linguistic, economic, and "rights of nature") inextricably linked to practices of inhabiting a territory, away from modes of possession that were foundational for the national project, has presented a challenge to the world envisioned by liberal notions of human rights.

On a different level, this historical *longue durée*, its political engendering of new subjects and visibilities, is paired with phenomena of cosmological implications that render human scale negligible. Partaking in the imperative to re-imagine the planet, in an effort to delink human rights discourse from its alliance with the autonomous subject of liberalism (the basis for Karl Marx's critique of human rights),[29] as well as from anthropocentrism, these films introduce a planetary perspective that regards water and calcium as central elements of life with cosmic origins. What appeared as the long historical duration of modernity traced back to colonial forms of violence becomes incommensurable with cosmic time, as the life/nonlife divide is regarded from the viewpoint of astrophysics, encompassing but reaching vastly beyond human-centered paradigms. A move with profound ethical implications, for if drowned bodies are lyrically conflated with the water composition of all biological entities, and bones buried in mass graves are reduced to the starry phosphorescence of their chemical elements, the metaphysical ground by which the expanded idea of human rights (which recognizes the atrocities of the dictatorship in continuity with colonial violence) dignifies the person above all other organic and nonorganic existences might also dissolve like stardust. What politics is conceivable when human bones are read within the same scale as minerals, "planetary accidents rather than global agents"?[30] In what forum might evidence conceived at such an unimaginable scale have any relationship to any form of world justice? How to think of (post?) human rights, then, when any conception of the integrity and dignity of the human might be both sustained in exploitative and colonial practices and crushed by planetary time-space?

I read this trajectory from human rights' discourse to planetary concerns as both problematic and compelling. Rearticulating the place of Indigenous peoples in the constitution of modernity, the films do not appeal to the nostalgia tokenized by the iconic "ecological indian"[31] as the subject embodying a repository of environmental practices—a ready-made elegiac narrative that the film *Avatar* (James Cameron, 2009) revived for the mainstream, as did *El abrazo de la serpiente* (*The Embrace of the Serpent*, Ciro Guerra, 2015) for the arthouse foreign film audience.[32] One reason environmental and Indigenous right claims are so entangled is that the social memory on which human rights claims traditionally have been grounded is generally conceived within the limits of a national community.[33] Indigenous memories, which from Western historiography appear retrospectively to be prenational or transnational, demand a radical critique of national history. Whereas Indigenous memories are intimately embedded in the biome, the notion of human freedom assumed both by human rights and modern nation-states is predicated on sovereignty and detachment, thus complicit with the colonization of "nature" understood as a providential, inexhaustible, albeit malleable resource. An imperative to re-imagine the planet goes hand-in-hand with the commitment to situate memory in time and space, an operation not exhausted by a local recovery of traditions that is easily recaptured by the national or global order.

At the end of *Nostalgia*, Guzmán's narrative voice explores an alternative by suggesting that "memory has gravitational force." In what follows, I unpack and deepen this metaphor, as I believe it is not only a metaphor. Both intimate and alien, memory blurs the distance between mind and world; its force aggregates unexpected elements, making them part of the same world, exerting on them the imperative to coexist. Rather than proposing the Indigenous as a master of atavistic memory, which might lead us along the path of a conservative and nostalgic essentialism, Guzmán develops a political articulation linking memory and planetarity.

In *Nostalgia*, astronomer Gaspar Galaz confesses that when he tries to imagine himself in the predicament of the relatives of the disappeared, the women of Calama searching for pieces of bone scattered by the military across the Atacama Desert, he pictures himself looking at the sky through the telescope, as if searching there for someone beloved. In what sense are the desert and the cosmos equally infinite, equally unknown, equally awe provoking and terrifying? These spaces are mutually incommensurable, so obviously incomparable in dimension, but the search for something alien yet so intimate, suggests the astronomer, would be equally anguishing—anguish being the modern response to this human confrontation of the immensely unknown, the space vacated by the gods, the opening where reason confronts its limitations. The astronomer's analogy, in dialogue with the film's treatment of the common matter of stars and bones, shows that this commonality is not proposed only as redemptive sublimation or compensatory poetic correspondence. It responds to the imperative of thinking about the disappeared on a planetary scale by making the human and the nonhuman collapse in our present end of the world, endowing planetary visions with an intimate, obstinately political affect.[34]

In a following sequence, a relative of a disappeared confesses that she dreams of a telescope that would look down at the earth, searching and finding bones in the desert: "to be able to thank the stars that we found them. . . . I can only dream." We might inscribe these painful dreams of hope within a genealogy of "inverted astronomy," which channels the desire to see and be seen from outer space, a desire that arguably gave way to ancient examples of what we would call "land art."[35] Walter Benjamin traced the Western genealogy of this vision from above, adding an important element manifest in its modern aftermath: "Mankind, which in Homer's time was an object of contemplation for the Olympian gods, now is one for itself. Its self-alienation has reached such a degree that it can experience its own destruction as an aesthetic pleasure of the first order."[36] In the midst of widespread apocalyptic anxieties foretold as the end of nature, the end of humanity, or both, the acceleration of capitalistic production and its global extermination of life-forms is presented as inevitable, or perceived as impossible to stop, even when the destruction that these forces bring about is increasingly evident. A sense of never-ending mourning, lived in the present but also felt in the imagination of possible futures, is supplemented by consumption jouissance. While these landscapes that Guzmán presents are imbued with a sense of the "end of earth," the inscription of the disappeared as an afterlife persisting in conditions that are perceived as inhabitable is a constant reminder of memory's gravitational force—aggregating life with the inorganic against the assurance of destruction.

Satellite or space travel images of planet earth, among other astronomical images, figure prominently in both *Nostalgia* and *The Pearl Button*, a visual archive that goes back to the iconic Blue Marble and Earthrise images, infinitely reproduced since they were first captured by the 1968 and 1972 Apollo missions. "Those two flights," geographer Dennis Cosgrove affirms, "left a pair of photographs of the globe that have subsequently achieved iconic status . . . throughout their capacity to incorporate and frame the Western inheritance of global meanings, from the Ciceronian somnium and Senecan moral reflection, through Christian discourse of mission and redemption, to ideals of unity and harmony."[37] The marvelously harmonic spell, as well as the notion of an object easily graspable to human comprehension, might certainly vanish upon close examination. What Cosgrove refers to as the "iconic status" of these pervasive images might be a form of detachment, a defense against planetary doom, considering that the development of planetary science that the Apollo missions helped advance was enmeshed with militaristic goals.[38] What modes of subjectivity are forged, what worlds generated with the visual technologies that are now freely available on Google Earth, when the vast and intimate web of life that sustains humanity is now perceived as the casualty, not just of war but of the normal state of affairs? This imagery opens up the surface of the earth, the depth of the ocean, and the atmosphere as potential "theaters of operation"—telescopes both pointing at us like guns and rendering the world superfluous, to come back to Huidobro's quote, because the destruction of the biosphere is the always unaccounted-for casualty of war. These layers are flattened when mobilized in support of comforting ideologies from corporate globalism to depoliticized ecological platitudes.

Are these world pictures intrinsic to technologies of detachment and planetary denial, to extraction and destruction? Is there perhaps, as the astronomer and Calama woman's painful hope seems to suggest, a way of engendering a planetary sensitivity to break through the glossy, rounded perfection of the view from nowhere? Memory's gravitational force, these films suggest, pulls toward something both intimate and inhuman. In a couple of sequences in which the montage produces a rearrangement of scale, *Nostalgia* pairs the image of the planet with a close-up of the surface of bones resembling minerals or vast topographies. Likewise, a collection of stones sculpted by Indigenous peoples is presented in *The Pearl* as analogous to planetary systems. The human-centered view is displaced while complemented by image-capturing technologies to suggest a capacity to grasp the planet as an entity that stands opposite to the glossy idealism of a Christmas tree decoration or the "blue marble"—the traditional images with which the Apollo pictures were first compared.[39] Complementarily, the desire expressed as a dream by the relative of the disappeared to visualize the scattered bones in the desert is another way of defamiliarizing, while making personal, disturbing, and painful, the world-picture and its projected illusion of rounded, self-sustaining perfection. *Nostalgia* disrupts the illusory transparency of the "blue marble" by simply zooming in on the Atacama Desert, visible as a brown stain in satellite imagery because of its absolute lack of atmospheric humidity. This coloration prompts Guzmán's comparison of the desert to the surface of Mars, the classic symbol of planetary alterity, but the film also endows this barren, inhuman landscape with intimacy—because the telescope, going back to the survivor's dream, might find there what is most dear, that piece of bone—the memory—that cannot be surrendered.

By the end of *The Pearl Button*, Guzmán presents his own dream, this time of a planet of water where the Indigenous inhabitants of the South Pacific, who used to cross the waters guided by the sky and stars above, still exist, enjoying refugee status ("un planeta de asilo")—and the film superimposes a moving canoe on water as a kind of ghostly appearance. This planet and other "celestial bodies" are no longer objects for distant contemplation or study, or radiant confirmations of an omnipotent dream of conquest and extraction, but specific entities where an ethics of preservation and regeneration of forms of life might be exercised, as human existence is inextricably tied to its material reality. Justice is reclaimed as a way to inhabit the planet, to read its traces, to care for its entities, and to imagine its future.

However, the imagination of a parallel planet where Indigenous people found refuge also points to the fact that Indigenous memories are memories of dis-location. They are experiences of the end of their world or, more accurately, of the recurrent ends of their worlds, the experience of the end reimagined from the end of the world where they have been confined to survive after their world has been turned upside-down, after "the eclipse of their world" (*Pearl Button*). There is a hint of this experience of living after the end, when Guzmán asks three Kawésqar speakers for versions of certain Spanish words. They translate for him; some of the words are borrowed from Spanish, showing linguistic hybridity and porosity; some have no translation (the words for "police" and "God"), pointing in the opposite direction of language as a particular world. Guzmán asks this word-by-word, which is the worst way to comprehend a language, perhaps because there is no true language left, just lone speakers of single words—words that don't make a world but are the remnants of a world both destroyed and persistent. He finally asks Kawésqar speaker Gabriela to narrate a 1,000-kilometer canoe trip that she embarked on with her family when she was a child. The camera moves on a traveling shot from a canoe through the land and waterscape, while Gabriela's narration is played on voice-over. The soundscape juxtaposes water and Kawésqar speech, as a memory that exceeds human agency.

The film also features anthropologist Claudio Mercado, who, after explaining that all matter—earth, air, cosmos—is ultimately water, and how water can be listened to, rehearses for the camera "the language of water" as expressed through his own voice, or as it passes through his body, as both sound and water are trans-corporeal. These segments of intense visual and sound sensitivity perform a continuity from sound to song to language to discourse, but not as partitioned and ordered by abstract, dematerialized reason. Thought itself might be comparable to water, both infinitely malleable, Guzmán affirms at one point. The film points to a linkage between the disappearance of a language and its distinctive worlds: a persistent regeneration after the end, an endless transformation.

Water is the matter with which *The Pearl Button* imagines a different form of inscription covering the planet, the channel by which the experience of displacement and oblivion turns into one of continuous becoming. Another scene focuses on a man, Martín Calderón, working on the maintenance of his canoe, which is sitting inside a building. He says he misses the time when his people, the Kawésqar, were able to "occupy" the ocean, suggesting the possibility of an ocean as habitation. The navy forbids them from continuing these practices today because, "They are not used to seeing such a small boat. They protect us, but not really." He identifies with this formulation the predicament of a protective, rather than repressive, state force, now committed to the preservation of life as long as it can separate it from the ecology where this existence flourishes. By literally grounding the Kawésqar, the navy men protect a paradigm that relies on mastery and detachment as the only way to relate to the so-called environment. He speaks of his childhood memories, of navigating Cape Horn with his father and of traversing the rough ocean during bad weather, pointing out that despite some setbacks, "we arrived well"; further explaining the navigation technique by which the boat is propelled by very short paddles against strong currents. Despite this, "se avanza" [one moves forward], he clarifies, as if to calm the anxieties of his interlocutor, Guzmán, who keeps asking questions. When confronted with the immensity of oceanic flows, the canoe doesn't shrink; it frames human senses in consonance with the flow of water. "We Chileans have lost this intimacy with the sea," Guzmán's narrative affirms.

Navigation stories do not acquire the accustomed epic tone of Man conquering immensity, but rather intimacy and habitation frame these relations. At the end of the sequence, as Guzmán explains that by the end of the nineteenth century there were three hundred canoes with approximately eight thousand people "moving around this immense archipelago," we are presented with the image of this man fixing a miniaturized version of this kind of canoe. This illustrates how scales are collapsed throughout Guzman's films: the navy ships set against the canoes, paddling in the face of the ocean's overpowering current, a final image of a man working on his miniatures in quiet domesticity next to the full-scale canoe, a home within a home, as boats used to double as a form of dwelling. There is no clarification regarding the nature of these crafts: perhaps they are collectibles, decorations, or tourist souvenirs.[40] Or perhaps, through a practice of substitution, they are transitional objects to work through the disappearance of the world being replaced by another in which matter is kept at a safe distance, where belonging to the world gives way to an adversarial relationship.

Another sequence of *The Pearl Button* presents an artifact created by Chilean artist Emma Malig, which Guzmán describes as a Chilean map united rather than divided into separate regions, as school maps dissect such a long and narrow territory for pedagogic absorption. The map as a work of art is unfolded as an epiphany, the viewer invited to partake in the revelation of seeing the country as a whole. Perhaps the promised wholeness of the landmass is anticlimactic in a film that insists on relationships, archipelagos, multilayered geophysical formations, aquatic habitations and transhistorical connections. But what unfolds is fragile; it takes a while to get it out of storage, to clean and position it in the right place. Made of wood paper, it cracks easily, and in its detachment, it could well be an island. Displayed on the floor of a long room, it is a very large scale for a map, but the power of its self-standing wholeness appears by the same token isolated and helpless, like the skin shed by an animal.

When displaying this fragile map, Guzmán himself explores practices of care and stewardship thematized in the films—the Kawésqar, the astronomers and archeologists, the relatives of the disappeared, all caring and curating objects close and distant in time and space. But mainly these subjects are being cared for in this relationship between human and matter, they themselves defined by the matter of their care.[41]

These film segments suggest that the representational challenge of re-imagining the planet goes beyond the difficulty of representing deep time and planetary scale while also attending to history both global and local at a human scale, as some influential environmental criticism has suggested. It is often impossible to trace and map the persistent and in many cases invisible "slow violences" enacted against environments.[42] To do so, we must eschew frames and scales prevalent in our modern conception of culture, history, and politics, as this violence originates in actors and impacts realities that are both vastly disseminated across time and space, and intimate, inside our bodies. Mapping the overarching catastrophe that is the silent mass extinction afflicting our present, thinking through and acting on its multidimensional causes—a difficult arrangement of the macro- and the microscopic, of frameworks intersecting cosmic time-space with histories on the ground—means mobilizing the imagination, affecting common notions of political spaces and historical times. Engaging this latent, interpersonal, and intermaterial geography, which only appears as negative and exceptional (in cases of manifest environmental degradation, toxicity, contagion across species and throughout vast distances), is a necessary component in the sensibility that might bring about a transformative political imagination.

Let me place this ethic of care suggested by Guzmán's films in dialogue with Bruno Latour's argument (in line with previously quoted observations by Arendt and Benjamin) that the moderns are the people who live after the apocalypse because their existence assumes that they have lost the world. Accordingly, there is in the Western resident "of the lovely global space of nowhere" a drive to leave its earthbound beings behind,[43] to leave behind "the world of the worldless people" as the ultimate condition for emancipating humanity from matter and biology, to ascend and look at the planet from a distance, to transcend the force of our attachments, of physical gravity.[44] Not surprisingly, the moderns have been keenly aware of rapid changes in climate patterns, accelerating biological extinction, loss of landscape due to mass-scale extraction, all punctuated by the perception of a world coming to an end that strikes public consciousness at times of catastrophic but rapidly forgotten events, one disaster after another managed for capital gains. The lack of care, negligence, and active denial are not an epiphenomenon of the modern enterprise but rather are at the heart of the matter. When Benjamin suggested that humanity was "experiencing its own destruction as aesthetic pleasure of the first order," he hinted that catastrophe might actually be desired with exultant exuberance as the consummation of the modern project.[45] Global crisis management for profit has become a favorite game of flexible capital accumulation, as disaster privatizes safety and security while yielding positive economic indicators by redistributing wealth upward. It is doubtful that the sheer force of catastrophe in and of itself would produce an imperative to imagine an alternative; moreover, there is a libidinal charge as suggested by Benjamin, invested (albeit unevenly distributed throughout "humanity") in experiencing disaster. So we shouldn't be surprised if the metaphysics of collective awakening so attractive to popular culture and hoped for by the environmentally aware after each catastrophic climate or other "natural" event (such as a pandemic) rarely gives way to the expected results—political insight, a shift in consciousness or consumer behavior, and so forth. This is because our modernity assumes a world that has already ended, because being, or just desiring to be, among the most privileged of the moderns means having left behind any attachment and having the right to render the planet superfluous.

I have hinted at two different endings of the world. One end is that of the people whose ways of life have been disappeared, and whose present is composed of practices of care, because survival depends on this exercise. The other is the end of the moderns, whose time was inaugurated by an act of colonization, extraction, and devaluation of the planet. The first end of the world confronts the present with an imperative to re-imagine the planet, as survival depends on a sense of continuity and regeneration, while the latter is compelled to neglect this task, as the availability of the earth as resource depends on this denial. The material wreckage of colonial and postcolonial disappearance is registered in Guzmán's films to invoke the legacy of survival, of living after the end of the world, of becoming undone and becoming something other,[46] thus articulating a reimagination of the planet that is capable of attending to the catastrophe of the present.

Notes

1. Vicente Huidobro, *Altazor, or, a Voyage in a Parachute* (Saint Paul, MN: Graywolf Press, 1988), 15.

2. I developed this thesis in my book *The Avant-Garde and Geopolitics in Latin America* (Pittsburgh: University of Pittsburgh Press, 2006).

3. Harun Farocki and Thomas Elsaesser, "Making the World Superfluous: An Interview with Harun Farocki," in *Harun Farocki: Working on the Sight-Lines* (Amsterdam: Amsterdam University Press, 2004), 188–89.

4. Hannah Arendt, "The Conquest of Space and the Stature of Man," *The New Atlantis* 18 (Fall 2007): 49.

5. Arendt quotes Franz Kafka's short parable, which resonates with Huidobro and Farocki: "Man . . . found the Archimedean point, but he used it against himself; it seems that he was permitted to find it only under this condition." Arendt, 53; 49.

6. According to Arendt (ibid., 51), "The simple fact that physicists split the atom without any hesitations the very moment they knew how to do it, although they realized full well the enormous destructive potentialities of their operation, demonstrates that the scientist qua scientist does not even care about the survival of the human race on earth or, for that matter, about the survival of the planet itself."

7. *Nostalgia de la luz*, directed by Patricio Guzmán (2010; Atacama Productions); and *El botón de nácar*, directed by Patricio Guzmán (2015; Atacama Productions). *La cordillera de los sueños* (2019; Atacama Productions) closes the trilogy.

8. In consonance with the "turn" in the humanities toward material cultures and object-oriented ontologies, some of the studies on Guzmán's films take this analytical perspective. See David Martin-Jones, "Archival Landscapes and a Non-Anthropocentric 'Universe Memory' in *Nostalgia de la luz/Nostalgia for the Light* (2010)," *Third Text* 27, no. 6 (2013): 707–22.

9. Gayatri Spivak, *An Aesthetic Education in the Era of Globalization* (Cambridge, MA: Harvard University Press, 2012), 335–50.

10. Elizabeth DeLoughrey summarizes Spivak's position by pointing out, "'planetarity' is a mode of interpreting the world that does not reduce it to the homogenizing reach of globalization, including its military forms, and recognizes its uncanny difference." Elizabeth DeLoughrey, "Satellite Planetarity and the Ends of the Earth," *Public Culture* 26, no. 2 (2014): 264.

11. *La batalla de Chile: la lucha de un pueblo sin armas—The Battle of Chile: The Struggle of an Unarmed People*, directed by Patricio Guzmán (2009; New York: Icarus Films Home Video).

12. *Memoria obstinada*, directed by Patricio Guzmán (1997; Les Films d'Ici and the National Film Board of Canada).

13. *El caso Pinochet*, directed by Patricio Guzmán (2001; New York: First Run/Icarus Films).

14. I discuss the relevance of the subgenre of "judicial documentary" and its relation to human rights in chapter 5 of my book *After Human Rights. Literature, Visual Arts, and Film in Latin America, 1990–2010* (Pittsburgh: University of Pittsburgh Press, 2016).

15. See Walter Mignolo, "Who Speaks for the "Human" in Human Rights?," *Hispanic Issues* 5, no. 1 (Fall 2009): 7–24.

16. Oswald de Andrade, "Cannibalist Manifesto," trans. Lesly Bary, *Latin American Literary Review* 19, no. 38 (1991): 39.

17. "Universal Declaration of Human Rights," http://www.un.org/en/universal-declaration-human-rights/.

18. Timothy Clark, "Scale. Derangements of Scale," in *Telemorphosis: Theory in the Era of Climate Change*, vol. 1 (Ann Arbor, MI: Open Humanities Press, 2012).

19. For a reading that attends to the stages of capitalist exploitation, see J. Sebastián Figueroa, "Landscapes of Extraction and Memories of Extinction in Patricio Guzmán's *Nostalgia de la luz* and *El botón de nácar*," *Ecozona* 11, no. 1 (2020): 152–69.

20. DeLoughrey, "Satellite," 274.

21. Elizabeth DeLoughrey, "Submarine Futures of the Anthropocene," *Comparative Literature* 69, no. 1 (2017): 33.

22. Bones were scattered in the desert when the military, sensing that their time in power was coming to an end, dug up the mass graves that they themselves created.

23. According to Mateo Martinic, interest in the area spiked during the sixteenth to seventeenth centuries with the search for the legendary city of Caesars. The exact contours of the archipelago became clear only after a 1944–45 US aerial survey, to which satellite images later added more precision. Mateo Martinic Beros, *Archipiélago patagónico: la última frontera* (Punta Arenas: Ediciones de la Universidad de Magallanes, 2004).

24. The film's archival photography was taken by late nineteenth- early twentieth-century explorers such as Austrian ethnographer Martin Gusinde, Italian Salesian priest Alberto María de Agostini, US explorer Charles Wellington Furlong, and Swedish botanist Carl Johan Fredrik Skottsberg, among others. Also featured is a photograph by contemporary Chilean photographer Paz Errázuriz, who is the only one mentioned by Guzmán as having inspired his quest. These photos are compiled in Margarita Alvarado, ed., *Fueguinos: fotografías siglos XIX y XX: imágenes e imaginarios del fin del mundo* (Santiago, Chile: Pehuén, 2007).

25. James Jaehoon Lee and Joshua Beckelhimer, "Anthropocene and Empire: Discourse Networks of the Human Record," *PMLA* 135, no. 1 (2020): 110–29.

26. Déborah Danowski and Eduardo Viveiros de Castro, *The Ends of the World* (Cambridge: Polity Press, 2017), 65.

27. Geologists are divided regarding the classification of pearls as stone. "Admittedly, the definition of living is equivocal, and so is the definition of mineral: whether it ought to include noncrystalline substances like opal, obsidian, and native metals or substances derived from life forms like amber, pearl, and petroleum are matters for debate, about which many mineralogists hold strong opinions." Paul Gillen, "Notes on Mineral Evolution: Life, Sentience, and the Anthropocene," *Environmental Humanities* 8, no. 2 (2016): 222.

28. Jeffrey Jerome Cohen, *Stone: An Ecology of the Inhuman* (Minneapolis: University of Minnesota Press, 2015), 3.

29. Karl Marx, "On the Jewish Question," in *Early Writings* (New York: McGraw-Hill, 1964), 1–40.

30. Spivak, *Aesthetic*, 339.

31. Salma Monani, "Evoking Sympathy and Empathy: The Ecological Indian and Indigenous Eco-Activism," in *Moving Environments: Affect, Emotion, Ecology and Film*, ed. Alexa Weik von Mossner (Waterloo, ON: Wilfrid Laurier University Press, 2014), 225–47.

32. Ecocritical studies and ecologically conscious films are not immune to these kinds of primitivist, exoticizing projections, illusions, and simplifications.

33. Andreas Huyssen, "Natural Rights, Cultural Rights, and the Politics of Memory," *Hemispheric Institute e-misférica* 6, no. 2 (2009).

34. It is debatable whether "rights of nature" might be a framework for investing the planet and all living beings with political force, Guzmán's films do not propose something along this line. But it is relevant to mention that neighboring countries such as Ecuador and Bolivia have included provisions in their newly reformed constitutions (2008 and 2009, respectively) to endow rights to nature, which intersect with and follow the renewed visibility of Indigenous rights in the 1990s. While rights of nature are a recognition of a nonhuman world that is irrevocably entangled with human history and culture, nature cannot be neatly circumscribed to local enclaves, contained within previously delineated jurisdictions. The transterritorial aspect of environmental concerns opens the possibility for any assumedly "local" entity to make potentially planetary claims. This was the rationale behind the criminal case leveled against British Petroleum for the 2010 oil rink leak in the Gulf of Mexico—not in defense of users but in defense of the environment. See Paulo Tavares, "Nonhuman Rights," in *Forensis. The Architecture of Public Truth*, ed. Anselm Franke and Eyal Weizman (Berlin: Sternberg Press and Forensic Architecture, 2014), 553–72.

35. The phrase "inverted astronomy" is cited by DeLoughrey ("Satellite," 263) from Wolfgang Sachs, who quotes Peter Sloterdijk.

36. Walter Benjamin, "The Work of Art in the Age of Mechanical Reproduction," in *Illuminations. Essays and Reflections* (New York: Schocken Books, 1969), 242.

37. Dennis Cosgrove, *Apollo's Eye. A Cartographic Genealogy of the Earth in the Western Imagination* (Baltimore: Johns Hopkins University Press, 2001), 257.

38. Joseph Masco, "Terraforming Planet Earth," in *Global Ecologies and the Environmental Humanities: Postcolonial Approaches*, ed. Elizabeth DeLoughrey, Jill Didur, and Anthony Carrigan (New York: Routledge University Press, 2015), 309–32.

39. Wolfgang Sachs, *Planet Dialectics. Explorations in Environment and Development* (Halifax, Nova Scotia: Fernwood Publishing, 1999), 113.

40. The Wikipedia page about the Kawésqar, which redirects the search to the name "Alacalufe," features "An Alacaluf woman selling handicrafts to tourists in Villa Puerto Edén, Chile."

41. Joanna Zylinska discusses this paradox by proposing an ethic of care that adopts "some minimal principles, the first one of which is the recognition of the entangled positioning of the human in, or rather with, the universe and a uniquely human responsibility for that universe. That responsibility is also minimal, in the sense that it does not involve any pre-decided values and rules. It only carries an

injunction to mobilize the human faculties." *Minimal Ethics for the Anthropocene* (Ann Arbor, MI: Open Humanities Press, 2014), 32.

42. See Robert Nixon, *Slow Violence and the Environmentalism of the Poor* (Cambridge, MA: Harvard University Press, 2013).

43. Bruno Latour, *Facing Gaia: Eight Lectures on the New Climatic Regime* (Cambridge, UK: Polity Press, 2017), 166.

44. Danowski and de Castro, *Ends of the World*, 30.

45. Benjamin, "Work of Art," 242.

46. The phrase "becoming undone" comes from the title of Elizabeth Grosz's inspiring book *Becoming Undone: Darwinian Reflections on Life, Politics, and Art* (Durham: Duke University Press, 2011).

Work Cited

Alvarado, Margarita. *Fueguinos: fotografías siglos XIX y XX: imágenes e imaginarios del fin del mundo*. Santiago, Chile: Pehuén, 2007.
Andrade, Oswald de. "Cannibalist Manifesto." Trans. Lesly Bary. *Latin American Literary Review* 19, no. 38 (July–December 1991): 38–47.
Arendt, Hannah. "The Perplexities of the Rights of Man." In *The Portable Hannah Arendt*, 31–45. New York: Penguin, 2000.
———. "The Conquest of Space and the Stature of Man." *The New Atlantis. A Journal of Technology and Society* (Fall 2007): 43–55.
Benjamin, Walter. "The Work of Art in the Age of Mechanical Reproduction." In *Illuminations. Essays and Reflections*, 217–51. New York: Schocken Books, 1969.
Clark, Timothy. "Scale. Derangements of Scale" *Telemorphosis: Theory in the Era of Climate Change*. Vol. 1. Ann Arbor, MI: Open Humanities Press, 2012.
Cohen, Jeffrey Jerome. *Stone: An Ecology of the Inhuman*. Minneapolis: University of Minnesota Press, 2015.
Cosgrove, Dennis. *Apollo's Eye. A Cartographic Genealogy of the Earth in the Western Imagination*. Baltimore: Johns Hopkins University Press, 2001.
Danowski, Déborah, and Eduardo Viveiros de Castro. *The Ends of the World*. Cambridge, UK: Polity Press, 2017.
DeLoughrey, Elizabeth. "Submarine Futures of the Anthropocene." *Comparative Literature* 69, no. 1 (2017): 32–44.
———. "Satellite Planetarity and the Ends of the Earth." *Public Culture* 26, no. 2 (2014): 257–80.
Farocki, Harun, and Thomas Elsaesser. "Making the World Superfluous: An Interview with Harun Farocki." In *Harun Farocki: Working on the Sight-Lines*, 177–89. Amsterdam: Amsterdam University Press, 2004.
Figueroa, J. Sebastián. "Landscapes of Extraction and Memories of Extinction in Patricio Guzmán's *Nostalgia de la luz* and *El botón de nácar*." *Ecozona* 11, no. 1 (2020): 152–69.

Gillen, Paul. "Notes on Mineral Evolution: Life, Sentience, and the Anthropocene." *Environmental Humanities* 8, no. 2 (2016): 215–34.
Grosz, Elizabeth. *Becoming Undone: Darwinian Reflections on Life, Politics, and Art.* Durham: Duke University Press, 2011.
Guzmán, Patricio, dir. *Memoria obstinada.* 1997; Les Films d'Ici and the National Film Board of Canada.
———. *The Pinochet Case.* 2001; New York: First Run/Icarus Films.
———. *La batalla de Chile: la lucha de un pueblo sin armas = The Battle of Chile: The Struggle of an Unarmed People.* 2009; New York: Icarus Films Home Video.
———. *Nostalgia de la luz.* 2010; Atacama Production.
———. *El botón de nácar.* 2015; Atacama Productions.
Huidobro, Vicente. *Altazor, or, a Voyage in a Parachute.* St. Paul: Graywolf Press, 1988.
Huyssen, Andreas. "Natural Rights, Cultural Rights, and the Politics of Memory." *Hemispheric Institute e-misferica* 6, no. 2 (2009). http://hemisphericinstitute.org/hemi/en/e-misferica-62.
Latour, Bruno. *Facing Gaia: Eight Lectures on the New Climatic Regime.* Cambridge, UK: Polity Press, 2017.
Lee, James Jaehoon, and Joshua Beckelhimer. "Anthropocene and Empire: Discourse Networks of the Human Record." *PMLA* 135, no. 1 (2020): 110–29.
Martin-Jones, David. "Archival Landscapes and a Non-Anthropocentric 'Universe Memory' in *Nostalgia de la luz/ Nostalgia for the Light* (2010)." *Third Text* 27, no. 6 (2013): 707–22.
Martinic Beros, Mateo. *Archipiélago patagónico: la última frontera.* Punta Arenas: Ediciones de la Universidad de Magallanes, 2004.
Masco, Joseph. "Terraforming Planet Earth." In *Global Ecologies and the Environmental Humanities: Postcolonial Approaches*, edited by Elizabeth DeLoughrey, Jill Didur, and Anthony Carrigan, 309–32. New York: Routledge University Press, 2015.
Marx, Karl. "On the Jewish Question." In *Early Writings*, 1–40. New York: McGraw-Hill, 1964.
Mignolo, Walter. "Who Speaks for the 'Human' in Human Rights?" *Hispanic Issues* 5, no. 1 (Fall 2009): 7–24.
Monani, Salma. "Evoking Sympathy and Empathy: The Ecological Indian and Indigenous Eco-Activism." In *Moving Environments: Affect, Emotion, Ecology and Film*, edited by Alexa Weik von Mossner, 225–47. Waterloo, ON: Wilfrid Laurier University Press, 2014.
Nixon, Robert. *Slow Violence and the Environmentalism of the Poor.* Cambridge, MA: Harvard University Press, 2013.
Rosenberg, Fernando J. *After Human Rights. Literature, Visual Arts, and Film in Latin America, 1990–2010.* Pittsburgh: University of Pittsburgh Press, 2016.
———. *The Avant-Garde and Geopolitics in Latin America.* Pittsburgh: University of Pittsburgh Press, 2006.

Sachs, Wolfgang. *Planet Dialectics. Explorations in Environment and Development.* Halifax, Nova Scotia: Fernwood Publishing, 1999.
Spivak, Gayatri. *An Aesthetic Education in the Era of Globalization.* Cambridge, MA: Harvard University Press, 2012.
Tavares, Paulo. "Nonhuman Rights." In *Forensis. The Architecture of Public Truth*, edited by Anselm Franke and Eyal Weizman, 553–72. Berlin: Sternberg Press and Forensic Architecture, 2014.
Zylinska, Joanna. *Minimal Ethics for the Anthropocene.* Ann Arbor: Open Humanities Press, 2014.

11

Sea Turtles and Seascapes

Representing Human-Nature Relations in the Central American Caribbean

MAURICIO ESPINOZA AND TOMÁS EMILIO ARCE

Though negligible for a long time, film production in Central America has reached an unprecedented output and maturity in the past decade, with new projects constantly developed and notoriety achieved in the international film festival circuit and among domestic audiences. In a region that has long been conceived of and depicted as a tropical and exotic paradise, many movies produced there (fiction and documentaries alike) have a particular inclination toward exploring and portraying its landscapes and fragile ecosystems, whether as an aesthetic strategy or a central theme. This chapter studies the filmic representation of conflict between human activity and nonhuman elements of nature in the Central American Caribbean, more specifically in Costa Rica and Nicaragua. We have chosen to concentrate on two recent productions: the feature film *Caribe* (2004), directed by Esteban Ramírez (Costa Rica), and the documentary *Lih Wina* (2012), directed by Dania Torres (Nicaragua). Although different in terms of genre, style length, and production values, both films pair well for analysis because they place emphasis on the ways economic development and conservation policies often clash with traditional cultural practices and/or efforts to preserve sustainable and locally based ways of living. Additionally, *Caribe* and *Lih Wina* take advantage of the southern Central American Caribbean's scenic coastal landscape and multiracial tapestry to visually construct a region that (despite national borders) shares a history of exotic representations, multicultural encounters, and exclusion from national imaginaries.

Caribe contrasts the paradisiacal and laid-back representation of Costa Rica's Caribbean coast (historically much less developed in terms of economic activity, including large-scale tourism, than its Pacific counterpart) with the corporate voracity of US oil companies that seek to exploit resources in the region. In the midst of this conflict are local constituents—environmentalists, ecotourism and agriculture entrepreneurs, Indigenous people, and Afro-Costa Ricans—who debate, argue, and mobilize over the pros and cons of petroleum exploration. Meanwhile, *Lih Wina* deals with the consumption of sea turtle meat as an ancestral tradition by people living in Nicaragua's Caribbean region, which is inhabited predominantly by native Miskitos. In addition to its cultural and ritualistic significance, turtle fishing is a profitable economic activity for impoverished coastal residents. However, the practice is under fire by environmental groups and the Pacific-based, central Nicaraguan government, which has attempted to prohibit it without consulting with and offering viable economic development alternatives to the region's often-ignored inhabitants.

With these considerations in mind, this chapter articulates how the Central American Caribbean coast is understood—at both the discursive and visual levels—as a paradisiacal and primitive postcard by Costa Rica's and Nicaragua's hegemonic regions; and how economic and environmental policies (often formulated from the outside without input from local residents) clash with ancestral traditions of the Caribbean's subaltern ethnic groups, without providing them with real and practical options to meet their financial needs and ensure cultural sovereignty. We also consider how the two films address agency (both human and nonhuman) and racial/ethnic power relations through elements such as characterization, plot, and photography.

Central America and Central American Film in the Twenty-First Century

Central America has experienced significant transformations since the 1970s, a period marked by the triumph of the Sandinista Revolution in Nicaragua in 1979 and its electoral defeat in 1990 following a decade-long, US-backed Contra-revolutionary war; the Salvadoran Civil War (1979–1992); the end of Guatemala's long civil war in 1996; the US invasion of Panama in 1989–90; and the implementation of neoliberal policies that have altered the region's economic and political landscape since the 1980s—a process that became fully consolidated with the ratification of the Dominican Republic-Central America Free Trade Agreement (CAFTA-DR) with the United States between 2006 and 2009. According to George Yúdice, among these transformations is "an increasing salience of the Caribbean, to the degree that it puts into question the national and regional imaginaries" that have long dominated the isthmus.[1] These imaginaries were shaped by elites and intellectuals from the Central Valley (in the case of Costa Rica) and the Pacific (in the case of Nicaragua). In Costa Rica, the Caribbean coast has been occupied mainly by Indigenous groups such as the Bribri and by West Indians who arrived in the late 1800s to work in railroad construction and later on banana plantations. Meanwhile, in Nicaragua, the Caribbean is dominated by the Miskitos (people of mixed African and Indigenous ancestry who have settled there since the mid-seventeenth century) and other Afro-Caribbean and Indigenous groups. As a result, the Caribbean landscapes of Nicaragua and Costa Rica have for centuries been racialized and represented as natural and cultural "others," with biodiversity and multiculturality operating metonymically in the construction of such representations.

Calling itself the "Switzerland of Central America," Costa Rica has paradoxically imagined itself as the isthmus' whitest and most egalitarian nation. This foundational myth arose from a prosperous agrarian system controlled by European descendants and mestizos in the country's temperate Central Valley—a direct result of colonial settlement patterns and coffee cultivation during the early Republican period in the nineteenth century. This myth has had a lasting impact on the constitution of Costa Rica's dominant national culture, which is full of ambivalences and contradictions in relationship with the country's Afro-descendant and Indigenous communities. Falling outside the national imaginary and challenging its tenuous existence, these non-white Costa Ricans have been historically discriminated against, exploited, rendered invisible, and viewed as roadblocks toward progress and assimilation.[2] For example, nineteenth-century Costa Rican scholars tended to ignore references to *aborígenes* in their writings, and when mentioned it would be to clarify that they were *reduced* in numbers and completely *isolated* from the "true" Costa Rican population, which was "blanca, homogénea, sana y robusta" [white, homogeneous, healthy, and robust].[3] Educational policies also reflected this attitude. A school text from the 1940s taught that Costa Rica was effectively "la nación blanca del Caribe" [the Caribbean's white nation],[4] even though a sizable Black population from the Antilles had settled in the Caribbean province of Limón since the turn of the century, and there were eight distinct ethnic Indigenous groups spread throughout the country. Because most Black and Indigenous Costa Ricans live in or near the Caribbean, this region has become associated with markers of otherness in the official imaginary: non-white individuals, languages others than Spanish, religious practices other than Catholicism, extensive plantation agriculture, and exotic tropical landscapes.

In the case of Nicaragua, the country's "Atlántico" has historically been isolated, semiautonomous, and largely outside Spanish and later Nicaraguan control. As Gloriantonia Henríquez puts it, the biologically rich but impoverished, vast but scarcely populated Caribbean region (which represents 56 percent of Nicaragua's territory yet less than 14 percent of its population)[5] is like a country inside another produced by a centuries-old conflict between a Spanish colony and the British crown.[6] Following these colonial disputes, Mosquitia's annexation by the independent Republic of Nicaragua in 1894 did little to change the region's fortunes. Either discriminated against or abandoned by the Nicaraguan government, this territory continued to be geographically, ethnically, and culturally distinct from the hegemonic construction of Nicaraguan-ness—which corresponds with the Spanish-speaking mestizo population living in the western part of the country.[7] The Sandinista government's effort to integrate the region into a unified nation ultimately failed because of its violent approach and because it did not take into account its racial and cultural complexity. As a result, these territories rebelled against the Revolution.[8] In an effort to quell civil war, the government passed a regional autonomy law in 1987 that recognized the individual and collective rights of Afro-descendants and Indigenous communities.[9] This reform divided the region into the Región Autónoma Costa Atlántica Norte (RAAN) and Región Autónoma Costa Atlántica Sur (RAAS), with Atlántica changed to Caribe in 2014. However, as we will see, the promise of this law has not always been upheld.

This Pacific- and Central Valley–centric construction of Central American mainstream identity can be observed in the region's literary and popular culture traditions, which represent the Caribbean as a wild and culturally/historically empty space, making few if any references to Black and Indigenous groups.[10] When they do, these groups are characterized in opposition to national goals or depicted in racist, dehumanizing, and stereotypical ways, such as Carlos Luis Fallas's *Mamita Yunai* (1941).[11] In this regard, Werner Mackenbach views the Central American Caribbean as a place subjected to a "double exclusion" in historical, political, and cultural terms.[12] Similarly, Yúdice lists three main reasons that the Caribbean coast has been left out of the Central American imaginary: it was historically insalubrious, inhospitable, and of difficult access from the Pacific and central areas; it was developed for export agriculture (coffee and bananas) by foreign powers; and the majority of the native inhabitants and labor brought there were non-Hispanic and non-mestizo, including Blacks, Chinese, Italians, and Arabs.[13]

However, Central America's new political, economic, and cultural landscape since the late 1900s—marked by increased migration inside and outside the isthmus, accelerated globalization, transregional drug trafficking and violence, neoliberal policies, free trade agreements, the emergence of multiculturalism discourses, tourism, environmentalism, and sustainable development efforts—has made the dominant criollo-mestizo national identity no longer viable. In response to these new realities, recent cultural production and criticism has moved away from an emphasis on traditional identity formations and national literatures, embracing instead revisionist narratives or transnational and transregional approaches.[14] Since 1990, the Caribbean has played a key role in this destabilization, making its way into the region's new cultural imaginaries—as evidenced in postwar literature, music, and (more recently) cinema.[15] The same is true in the fields of literary and cultural studies, which according to Alexandra Ortiz Wallner have finally "discovered" the Afro-Caribbean roots of Central American cultures and societies.[16]

Just as the Caribbean has gained more prominence in the region's cultural production and criticism, Central American film is experiencing an unprecedented boom in this century. According to María Lourdes Cortés, Costa Rica's film industry (the most active in the region) has gone from having only nine locally produced fiction feature films shown in the country's movie theaters during the entire twentieth century to thirty-seven exhibited between 2001 and 2015.[17] Filmed in 2004, *Caribe* was one of the first movies that proved that feature films with international reach could indeed be made in Costa Rica, paving the way for future, more ambitious projects. By contrast, Nicaragua's cinema has had much less support and commercial success, among other factors because of the demise of the revolutionary project—which had enthusiastically supported audiovisual production through the Nicaraguan Film Institute (INCINE).[18] However, movies such as *La Yuma* (2009) have gained international recognition, and the production of documentaries on a variety of topics has been aided by the availability of new digital technologies and international NGO funds.

Caribe and *Lih Wina* not only are representative of Central America's new film era, but also reflect the isthmus' new realities and preoccupations regarding the environment, tourism, and diversity—both biological and human. Ecocriticism-based scholarship of this emergent regional cinema is just now starting to appear, following in the footsteps of pioneering ecocritical studies of isthmian literature and travel writing by scholars such as Tatiana Argüello, Laura Barbas-Rhoden, Niall Binns, Meghan Ann Casey, Scott DeVries, Carolyn Fornoff, Gisela Heffes, Adrian Taylor Kane, Sofía Kearns, Marisa Pereyra, Walter Pérez Rojas, Joel Thomas Postema, Jacob G. Price, and Steven White. This chapter contributes to this growing body of work by bringing together film studies and ecocriticism in a specifically Central American context.

Film and Environment: Between Tourism and Activism

One key characteristic that ties together the two films studied here is the preponderance of place. This place (the Caribbean coast) is represented through difference and otherness in both human and nonhuman terms—it is at once home to human communities that differ ethnically and culturally from the majority populations of their countries and to exotic natural landscapes anchored by the omnipresence of the Caribbean Sea and rainforest ecosystems. That film and nature should be connected in this manner is not novel or unique. As Adrian Ivakhiv indicates in *Ecologies of the Moving Image: Cinema, Affect, Nature*, "travel, exploration, and touristic consciousness have been with cinema from its very beginning," and so a powerful link has been established over time between the practice of filming and the depiction of nature and its multiple components.[19] Films bring places to us, Ivakhiv writes, "but this bringing cannot leave those places unaffected."[20] Several of the first great voyages of cinematic discovery (*Nanook of the North*, 1922; *Black Journey*, 1924) took place in the service of advertising. As a result, "seeing a place in film can elicit in viewers a desire to visit that place in reality. Cinematic portrayals can contribute to the popularization and overuse of certain places or to their neglect, to the construction of a certain aura around them or to the dispersion of a pre-existing aura."[21] According to Don Gayton, cinema's indiscriminate and interchangeable way of "using" places to stand in for others (in this case, the Caribbean as mythical or virginal paradise) can have the effect of turning that place into a mere commodity that can "be traded and substituted at will."[22] Ivakhiv argues that this practice can also have the opposite effect: that is, elevating that place so that it generates recognition and economic development for the region (such as the case of the American West) and placing value on that particular landscape for its iconic qualities, which can lead to preservation efforts.[23]

While place is central to understanding both films, they approach and construct it differently, leading to varying discursive and aesthetic results. In this regard, one of the main criticisms *Caribe* has received is that it overemphasizes the region's gorgeous landscape while downplaying or even ignoring the harsh social and economic realities of its inhabitants and the discrimination and abandonment they face. This combination effectively renders the film little more than a promotional travel video packaged for consumption by would-be tourists. The film's opening scene, which lasts for one minute and twenty-two seconds, establishes this visual emphasis, showing the ocean waves and the coastline in the background, followed by a forest canopy teeming with life, the beach, serene landscapes, boats, lush forest views, and the sound of drums as the expected extradiegetic supplement that unmistakably signifies a stereotyped Caribbean scene. Cortés views *Caribe* as an exoticizing "postcard," a film that lacks in character development and plot intricacies but is rich in its cinematography.[24] *Caribe* was the first Costa Rican fiction feature film shot outside the country's Central Valley, which is the center of population, commerce, and national culture. Cortés associates this move with the drastic transformation of the country's economy and international reputation—from an agrarian nation known for its coffee and bananas to a popular tourist destination, to the point that by the end of the 1990s, tourism became Costa Rica's number-one industry. The Caribbean that is depicted in *Caribe* is, according to Cortés, "idealizado, como había sido el Valle Central en el siglo precedente, y la pobreza de la región nunca se exhibe" [idealized, as the Central Valley had been the century before; regional poverty is never shown].[25] What director Ramírez achieves in this movie is a sterilization and romanticization of the Caribbean environment, with unspoiled nature serving as the alluring and carefully photographed backdrop against which equally good-looking protagonists face conflict but manage to resolve it without compromising their bonds—and without resolving (or even showing) the socioeconomic and environmental issues that plague Costa Rica's Limón province.[26]

Sterilization as an aesthetic strategy is not unique to *Caribe*'s photography and its treatment of nature. Even the environmental struggle (which is central to the movie's plot and message) is sanitized for the purpose of disrupting as little as possible the ideal of a tropical and democratic paradise. In the film, Vicente (played by Cuban actor Jorge Perugorría) is a biologist who has inherited land in the Caribbean and moves there with his wife, Abigaíl (Spanish actor Cuca Escribano). Together, they operate a small banana farm and grow ornamental plants for export—a combination that perfectly blends the region's traditional agricultural past with new ventures typical of the neoliberal period. The seemingly idyllic life of the protagonists and their beach-town community is suddenly disrupted by three events that occur almost simultaneously: Abigaíl's half-sister, Irene (played by Mexican actor Maya Zapata and whose existence was unbeknownst to Abigaíl) shows up in town to inform her of their mother's passing; Vicente's broker tells him he no longer will be able to buy his harvest because of changing international market conditions; and news arrives that the Costa Rican government is considering granting a foreign oil company permission to explore in the region. *Caribe* is partly based on the fictional short story "El solitario" by the Costa Rican writer Carlos Salazar Herrera (from which it borrows the setting, main characters, and the story's love triangle) and the real-life saga of US-based Harken oil company, whose controversial petroleum exploration and drilling rights contract with the Costa Rican government was rescinded in 2002 following stern protests from environmental and civil society groups.[27]

The film skillfully incorporates the Harken story (still fresh in the memories of Costa Ricans and international observers) to introduce in the plot a foreign threat that seeks to undermine the country's environmental riches, its reputation as an ecotourism destination, and its autonomy in the face of rampant economic globalization. In this regard, *Caribe*'s ecological dilemma reminds us of Anacristina Rossi's 1991 novel *La loca de Gandoca* (*Madwoman of Gandoca*), a popular subject of ecocritical scholarship in which a foreign development corporation threatens to destroy a Caribbean coast wildlife refuge.[28] However, *Caribe* fails to provide a nuanced representation of Costa Rica's ecological paradox in the neoliberal period: a carefully crafted international reputation that often clashes with realities on the ground, including blatant disregard for environmental regulations, corruption, and even the murder of conservationists.[29] Choosing image over substance, *Caribe* mentions environmental degradation but never shows it, blaming problems with local fishing resources on actions taken by the oil company. The plan for petroleum exploration in the region looms as a threat during the entire narrative, but it is defeated in the end by local activists and never materializes. Initial disagreements between the locals over the decision to allow or reject the oil company are presented. On the one hand, ecologists, those involved in ecotourism and sustainable agriculture, fishermen, Indigenous groups, and surfers vehemently oppose the idea. On the other hand, young people concerned about their employment prospects and members of the Black community who criticize the Costa Rican government's lack of development strategies for the Caribbean region agree to give petroleum a chance. While the issue divides the community, it never fractures it. In the end, the power of democracy—a tradition that most Costa Ricans proudly adhere to—prevails, as mounting public pressure and a local referendum leave the government no choice but to rescind the oil company's permit. Friction is neutralized with a series of celebratory scenes toward the end of the film that show a unified community (old, young, mestizo, Black, Indigenous, white) coming together to heal. The initial paradisiacal order is restored, visually and discursively.

Trapped in the midst of these tensions is Vicente. A man trusted in the community because of his scientific knowledge and commitment to sustainable development, Vicente is quick to speak out against petroleum exploration at a town hall meeting and rejects offers from the oil company's lobbyist to change his mind. However, fear of losing the farm because of his voided contract and mounting debt push him over the edge: he takes money from the company and, against his principles, lends public support to oil exploration. If this weren't enough, Vicente has begun an affair with Irene, his wife's sister. When he decides to end the relationship, he finds out that she is pregnant. Tormented by the rifts his actions have created, Vicente returns the oil bribe and tells his fellow *limonenses* to vote against petroleum exploration. In the movie's climax, Abigaíl learns of her husband's infidelities (both ethical and sexual) and then hears the shot that would end his life in the dead of a dark, rainy night. The problem with *Caribe* is that even Vicente's murder (supposedly by thugs acting on behalf of the oil company) is stylized and sublimated. The brief moment of mourning that follows his demise is quickly taken over by the joyful scenes of community celebration. This is followed by the movie's closing scene, which shows the two reconciled sisters playing with Vicente and Irene's son on the beach.

In this manner, Vicente's death is portrayed as a necessary atonement to guarantee continued life and community cohesion, downplaying what this action truly means—the ruthless and cowardly murder of a nature defender who angered a power-hungry transnational corporation. There is no public uproar, no judicial investigation, no resolution of the murder. *Caribe*'s emphasis on sacrifice and restoration of a pristine and idyllic order (which does not exist in the reality of Costa Rica's Caribbean coast) is important. In the end, this strategy helps to preserve the film's postcard-perfect representation of space and the touristic appeal of a country that often glosses over internal strife and imperfections in favor of its international reputation as a peaceful, welcoming, and nature-loving destination. As Liz Harvey-Kattou indicates, *Caribe*'s cinematography undoes its anti-imperialist plot by performing "for the tourist gaze, inviting the viewer to take part in the neo-colonialism of the nation through tourism."[30]

Figure 11.1. Esteban Ramírez, *Caribe*, 2004, video still.

Meanwhile, *Lih Wina* portrays the Central American Caribbean landscape and sense of place in a completely different fashion. There is no sterilization here. The documentary subverts the traditional postcard approach of representing the "tropical paradise," beginning with a sequence shot of two men carrying turtle meat for sale in a wheelbarrow through the city of Bilwi (Puerto Cabezas), capital of the RAAN. Against the audience's expectation of magnificent wildlife put on the screen for their pleasurable consumption (which *Caribe* often does), what we encounter here is a different type of consumption. The capture, killing, butchering, and eating of sea turtles is shown without hesitation but not for its shock value—although the images can be disturbing for viewers who sympathize with the plight of any animal, wild or domesticated. What Torres does is document the connection between turtle fishing and consumption and everyday life for the Miskitos. They eat turtle meat as part of their basic diet, use it for ritualistic purposes associated with enhanced vitality and overall well-being, and their livelihoods depend on its commercialization. What is shown in the film is unfiltered, even if such realism might upset viewers or go against the documentary's implicit goal of getting viewers to empathize with the struggles of impoverished and discriminated Nicaraguan Caribbean residents.

To be fair, the film does include gorgeous cinematography, but it serves a different purpose than in *Caribe*. For example, beauty shots of turtles hatching in the sand and rushing toward the ocean waves appear in the second scene, but they are punctuated by the documentary's somber subtitle: "El viaje sin retorno" ("The Journey of No Return"). Carefully composed shots of the sea and fishing vessels also appear throughout the documentary, but they are used to illustrate how sailing and turtle fishing hold great historical significance for the Miskitos, who gained remarkable navigational skills as a result of engaging in this practice—skills that led to their territorial expansion and dominance along the Central American Caribbean coast during colonial times.

While in *Caribe* space and nature serve mainly aesthetic and touristic goals, in *Lih Wina* they are an integral part of the narrative and of the cultural-historical legacy the documentary is trying to portray and asking viewers to engage with. According to Karl Offen, for Miskitos the environment is "much more than a physical space, it provides people with a set of sensory and emotive resources that they use to narrate their lives."[31] To quote Macarena Gómez-Barris, the Mosquitia is represented in the documentary as one of those "many spaces within the Américas [that] have never been fully inserted into Western capitalism" and more specifically as one of those "complex Afro-Indigenous spaces of coexistence with the nonhuman world that have been formed in relation to the colonial Encounter."[32] Consequently, ecosystems are extremely important for the Miskitos' sense of culture and identity, as members of this ethnic group "establish a dialogue with their landscape in ways that inform their historical consciousness and anchor their identity to a uniquely Miskitu place, the Mosquitia."[33] This dialogue is fundamental, as it has shaped the Miskitos' cosmogony and spirituality over centuries. In other words, the Miskitos would not have been able to forge their particular culture without the natural elements that surround them and the relationship this community has established with them. It is no surprise then that the two most important of these elements—sea turtles and the Caribbean Sea—are the ones Torres portrays in the first two scenes. These visual cues establish the tone for the documentary, which ultimately interrogates whether the ancestral practice of fishing and eating green turtles can coexist with modern environmental concerns regarding the survival of this endangered species.

The short thirty-two-minute documentary is not able to provide audiences with a detailed account of Miskito history in Nicaragua's Caribbean region, but it invites viewers to become more acquainted with it through the lens of contemporary struggles. Implicitly, the film works with this rich history through its emphasis on place and nature (the sea, the Miskito coast, the turtles), but it is difficult to gain a real sense of why turtle fishing by Miskitos (and Miskitos's way of life in general) is such a divisive issue without understanding more about the cultural-historical peculiarities of this community and the region they inhabit. The "journey" proposed in the documentary's title and embodied by the turtle that swims toward the horizon in the second sequence is also an invitation for audiences to embark on a voyage through a complex and little-understood space.

The Caribbean region did not experience the same colonial process to which other regions of the Nicaraguan nation were subjected. According to José Miguel González Pérez, native inhabitants of the Caribbean—Miskitos, Sumos-Mayagnas, and Ramas among them—successfully resisted the Spanish colonial incursion during the seventeenth and eighteenth centuries.[34] This was the result of two factors: the hostility with which Indigenous populations fought off Spanish attempts to settle there and the mountain ranges that divide the Caribbean from Nicaragua's central and Pacific regions, which became a sort of cultural border.[35] Taking advantage of the Spanish Crown's failed attempts to settle the Caribbean, the British Empire subsequently launched a colonization process in a region inhabited by heterogeneous ethnic groups. The English gave the Miskitos symbolic power that according to González Pérez would turn them into the Nicaraguan Caribbean's hegemonic group.[36]

The relative power and autonomy achieved by the Miskitos was the result of their exceptional navigation and fishing skills. They served as sailors in British pirate ships that assailed Spanish trade routes, helping them secure enough seafood to feed their crews. Among those resources were green turtles.[37] As Offen indicates, commercialization of turtle meat with outsiders has been a staple of the region's economy since the early times of British-Miskito interaction.[38] Because of their distinct relationship with the British and their dominance among regional groups, the Miskitos developed an elevated sense of ethnic pride, as they "began to see themselves as co-equals among European nations."[39] The British did not mind the Miskitos' nonsubmissive stance, as they were more interested in the resources and logistical support they could obtain from the natives than in exerting control over them.

Even though the Miskitos obtained a reputation as a people who successfully challenged colonial and state authority, it is also true that despite their heroic resistance, Nicaragua's Caribbean coast experienced a type of colonization that can be described as domination by consent.[40] By 1844, the British Empire had formally established a protectorate in the Caribbean. This official recognition coincided with the impetus to form the Nicaraguan state, emanating from the Pacific region. According to González Pérez, this nation formation would have a definite impact on the Caribbean zone, as the Nicaraguan government encountered the problem of exercising national sovereignty over a territory controlled by a military power such as Great Britain. The United States would play a key role in the incorporation of the Caribbean region to Nicaragua's national project, securing from the British recognition of Nicaragua's sovereignty over the Costa de Mosquitos.[41] Finally, in 1894, during the liberal government of José Santos Zelaya, the Caribbean was formally annexed to the Republic of Nicaragua. Since then, the region has endured a variety of disadvantageous policies and discriminatory treatment by liberal and conservative governments, the Somoza dictatorship, and the Sandinista Revolution—highlighting a significant rift between mestizos in the Pacific and Indigenous and Black communities in the Caribbean. This region continues to experience a sort of "lettered violence" that began in the eighteenth century—particularly through central government decrees that fail to recognize the autonomy and cultural differences of this multiethnic and complex territory.[42]

Against this historical backdrop, it is easier to understand the plight of coastal residents regarding their assumed right to fish for turtles and consume

Figure 11.2. Dania Torres, *Lih Wina*, 2012, video still.

their meat—as turtles and the ocean where they live are intimately tied to their ancestral sense of space and being. At the core of the story told in *Lih Wina* is a 2005 turtle-fishing ban enacted by Nicaragua's Environmental Ministry, which is related via voice-over narration.[43] This decision has been vehemently opposed by the Miskitos. In some of their communities, up to 85 percent of the population depends on turtle fishing and commercialization for their livelihood and sustenance. Members of the local government in Bilwi talk about the measures they have implemented to control the number of turtles that fishermen can capture and bring to market, while still allowing them to keep their livelihood. This emphasizes efforts for regional self-determination in the face of national pressure to eradicate turtle fishing completely. However, community members complain that the restrictions hurt them and insist that the national and local governments should consult and work with them to find viable solutions—for the conservation of turtles and for increasing their economic opportunities by means of alternative activities. This is crucial for Nicaragua's most underdeveloped region, which has been systematically excluded from national growth.[44]

There is also an insistence in the documentary that the decline in the populations of green turtles off Nicaragua's Caribbean coast is mainly due to outside demand: from the Caribbean islands in times past and from Nicaragua's capital, Managua, in recent decades. As a result, the point of view that ultimately comes through in the film is that the problem of endangerment rests with outside consumption and the demand it creates, not with local practices. The documentary ends with images of people eating turtle at a restaurant (the reality of demand), followed by what could be interpreted as a sign of hope for the future: a newly hatched green turtle emerging from the sand and racing toward the ocean as the sun sets.

Neoliberal Subjects: The Characterization of People and Nature

The act of seeing and experiencing a new place in film (whether fiction or documentary) inevitably leads to the encounter between an "us" (viewers) and "them" (the elements that constitute that place, whether landscape, nature, animals, and/or people). In the case of documentaries, there is also an encounter between the researcher/interviewer (standing in for and guiding "us") and the film's subjects ("them"), who often come from different worlds, worldviews, or understandings of reality. In the diegesis, there tends to be another encounter (sometimes a collision) between outsiders or natives (whether actual locals or natural elements that represent the place gazed at and explored). In this case, too, we as the audience tend to identify with the outsider, through whom we vicariously come into contact with the "other." In *Caribe* and *Lih Wina*, both people and natural elements emerge as characters whose construction is often intertwined, and which are squarely configured within the neoliberal discourses of multiculturalism, subaltern agency, conservation, and tourism.

While Ramírez carefully attempts to depict an inclusive and multicultural society in *Caribe*, the film is problematic in the way it creates a distinction between whites/mestizos (with whom we as viewers are automatically asked to identify) and the majority Black and Indigenous communities that have traditionally inhabited and shaped the Caribbean coast. One issue is agency and voice. For example, during a town hall meeting in which citizens are first informed about the oil company's plans, a mestizo environmental activist, Ezequiel, is the one who does almost all of the talking and is the only person standing, commanding all visual and vocal authority. Afro-Costa Ricans, Indians, and other citizens are present and shown, but they barely speak, and their main function is to display the diversity of the region and the idea of tolerant ethnic/racial coexistence in a neoliberal, democratic, multicultural paradise. We also see this portrayal at the end of the film, when the community is reconciled and celebrates the victory over the "evil gringo outsiders." It is a true kumbaya moment, with Blacks, whites, Indigenous people, and mestizos embracing—the filmic framing of a postracial utopia that erases the country's continued racist attitudes and socioeconomic inequalities. But even in this moment of diversity, visual relevance is again given to the mestizo hero: the sequence shot that shows a group of Afro-Costa Rican children performing a ceremonial dance dissolves into a close-up of Ezequiel, who once again achieves visual prominence over the rest of the cast.

Dissent and criticism from other members of the community are also downplayed or given little screen time in *Caribe*. At the same town-hall meeting, Rupert, a young adult, speaks up: "Si la petrolera nos va a dar trabajo, y bien pagado, ¿para qué carajo queremos pesca?" [If the oil company will give us well-paid jobs, why in the hell would we want to fish?]. Ezequiel shuts him down categorically: "No le van a dar trabajo calificado a nadie de la zona. Y se fue al carajo la pesca y el turismo" [They are not going to give good jobs to anyone from the region. And fishing and tourism have gone belly-up].[45] Black leaders also lend their support to the oil exploration project, expressing disappointment with San José's historical abandonment of Limón and racist attitudes toward their community. Jackson, a Black handyman, summarizes this sentiment: "Es que Limón nunca le ha importado a nadie" [Limón has never really mattered to anyone]. And by Limón he really means "Black Limón." At the end, the oil exploration project is shelved, but no employment or other economic development alternatives for the region are proposed. Just like the environmentalist Ezequiel, the movie's main characters are white or mestizo. Blacks, Indians, Chinese, and other *limonenses* are minor characters—literally, local color. Vicente, Abigaíl, and Irene are also outsiders: relatively recent arrivals who cannot possibly embody or fully understand the historical plight of the region's Black and Indigenous people. Harvey-Katou views this couple as representing the marriage of tourism and coloniality, as theirs is "the story of the tourists who decide to settle in a land that is not their own—not due to forced migration but out of a colonial desire to appropriate land."[46]

Caribe also represents and often exoticizes the environment by constructing key characters both visually and discursively as intimately connected with various elements from nature. Jackson, a middle-aged Afro-Costa Rican who works for Vicente and Abigaíl, is dark (literally and figuratively), quiet, secretive, and contemplative, just like the jungle where he lives in a humble cabin. Irene has black hair and tanned skin and is associated with the seductive, exuberant, sensual, exotic nature of the wild rainforest; she is often shown amid nature. In one beautifully shot scene, we see a colorful toucan on a tree, which in the next shot we realize is perched just outside Irene's window. Irene is shown in a seductive pose, her white panties emphasizing her darker skin tone. The toucan and Irene become one in this scene: both framed as beautiful wild creatures to be looked at. In contrast with her half-sister, Abigaíl is white and has light hair, not fitting the seductive, sensual trope already established in the film via nature shots and Irene's depiction. Fittingly, Abigaíl's passion and occupation is the cultivation of bromeliads in a greenhouse. She is beautiful, too, but her beauty is tamed and contained just like the plants she grows in a controlled environment. As a biologist and small farmer, Vicente is associated with the land, its protection, and its conquest. At one point, Abigaíl says: "Lo de mi esposo es la tierra" [my husband's thing is the land]. It is not surprising then that he becomes strongly attracted to Irene, who represents the unbridled seduction of the land. Vicente's betrayal of the environment by choosing to support the oil company is metonymically tied to his decision to stop seeing Irene, who embodies the lush landscapes of the Caribbean—and not with the betrayal of his wife's trust.

Unlike *Caribe*, *Lih Wina* belongs to a type of more recent cinematic productions where locals tell their own stories and control the way in which they are portrayed. In *Lih Wina*, we enter Nicaragua's Miskito coast through the lens and guidance of the documentarist, Torres, who is from the region. This point of view shapes our understanding of the struggle to preserve both endangered sea turtles and a way of life that depends on their consumption. Torres clearly takes the side of the local inhabitants, giving them as much agency as subjects can possibly have in a traditional documentary that narrates from the perspective of the camera rather than from the point of view of the people whose story is being told. The film employs two strategies to maximize agency: language and letting subaltern subjects' voices guide the story, which prompts viewers to identify with them.

Language is key to the relationship the documentary creates between viewers/outsiders and the Indigenous subjects. This is established from the opening sequence, when two men selling turtle meat door-to-door repeatedly yell "lih wina" (green turtle in Miskito). The words are untranslated (no subtitles provided), meaning non-Miskito viewers (for whom the film is intended) are left wondering what it means. In this way, the documentary from the outset forces the audience to grapple with the challenge of not understanding the culture and ways of life portrayed onscreen—and to engage with them to try to get a sense of what's happening. The reiteration of this phrase in the Miskito language, which has a similar function to anaphora, reveals the Nicaraguan nation's multicultural complexity by showing that it houses in its territory tongues and cultural traditions that vastly differ from the official Spanish language and Pacific-dominated "national" culture. Through this opening sequence, Torres generates a culture shock for viewers not acquainted with the Miskito language. Even for Nicaraguans from the Pacific or central regions, Miskito, Rama, or creole English from the Caribbean are basically foreign languages.[47] In the case of Miskito, the differences go beyond the purely linguistic. According to Offen, Miskito language "connects the commonplace landscape of the everyday world to the landscape of the past and the landscape cosmos by utilizing place-names and stories about places in everyday life."[48] In other words, this is a language that is totally foreign to Western ways of understanding the world to begin with. When the seller utters "lih wina," he is not just advertising a product: he is connecting the practice of capturing and consuming green turtles today with his people's ancestral traditions and the specific place where this practice has always taken place.

Another important decision made by Torres in *Lih Wina* is to let Miskitos and creole-speaking Afro-Nicaraguans present their stories and concerns in their native languages. Language reinforces the ideas of cultural heritage, cultural pride, and self-determination of the Caribbean's many ethnic groups. By having to read subtitles or attempting to understand the creole English spoken, we as the audience are placed in a humbling position where we may be more likely to pay attention to the voice of "others" and acknowledge their agency. This is the opposite of what usually happens in Hollywood films depicting Indigenous people and a host of other "others," where as if by magic they all suddenly communicate in perfect English to eliminate the viewers' uneasiness with difference. Something similar tends to occur in Latin American touristic experiences designed for English-speaking visitors. In the documentary, Torres rejects this neocolonial practice and engages in a bit of decoloniality of her own. The three main subaltern voices and faces that we hear and see in the film—butchers Rosa Richard and Elba Humphreys and Dino Daniel, elder of the Awastara community—bear witness to the cultural significance of sea turtle consumption and the many rituals associated with it. For example, Richard explains that it is imperative for a butcher not to have engaged in sexual relations with a woman before handling the turtles, as this may cause the meat to acquire bad odor and taste.

These candid interventions make it clear that turtle fishing is much more than an economic activity for Miskitos and that banning it would not just hurt their ability to provide for their families—it would endanger their cultural survival as well. By giving agency to these voices, Torres takes a political stance against how environmental policies are issued by the central government without taking into consideration the communities that might be affected.[49] Such policies have been historically drafted by government officials who ignore and consequently cannot understand the realities of the people impacted by them. As Ángel Rama explains, this practice perpetuates a tradition that began during the colonial period, when laws, rules, proclamations, edicts, and other legal instruments were used to exercise power.[50] In addition to this continued violation of their autonomy via legal instruments, Miskitos and other native communities from the Caribbean face the usurpation of communal lands by non-Indigenous *colonos* [settlers], the destruction of virgin rainforest as the agricultural frontier is illegally expanded, and even the death of community leaders.[51]

Concluding Remarks

Despite the Caribbean's newfound role in Central America's economic and discursive configuration, native Caribbean inhabitants are still left out of the riches that come from tourism and other types of development, just as they were exploited by the enclave economies of banana and cacao plantations in the past.[52] On the other hand, alluring nature and quaint local cultural color—two key visual elements of ecotourism's postcard-perfect promise—need to be preserved for this industry to continue to thrive in a neoliberal and globalized reality. Consequently, *Caribe* highlights the natural beauty and exoticism of Costa Rica's Caribbean coast the way a tourism promotional video would. The possibility of environmental degradation is hinted at but never quite materializes, thus maintaining the promise of an idyllic tropical getaway in a peaceful Latin American democracy for would-be tourists who watch the film.[53]

In the case of *Lih Wina*, the film successfully presents the perspective of native Miskitos who fear that a complete ban on turtle fishing would jeopardize not only their ancestral diet but also their cultural identity, while at the same time denouncing the impact that external demand for turtle meat and the lack of alternative employment options for Indigenous communities have on this endangered species. The pressure put on the Miskitos to stop their ancestral practices and basic means of survival in order to protect endangered sea turtle species contrasts with ecologically destructive actions taken by the Nicaraguan government. The most salient example has been the plan to build a $50 billion interoceanic canal with Chinese investment. The project (currently on hold) has been exempted from the required independent environmental impact review, even though international scientists have warned it would cause staggering environmental devastation, displacement of thousands of people, and expropriation of land otherwise protected by law—most of it affecting the Caribbean coast.[54] The unequal enforcement of conservation policy has also proven to be closely connected to issues of national governance in Nicaragua. For instance, the government's slow and indifferent response to a fire that ravaged the southern Caribbean's Indio Maíz Biological Reserve in April 2018 helped spark a national protest movement (and subsequent state repression) that is still ongoing—threatening the government of former Sandinista rebel leader Daniel Ortega.[55]

Despite significant differences between the two films, *Caribe* and *Lih Wina* raise similar questions about the relationships between human and nonhuman subjects in cinematic portrayals of environmental struggle. In both cases, attempts to preserve threatened natural resources in the exuberant yet extremely fragile Central American Caribbean coast leads to a) the limiting of much-needed socioeconomic development alternatives for impoverished residents, mainly Black and Indigenous and b) the prohibition of traditional ways of subsistence that are essential for the preservation of native cultures.

After watching both films, one can't help but ask if top-down environmental protection policies and large-scale ecotourism can coexist with the needs of disadvantaged communities of color. In the case of Costa Rica, the risk of building an economy dependent on international tourism has been highlighted by the Covid-19 pandemic, which halted foreign travel into the country in early 2020 and brought the industry to a standstill.

A reading of these films from the perspective of human-nonhuman relations should also make us realize that the concepts of "endangerment" and "fragility" typically employed in the language of ecology not only apply to animal species or forests—but also to the precarious human communities that coexist in those habitats and that have been subjected to the same historical forces of colonial, racial, environmental, cultural, and economic violence. In this regard, *Caribe* and *Lih Wina* denounce extractive capitalism in its various facets.

Notes

1. George Yúdice, "The Central American Caribbean: Rethinking Regional and National Imaginaries," in *El Caribe y sus diásporas: Cartografía de saberes y prácticas culturales*, ed. Anja Bandau and Martha Zapata Galindo (Madrid: Editorial Verbum, 2010), 96.

2. Iván Molina Jiménez, "*Limón blues*: una novela de Ana Cristina Rossi," *Revista de Filosofía de la Universidad de Costa Rica* 42 (January–April 2004): 185–88; Víctor Hugo Acuña, "La invención de la diferencia costarricense, 1810–1870," *Revista de Historia*, no. 8 (January–June 2002), 191–228.

3. Joaquín Bernardo Calvo, *República de Costa Rica. Apuntamientos geográficos, estadísticos e históricos* (San José: Imprenta Nacional, 1887), 34.

4. Jorge León, *Nueva Geografía de Costa Rica* (San José: Soley y Valverde Editores, 1943), 33.

5. Based on 2012 data from the Instituto Nacional de Información de Desarrollo (https://www.inide.gob.ni/).

6. Gloriantonia Henríquez, "La Costa Atlántica de Nicaragua: ¿Un país inserto en otro o la heterogeneidad cultural como frontera?," *Cahiers du CRICCAL* 8 (1991): 103.

7. Ibid., 110.

8. Mateo Jarquín Chamorro, "A la sombra de la revolución sandinista: Nicaragua, 1979–2019," in *Anhelos de un nuevo horizonte. Aportes para una Nicaragua democrática*, ed. Alberto Cortés Ramos, Umanzor López Baltodano, and Ludwing Moncada Bellorin (Costa Rica: FLACSO, 2020), 56.

9. Lottie Cunningham Wren, "Pueblos indígenas y afrodescendientes: La lucha por sus derechos humanos," in *Anhelos de un nuevo horizonte. Aportes para una Nicaragua democrática*, ed. Alberto Cortés Ramos, Umanzor López Baltodano, and Ludwing Moncada Bellorin (Costa Rica: FLACSO, 2020), 633.

10. Alexandra Ortiz Wallner, *El arte de ficcionar: La novela contemporánea en Centroamérica* (Madrid: Iberoamericana, 2012), 230.

11. Valeria Grinberg Pla and Werner Mackenbach, "Banana novel revis(it)ed: etnia, género y espacio en la novela bananera centroamericana. El caso de *Mamita Yunai*," *Iberoamericana*, no. 6 (September 2006): 167–68.

12. Werner Mackenbach, "El Caribe y la literatura centroamericana: de la doble exclusión al doble espejo," in *Caribbean(s) on the Move—Archipiélagos literarios del Caribe. A TransArea Symposium*, ed. Ottmar Ette (Frankfurt: Peter Lang Verlag, 2008), 107–8. This exclusion also takes place in ecocritical studies about the Caribbean; for instance, the influential collection *Caribbean Literature and the Environment: Between Nature and Culture*, ed. Elizabeth M. DeLoughrey, Renée K. Gosson, and George B. Handley (Charlottesville: University of Virginia Press, 2005) includes studies about the Antilles and South America's continental Caribbean, leaving out Central America's eastern coast and its circum-Caribbean connections.

13. Yúdice, "The Central American Caribbean," 98.

14. Ana Patricia Rodríguez, *Dividing the Isthmus: Central American Transnational Histories, Literatures, and Cultures* (Austin: University of Texas Press, 2009), 3.

15. Other recent Central American films dealing with the Caribbean include *El barco prometido* (Luciano Capelli, Costa Rica, 2000), *Paso a paso: A sentimental journey* (Julio Molina and Daniel Ross, Costa Rica, 2006), *Three Kings of Belize* (Katia Paradis, Belize, 2007), *Pikineras* (Rossana Lacayo, Nicaragua, 2012), *Garifuna in Peril* (Ali Allie, Honduras, 2012), and *Dos Aguas* (Patricia Velásquez, Costa Rica, 2014).

16. Ortiz Wallner, *El arte de ficcionar*, 235–36.

17. María Lourdes Cortés, *Fabulaciones del nuevo cine costarricense* (San José: Uruk Editores, 2016), 18.

18. María Lourdes Cortés, *La pantalla rota: Cien años de cine en Centroamérica* (México: Taurus, 2005), 346.

19. Adrian J. Ivakhiv, *Ecologies of the Moving Image: Cinema, Affect, Nature* (Waterloo, ON: Wilfrid Laurier University Press, 2013), 125.

20. Ibid., 120.

21. Ibid., 121.

22. Don Gayton, "In Film, Out of Place," *Alternatives* 24, no. 4 (1998): 8–9.

23. Ivakhiv, *Ecologies of the Moving Image*, 121.

24. Cortés, *Fabulaciones*, 46.

25. Ibid.

26. Limón province, which encompasses Costa Rica's Caribbean region, has some of the highest rates of poverty, unemployment, and crime in the country. According to an October 16, 2016, article in the newspaper *El Financiero*, extreme

poverty in Limón rose from 7.5 percent in 2010 to 11.1 percent in 2015; and the murder rate was 19 per every 100,000 people, compared to the national average of 11.4. In the 2018 presidential elections, *limonenses* turned their backs on the ruling-party candidate, overwhelmingly supporting populist and evangelical newcomer Fabricio Alvarado. Analysts viewed this as a clear sign that the locals were tired of decades of neglect by the central San José government.

27. "Harken Oil Company Requests $13 Million," *The Tico Times*, July 7, 2006, http://www.ticotimes.net/2006/07/07/harken-oil-company-requests-13-million.

28. See Sofía Kearns's "Otra cara de Costa Rica a través de un testimonio ecofeminista," *Hispanic Journal* 19, no. 2 (Fall 1998): 313–39; Joel Postema's "Ecology and Ethnicity in Anacristina Rossi's *La loca de Gandoca*," *Cincinnati Romance Review* 27 (2008): 113–24; and Laura Barbas-Rhoden's *Ecological Imaginations in Latin American Fiction* (Gainesville: University Press of Florida, 2011).

29. A highly publicized recent case that weaves together issues depicted in both *Caribe* and *Lih Wina* was the 2013 murder of Jairo Mora, a sea turtle conservationist working near the Caribbean port city of Limón, Costa Rica.

30. Liz Harvey-Kattou, "Performing for Hollywood: Coloniality and the Tourist Image in Esteban Ramírez's *Caribe/Caribbean* (2004)," *Studies in Spanish & Latin American Cinemas* 15, no. 2 (2018): 254.

31. Karl Offen, *The Miskitu Kingdom: Landscape and the Emergence of a Miskitu Identity, Northeastern Nicaragua and Honduras, 1600–1800* (PhD diss., University of Texas, 1999), 55.

32. Macarena Gómez-Barris, *The Extractive Zone: Social Ecologies and Decolonial Perspectives* (Durham: Duke University Press, 2017), 2–3.

33. Offen, *The Miskitu Kingdom*, 89.

34. José Miguel González Pérez, *Gobiernos Pluriétnicos. La Constitución de Regiones Autónomas en Nicaragua* (Ciudad de México: Plaza y Valdés, 1997), 43.

35. Richard N. Adams, *The Dynamics of Societal Diversity: Notes from Nicaragua for a Sociology of Survival* (Austin: University of Texas, 1981), 3.

36. The first encounters between the Miskitos and the British took place between 1633 and 1634. The Miskitos engaged in slavery, contraband, and even launched systematic attacks on Spanish settlements in Central America's central valleys. González Pérez, *Gobiernos Pluriétnicos*, 65–67.

37. Mario Rizo, *Pueblos Indígenas de Nicaragua y su cultura del agua* (Managua, 2005), 19; 26. Miskitos still employ ancestral turtle fishing techniques, including the construction of corrals in the sea using native woods such as mangrove.

38. Offen, *The Miskitu Kingdom*, 114.

39. Offen, *The Miskitu Kingdom*, 112.

40. González Pérez, *Gobiernos Pluriétnicos*, 71.

41. US support was due to its geopolitical interests in the region, especially the construction of an interoceanic canal through Nicaragua, for which incorporating the Caribbean coast into the young Central American nation was crucial. González Pérez, *Gobiernos Pluriétnicos*, 117.

42. Development policies carried out during the twentieth century caused a series of regional clashes that ranged from confrontations between mestizos and Indigenous people along the agricultural frontier as well as timber and mining concessions. González Pérez, *Gobiernos Pluriétnicos*, 438.

43. *Lih Wina*, directed by Dania Torres (2012, Nicaragua), DVD.

44. Cunningham Wren, "Pueblos indígenas y afrodescendientes," 634.

45. *Caribe*, directed by Esteban Ramírez (2004, Costa Rica), DVD.

46. Harvey-Kattou, "Performing for Hollywood," 256.

47. Regarding the issue of linguistic difference, coauthor Tomás Arce, who is Nicaraguan, states: "Even though I'm Nicaraguan and the Miskitos are my compatriots, I'm only able to understand what the sellers are saying because the documentary has subtitles. However, I know that those men could understand me, because since the time of the Zelaya government in the late 1800s, the ethnic groups living in the Caribbean were forced to learn Spanish."

48. Offen, *The Miskitu Kingdom*, 78.

49. This idea of political action is taken from Paula Willoquet-Maricondi, "Shifting Paradigms: From Environmentalist Films to Ecocinema," in *Framing the World: Explorations in Ecocriticism and Film*, ed. Paula Willoquet-Maricondi (Charlottesville, VA: University of Virginia Press, 2010).

50. Ángel Rama, *La ciudad letrada* (Hannover: Ediciones del Norte, 1984), 41–71.

51. Lidia López, "Líderes indígenas dicen que versión policial sobre ataque pone en peligro la vida de los comunitarios," *La Prensa*, February 21, 2020, https://www.laprensa.com.ni/2020/02/21/nacionales/2643375-lideres-indigenas-sobre-ataques-de-colonos-ellos-creeran-que-como-somos-negritos-somos-animales-salvajes-que-nos-cazan. In this article, community leader Susana Marley protests: "Ellos (colonos) creerán que como (somos) negritos, somos animales salvajes que nos cazan," underscoring racial tensions in the region.

52. Yúdice explains: "With neoliberal restructuring from the 1980s on, the rise of environmental protection, and tourism as the major industry in Central America (over 10% of the Gross Regional Product), the activism of indigenous and Afro-Central Americans since 1992, buttressed by international organizations (European International Cooperation, Ford and Rockefeller Foundations, UNESCO) that promote cultural diversity and citizenship, it is no wonder that the Caribbean has acquired value and receptivity in this new formation. But that does not guarantee that non-elites will derive value within this context. It may only mean that elites and transnational corporations have captured the discourse of diversity and sustainability." Yúdice, "The Central American Caribbean," 109.

53. Some critics argue that sustainable development is a neoliberal ploy designed to maintain unsustainable levels of production and consumption, which has failed to heal the planet, eradicate poverty, and reduce inequality. Instead, they advocate for Indigenous-centric worldviews and other strategies that deemphasize the capitalist concept of "development." See Ashish Kothari, Federico Demaria, and Alberto

Acosta, "Buen Vivir, Degrowth and Ecological Swaraj: Alternatives to Sustainable Development and the Green Economy," *Development* 57, no. 3–4 (2014): 362–75.

54. Adrian Taylor Kane, "The Nicaragua Canal and the Shifting Currents of Sandinista Environmental Policy," in *Ecological Crisis and Cultural Representation in Latin America: Ecocritical Perspectives on Art, Film, and Literature*, ed. Mark Anderson and Zélia M. Bora (New York: Lexington Books, 2016), 269–73.

55. Tania Paz, "The Flame That Ignited Nicaragua's Protests," *AIDA*, May 31, 2018, https://aida-americas.org/en/blog/the-flame-that-ignited-nicaragua-s-protests.

Works Cited

Adams, Richard N. *The Dynamics of Societal Diversity: Notes from Nicaragua for a Sociology of Survival*. Austin: University of Texas, 1981.

Barbas-Rhoden, Laura. *Ecological Imaginations in Latin American Fiction*. Gainesville: University Press of Florida, 2011.

Calvo, Joaquín Bernardo. *República de Costa Rica. Apuntamientos geográficos, estadísticos e históricos*. San José: Imprenta Nacional, 1887.

Cortés, María Lourdes. *Fabulaciones del nuevo cine costarricense*. San José: Uruk Editores, 2016.

———. *La pantalla rota: Cien años de cine en Centroamérica*. México: Taurus, 2005.

Cunningham Wren, Lottie. "Pueblos indígenas y afrodescendientes: La lucha por sus derechos humanos." In *Anhelos de un nuevo horizonte. Aportes para una Nicaragua democrática*, edited by Alberto Cortés Ramos, Umanzor López Baltodano, and Ludwing Moncada Bellorin. Costa Rica: FLACSO, 2020.

Gayton, Don. "In Film, Out of Place." *Alternatives* 24, no. 4 (1998): 8–9.

Gómez-Barris, Macarena. *The Extractive Zone: Social Ecologies and Decolonial Perspectives*. Durham: Duke University Press, 2017.

González Pérez, José Miguel. *Gobiernos Pluriétnicos. La Constitución de Regiones Autónomas en Nicaragua*. Ciudad de México: Plaza y Valdés, 1997.

Grinberg Pla, Valeria, and Werner Mackenbach. "Banana novel revis(it)ed: etnia, género y espacio en la novela bananera centroamericana. El caso de *Mamita Yunai*." *Iberoamericana* 6, no. 23 (2006): 161–76.

"Harken Oil Company Requests $13 Million." *The Tico Times*, July 7, 2006. http://www.ticotimes.net/2006/07/07/harken-oil-company-requests-13-million.

Harvey-Kattou, Liz. "Performing for Hollywood: Coloniality and the Tourist Image in Esteban Ramírez's *Caribe/Caribbean* (2004)." *Studies in Spanish & Latin American Cinemas* 15, no. 2 (2018): 249–66.

Henríquez, Gloriantonia. "La Costa Atlántica de Nicaragua: ¿Un país inserto en otro o la heterogeneidad cultural como frontera?" *Cahiers du CRICCAL* 8 (1991): 103–17.

Ivakhiv, Adrian J. *Ecologies of the Moving Image: Cinema, Affect, Nature*. Waterloo, ON: Wilfrid Laurier University Press, 2013.

Jarquín Chamorro, Mateo. "A la sombra de la revolución sandinista: Nicaragua, 1979–2019." In *Anhelos de un nuevo horizonte. Aportes para una Nicaragua democrática*, edited by Alberto Cortés Ramos, Umanzor López Baltodano, and Ludwing Moncada Bellorin, 55–77. Costa Rica: FLACSO, 2020.

Kane, Adrian Taylor. "The Nicaragua Canal and the Shifting Currents of Sandinista Environmental Policy." In *Ecological Crisis and Cultural Representation in Latin America: Ecocritical Perspectives on Art, Film, and Literature*, edited by Mark Anderson and Zélia M. Bora, 269–75. New York: Lexington Books, 2016.

Kearns, Sofía. "Otra cara de Costa Rica a través de un testimonio ecofeminista." *Hispanic Journal* 19, no. 2 (Fall 1998): 313–39.

Kothari, Ashish, Federico Demaria, and Alberto Acosta. "Buen Vivir, Degrowth and Ecological Swaraj: Alternatives to Sustainable Development and the Green Economy." *Development* 57, no. 3–4 (2014): 362–75.

León, Jorge. *Nueva Geografía de Costa Rica*. San José: Soley y Valverde Editores, 1943.

López, Lidia. "Líderes indígenas dicen que versión policial sobre ataque pone en peligro la vida de los comunitarios." *La Prensa*, February 21, 2020. https://www.laprensa.com.ni/2020/02/21/nacionales/2643375-lideres-indigenas-sobre-ataques-de-colonos-ellos-creeran-que-como-somos-negritos-somos-animales-salvajes-que-nos-cazan.

Mackenbach, Werner. "El Caribe y la literatura centroamericana: de la doble exclusión al doble espejo." In *Caribbean(s) on the Move—Archipiélagos literarios del Caribe. A TransArea Symposium*, edited by Ottmar Ette, 107–19. Frankfurt: Peter Lang Verlag, 2008.

Molina Jiménez, Iván. "*Limón blues*: una novela de Ana Cristina Rossi." *Revista de Filosofía de la Universidad de Costa Rica* 42 (January–April 2004): 185–88.

Offen, Karl. *The Miskitu Kingdom: Landscape and the Emergence of a Miskitu Identity, Northeastern Nicaragua and Honduras, 1600–1800*. PhD diss., University of Texas, 1999.

Ortiz Wallner, Alexandra. *El arte de ficcionar: La novela contemporánea en Centroamérica*. Madrid: Iberoamericana, 2012.

Paz, Tania. "The Flame That Ignited Nicaragua's Protests." *AIDA*, May 31, 2018. https://aida-americas.org/en/blog/the-flame-that-ignited-nicaragua-s-protests.

Postema, Joel. "Ecology and Ethnicity in Anacristina Rossi's *La loca de Gandoca*." *Cincinnati Romance Review* 27 (2008): 113–24.

Rama, Ángel. "La ciudad escrituraria." In *La ciudad letrada*, 41–71. Hannover: Ediciones del Norte, 1984.

Ramírez, Esteban, dir. *Caribe*. 2004, Costa Rica, DVD.

Rizo, Mario. *Pueblos Indígenas de Nicaragua y su cultura del agua*. Managua, 2005.

Rodríguez, Ana Patricia. *Dividing the Isthmus: Central American Transnational Histories, Literatures, and Cultures*. Austin: University of Texas Press, 2009.

Torres, Dania, dir. *Lih Wina*. 2012, Nicaragua, DVD.

Willoquet-Maricondi, Paula. "Shifting Paradigms: From Environmentalist Films to Ecocinema." In *Framing the World: Explorations in Ecocriticism and Film*, edited by Paula Willoquet-Maricondi, 43–61. Charlottesville, VA: University of Virginia Press, 2010.

Yúdice, George. "The Central American Caribbean: Rethinking Regional and National Imaginaries." In *El Caribe y sus diásporas: Cartografía de saberes y prácticas culturales*, edited by Anja Bandau and Martha Zapata Galindo, 96–115. Madrid: Editorial Verbum, 2010.

12

Refracting Lenses on the Atlantic Coast of Nicaragua

Documenting Social Ecologies and Biospheres in *El ojo del tiburón* and *El canto de Bosawas*

JULIA M. MEDINA

> Acknowledging the uncommon that brings them together . . . these alliances may also be capable of refracting the course of the one world world and proposing, as in the Zapatista declaration, the practice of a world of many worlds, or what we call a pluriverse: heterogenous worldings coming together as a political ecology of practice.
>
> —Blaser and de la Cadena[1]

The Atlantic or eastern coast of Nicaragua has been a crossroads of all sorts of (proto)imperial prances and glances.[2] Within an anthropocentric scale of time and perspective, this includes the precolonial interface of various ethnic groups (including but not limited to the Maya, Nahuas, and Chibcha), Columbus's fourth voyage to the Americas and the African flux, the British declaring kingdoms upon the chief-led society of the Miskitu, the United States' imperial meanderings, Chinese canal dreams, and the ongoing onslaught of expanding extractive economies, such as mining, cattle, timber, and monocrop production. The relationship of the Autonomous Regions of the Atlantic Coast with the nation-state of Nicaragua continues this pattern, with its late incorporation into the nation in 1893, and its continued assault by the state throughout the twentieth century and into our present.[3]

A crossroads of people and geography, the Atlantic coast has long trafficked in the various things implicit in imperial domination, now manifest in the form of arms, drugs, livestock, timber, metals and more. In the era of the Anthropocene, these trafficked goods continue the colonial legacy through violent forms of extraction, both material and abstract, that deplete ecologies and ontologies. Those forests, mountains, and rivers are the living legacy of the original peoples whose livelihood remains under constant assault.[4] Despite or because of its geopolitical position, the Atlantic coast is an area marked by imperial imagery and imaginaries.[5] Is it possible to overcome this pervasive imagery in twenty-first-century documentary film? This chapter explores how two films portray the complex alliances that are necessary, as suggested in the epigraph, in order to represent an environment under siege that resists the estrangement of place.

Despite their titles, *El ojo del tiburón* (*The Eye of the Shark*, Argentina, Spain, 2012) by Alejo Hoijman,[6] and *El canto de Bosawas* (*The Song of the Bosawas*, United States, Nicaragua, 2014) by Camilo Castro and Brad Allgood, both approach the socioecological complexity of the Atlantic Coast of Nicaragua from an anthropocentric perspective that corresponds to transatlantic and continental angles respectively. These films stand on different spectrums of the documentary gamut, in that the first emphasizes artistic production and aesthetic effect, whereas the second focuses on activism to advocate for the conservation of the Bosawás Biosphere. The artistic take of *El ojo del tiburón* aligns with the tradition of direct cinema through a coming-of-age story of two boys who must choose between "traditional" shark fishing and drug trafficking. The activist approach of *El canto de Bosawas* is a conventional expository documentary that registers the musical practices of the Mayangna. In both cases, the human subject (in its Western male iteration) is the subject and point of departure, although both purportedly seek to register posthuman ontologies and imperatives.

While these films register different angles within the documentary film genre, it is fruitful to consider them concurrently because of the geography and ecologies they document: the northern and southern autonomous regions of the Atlantic Coast. These films provide a glimpse into the tension of being able to push, or not, past the human in film, in the context of biological reserves and biospheres in Nicaragua: threatened, peripheral areas.[7] To understand the general situation of such ground zeros, Macarena Gómez-Barris's elaboration of the "extractive zone" is particularly useful, which she defines as "geographies where coordinated forms of capitalist power advance," and whose "universalizing idiom and viewpoint . . . hides the political geographies embedded within the conversion of complex life."[8] Within these zones, Gómez-Barris excavates "submerged perspectives" that make local knowledge visible and "displace the ocular centricity of human development [in order to reveal] a submerged, below-the-surface, blurry countervisuality."[9] The films at hand attempt that gaze from different approaches.

In their form, content, and production, these two films register the contradictions of how the extractive gaze captures submerged perspectives. In doing so, we will see that they reproduce the cultural, political, and ontological tension that characterizes the divide between the Pacific and Atlantic sides of Nicaragua. This divide incarnates the split between "Western" and "non-Western" paradigms as it relates to being in place.[10] As these films indicate, to push past the human in Latin American film or otherwise requires reckoning with the human/nonhuman interface in place.

Each of these films portrays the southern and northern autonomous regions of the Atlantic coast of Nicaragua, producing a refracted perspective of that peripheral range. The area was declared as autonomous, and split into North and South regions, in 1987 during the first presidency of Ortega, at the height of the Contra war. They were then designated as protected biospheres in the 1990s during the neoliberal government of Violeta Barrios de Chamorro. The Sandinista government had previously promoted the creation of these protected zones during the mid-1980s. However, instead of aiming for achievable transnational conservation, at that time ecological discourse was used to pressure US military operations to end in Honduras, Nicaragua, and Costa Rica.[11] Perhaps anticipating the current cynical rhetoric of the Ortega-Murillo regime, the proposal was called "Natural Reserves for Peace."

In film proper, the Oscar-nominated film *Alsino y el cóndor* (*Alsino and the Condor*, Nicaragua, Cuba, México, Costa Rica, 1982), by Miguel Littín, launched Nicaragua on the international cinematic map during the height of the armed struggle between the Contras and the Sandinistas.[12] Just a few years later, the Atlantic Coast entered the film circuit with a Sundance-nominated documentary by Lee Shapiro, *Nicaragua Was Our Home* (United States, 1985), which depicts the struggle of the Miskitu, an Afro-Amerindian community violently forced out of their ancestral lands.[13] On the commercial end of the spectrum, the mega-production *The Mosquito Coast* (United States, 1986) emptied the area of its history and people to enact a twentieth-century take on *Robinson Crusoe*.[14] *The Mosquito Coast* was released at the height of the Contra War, which in part took place in the Atlantic Region of Nicaragua and Honduras, where the US military set up camp and trained Contra operatives.[15]

More recently the area was included in a Spanish documentary made for the Discovery Channel: *Caribe salvaje: tierras desconocidas (Wild Caribbean: Unknown Lands,* 2013). Here the region is described as extending for more than 2,700 kilometers that stretch from Panama to Mexico: delicate ecosystems, almost void of people. As this production illustrates, the visual decentering of the human under the guise of ecotourist perspective, much like earlier European discovery and travel narratives, reinforces colonial paradigms of Eurocentric humanism. In contrast to these films' external gaze, films of this region produced from a Latin American perspective allude to other-than-human subjects and subjectivities, as in the case of *Alsino y el cóndor* and the two films under discussion. Directed and adapted by the Chilean director Miguel Littín, from a novel titled *Alsino* (Pedro Prado, 1920), the film references an extension of Operation Condor (1968–1989) in effect at the time in South America. Although the films coproduced in the South allude to a posthuman approach, both get caught up in the poetics of "nature or open spaces" as a backdrop for individual male experiences. In the most recent cases of the first film we consider, an Argentinian/Spanish coproduction, they also provide a graded perspective that foregrounds the humans who are intertwined with the Atlantic coast and their relationship with those surroundings.

Consistent with its transnational production, and as the title suggests, *El ojo del tiburón* (2012) strives to universalize and aestheticize a localized other-than-human experience.[16] The title is a nod to the poetry collection by Mexican writer Homero Aridjis, *El ojo de la ballena* (*The Whale's Eye*, 2001), which Scott De Vries hails as a pioneering example of environmentalist literature.[17] The intertextual allusion is significant, as the film posits itself as part of an ecologically minded canon. Despite the titular reference to nonhuman life, the story follows Bryan and Maicol, two boys who must choose between the dwindling practice of artisanal shark hunting and the enticing option of drug trafficking.

The action is set in the San Juan River, in El Castillo and San Juan del Norte, located in the southeast quadrant of the Southern Autonomous Atlantic Region of Nicaragua. San Juan del Norte was occupied and contested by the British, and the region represents the bastion of hegemonic struggles between the old empire and the rising United States. As such, the town is also known as Graytown. The nearby Reserva Indio Maíz, not mentioned in the film, is an integral part of the San Juan River Biosphere and region.[18] When it was established in 1994, it was called "La gran reserva" and included all of this southern region. In 1998, because of conflict with *colonos*/settlers, it broke up into four adjacent reserves.[19] The film's first sequence sets the two boys on a barren and littered shore of the Caribbean Sea, the mouth of the San Juan River, all part of this unique ecosystem.

According to Pablo Piedras, *El ojo* is an example of the Argentinian tradition of direct cinema, although in this case with a more controlled mise-en-scène.[20] This style of documentary filmmaking is characterized by the open relationship between filmmaker, camera, and filmed material to capture unexpected gestures of reality. This approach is about not controlling the image nor providing explanatory narration or script. The advantage of this style is that it allows access to private spaces through observational representation. Piedras admits that the approach has gained currency in contemporary Argentinean documentary filmmaking because it avoids political commentary that historicizes state violence. In effect, the film may be considered a poetic mode of documentary filmmaking, one that is "particularly adept at opening up the possibility of alternative forms of knowledge to the straightforward transfer of information."[21] Displacement and interaction through bodies of water provide a medium of socialization for the characters.

Formally, the river—and the boys' lives through it—structures the visual narrative of the film as an important nonhuman agent that is more than mere setting. The San Juan river connects the Atlantic Ocean to the Lake of Nicaragua, which once facilitated the Spanish colonization of the Pacific Coast and would later incite dreams of an interoceanic canal. Mark Twain registered these pretentions, as well as filibustering remnants of Walker's incursion, in his 1866 account of his crossing through the country, published at the time in newspapers in San Francisco.[22] Because of disputes generated at this crossroads, embodied by the William Walker affair, in the mid-nineteenth century the river became a contentious, tangible border between Costa Rica and Nicaragua. During the production of this film, several ecological threats endangered the area, including a road built by Costa Rica that ran parallel to the aforementioned river.[23]

Through the situated human experience, the film registers the river as a transitory place in a historical juncture of shift between local traditional practices and other ways of being. A striking sequence framed at water level, with visible water droplets on the lens, depicts a group of seven boys climbing up a huge sphere made of rubber car wheels tied with chains that turns as they climb (figure 12.1). The dark-skinned boys laugh as they climb

Figure 12.1. Alejo Hoijman, *El ojo del tiburón*, 2012, video still.

up this toy made of vehicular rubbage. It is a contraption more in synch with a dystopian *Mad Max* setting than the riverbank's shrubbery. A common joke in Nicaragua is that the national flower is the plastic bag, which litters most urban and rural settings. Mass production and consumption, evidenced by the buildup of nondegradable materials, such as plastics or rubber, are portrayed through the repurposed car wheels in this scene.[24] The camera closes in almost uncomfortably on the massive rubber ball and the boys, whose wristwatches, in line with the prop, contrast with an otherwise rustic setting. An affirmation of displaced modernity, these objects mediate the boy's experience of the water. The river is rendered modern, a site of diversion and current time because of the presence of artisanal plastic-/rubber-based props. The boys' nascent masculinity is displayed in a game suggestive of aqua-military training.

The next scene is a wide angle shot at water level or slightly below that puts the game at a distant foreground and shows Maicol in the first plane, preparing a snorkel. The wider angle displays the riverbank's exuberant vegetation. Shifting perspective, the camera submerges underwater in a sequence that lasts about thirty-five seconds, capturing a sediment-filled brownish substance and aqueous sounds. Gómez-Barris refers to such tactics as producing a "fish-eye epistemology that changes how we might relate to [the river] as a sentient being, rather than an extractible commodity."[25]

The two protagonists are not part of the other boys' game of climbing up the rubber ball, and individually they experience water in different ways and frames, as subjects of that fish-eye perspective. After a few seconds of silence in the underwater sequence, we see Bryan free-dive, submerged in the murky substance that hardly seems potable. The spectator, also plunged in the scene, is immersed in the tension of lively games in that almost abject setting. Anticipating the paths each character will later chose, Maicol employs a snorkel, while Bryan freely submerges into the river. In addition to the juxtaposition between disposable materials in a body of water, thematically, the frame anticipates that Bryan is the boy open to continuing traditional shark fishing practices. Visually and symbolically the water sequence synthesizes the story, as it relates to male socialization and technologies in that space.

Given the film's title, it is imperative to consider the presence of sharks, whose bodies only appear dead, as bodies to be manipulated and slaughtered by humans.[26] One of the final scenes shows the fisherman butchering several specimens, throwing the bloody bodies on a boat floor. Bryan appears among the men cutting up the sharks. Distanced from any vocational activity, in the following scene his counterpart, Maicol, is seen at a barbershop, bending his head down while his hair gets tightly cropped with a blade. Given the sequential chain's insistence on the blade, this scene alludes to some sort of sacrificial rite, produced by the changing position of his head to get trimmed around the ear, in contrast to the fin.

Foreshadowing the scene with the shark, earlier in the film there is a sequence of the boys in the forest hunting with a slingshot. Under the guidance of the Maicol, after many attempts Bryan shoots and kills a small lizard. With pride, Bryan holds the reptile's body by the tail and walks it to his mentor, who crudely operates on the lifeless creature by throwing it on the floor and stomping on it. The camera does not follow the implied violence, but registers its sounds. Although the shark fishing/processing scene depicts the handling of the dead shark, as the fin is the most valued part of the animal for the Asian market, it does so matter-of-factly: an economic transaction that involves humans, blood, and animals. The purposelessness of Maicol's stomping on the lizard, however, speaks to a destructive inter-species dynamics. Killing the lizard with the slingshot, a gained skill in and of itself, is not enough; Maicol must assert its obliteration.

Physical male contact exposes an equally bellicose underpinning, as can be seen on a scene set on the beach, where two boys fiercely wrestle while three older boys watch from a distance. A younger mate serves as referee to playfully legitimize the combat. The film is a testament to intergenerational socialization of masculinity, as conditioned by place, at that specific historical juncture. The place is embedded in a natural reserve, located in a geographical and political frontier between the Caribbean Sea and Costa Rica; between the lively Indigenous people of that region and the economic demands of (neo) colonial/settler economies. The historical stage is at the height/fall of capital, at the inflection of the Anthropocene, or rather the Capitalocene, understood as the "era shaped by relations privileging the endless accumulation of capital."[27] How are boys on the verge of adulthood socialized at this liminal time, in an extractive zone though an extractive gaze?

Much like the river, the forest is setting to intergenerational male socialization where the protagonist learns to decipher the sounds of the mountain, "el monte," from an elder, Juan Inocencio García Meléndez, presumably Maicol's father. The boy expresses bewilderment and vulnerability by asking about the sounds he hears. Visually anchoring indigeneity, the paternal figure traces a parallel between the rustling sound the wild boars (*wari*) make on the leaves and the waves of the ocean, thus weaving through verbal image a synesthesia of ocean and forest. As part of the beyond human interaction, the father shows his son jaguar prints in the dirt, as well as dwellings of other animals such as armadillos, while warning of the dangers of snake. Although Juan Inocencio is able to share with his son the forest's sounds and secrets, perhaps because of his son's rejection of his vocation, shark fishing is something he can only impart on Bryan, his son's best friend. Decoding the sounds of the forest is portrayed as an intergenerational platform of male socialization. Shifting roles, Maicol at one point indicates that "it smells like iguana" and instructs Bryan to imitate the howling monkeys. Prolonged takes of the boys' intent interactions with the rustling of leaves, or the howling, chirping, and buzzing of various monkeys, birds, reptiles, and insects, point to forms of other than human socialization.

Although neither crew nor cameras appear on-screen, the references to production, and its effect on the character's lives, shape the narrative. One scene shows the back of the boys' heads watching and commenting on footage of the documentary the audience has just seen. Another shows them watching Bryan in the shark-hunting expedition on a television screen. They gaze, like us, as spectators of the traditional shark fishermen, which include Bryan, Maicol's father, and others on the crew. With a hint of envy for having missed out on the action, Maicol mocks his friend for looking scared. In turn, and to highlight his friend's absence, Bryan mentions "there is Maicol" as the camera focuses on his father. The temporal simultaneity is visually captured and verbally extended onto the story.

The film's conclusion focuses on Maicol having a conversation on a wooden pier by the river with Elba. This end closes the cycle of male socialization; Elba's appearance contrasts with most of the film, where women are scantly included and only in relation to men. Their conversation turns to the film's production. After lamenting that she could not join the filming because of her gendered obligations, Elba wonders why a crew would want to record such a dull place. To this, Maicol responds that the crew deems the place a paradise. The protagonists voice the filmmakers' intentions, symbolically closing the story with their projected desires, where they wish they could live. What is considered ordinary to the actors represents an ideal for the film crew, a revelation uttered by the filmed subjects as the credits start to roll. Much is suggested by this narrative structure as the final aerial take confirms. It shows Maicol sitting behind a heavyset man associated with drug trafficking with a prominent wristwatch on a jet ski, loudly and rapidly motoring down the river. This last sequence of humans in water and forest visually depicts, from a distant perspective, the gaze of a traveler or witness that leaves by air. Thematically the film leaves us with the suggestion that traditional shark hunting is a bloody, violent, mechanical task, and the lures of trafficking offer wistful possibilities of success and mobility. The intricacies of drug trafficking are never made explicit, just suggested. The lure of this form of economic subsistence is suspended, omitted, remitted to the viewer's imagination. Drug trafficking is portrayed as it might operate in reality: understated, unexpected, implied.

Shifting north and a couple of years later, the second film under consideration here is the documentary *El canto de Bosawas,* a local attempt to advocate for the preservation of the Biosphere Bosawás as inseparable from the musical practices of its human inhabitants.[28] To personify and approach the place, the filmmakers set out to record the musical tradition of the Mayangna people who live in that region.[29] In the opening sequence, before the title screen, the frame depicts two Indigenous women singing in their language, while a man holds a recorder against the backdrop of lush green mountains, in a shared frame with pigs grazing nearby. The visual and auditory recordings of singing (by human or birds) is limited to a few scenes that present the sounds and voices of the Mayangna people. By privileging the human in the pre-title scene, the film centers the biosphere through Western human ecologies and perspectives. The title scene lets us hear the songs of the women, while the words "El canto de Bosawas" appear superimposed on a stunning shot of rolling mist in the green forest hill. Unbeknownst to most viewers, the word Bosawás, as a proper name, depicts a different ontology. The name is composed of the first syllable from the River Bocay, Saslaya Hill, River Waspuk, all constitutive parts of that area. The lyrical quality of the title is bound to the fragmentary conception of ecological corridors. To the north of Bosawas, the ecosystem continues on to the National Park Patuca in the Biological Reserve of Tawahka in Honduras, and together they constitute $50,000^2$ kilometers of protected area, constantly under siege. Since the beginning of 2020, more than a dozen Mayangnas community members have been killed in Nicaragua because of aggressive settler encroachment.[30] North of that national border, the situation does not fare any better for first nations of Honduras that are part of this reserve.

The premise of *El canto de Bosawas* follows the code of documentary activism and reflects on the advances and shortcomings of new technologies and new networks of geocultural collaboration. Unlike the previously analyzed film, where the focus is on the local cast and setting, here the local human and nonhuman agents are the background to the Western traveler's saga. Moreover, unlike the first film, where the metanarrative does not include the camera or the technologies of recording, in this case the documentary centers on the complexities of production in a remote region, not necessarily on the music itself, the Mayangna, or the place being depicted. Somewhat like novels, *testimonios*, or other forms of narrative, the documentary visually portrays ecological assemblages, *collectives*[31] through the narrator's travel experience. The question is, as Blaser and de la Cadena point out, "can conditions be created so that heterogeneous knowledge practices (Indigenous and non-Indigenous, for example) do not encounter each other in a relation of subject to object (or not only as such relation)?"[32] A close look at this film allows us to consider this question.

Consistent with the traditional format of participatory documentary filmmaking and the expository mode, the camera follows the perspective of Ernesto "Matute" López, a Nicaraguan percussionist in the band *La cuneta Son Machín,* a clear nod at *Miami Sound Machine*. This local celebrity from the Pacific Coast of Nicaragua narrates and mediates the North American crew's gaze and the Indigenous cultural expressions they seek to capture in Bosawás. Matute could not finance or produce a documentary of this scope. The question of whether he sought out support from the Nicaraguan government is never raised. To compensate for the lack of local and national infrastructure, Matute joins forces with two sound engineers and an art historian from the United States to record the human songs of Bosawás.[33] Through music, Matute aims to raise support for the conservation of the biosphere.

The documentary's main contribution is that it documents the voices and musical practices of the Mayangna people. In the process, it also captures the richness and vulnerability of the biosphere, thus encapsulating a contemporary example of the (neo)imperial gaze and friction inherited from Spanish and US travel writing traditions.[34] In reference to nineteenth-century travel writing on New Zealand, Linda Tuhiwai Smith notes that in accounts of the colonized world, "There was a consciousness expressed in some accounts of the 'need' to record what was seen in the interest of expanding knowledge and to write things down before too many changes occurred to the peoples being observed."[35] In *El canto de Bosawas*, music functions as a transnational language that is the anthropomorphized extension of the ecosystem, and a relatable practice for the Western audience. Irrespective of humans, ecosystems have their own music or soundscapes composed of birds, insects, fauna, wind, and vegetation. Film technology registers Mayangna voices, places, and images, albeit mostly male, that assert other ontologies and collectives that push past the human, as the testimony from the chief and others confirm. The question is if the viewer can decipher or receive those messages within the melodrama of the cast.

In terms of gender, with the exception of the opening scene and one other brief sequence, the female voice is relegated to a marginal role. Mayangna women never address the camera to comment or talk about their livelihoods. The Western woman does not fare any better, in that the art historian and fourth integrant of the crew never speaks directly to the camera to share her professional expertise. Whereas in the first documentary at least one woman speaks to the disproportionate labor obligations of women, in this second documentary the female voice is rendered object, not a subject of agency.

The first recording of Indigenous voices is set in the Mayangna territory of Sauni As, in the community of Sakalwas. The spokesman for the community expresses support for recording their musical practice, and the musicians are eager to share songs that decry threats to the ancestral livelihood in that land.[36] This references the real and daily threats imposed by the growing demands of livestock, logging and mining industries. At the beginning of the musicians' recording, they dedicate their singing to two hills called Kirahbu, named thus by the ancestors in reference to a beautiful, lush tree that bears fruit. The musicians offer their songs to those hills, to the Sakalwas, and to the population gathered for the recording. The screen moves between two men singing with microphones, while a guitarist and supporting vocals join in. The end of that sequence includes a brief depiction of two women singing. This recording lasts less than a minute and includes voice-overs by a North American sound engineer, Izzy, and Matute. The former points to the Caribbean character of the music, and the latter specifies that is reminiscent of Miskitu and Garifuna influence.

The experts' narration overpowers the showcased music. Seemingly the value of the music itself does not suffice, nor does the viewer's criteria, for it is the narrator's voice and perspective that dominate this first official scene of recording. This is more problematic in that although undoubtedly Caribbean rhythms mark this sample of music, in this first example there is more of a Mexican-Norteño beat, overlooked by the musical experts. It may have been inconceivable for Izzy to consider the convergence of Mexican and Caribbean sounds as transareal historical experiences. Echoing rigid nationalist parameters, this compartmentalized thinking obviates the geo-cultural history and ecological reality of the region.

A second scene from this performance focuses on the staging of the recording rather than its execution. In this instance, thirty seconds of uninterrupted music are directly aligned with a Caribbean sound. This sequence is followed by brief words from one of the musicians, Arnoldo "Arkin" Taylor, who sees in this experience the realization of his dream of recording music for distribution and posterity. Izzy self-congratulatorily comments that he is carrying out "guerilla recording." The tone-deaf comment trivializes the region's history as guerrilla history, capturing the asymmetrical underpinnings of this film. Once in Bosawás there are only two or three other brief scenes of Mayangna music. Taken as a whole, despite the documentary's title and intent, *El canto de Bosawas* is less about the songs, sounds, voices, and other subjectivities of Bosawás and more about the drama of its production. It comes across as a prelude to the sounds and songs recorded on that trip, which one hopes to find soon in local music stores, bookstores, or online. Unfortunately, as of 2020, the release of the recorded music has not materialized. Nonetheless, by virtue of its setting, the documentary also exposes the ecosystem's vulnerability, as it is intrinsic to Mayangna's ways of being.

Music, as seen by the introductory dedication of song to the two mountains of Kirahbu, is part of a way of being that includes an indivisible relationship to other-than-human earth beings, as described in de la Cadena's work. Although the film does not present it sufficiently, the conservation of Mayangna culture is interwoven with the conservation of place. The ecology of Bosawás, as a reserve, is indivisible from the Mayangna, not as mere stewards of place, but co-constitutive. As for *other-than-human beings*, in addition to the topographical entities that include rivers and mountains, a few separate close-ups focus on different species of insects and reptiles, along with the sounds of their surroundings. On the domesticated side of things, swine, dogs, equines, and chickens are shown in interaction with humans. As part of their journey registering those sites, Matute's focus turns to the region's fragile beauty with a romantic gaze.

His ecocritical commentary is accompanied by scenes of cattle in the green but barren mountainside, oblivious culprits of much of the ecological devastation experienced in the region today.[37] The bovine is sequenced with scenes of deforestation that show the cut trunk of a large tree against the backdrop of burned ones. The slash-and-burn assault on ancient forests and protected areas is enacted to meet the demands of the growing meat industry, palm tree, rice, or other single-crop economy. Though not named as such, the Capitalocene is another culprit. The auditory commentary of this visible ecocidal logic is critically self-reflective and seeks to distance itself from the otherwise romantic encounter with place. Matute acknowledges that he is a *colono* or settler himself, complicit in the pressures on protected areas. His own positioning in relation to this category condemns the colonial enterprise and points to a clear understanding of the economic forces that drive destruction, apathy, and neglect. Matute's assessment, in relation to the chief's perspective, points to interesting "partial connections" or cooperation between non-native and Indigenous leaders and activists.[38]

Given the remoteness of this community and reserve, following the tropes of explorer narratives, the local *colono* Pacific Coast Afro-mestizo, must navigate through rivers and jungles to reach his altruistic objective. After a sequence of the boat going down the river with the crew, representing two days of travel, Matute expresses his gratitude for arriving in Bosawás. The first impromptu recording of music is set in the community plaza, a troupe of several men dance with sticks and masks made of cardboard. In addition to a large audience of children, a group of four musicians with different types of guitars play and sing. Through a close-up, we can see that some of the masks depict a jaguar and also the devil, as the narrator explains. Following the welcome dance, as music plays, the camera shows the crew meeting with musicians in the school, along with a public mostly composed of young boys. The camera focuses on the captivated faces of children intently listening to two male singers wearing baseball caps. Intergenerational male socialization here too is at the center of the action. Young people are learning not just about their cultural traditions, but also about how these are performed for outsiders. Speaking over the song, Izzy's voice explains that this is like listening to 1960s Jamaican music.

To contextualize the level of common misunderstandings around Mayangna cultures, the following sequence shows Matute talking with Econayo Taylor, a leader of the Mayangna Territory of Sauni As, a place he apologetically explains that many educated Nicaraguans and policy makers ignore. This is a regrettable reality in the complex multiethnic context of the Atlantic Coast of Nicaragua. The local leader explains that Mayangna are very different in their ways of being, and that such recordings serve to create understanding of their livelihoods and their plight. A second leader, Pedro Justo, follows up with commentary to condemn the neglect of the government against invaders. A third leader, Rolando Davis Jacobo, describes the need to safeguard their cultural patrimony for humanity, not just for locals. His appeal has to go beyond the national, in part to protect his community from the national, as the production also suggests. Throughout the film, Mayangna voices insist on the significance of a *pluriverse,* that is, "the practice of a world of many worlds [. . .] heterogeneous worlding coming together as a political ecology of practice, negotiating the difficult being together in heterogeneity."[39] Indeed, the recording of musical practices in this context cannot be disentangled from political ecological practices of these communities.

Shifting from leaders to the community, and subtly reifying the supremacy of a singular world, the next sequences show people attending mass, where they sing and chant in unison. Singing and chanting practices are linked to official religion, or forms of spirituality, that may involve earth beings, or not. Unlike most other male-centric representations, here visual focus is given to children and women, as well as to elders. The narrator's voice hails the communion among the people, as well as the environmental motivation of their gathering. Closing this sequence, the camera follows four men navigating the river in a traditional canoe. The narration of Gustavo Lino, the vice president of the GTI Mayangna Sauni As from 2011–2013, expresses fear of losing the culture, their practice of everyday life, and the place that sustains it. Expressing part of this pluriverse, he explains that maintaining culture is a way that allows them to safeguard the land as part of their identity. As the lens takes us through the misty forest, Matute confirms that the existence of the biosphere depends on the Mayangna, as do the rest of us.

After digressions that detail the intercultural drama of production among the crew, we finally reach a highlight of the whole documentary. That sequence takes place at night in a school, and it includes some community members. The climax documents a song that lasts around one minute and forty-five seconds, the longest uninterrupted focus on sound from Bosawás. While the spectator listens to the sweet music that combines male voices and melody, the camera shifts between the playing musicians, the listening public, and the pleased expressions of Matute and the other sound engineers. The delight of the production is extended in scenes of local musicians listening to the recording of their music, and the crew's commentaries on their professionalism. The narrator closes the sequence by noting the magical quality of the experience and his feeling of achievement. The archival value of the recording lies not just in the content and in the platform for cultural agency that it provides, but also in what it represents to the chief and the people as they first experience listening to their own recorded music, a refraction of their pluriverse.

The significance of the occasion is structurally interrupted by accounts of the ailments of one of the crew and efforts to find adequate health care. The remaining sound engineer prepares for another recording in the church that they had planned prior to the news of the ailment. As the camera focuses on three men singing in a microphone, we hear Izzy lament that this group had no clear concept of their style. Perhaps in what may be considered the most problematic part of the whole documentary, the expert insists that the group sounded as though "they were trying to play reggae." He arrogantly instructs the musicians to play more "como piedra" [like a rock] so that the music can sound more like reggae, which he equivocally envisions as the ultimate expression of the music they are recording. His imposing attitude misses that the translation, in this case, does not always work.

The contrast between the musician's visual depiction and Izzy's instructions renders his opinion objectionable. Limited to his own repertoire, which he tries to project onto the Mayangna musicians, the sound engineer laments the poor quality of the musical production but acknowledges the vocals' merit. The imposed referent upon the Mayangna cultural and musical expression suggests an impossibility of pushing past the human if the human cannot be heard or understood. The unfortunate attempt to classify Mayangna music within preconceived genres parallels the inadequacies of parceling an ecological corridor according to national boundaries, as is currently practiced in political and academic terms.

The imperial projection is trailed by the chief's arrival to the makeshift studio. Visually, his status is inscribed by the painted jaguar on the back of his jacket and an improvised headdress. Matute explains to the viewing public the chief's significance as the sage of the people, the philosophical leader who keeps tradition and history alive. The sequence of the chief listening to the playback of the previous night's recording is the second highlight of the film. Refocusing on space and Western perspective, after thanking the work that the recording entailed, the chief of the Mayangna Suni As territory, Nirio Simion, states that he would like to hear "more songs about the forest in our mountains and the life of the Mayangnas" and that "we are also happy singing to our forests, rivers and animals. And that is why it is important to extend this work and give it continuity." He emphasizes that the people are bound to that land because they chose to settle there because of its richness. It is their last frontier, their last place. Nirio grieves that he and his people have been mistreated everywhere and refuse ill treatment there because they will not leave that place. And so he declares that they will not leave, for Mayangna have been pushed to the limit, the biosphere reserve, a collective of human and nonhuman beings necessary for each other's survival.

This brief scene features a headframe of Nirio directly addressing the camera and includes his name and title in caption. Captions are necessary to translate his words from his native language to Spanish. Mayangna is from the Sumalpa/Misumalpa family, part of the macro Chibcha. By addressing the camera in his language, he asserts its continued existence. From that angle

Figure 12.2. "But here we do not want more harassment. We are not going to leave this place." Nirio Simion, chief of the Mayangna Sauni As territory. Brad Allgood and Camilo de Castro, *El canto de Bosawas*, 2014, video still.

the viewer can read that the headdress, in addition to a couple of feathers on either side, depicts three drawn mountains, with a text below that reads "NG. Rarah." It's frustrating to the curious viewer not to understand the meaning of signs here. Ng is a consonant in Mayangna, although also "of" in Tagalog and other possibilities. My limited research indicates the Rarah is a part of broader concepts, such as Asang Rarah, a supreme being of sacred and mythical places.[40] As a suffix it appears in mamahrarah, a bird that arrives at the region as summer begins. Though viewers do not understand this nor its intended reference, the urgency of the chief's message is clear: the sounds and visual representations of the language's concepts matter, be it in music or otherwise, as his headdress illustrates.

Hailing the crew's effort, and the advances of technology, Nirio expresses hope and joy in the recording of their songs, which allows the Mayangna to reclaim and register their silenced voice. As the narration is set against scenes of different collectives of the biosphere and their ways of being, the documentary serves as a contemporary rendition of testimonial narrative in the form of audiovisual recording. Whereas literary testimony in Central America dealt with military violence enacted against the subaltern, the cinematic testimonial form in the twenty-first century must reckon with ecocidal and epistemic violence that threatens Indigenous livelihoods and collective with the other-than-human counterparts. It also must reckon with the narcissistic tilt of projects that seek to visually document or experience certain areas without reciprocal exchange.

Against the visual backdrop of human-nonhuman collectives, Chief Nirio firmly states that "[e]very mountain covered in mist has its own history that the next generation must know. They don't know it. We must teach them so they can share with other cultures." This recording of the chief's pluriversal testimony, even if it is over piano instead of local sounds, along with the voices of other leaders as they envision the Mayangna relationship to place, is compelling. This is further substantiated by subsequent scenes that frame the mountains, sky, river, animals, and collectives to corroborate the imperative of place, while unpacking it. The refracting form of the sequencing captures a "fractal" collective through the "fractal self" of Nirio, the Chief. "The fractal self" articulates "an emergent human spirit in our ancestors seeking connections in the grand milieu of nature."[41]

Despite the narrative focus on the drama of the traveler's return, the imposition of place is set by visual sequences of the land and the landscapes. The significance of Bosawás is marked by the density and layers of greens amid mist and is deciphered by the explanatory text in the final shot.[42] The plight of Bosawás is visually, audibly, and textually transcribed in this filmic testimony. The documentary seeks to illustrate the reach of ecocidal threats while linking the biosphere to its protectors' future, and by extension to ours. Invariably, the film extends the nineteenth-century trope of the declensionist narrative: stories that raise awareness of nature's value as linked to a sense of looming destruction.[43] A fractal perspective of this dynamic points to the axiom of that approach, in that it reveals the tensions of cooperation versus the dominant mode of competition. Agency as a contested platform is entangled to the (neo)imperial frictions that frame documentary production, in form and content.

Recording, whether it be a coming-of-age story, as in the case of *El ojo del tiburón*, or the music of the people of the region, as in the case of *El canto de Bosawas*, underlies both films thematically and formally. These efforts of documentation are shaped by male practices and socialization and redefined by new technologies and its by-products. As such, they engage in the extractive view, which "sees territories as commodities, rendering land as for the taking, while also devalorizing the hidden worlds that form the nexus of human and nonhuman multiplicity."[44] Consequent with their respective aesthetic and activist intent, *El ojo del tiburón* is not readily available online, like an artwork, whereas *El canto* is readily available, as a pedagogical tool to diffuse information. A refractive reading of these documentaries conveys the complexities of ecocritical representations and approaches to contested marginalized and endangered places, like the biospheres in the Atlantic Coast of Nicaragua. Dialectically, the chronicling and recording of fragile and endangered being-ness in place reveals an imperial underpinning to the new form of testimonial gesture in the Anthropocene. In centering the human, both films denote the precariousness of ecologies and ontologies under siege, exposing the split between Western and non-Western paradigms. In their strengths and shortcomings, these films reveal the messy and contradictory forms of cooperation. They ratify the mounting task of pushing past the human in the context of the Atlantic Coast of Nicaragua, not to mention the isthmus and beyond.

Notes

1. Mario Blaser and Marisol de la Cadena, "Pluriverse: Proposal for a World of Many Worlds," in *A World of Many Worlds* (Durham: Duke University Press, 2018), 4.

2. An earlier version of this paper was presented at the *International Symposium of Transcultural Convergences of the Caribbean* (Bowling Green State University, Ohio, February 22–24, 2018). This draft was enriched by the fruitful exchange on that occasion, by conversations with the Decolonization working group at the University of San Diego, as well as by the input of the editors of this volume, in particular Carolyn Fornoff's dedicated exchange.

3. Charles Hale, *Resistance and Contradiction: Miskitu Indians and the Nicaraguan State, 1894–1987* (Palo Alto: Stanford University Press, 1994), 89–94. Or see Carlos Vilas, *La Costa Atlántica en Nicaragua* (México: Fondo de Cultura Económica, 1992).

4. The Humboldt Center has reported that from 2011 to 2018, 1.4 million hectares of forest have been cut in Nicaragua, totaling 11 percent of the country.

5. Julia Medina, "Propaganda política en las ilustraciones de *Waikna, Aventuras en la Costa de la Mosquitia,* el imperialismo visual del siglo XIX," in *América Central en siglo XIX: Retratos en Tinta en de la region,* ed. Paúl Martínez (Honduras: Fototeca Nacional, 2018), 70–93.

6. I am grateful to Mora Juarez Allen for generously sharing with me *El Ojo del Tiburón*, co-produced by her sister.

7. The Indio Maíz reserve was devastated at the beginning of April 2018 by a fire caused by a *colono* seeking to expand the agricultural frontier. For more than 10 days the reserve burned 5,000 hectares of a precious ecosystem, as the Ortega government refused assistance offered by Costa Rican firefighters. The state's disproportionate response to student protests of this ecocide was a somber preamble for the April 18 insurrection that ensued.

8. Macarena Gómez-Barris, *The Extractive Zone: Social Ecologies and Decolonial Perspectives* (Durham: Duke University Press, 2017), xv, 4.

9. Ibid., 15.

10. In describing Indigenous ontologies/epistemes, Linda Tuhiwai Smith explains that there is a "different orientations towards time and space, different positioning within time and space, and different systems of language for making time and space 'real' underpin notions of past and present, *of place* and of relationship to the land." Linda Tuhiwai Smith, *Decolonizing Methodologies: Research and Indigenous Peoples* (London: Zed, 1999), 55.

11. The stipulation for this proposal was that it would be a multinational plan that included Costa Rica and Honduras, in order to establish an ecological corridor. During this time, the Contra War was taking place on both northern and southern borders, which greatly affected local communities.

12. In addition to the Chilean director, the film was a coproduction by Nicaragua, Cuba, Mexico, and Costa Rica. In 1991 Miguel Littin featured another film titled *Sandino*, full of contradictory implications given the time of production. On the plus side, scenes were shot on location and the film provided a critical perspective on the historical figure. Negatives include the casting of the main character, inaccuracies regarding Sandino's biography, and the film's melodramatic tone.

13. This episode centers the novel by Erick Blandón *Vuelo de cuervos* (Managua: Editorial Vanguardia, 1997).

14. Allegedly, the inspiration for Mr. Friday was a pirate called Will, a Miskitu man who had been stranded on the Juan Fernandez Island (1681), and whose story was recorded by William Dampier, *A New Voyage Round the World*. Thomas Roscoe connects the story of Will/Dampier to Crusoe in his annotated edition of Defoe's text (1831). Holden and Ruppel have noted that "Crusoe's relationship with Friday establishes a paradigm for other relationships between colonizers and colonized in Victorian adventure fiction, fiction that served a series of conduct books for the creation of a certain style of colonial and metropolitan masculinity." Philip Holden and Richard J. Ruppel, *Imperial Desires: Dissident Sexualities and Colonial Literature* (Minneapolis: University of Minnesota Press, 2003).

15. The so-called Mosquito Coast is a geocultural area, a triangular territory that lies in the Atlantic coast of Nicaragua and Honduras. The term replaced the earlier colonial term Taguzgalpa. It also refers to a polity of African Amerindian groups. Karl H. Offen, "Race and Place in Colonial Mosquitia, 1600–1787," in *Blacks and Blackness in Central America: Between Race and Place*, ed. Lowell Gudmundson and Justin Wolfe (Durham: Duke University Press, 2010), 94.

16. *El ojo del tiburón* was funded by the Ministry of Culture of the Spanish Government, Argentinean National Institute of Science and Audiovisual Art in (INCAA) with the support of Ibermedia, Cinereach, Media Tribeca Film Institute, and IDFA Fund BAL. Upon its release in 2012, the film was officially selected in the International Film Festival of Guadalajara México, the International Film Festival in Roma Italy, and the International Film Festival of Mar de la Plata, Argentina. In 2013 it received the prize for best Argentine feature film at the International Festival of Documentary Film in Buenos Aires (FIBDA), and Hoijman was awarded the prize for best director at the International Film Festival of Cartagena de Indias, Colombia.

17. Scott De Vries, *A History of Ecology and Environmentalism in Spanish American Literature* (Lewisburg: Bucknell University Press, 2013), 251.

18. Located in the southwestern quadrant of the country, the Indio Maíz Biological Reserve is nestled between the Indio River in the north and the San Juan River in the South over a stretch of 3,180 km^2. It was declared a protected Biological Reserve in the 1990s.

19. The government established the creation of Natural Protected areas of Southeast Nicaragua in 1990, which was consolidated in 1994 as Southeastern Territory of Sustainable Development, and in 1999 broken up into Refugio de Vida Silvestre Río San Juan, Reserva Natural Punta Gorda, and Reserva Natural Cerro Silva y Reserva Biológica Indio-Maíz.

20. Pablo Piedras, "La tradición del cine directo en el documental argentino contemporáneo," *Palimpsesto* VII, no. 10 (2016): 6.

21. Bill Nichols, *Introduction to Documentary Film* (Bloomington: Indiana University Press, 2001), 103.

22. *Mark Twain's Travel with Mr. Brown: Being Heretofore Uncollected Sketches*, ed. Walter Franklin and Dana Ezra (New York: Alfred Knopf, 1940).

23. In 2011 Nicaragua filed a complaint at the International Court of Justice to denounce construction of a road along the San Juan River, in Costa Rican territory, because of the environmental threat it posed to adjacent ecosystems, namely the river. In 2013 the Court rejected the claim and dispute ensued. In addition to other questions of sovereignty and rights to navigation, in 2015 the Court found that Costa Rica violated general international law because it did not carry out the necessary environmental impact assessment on construction along parts of the river. Jacob Katz Cogan, "Certain Activities Carried Out by Nicaragua in the Border Area (Costa Rica v. Nicaragua); Construction of a Road in Costa Rica Along the San Juan River (Nicaragua v. Costa Rica)," *American Journal of International Law* 110, no. 2 (2016): 320–26.

24. Gisela Heffes, in her book *Políticas de la destrucción/Poéticas de la preservación: Apuntes para una lectura (eco) crítica del medio ambiente en América Latina* (Beatriz Viterbo Editora, 2013), makes reference to the trope of waste/garbage dump in the recent cultural production of Latin America.

25. Gómez-Barris, *The Extractive Zone*, 103.

26. Despite what may be traditional fishing practices, such as controversial turtle egg consumption, shark fishing has been more scrutinized because the animals are usually thrown back to die at sea, without the coveted fin, a prized commodity for the Asian market, and without which, the sharks cannot swim.

27. Jason W. Moore, *Anthropocene or Capitalocene?: Nature, History, and the Crisis of Capitalism* (Oakland: PM Press, 2016), 94.

28. The Bosawás reserve consists of $20,000^2$ kilometers situated between Jinotega and the Autonomous Region of the North Caribbean Coast (RAAN). It was declared a National Resource Reserve in 1991 and was recognized as part of Biosphere World UNESCO Reserve in 1998. It is under serious siege by cattle and logging interests.

29. Traditionally the derogatory term of Sumu was used to describe this group, which has managed to resist advances of the *colono* mestizos, as well as tensions with the Miskitu. The Mayangna, which consists of about 8,000 individuals, is divided into three separate peoples (Twahka, The Panamaka, and the Ulwa), with distinct dialects of the Mayangna language. Other than the Ulwas, these groups live in villages along the rivers of the RAAN North Atlantic Autonomous Region.

30. Laura Hobson Herlihy and Brett Spencer, "As Covid-19 Starts in Nicaragua, Settler Violence Continues," *Cultural Survival*, April 17, 2020.

31. The concept of "collective" refers to a process of associations between human and nonhumans, and is elaborated by Bruno Latour in *Políticas de la naturaleza, por una democracia de las ciencias* (Barcelona: RBA Libros 2013): 97–145, 389.

32. Blaser and de la Cadena, "Pluriverse," 10.

33. Produced by CaLé Video, Fall Line Pictures, Misión Bosawás, and Dúo Guardabarranco Foundation, as part of the "Project for the development of a culture

of respect and human rights promotion for the Indigenous inhabitants of BOSA-WAS," financed by members of the Common Fund of Democratic Governability (FGD), NGO Initiative of Germany, Swiss agency for cooperation and development (COSUDE), Finland, Luxembourg, etc.

34. This idea is developed by Mary Louise Pratt, *Imperial Eyes: Travel Writing and Transculturation* (London: Routledge, 1992).

35. Tuhiwai Smith, *Decolonizing Methodologies*, 82.

36. An important case filed in 2001 at the Inter-American Court of Human Rights, the Mayangna Awas Tingi Community versus Nicaragua, involved the state's failure to demarcate and protect communal land and Indigenous people's right to it. This case was the first time a court of this stature judged in favor of Indigenous peoples' right to their ancestral lands. S. James Anaya and Claudio Grossman, "The Case of Awas Tingni v. Nicaragua: A New Step in the International Law of Indigenous Peoples," *Arizona Journal on International & Comparative Law* 19, no. 1 (2002): 1–15.

37. Cattle is one of Nicaragua's main exports. The effect of this industry on protected areas and Indigenous land is a documented fact. An article by Cinthya Tórrez García, "Bosawás pierde bosque y nadie hace nada por evitarlo," in *La Prensa: El Diario de los Nicaragüenses*, February 2, 2017, reports that Bosawás lost 6 percent of its territory because of deforestation, from 2011–2016, for a total of 92,257 hectares, concurrent with the accelerated growth of the cattle industry.

38. Marisol de la Cadena, *Earth Beings: Ecologies of Practice Across Andean Worlds* (Durham: Duke University Press, 2015), 33.

39. Blaser and de la Cadena, "Pluriverse," 4.

40. Taymond Robins Lino et al., *La naturaleza está poblada de espíritus: cuaderno cultural sumu mayangna* (Managua: CRAAN, 2012), 56.

41. John L. Culliney and David Edward Jones, *The Fractal Self: Science, Philosophy, and the Evolution of Human Cooperation* (Honolulu: University of Hawai'i Press, 2017), 29.

42. The last frame reads, "Bosawás produces 264 million tons of oxygen per year and holds 3.5% of terrestrial biodiversity of the world. The reserve is losing 42,000 hectares of forest per year and could disappear in the next 20 years. The future of the Mayangna and ours depends on what we do today to guarantee the conservation of the forest."

43. Ursula K. Heise. *Imagining Extinction: The Cultural Meaning of Endangered Species* (Chicago: University of Chicago Press, 2016), 7.

44. Gómez-Barris, *The Extractive Zone*, 5.

Works Cited

Anaya, S. James, and Claudio Grossman. "The Case of Awas Tingni v. Nicaragua: A New Step in the International Law of Indigenous Peoples." *Arizona Journal on International and Cooperative Law* 19, no. 1 (2002): 1–15.

Blaser, Mario, and Marisol de la Cadena. "Pluriverse: Proposal for a World of Many Worlds." In *A World of Many Worlds*, edited by Marisol de la Cadena and Mario Blaser, 1–22. Durham: Duke University Press, 2018.

Cadena, Marisol de la. *Earth Beings: Ecologies of Practice Across Andean Worlds*. Durham: Duke University Press, 2015.

Culliney, John L., and David Edward Jones, *The Fractal Self: Science, Philosophy, and the Evolution of Human Cooperation*. Honolulu: University of Hawai'i Press, 2017.

DeVries, Scott. *A History of Ecology and Environmentalism in Spanish American Literature*. Lewisburg, PA: Bucknell University Press, 2013.

Gómez-Barris, Macarena. *The Extractive Zone: Social Ecologies and Decolonial Perspectives*. Durham: Duke University Press, 2017.

Hale, Charles. *Resistance and Contradiction: Miskitu Indians and the Nicaraguan State, 1894–1987*. Palo Alto: Stanford University Press, 1994.

Heffes, Gisela. *Políticas de la destrucción/Poéticas de la preservación: Apuntes para una lectura (eco) crítica del medio ambiente en América Latina*. Argentina: Beatriz Viterbo Editora, 2013.

Heise, Ursula K. *Imagining Extinction: The Cultural Meaning of Endangered Species*. Chicago: University of Chicago Press, 2016.

Hobson Herlihy, Laura, and Brett Spencer. "As Covid-19 Starts in Nicaragua, Settler Violence Continues." *Cultural Survival*, April 17, 2020.

Holden, Philip, and Richard J. Ruppel. *Imperial Desires: Dissident Sexualities and Colonial Literature*. Minneapolis: University of Minnesota Press, 2003.

Katz Cogan, Jacob. "Certain Activities Carried Out by Nicaragua in the Border Area (Costa Rica v. Nicaragua); Construction of a Road in Costa Rica Along the San Juan River (Nicaragua v. Costa Rica)." *American Journal of International Law* 110, no. 2 (April 2016): 320–26.

Latour, Bruno. *Políticas de la naturaleza, por una democracia de las ciencias*. Barcelona: RBA Libros, 2013.

Medina, Julia. "Propaganda política en las ilustraciones de *Waikna, Aventuras en la Costa de la Mosquitia*, el imperialismo visual del siglo XIX." In *América Central en siglo XIX: Retratos en Tinta en de la region*, edited by Paúl Martínez, 70–93. Tegucigalpa: Universidad de Honduras, Fototeca Nacional, 2018.

Mirzoeff, Nicholas. *How to See the World: An Introduction to Images, from Self Portraits to Selfies, Maps to Movies, and More*. New York: Basic Books, 2016.

Moore, Jason W. *Anthropocene or Capitalocene?: Nature, History, and the Crisis of Capitalism*. Oakland: PM Press, 2016.

Nichols, Bill. *Introduction to Documentary*. Bloomington: Indiana University Press, 2001.

Offen, Karl H. "Race and Place in Colonial Mosquitia, 1600–1787." In *Blacks and Blackness in Central America: Between Race and Place*, edited by Lowell Gudmundson and Justin Wolfe, 92–129. Durham: Duke University Press, 2010.

Piedras, Pablo. "La tradición del cine directo en el documental argentino contemporáneo." *Palimpsesto* 7, no. 10 (2016): 1–13.

Pratt, Mary Louise. *Imperial Eyes: Travel Writing and Transculturation.* London: Routledge, 1992.
Robins Lino, Taymond et al. *La naturaleza está poblada de espíritus: cuaderno cultural sumu mayangna.* Managua: CRAAN, 2012.
Tórrez García, Cinthya. "Bosawás pierde bosque y nadie hace nada por evitarlo." *La Prensa: El Diario de los Nicaragüenses,* February 2, 2017.
Tuhiwai Smith, Linda. *Decolonizing Methodologies: Research and Indigenous Peoples.* London: Zedbooks, 2012.
Vilas, Carlos. *La Costa Atlántica en Nicaragua.* México: Fondo de Cultura Económica, 1992.

13

The Sacred Space of Motoapohua

Intercorporeal Animality and National Subjectivities in
Nicolás Echevarría's *Eco de la montaña*

IVÁN EUSEBIO AGUIRRE DARANCOU

In November 2009, thirty-eight mining concessions were given by the Mexican government under President Felipe Calderón to the Canadian First Majestic Silver Corporation for the price of 3 million dollars. These concessions later grew to seventy-eight and expanded to include Proyecto Universo, summing a total of more than 60,000 hectares, with more than 40 percent of these in the Natural and Cultural Ecological Reserve of Wirikuta, a sacred location for the Wixáritari (Huichol) people of Northern Mexico who live across the states of Nayarit, Jalisco, Zacatecas, Durango, and San Luis Potosí. Rapidly responding to this ecological threat, the Wixáritari commenced political and social mobilization and in 2011 gathered in the sacred space of Wirikuta to organize in peaceful defense of their sacred territories. They also mobilized lawyers and civil organizations in Mexico, the United Nations, and Canada to defend the sacred lands from mining exploitation, water contamination, and extensive illegal agricultural projects.

In this political milieu, mara'akame (shaman and elder) Jose Luis "Katira" Ramírez from the San Andrés Cohamiata community in Jalisco contacted director Hernán Vilchez to produce the documentary *Huicholes: los últimos guardianes del peyote* (*Huicholes: The Last Peyote Guardians*, 2014).[1] The film, a classical expository documentary, follows Katira and his family as they carry out a pilgrimage to their sacred sites, culminating in Wirikuta. It weaves their story in a fragmented manner with voices from academic and political activists, mining employees, and community members from the various towns (positively and negatively) affected by mining. Through this cacophony of voices, the viewer is exposed to a limited self-representation of the Wixáritari peoples as they mobilize to defend Wirikuta, as well as to hard facts about the mining industry and its catastrophic effects on the environment. The commissioned film functions as a visual documentation of the political actions the Wixáritari and their allies have taken, with the effect of having the seventy-eight mining concessions canceled by 2015. In doing so, however, it mobilizes an emotional gaze toward both indigeneity as tied to an ancestral past and activism as the only political action available; by emotional I refer to a subjugating of the affective-political potential of the film to a specific relation constructed between the viewer and the humans on-screen, a relation that generates hierarchical feelings of sympathy and solidarity with the Wixáritari peoples as they appear, particularly through a visual process of Othering. In other words, the film represents activism and indigeneity using an emotional tone, relying on images that place the Wixáritari peoples in their "proper" space of proximity to nature as well as sequences that follow mass demonstrations in Mexico City.

While functioning as an important political tool, these representational limitations of the film must be underscored. Although framed by the Wixáritari request to film the documentary, *Los últimos guardianes* perpetuates an expository documentary gaze that reinforces the limits of human subjectivity. It does so first by representing "nature" as an isolated and rural space that must be defended from human exploitation, and second by visually emphasizing how non-Western humans (Wixáritari) are intrinsically related to nature in ways Western subjects cannot achieve.[2] In constructing an image of "nature" as separate from the social and economic organization of the non-Wixáritari peoples (both Mexican and Canadians), the film unconsciously reproduces the separation of man-nature and thus limits the possibilities of generating an affective response in the viewer that reconfigures their subjectivity in proximity to nonhuman life.[3] Rather, what the viewer experiences is the urgency to mobilize a political subjectivity in defense of the Wixáritari people's territory. On the one hand, the developed world of laws, institutions, mining companies, and Western experts; on the other, the Wixáritari people, whose subjectivity is so alien and unrepresentable that when their myths are referenced, they must appear in animated sequences. Even though the camera follows Katira and other elders as they travel to offices—including the United Nations—to petition their cause, their political engagement remains at an institutional level, and thus any possibility of subjective redefinition or rupture is bracketed.

Filmed during the same period as *Los últimos guardianes*, experienced filmographer and documentalist Nicolás Echevarría intervenes in the Wixáritari political and representational struggle with the film *Eco de la montaña* (*Echo of the Mountain*, 2015). This documentary tells the story of two murals created by internationally recognized artist Santos de la Torre "Motoapohua" through the medium of *shakira* or beads.[4] Although the two films use similar tropes—the sacred pilgrimage to Wirikuta and its defense—*Eco de la montaña* avoids the emotional retelling of a "troubled" people and an endangered "wilderness." Instead, it functions by generating a distanced gaze that moves between the poetic, observational, and performative documentary modes, following Santos and his family on their pilgrimage while also documenting the creation of a mural to register their presence in a national space. In doing so, it exemplifies what has been described as ecocinema, films that "incorporate nature and environmental issues into their narratives but whose modes of representation reveal the ideological limitation or shortcomings of the culture vis-à-vis the environment."[5]

Echevarría resists an othering gaze toward Santos de la Torre and the Wixáritari people represented on-screen and uses various experimental strategies, including a fusion of the experimental music of longtime collaborator Mario Lavista with the unmistakable Wixáritari violin, in an attempt to construct a space of political representation that reduces the distance between the *mestizo* national identity underpinning modern Mexican politics and the reality of the Wixáritari peoples as living political subjects.[6] Contra the exclusively human subjectivities that appear in *Los últimos guardianes*, Echevarría's documentary populates the representational space (Wirikuta, cities and towns in Zacatecas, Santos's home in the mountains) with humanimal subjectivities whose limits are not confined to the human body. These other subjectivities, which are seen to be characteristic of Santos and his family but seek to be extended to the global audience that consumes the film, are constructed in the relations established through the enactment of the pilgrimage, relations that without explicating verbally their significance gradually build Santos's, his family's, and the viewers own subjectivity as intercorporeally related to plants, animals, and natural spaces.

To develop what I refer to as humanimal intersubjectivities in the context of *Eco de la montaña*, Wixárika ethos and cosmology provide useful explanations. I emphasize that I am attempting to define and describe the intersubjectivities as they appear in the film, and by no means am seeking to define, categorize, or provide meaning to Wixárika way of life or realities. I recur to these cultural concepts as a particular and contingent mode of approaching Echevarría's particular visual construction of intersubjectivities. As delineated by anthropologist Arturo Gutiérrez del Ángel, the Wixárika comprehension of the (human) body rests on the concept of *iyari,* literally meaning heart as in the biological organ, but also referring to the historically continuous and constantly reactivated collection of memories, rituals, and experiences that the individual must enact through practicing *el costumbre,* the series of traditions that are continuously updated while revolving mainly around the yearly pilgrimage to the sacred space of Wirikuta.[7] Put differently, the (human) body is a person insofar as a series of relations is established and enacted with other community members, but also with the variety of plants (maize, beans, peyote) and animals (deer) that compose the specific cosmology of the Wixárika. The body becomes an intersubjective person in these relations; it is not just that rituals—social and religious—inform and shape the individual's subjectivity, but rather that (inter)subjectivity itself is anchored in a body insofar as the heart—physically and spiritually—is nurtured and established in these relations. That is, a body's *iyari* (heart) becomes or develops through the enactment of the ritual, quotidian and sacred. Understanding the body in these terms brings to the forefront the political possibilities of Echevarría's film as it embeds a series of Wixárika artists, elders, and families onto a geographic space that is both rural and urban, *mestizo* and Wixárika, human and nonhuman (animal and plant). Rather than being saturated with information about environmental destruction, the viewer is exposed only to the story of Santos as told by himself, and a series of fragments about Wixárika philosophy, ethics, and politics in the scenes when Santos explains certain mosaics that will be part of the mural. While the underlying political injunctive is the preservation and protection of the sacred lands (and all of Mexican territory with it), the documentary resists saturating the viewer with information about the specifics of the locations. It allows for the viewer to engage with Santos and his family not as Othered Wixárika people, but as bodies whose *iyari,* cultured heart, rest in the lands as much as the relations among its peoples, both mestizo and Wixárika.

Through this mural revealed in its totality only in the final sequence—itself an interrelational construction that not only involves the group participation of the whole family but also requires a pilgrimage from the artists—humanimal subjectivities are constructed that allow for a politicization and a push toward protecting Wirikuta. This push is grounded in a new comprehension of national subjectivities, because Echevarría's editing makes a continual emphasis on the presence of the Wixárika peoples in relation to the Mexican nation. The sparse mise-en-scène of the documentary highlighted by shaky camera movements and meager lighting emphasizes the participatory mode that Bill Nichols underlines. The presence of the filmmaker is silent but present in the various sequences where Santos speaks directly to the camera. The effect of this direct address is that the viewer affectively becomes another body related to the human and nonhuman bodies appearing on-screen. The contingent political subjectivities of Santos and the other Wixárika are activated not through their engagement with the legal institutions of Mexico, Canada, and the United Nations, but rather in their interrelational encounters with mestizo citizens and, most importantly, with the variety of sacred sites they visit and the animal and plant life they engage with in these moments. The political subjectivities on-screen are thus interrelationally embodied, and animality—both sacred and profane—becomes a defining component that resists the position of the human protecting a defenseless nature.

Eco de la montaña opens with found footage from 1997 public television, showing the moment when a mural commissioned by the Mexican government from Santos de la Torre is unveiled in the Louvre metro stop of Paris. Quickly, Santos's voice-over takes over the sonic space of the footage to explain how he was not invited to the mural's installation, how it was incorrectly set up, and how he experienced the whole situation as a physical and spiritual wound, a devastating act of cultural exploitation. The film then switches to a road movie narrative, following Santos and his family as they leave their home in isolated Mesa del Venado to the city of Zacatecas to work on a new mural, whose political purpose is to visualize the defense of Wirikuta. As the mural is being created, Echevarría follows Santos and his family as they make the pilgrimage to Wirikuta and other sacred spaces to commune with the gods and other members of their community. This framing of the film through an old mural and the creation of a new one constructs the film as a political intervention by understanding Wixáritari not only as Indigenous peoples, but also as citizens of Mexico and ultimately as human beings living alongside the sacred and quotidian animals and plants of their lands. The Wixáritari are presented not just as guardians of a sacred space but also as active participants in current political debates through the use of an art form that is at the heart of the *mestizo* nation: the mural.

By telling the story of Wirikuta and visualizing—but not explaining or detailing—a cosmology through the mural artist's past and present work representing the Wixáritari in modern Mexico, Echevarría's film achieves a double purpose. First, it historicizes the modern abuses of the Wixáritari in contemporary Mexico, from land and resource exploitation to cultural appropriation and theft. Second, it cinematically stages a feature-length ritual similar to the peyote (*hikuri*) ceremony central to the Wixáritari cosmology and ethos where the sacred animals become integral components in the construction of interpersonal and humanimal subjectivities. *Eco de la montaña* (as a film and as the message that Santos himself is communicating) directly intervenes in both the current environmental situation and the ideological debates about (political) representation and subjectivities.

The film then becomes a collective act of assembling and presenting a political subjectivity that is thoroughly grounded and embodied in Santos de la Torre, who participates in the weaving of the nation's fabric.[8] *Eco de la montaña* fluctuates between a poetic and participatory mode, rejecting the expository and observational modalities that construct a level of truth of the Other accessible via the camera.[9] In this way, the humanimal aspects of the Wixáritari cosmology cease to be visualized as exoticized individual and collective subjectivities of an-other nation and start to be understood, especially by a *mestizo* audience, as a (national) subjectivity participating in the political practices of the nation.[10]

Aware of the *mestizo* audience who will consume the film in various specialized circuits (including festivals and cinetecas), Echevarría directly engages this ideal viewer in order to subvert paradigmatic power dynamics, especially those established in the filming process where the *mestizo* cameraman captures the Indigenous subject. The director carries out this subversion through a series of critical representational strategies that give Santos control over the narration, such as camera movements that follow the Indigenous subjects and situate them in national and sacred spaces where they now assume the conventional role of a contemporary metropolitan subject who witnesses and comments on what is seen. *Eco de la montaña* creates these intercorporeal national subjectivities crossed by animality through the focalization on Santos first as an individual artist, second as a member of a community, third in that particular community's (now signified as politically legitimate in the nation) intercorporeal subjective relation with nonhuman life, and finally by using the mural as a framing device that remits to the Wixáritari concept of *iyari*, heart and genetic memory given life through ritual action.

In focusing on Santos as an artist, the film takes a self-reflexive turn. Echoing the way that Santos incorporates Wixáritari cosmology and ethos into the mural, Echevarría, as a *mestizo* documentary maker, weaves that story into the fabric of the nation. This placement of Santos as a legitimate Mexican citizen engages a *mestizo* audience familiar with Indigenous political struggles, a topic of intense media attention, but who nevertheless constructs the Wixárika—and other Indigenous subjects—as outside the nation. Santos's subjectivity, and his relationship to plants (specifically the peyote cactus or *hikuri*) and animals (deer, tigers, bulls, serpents, and fishes) that populate Wirikuta and other sacred spaces, are spliced into a new paradigm for the viewer to follow: a spiritual-political guide as well as a living document. As Rafael Mejia Guzmán and María del Carmen Anaya Corona specify, for the Wixárika peoples, following *el costumbre* is a ritual but also a political act that holds community (and in the film, community is expanded to include the nation) together through quotidian actions where individuals establish and nurture relations with the nonhuman life surrounding them.[11] The humanimal subjectivities that Santos points at in the close-ups of the mural are visualized as processes that every citizen-viewer must enact, a redefinition of subjectivity whose political component rests not in protecting nature, but in becoming it, and nature becoming subject through the body of this redefined citizen. As any political action, subjectivity (particularly humanimal) is represented as a process that the individual, Santos in this case, must enact, through pilgrimage and ritual but also through quotidian and political engagements.

Eco de la montaña continually emphasizes Santos not as an exceptional individual, but as one more member of an intergenerational community navigating both the rural spaces literally abandoned by the state and the urban spaces where they negotiate nationality. Santos and his family are accompanied by Don Julio, a *mara'akame* (shaman) who becomes their spiritual protector. These individuals become representatives of the Wixáritari nation as a whole. However, instead of being attached exclusively to an isolated and idealized rural lifestyle, Echevarría documents their existence through quotidian acts of meaning-creation as they navigate the city and their national experience. Geographer Diana Negrin da Silva foregrounds the concept of *makuyeika*, s/he who walks in many places, as a way in which Wixárika peoples conceptualize members who navigate urban education while conserving and reproducing traditional responsibilities.[12] In a similar manner, the camera follows Santos and Julio as they negotiate *mestizo* space to equip themselves for the pilgrimage; in a religious shop, they negotiate the purchase of incense, explaining its ceremonial use, and in a church they obtain holy water, resignified in a later scene when they visit the sacred well of Tatei Manieri. Intersubjectivity is embodied in the fusing of Catholic tradition with Wixárika ritual (*el costumbre*), activated in the ritual and embedded in the mural as the final product, which now contains not only Wixárika but also national elements.[13]

These negotiations, however, are not without tension, because their success rests as much on the affective response of the viewers as on the actions of Santos and his community. A central scene takes place in the Museo de Arte Abstracto, where Santos and his grandson fluctuate between speaking Wixárika and Spanish while discussing their difficulty in understanding Western codes of representation in abstract art. Their conversation embodies these negotiations: "yo me siento más triste al verlo, el cuadro. Más bien, no lo entiendo" (I feel sadder upon seeing the painting. Or rather, I don't understand it).[14] As Negrin da Silva specifies, in their entering and exiting of activist, institutional, and national spaces, *makuyeika* Wixárika face the double challenge of interracial (and I would argue interspecies, in that their understanding of embodied subjectivity is relational with nonhuman life) relations, first of being understood as the noble savage protecting nature, and second as being perceived to be an obstacle to modernity.[15] In this scene, Santos and his grandson make visually explicit the pitfalls of these two misreadings and the urgent need to reconfigure the ways in which Wixárika subjectivity is understood by the Western subject and polis. Santos wears traditional clothing while his grandson sports jeans and a cowboy shirt; they speak in both languages; they affectively and rationally engage with abstract painting. Their embodied subjectivities are presented as cultural crossers, as in-between subjects who navigate and negotiate the interstices of religion, nation, and, ultimately, the human.

The use of the mural as a framing device is Echevarría's most skillful negotiation of symbolic registers, as it mobilizes a Wixáritari storytelling medium to incorporate the various represented humanimal subjects into the nation itself. The pilgrimage, which takes Santos and his family from their remote home to the urban center of Zacatecas, and along a sacred voyage that includes visits to Haramara (San Blas, Nayarit), Cerro Quemado (Wirikuta, San Luis Potosí), Tiu Migate (San Luis Potosí), La Nariz (San Luis Potosí), Tatei Manieri (San Luis Potosí), Tiu Maye'u (San Luis Potosí), and Isla del Rey (Nayarit), becomes a central component of the mural. Thus, the object that was initially appropriated/stolen from Santos and wrongly assembled gives way to a new material manifestation of *iyari*: "a body of conscious and unconscious cultural knowledge accumulated during generations of observing, experimenting with, and utilizing the natural phenomena and resources of the environment."[16]

This new mural, the historic medium that underpins *Mexicanidad*, is transformed into a constructed collection of knowledge to which viewers are only privy in the final sequence, when the camera leaves Santos's side via a crane shot that encompasses what previously had been seen exclusively through close-up fragments. In the tradition of nation building inaugurated with the official support of the muralist movement headed by Diego Rivera, David Alfaro Siquieros, and José Clemente Orozco in the 1920s and 1930s, murals have become the privileged artistic medium through which to represent the Mexican nation. However, the variety of Indigenous subjects depicted in them have been symbolically subjugated to the colonial ideologies of *mestizo* nationalism.

In *Eco de la montaña*, the murals of Santos de la Torre become a counternarrative to this official use of mural as nation-building tool. In the final mural, Santos places the Wixárika peoples alongside mestizo citizens, plants, and animals nurturing and relationally assembled with Wirikuta. Echevarría demands the viewer actively participate in the deciphering and interpreting of the mural's complex symbology, an activation of a genetic memory whose national symbols are both *mestizo* and Wixáritari. The humanimal subjectivities that appear represented in the beadwork are extended then not only to the Wixáritari people themselves, but also to the range of political subjects who now populate national spaces: from those who promote the destructive extraction of resources in Wirikuta (the tiger) to those who come together to become the embodied subjectivities protecting the (national) territory.

Figure 13.1. The final shot reveals Santos de la Torre's mural in its totality. Nicolás Echevarría, *Eco de la montaña*, 2014, video still.

This critical space is reactivated in *Eco de la montaña* in the conflicting opening sequence that evidences the traumatic relationship between Santos—as representative of the Wixáritari people he belongs to—and the Mexican government, representing the *mestizo* nation as a whole. As Santos details, "me transearon, porque lo agarran desaprevenido, pero así me pasó . . . Y así pasó, así fue . . . No me dejaron lisiado ni herido ni nada, pero en el alma sí . . . eso fue" [they swindled me, because they caught me unawares, but that is what happened to me . . . And that's how it was . . . They didn't damage or wound me or anything, but in my soul they did]. Made explicit through the use of the found footage of the mural's unveiling, instead of a retelling of the event, this wound indicates the power of the camera as a potential weapon used against Santos to injure the soul. The next sequence, set in 2011 in the same geography of Mesa del Venado, generates a resistance to this understanding of the camera. Santos holds a human skull found in the field and says, "yo no soy antropólogo para explicar todo el contenido, nada más que mi hijo lo encontró por ahí encajado en un poste" [I am not an anthropologist to explain all of its context, my son just found it there on a post]. The film establishes Santos as a subject in control of the narration, while simultaneously resisting the understanding of anthropology's epistemological placement as the revealer of cultural codes.[17] In the first minutes of this ecocinematic documentary, the viewer becomes aware of the power relations embedded in the genre. Most importantly, as Willoquet-Maricondi emphasizes when approaching ecocinema, the viewer—and especially the explicitly *mestizo* viewer as opposed to the more "neutral" spectator position that a documentary such as *Los últimos guardianes* interpellates—is put in a position of negotiation, of understanding the representation she sees as a mediated experience in which Santos (and the intersubjective space he inhabits/that inhabits him) is as much an active knowledge-creator as Echevarría.[18]

The creation of the new mural becomes the moment of healing the symbolic wound in Santos's soul through the collaboration between the ever-present but silent *mestizo* filmmaker and the Wixáritari artist. As it registers the mythic walk of the Wixáritari from the ocean to Wirikuta, the mural embeds the current pilgrimage that Santos and his family take into a ritual space that remains within the nation. In following them, the camera captures the humanimal subjectivities that Santos vocally alludes to in the peyote hunt and situates them in the mural itself (figure 13.2). The (human/nonhuman) eyes that look back at the viewers are those of a subjectivity whose intercorporeality alludes to Santos, his family members,

Figure 13.2. Close-up of Santos de la Torre's mural: humanimal and vegetal intersubjectivities. Nicolás Echevarría, *Eco de la montaña*, 2014, video still.

the sacred beings they encounter and relate to (deer, maize, peyote), and the viewer herself as she recognizes her own presence in the national space that Santos weaves. This looking back at the viewer activates what bell hooks describes as one of the aspects of the oppositional gaze, where "by courageously looking, we defiantly declared: 'not only will I state. I want my look to change reality.'"[19]

The camera in *Eco de la montaña* constructs a viewer-position that is intrinsically oppositional, from the moment of going against the official state narrative, to the intercorporeal animality embedded in the mural as political resistance, to the development of Wirikuta as a national space. Because it is only Santos's voice that directs the physical and cinematic journey, Echevarría's camera assembles the looking back in the mural as analogous to Santos's own looking back into the national space, generating a position from which the *mestizo* viewer can exist alongside the Wixáritari subject, political and representational. The defense of sacred ecological spaces is undertaken then precisely *from* the position of the intercorporeal subjectivities that Santos is creating in the mural, a position that is open to incorporate the viewer and not a closed, essentialized indigeneity.

This critical and oppositional gaze that Santos generates and Echevarría documents crystalizes in Santos's engagements with the various *mestizo* institutions he encounters. Throughout the film, the camera focuses on several key moments of Santos and his family looking back at the *mestizo* society they inhabit. They visit a regional *feria*, and after strolling through and watching the spectacle of a military band and a group of Indigenous dancers, they end up on a hill overlooking Zacatecas. The camera zooms in to a close-up of their faces and gazes over the city as Santos talks about conserving cultural traditions while coming in contact with *mestizos*, switching to point-of-view shots of the landscape and peoples they are seeing. The Wixáritari political subjectivity that Santos embodies is relational, not only in connection with the natural, vegetal, and animal inhabitants of the national geography but also with the subjects and institutions of *mestizo* Mexico. This looking back, exemplified in the mural eyes looking back at the viewer but continuously referenced in the scenes where Santos and his family look back at us, is solidified in the self-encounter that Santos has in the Museo Zacatecano. In powerful sequence, the camera follows Santos from a low angle shot as he enters the Museo; a Wixáritari violin plays softly and increases in volume as he approaches the exhibit of the "native" peoples of Zacatecas. The sequence ends with Santos looking at one of his murals, and the camera gives a point-of-view shot: a contemporary Indigenous subject looking back at the past and the present. The camera zooms in on the mural to focus on a pair of eyes staring back at the viewer, and the violin slowly gives way to Mario Lavista's experimental and haunting music. This enacts an intercorporeal fusion of gazes: from Santos to the mural to the viewer's own looking at the screen and the mural staring back. As bell hooks underlines, the oppositional act of staring back is powerful in the sense that it opens up a possibility of agency, especially when it is done in the face of structures of domination, that is, the museum as an institution of the state.[20]

In this intercorporeal construction, the eyes looking back are crossed with animality. While animals make few appearances as living being in the film, their presence is felt in the various images that Santos generates as political instances (i.e., mural fragments where animals represent political/activist groups standing up to multinational corporations). In this way, animality is defined less as something that is outside the limits of human subjectivity and more as an intrinsic and relational component of the latter. In this particular sequence, where Santos, the viewer, and the (human) animal eyes in the museum mural look at each other, the subject-position that Echevarría, cinematographer Sebastián Hoffman, and Santos construct is embedded with aspects of animality, political engagement, and indigeneity not as a museum artifact, but as a living body. This other subject-position pushes back against the limits of the museum as a physical and ideological construction, while at the same time using it as a repository of history where the living Indigenous subjects re-create themselves through looking back at and intervening.

As the film progresses, the viewer follows Santos's family on their pilgrimage to the aforementioned sacred sites, some in urban areas but most in isolated regions. Greg Garrard defines the idea of wilderness in opposition to civilization as a tool for environmentalism that nevertheless reproduces the separation between man and nature.[21] In their travels, Santos and his family inhabit these spaces not as a pristine wilderness offering refuge and safety from the perils of modern life, but as a space that is intrinsically connected to humanity via the Wixáritari people and their intercorporeal and interdependent relationships with the plants, animals, and natural forces living there. At the core of these interrelations is the peyote cactus, *hikuri* for the Wixáritari, born out of the primordial sacrifice of the sacred Brother Deer whose life birthed the sun in Cerro Quemado, Wirikuta.[22] The ritual ingestion of the cactus becomes a sympoietic moment, as Hediger, inspired by Haraway, explains, one that involves "the way that all forms of life are ecological through and through, relying upon not just other organisms but the material environment itself."[23] Opposing *Los últimos guardianes*, which includes a thorough explanation of the ritual in both a Wixáritari and an anthropologist voice-over, *Eco* presents the ritual hunt of the peyote, neither exoticizing nor explaining it, simply following Santos's family and the *mara'akame* Don Julio as they explore the desert and prune the cactus.

The visual narrative device that Echevarría uses to explain the importance of the human-plant-animal relationship is the mural, switching from shots of the group in the desert to close-ups of the mural showing the peyote buds and the sacred animals in the beadwork. Lavista's music, interspersed with Wixáritari violin, provides an audial and affective bridge between the desert, mural, and humanimal subjects inhabiting both. The viewer experiences this intercorporeality visually and aurally and is invited to understand the ritual consumption as entheogenic (and not hallucinatory nor psychedelic), an act of knowledge-construction and interspecies communication as opposed to a human-centered experience. In this way, the animality of the deer and the serpent become core components of the intersubjective experiences that Santos relates to the camera, grounded in a caring and co-creative stance toward the nonhuman other.[24] Rather than consume peyote, Santos stresses the need to "ser peyote con raíz," to become the cactus. Consumption is sidelined, although visually referenced, to give more importance to the humanimal ethics that comes as a consequence of a human-plant-animal becoming, an intersubjectivity whose relationality is constructed through the quotidian ritual of *el costumbre* that is made visible (but not solely contained) by the ritual ingestion of the cactus. The mural revealed in the final sequence is to be understood then as a road map, the codex that contains the essence of the Wixáritari knowledge of the natural world and the interrelatedness of the human species with it. The viewer is privy to that knowledge not via the spoken word, as it is never explained, but via the active engagement and deciphering of mural representations and the real places to which Santos's family travels. In this act of deciphering, the viewer is then inevitably placed in the space of a series of humanimal intersubjectivities, at times looking at and other times being stared back at by the human subjects as well as by empty landscapes.

Moving toward a conclusion, I want to focus on a final sequence in *Eco de la montaña* that coalesces the subjectivities I have been delineating. As Santos is with his family in their temporary home in Zacatecas, sketching what will eventually become the mural, he historicizes the relations embedded in the creation myths of the Wixáritari: "nosotros somos del mar, venimos del mar, salimos para buscar la luz, y ahora que encontramos la luz, no nos acordamos del mar, pero somos del mar, de la oscuridad" [we are of the sea, we came from the sea, we emerged to look for light, and once we found it, we stopped remembering the sea, but we are of it, of the darkness]. The mural visualizes the mythical transformation of fish into humans, which will be resignified in a current sociopolitical context when the camera shows us Santos's family visiting Haramara, the sacred beach in Nayarit. These mythical humanimal intersubjectivities are recontextualized as a historical and politically powerful intervention when in his explanation Santos focuses on the Consejo Regional de Wirikuta gathering in 2011 to defend the sacred land. The "nosotros" that Santos includes in the mural ceases to be the exclusively ethnocentric Wixáritari community to become all those who defend the land (and the nation) with them. The camera show Santos working on the mural detail of a tiger attacking Wirikuta while a bull stands in its way. Santos explains that the tiger represents President Felipe Calderón and anyone exploiting the natural resources, while the bull stands for "nosotros que estamos defendiendo el lugar sagrado" [we who defend the sacred place]. In this moment, the pilgrimage, the mural, and the film become a political intervention in the face of politicians, transnational mining corporations, and farmers who seek control of the land. The words of Santos produce a dual image. On one level, the artistic endeavor of the mural is transformed into a political act of resistance, as the appropriation experienced by Santos in the first mural is reconfigured into an act of self-representation. On another level, the mural transcends this representation of indigeneity to map a plural "nosotros," a collective that is not solely Wixárika, but a greater political community that includes animals and other natural forces as well as *mestizo* citizens who stand in the way of extractive capitalism.

As Diego Salgado signals, "los trazos de Santos se convierten en signos de sus razonamientos, de la forma en que explica los fenómenos actuales" [Santos's designs index his reasoning, the way in which he understands current events].[25] Santos becomes a knowledge-producer who splices experiences, words, sketches, and beads into a mural that, though fully represented on-screen in the final sequence, far surpasses the limits of the camera. Jumping from the panel close-ups and explanation to the final revelation, the mural places the viewers in a critical para-hegemonic position in between the Wixáritari cosmology and the *mestizo* nation, without being fully situated in either.[26] The viewer, especially the *mestizo* viewer, is pushed to consider the limitations of words (the anthropological medium of representation) and even moving images and sounds (the cinematic mode) as hegemonic codes of understanding and ordering reality. The words of political agreements and international treaties controlling land—which make a powerful appearance in *Los últimos guardianes* when the Wixáritari leader gives their written demands to President Calderón, the United Nations, and even First Majestic Silver Corporations—give way to the signs and images contained in the mural and, most importantly, to the eyes of the different (human)animals that appear in it and look back at us. It is here that Santos signals how the political struggle includes a different conception of subjectivities, from the Western notion of human individual to intercorporeal humanimality. What is more, the film emphasizes how this different conception of subjectivity is positively constructed by Santos, but is not exclusive to Wixárika peoples. In a close-up, the camera focuses on the eyes of the tiger, the humanimal figure that embodies both tangible (President Calderón) and intangible (global corporations) bodies. By not being exclusive to the Wixárika peoples or their allies, this negative humanimality crystalizes the urgent need to push back against the othering modes of representation that equate Indigenous peoples with an essential bond with nature, a bond that in *Eco de la montaña* is constructed to be political, subjective, and ultimately collective.

As the scene progresses, Santos explains the importance of defending Wirikuta and the surrounding lands as homes of the gods, but he describes these geographical places in bodily terms: "la mina es como nuestro cuerpo, el oro es como la vida, la plata es como el hueso de nosotros mismos, el agua es como las venas de sangre, la tierra tiene todo lo que tenemos nosotros" [the mine is like our body, gold like our life, silver like our bones, water like the blood in our veins, the earth has everything that we need]. In this moment, the mural becomes the key to deciphering the documentary's codex, containing the core concepts of Wikáritari cosmovision without explaining them verbally.[27] For the purposes of my argument, I want to underscore another aspect that is added onto this understanding of Wirikuta and nature in the words of Santos. As Santos trails off, the camera cuts to an extreme long shot of Wirikuta and the surrounding area, ending with a shot of a small Mexican flag lying on the ground, slowly fading. Santos's words echo ominously and achieve two purposes. First, the viewer understands that the extension of land that Santos is talking about is larger than Wirikuta itself, covering the whole Mexican territory. Second, it places Santos as a member of a national community beyond his ethnicity, a position that Santos himself seems reticent to embrace but that he recognizes in the self-description of his temporary living situation in Zacatecas during the creation of the mural: "mi vida ha sido muy rara en Zacatecas, porque como no soy de aquí, pero cumpliendo con la obligación de nuestro trabajo, me tengo que aguantar" [my life has been very strange in Zacatecas, because I am not from here, but in order to fulfill our obligations to the work, I have to endure]. Though there is a recognition of a distance between his own culture and the *mestizo* nation, Santos's life in Zacatecas is nevertheless compelled by an obligation of labor, which simultaneously places him in the national space in economic and subjective terms. Combined with the scenes where military bands, national flags, state museums, and other representatives of the nation make an appearance alongside Santos and his family, this shot of the flag lying on the ground can be read as a key moment when the film generates an understanding of nation thoroughly populated with the humanimal intersubjectivities associated with the Wixáritari cosmology.

The film continues to develop these generational moments of intercultural subjectivity by focusing on significant shots that evidence the Wixáritari's negotiation of nationality. After the traumatic opening sequence where the mural is incorrectly installed without his input, Santos and his family ask for a blessing from the gods before departing on the mural-making pilgrimage to Zacatecas, and the camera shows their familial ceremonial altar containing small national symbols. Contrasting with the absence of the state in material terms (lack of electricity, running water, roads, or other services), the presence of these symbols allows for an understanding of Santos's and the rest of the Wixáritari's ethicoecological commitment not only as ethnic survivors of the Conquest and the violence it embedded in the social fabric, but as contemporary citizens. In spite of the real marginalization the documentary foregrounds, it pushes for a consideration of Santos's Indigenous community as national-political subjects and not as Indigenous aliens. By emphasizing these kinds of shots in several key moments, embedding national symbols in sacred space and foregrounding the negotiation of Indigenous peoples between state, nation, and ritual, *Eco* focuses on representing indigeneity as actively negotiating nationality, thus extending the activist-environmentalist work not simply as a defense of sacred territories but also as a defense of the greater Mexican nation itself.

In conclusion, in the milieu of media attention of which the Wixáritari people have been the focus since 2011, this particular example of ecocinema can be read as a political intervention in the creation of alternative subjectivities. Rather than using an expository or observational documentary mode to generate an image of indigeneity that stands outside the ideological and political realm of the nation, Echevarría takes the opportunity to construct a critical mode of viewing indigeneity, nature, and political activism through his collaboration with Santos de la Torre. They together generate a parahegemonic third space from which to understand Wixáritari indigeneity and cosmology, and the environmental and political crisis the nation is facing.[28] In this way, the camera is transformed from an objective witness that captures the pilgrimage to a subjective participant invited or allowed to travel alongside the Wixáritari in their ritual defense of the sacred spaces. During the Isla del Rey sequence, where Santos joins a greater group of Wixáritari camping in the sacred island, the fixed camera captures Indigenous bodies traversing the space but then starts walking alongside them, generating a viewer-position whose physicality is made evident. It is in this position that Echevarría and Hoffman, as the controllers of the technology, are made visible in their *mestizo* identity, and it is this position that holds the key of the documentary: the powerful force of resignification that politicizes the modes of representation themselves, beyond being a call to political action.

It is here that I read Echevarría's contribution—based on his decades-long documentary experience with Indigenous people (including the Wixáritari) and the representational crisis he makes explicit in *Cabeza de Vaca* (1992)—not as providing knowledge about the environmental situation in Wirikuta or anthropological information about the Wixáritari or even legitimizing Santos with regard to his previous experience with the Mexican government, but as collaboratively creating a visual, audial, and representational space where alternative national subjectivities, crossed with animality and other natural forces, can be collectively assembled. In this way, the viewers are subjected to a series of institutional spaces (museums, *ferias*, churches, shops, and the natural homes of the gods) where subjectivities are redefined both by the *mestizo* nation and the Wixáritari peoples. It is within these spaces, audibly assembled with Santos's voice, the ever-present violin, and Lavista's experimental music, where the viewer is politically engaged, not precisely to take to the streets and demand the protection of Wirikuta but rather to construct a subjectivity crossed through lines of animal, vegetal, and human experiences. Thus, instead of striving to represent Wixáritari singularities, Echevarría pushes the viewer to question the relationship between the Wixáritari and *mestizo* nations and reassemble herself in the mural, the museums, and the natural environments of Wirikuta and Mexico as a whole. Aware of the film's implied audience, *Eco de la montaña* constructs a space where an Indigenous subject is placed in control of the knowledge-production while constantly self-reflexive of the presence and power of the camera.

Notes

1. *Huicholes: The Last Peyote Guardians*, directed by Hernán Vilchez (2014; México: Kabropro Films).

2. I want to make explicit that I do not dismiss Vilchez's film, especially because it exemplifies the contingent politics that have characterized Indigenous political activism and their use of media in the last decade of struggle. *Los últimos guardianes* is valuable precisely because of its political effect, but I place it next to *Eco de la montaña* given their temporal proximity and the radically different modes of representation each mobilizes.

3. Anat Pick and Guinevere Narraway, "Introduction," in *Screening Nature. Cinema Beyond the Human,* ed. Anat Pick and Guinevere Narraway (New York: Berghahn Books, 2013).

4. While Motoapohua is Santos de la Torre's Wixáritari name, meaning "Echo from the mountain," I use Santos throughout the rest of this intervention because it is the one he uses in his own presentation.

5. Paula Willoquet-Maricondi, "Introduction," in *Framing the World. Explorations in Ecocriticism and Film,* ed. Paula Willoquet-Maricondi (Charlottesville: University of Virginia Press, 2010), xii.

6. *Los últimos guardianes* constantly showcases scenes in which the *mestizo* miners, activists, politicians, academics, and population at large mobilize a dichotomy of "them" versus "us," understanding that the Wixáritari peoples are included only geographically in the national territory. For the remainder of this intervention, I use

the word *mestizo* to refer to the non-Wixáritari people and political subjectivities that both Vilchez and Echevarría represent, in order to better understand Mexican creation of subjectivities grounded in ideas of racial mixing while clearly setting up limits of political representation and participation.

7. Arturo Gutiérrez del Ángel, "Las metáforas del cuerpo ¿Más allá de la naturaleza . . . o con la naturaleza?," *Revista del Colegio de San Luis* 3, no. 5 (January–June 2013): 258–86.

8. Diego Augusto Salgado Bautista, "La significación en el documental *Eco de la Montaña* de Nicolás Echevarría: un discurso de lo real histórico," in *Mexican Transnational Cinema and Literature*, ed. Maricruz Castro Ricalde, Mauricio Díaz Calderón, and James Ramey (Oxford: Peter Lang Ltd., 2017), 231. Salgado specifies how, more than representing an Indigenous reality, Echevarría enters into a public debate on representation and how to provide an alternative to an othering gaze.

9. Bill Nichols, *Introduction to Documentary*, 2nd ed. (Bloomington: Indiana University Press, 2010), 31.

10. I am particularly grateful to Olivia Cosentino for this critical insight.

11. Rafael Guzmán Mejía and María del Carmen Anaya Corona, *Cultura del maíz-peyote-venado. Sustentabilidad del pueblo Wixaritari* (México: Universidad de Guadalajara, 2015), 93.

12. Diana Negrín da Silva, "*Makuyeika:* la que anda en muchas partes," *Cuicilco* 62 (January–April 2015): 37–59.

13. Joanne Hershfield, "Assimilation and identification in Nicolás Echevarría's *Cabeza de Vaca*," *Wide Angle* 16, no. 3 (1995): 6–24. Her reading of *Cabeza de Vaca* "suggests, perhaps in what some might brand utopian language, that a Mexican national identity can no longer be located in the nostalgic myth of history but may instead be found in the various dialogical processes of everyday interactions between selves and others" (21). In the same way, *Eco de la montaña* suggests the possibility of constructing a national subjectivity located in the interstices between *mestizo* and Indigenous cultures, between human and animal, and between human and vegetal.

14. *Eco de la montaña*. directed by Nicolás Echevarría (2015; México: Cuadro Negro/Cinepolis).

15. Negrín, "*Makuyeika*," 57.

16. Stacy B. Schaefer and Peter Furst, "Introduction," in *People of the Peyote: Huichol Indian History, Religion & Survival*, ed. Stacy B. Schaefer and Peter T. Furst (Albuquerque: University of New Mexico Press, 1996), 24.

17. Salgado, "La significación," 236.

18. Paula Willoquet-Maricondi, "Shifting Paradigms: From Environmentalist Films to Ecocinema," in *Framing the World. Explorations in Ecocriticism and Film*, ed. Paula Willoquet-Maricondi (Charlottesville: University of Virginia Press, 2010), 43–61.

19. bell hooks, "The Oppositional Gaze. Black Female Spectators," in *Black Looks: Race and Representation* (Boston: South End Press, 1992), 116.

20. Ibid., 116.

21. Greg Garrard, *Ecocriticism* (New York: Routledge, 2012), 66.

22. As Schaefer and Furst detail, "peyote is the focus of much of Huichol religious emotion, the annual cycle of communal and extended family ceremonial and ritual activities, and the common intellectual culture. That includes rites intended to promote the growth of maize and other useful cultivated and wild plant life, hunting, rain, human and animal fertility, and so forth, for peyote and its effects also key into their welfare." Schaefer and Furst, "Introduction," 23.

23. Ryan Hediger, "Becoming with Animals: Sympoiesis and the Ecology of Meaning in London and Hemingway," *Studies in American Naturalism* 11, no. 1 (2016): 7.

24. Barbara Smuts, "Encounters with Animal Minds," *Journal of Consciousness Studies* 8, no. 5–7 (2001): 308.

25. Salgado, "La significación," 236.

26. In using the term para-hegemonic, I refer to Kathryn Mayers's interpretation of Echevarría's earlier film *Cabeza de Vaca* (1992) as an ideological intervention that seeks to problematize representations of indigeneity from the hegemonic position of Western codes of representation. Kathryn Mayers, "Of Third Spaces and (Re)Localization: Critique and Counterknowledge in Nicolás Echevarría's *Cabeza de Vaca*," *Confluencia* 24, no. 1 (Fall 2008): 12.

27. Salgado, "La significación," 241.

28. Nichols, *Introduction to documentary*, 31.

Works Cited

Echevarría, Nicolás, dir. *Eco de la montaña*. 2015; México, D.F.: Cuadro Negro/Cinepolis.

Garrard, Greg. *Ecocriticism*. New York: Routledge, 2012.

Gutiérrez del Ángel, Arturo. "Las metáforas del cuerpo ¿Más allá de la naturaleza . . . o con la naturaleza?" *Revista del Colegio de San Luis* 3, no. 5 (January–June 2013): 258–86.

Guzmán Mejía, Rafael, and María del Carmen Anaya Corona. *Cultura del maíz-peyote-venado. Sustentabilidad del pueblo Wixaritari*. México: Universidad de Guadalajara, 2015.

Hediger, Ryan. "Becoming with Animals: Sympoiesis and the Ecology of Meaning in London and Hemingway." *Studies in American Naturalism* 11, no. 1 (2016): 5–22.

Hershfield, Joanne. "Assimilation and Identification in Nicolás Echevarría's *Cabeza de Vaca*." *Wide Angle* 16, no. 3 (1995): 6–24.

hooks, bell. "The Oppositional Gaze. Black Female Spectators." In *Black Looks: Race and Representation*, 115–31. Boston: South End Press, 1992.

Mayers, Kathryn. "Of Third Spaces and (Re)Localization: Critique and Counterknowledge in Nicolás Echevarría's *Cabeza de Vaca*." *Confluencia* 24, no. 1 (Fall 2008): 2–16.

Negrín da Silva, Diana. "*Makuyeika:* la que anda en muchas partes." *Cuicilco* 62 (January–April 2015): 37–59.

Nichols, Bill. *Introduction to Documentary*. 2nd ed. Bloomington: Indiana University Press, 2010.

Pick, Anat, and Guinevere Narraway. "Introduction." In *Screening Nature. Cinema Beyond the Human*, edited by Anat Pick and Guinevere Narraway, 1–12. New York: Berghahn Books, 2013.

Salgado Bautista, Diego Augusto. "La significación en el documental *Eco de la Montaña* de Nicolás Echevarría: un discurso de lo real histórico." In *Mexican Transnational Cinema and Literature*, edited by Maricruz Castro Ricalde, Mauricio Díaz Calderón, and James Ramey, 231–46. Oxford: Peter Lang Ltd., 2017.

Schaefer, Stacy B., and Peter Furst. "Introduction." In *People of the Peyote: Huichol Indian History, Religion & Survival*, edited by Stacy B. Schaefer and Peter T. Furst, 1–25. Albuquerque: University of New Mexico Press, 1996.

Smuts, Barbara. "Encounters with Animal Minds." *Journal of Consciousness Studies* 8, no. 5–7 (2001): 293–309.

Vilchez, Hernán, dir. *Huicholes: The Last Peyote Guardians*. 2014; México: Kabropro Films.

Willoquet-Maricondi, Paula. "Shifting Paradigms: From Environmentalist Films to Ecocinema." In *Framing the World. Explorations in Ecocriticism and Film*, edited by Paula Willoquet-Maricondi, 43–61. Charlottesville: University of Virginia Press, 2010.

———. "Introduction." In *Framing the World. Explorations in Ecocriticism and Film*, edited by Paula Willoquet-Maricondi, 1–9. Charlottesville: University of Virginia Press, 2010.

14

Undisciplined Knowledge

Indigenous Activism and Decapitation Resistance

GISELA HEFFES

Technology, it can be argued, creates "miracles." Who would believe that mountains could drift away, come closer into view, or even vanish? Because of modern extractive mechanisms as well as the use of cutting-edge gear today, we are witnessing this spectacle of removal. In the last two decades, Latin American cinema has brought a landscape of decapitated mountains into view. Mountains with no head, with their top chopped off, bold and bare, like the head of a Dominican friar. This violent landscape reproduces itself in various and multiple scenarios, from the Andes in Argentina to the Appalachian Mountains of West Virginia. I use the term *decapitated* acknowledging the ferocity of its meaning, but, more importantly, to directly address the violence embedded in the images of what Sunaura Taylor has defined as disabled ecologies: "the webs of disability that are created spatially, temporally, and across species boundaries when ecosystems are contaminated, depleted, and profoundly altered."[1] Decapitated mountains entail the violence of a spectacle: the degradation of magnificent landscapes, the curtail of living organisms. A visual spectacle that depicts how thousands of bodies (human and nonhuman alike) are wounded daily, and gratuitously, for no apparent reason except the ongoing machinery put into practice by the Capitalocene.[2]

Specifically, I refer here to a well-known reason: coal, copper, gold, and silver. All of these precious commodities, except for coal, have an ongoing demand in the current markets of this globalized era.[3] Let's take, for example, gold mining. As Joan Martinez Alier suggests in *The Environmentalism of the Poor*, this type of mining is "similar in a way to shrimp farming, or to the extraction of tropical wood like mahogany or to exports of ivory and diamonds from Africa. About 80 per cent of all gold that is dug out of the ground ends up as jewelry."[4] Consumption, or the wish to obtain positional goods, is a more culturally than biologically driven phenomenon.

Gold mining is particularly destructive. At the mine, daily dynamite explosions break up gold, which is then piled onto large filter pads to be sprayed twenty-four hours a day with a cyanide solution. Sodium cyanide used in gold mines can kill fish and cause other ecological damage. As Martinez-Alier argues, gold mining pollutes not only the rivers downstream but also local water sources. While the cyanide technique has been used as an alternative to amalgamation with mercury, consisting of "spraying a solution of cyanide over crushed ore heaped into open piles," mercury is also used.[5]

In 2000, a truck traveling from the Yanacocha Gold Mine in Northern Peru spilled 150 kilograms (330 pounds) of liquid mercury along a twenty-seven-kilometer stretch of a highway traversing the towns of Choropampa, Magdalena, and San José. As Fabiana Li noted, until the spill, "local people had not been aware that mercury is a byproduct of the gold mining process, since the company had not made this information public."[6] It was not until then that the potential risks of modern mining were made evident. As a result, children and adults came into contact with mercury. Because this happened before the town was warned of the potential toxic risks, more than 750 people sought medical aid, and more than one hundred people ended up in the hospital with mercury poisoning. The Choropampa spill brought into public question how mining companies—in this case Minera Yanacocha—handled their daily operations. Although extractive corporations usually insist that their procedures are safe and do not create pollution or negatively impact the environment, gold mining leaves behind enormous ecological rucksacks, along with pollution from mercury or cyanide, and wreaks immense damage on both humans and nonhumans beings alike. In addition to polluting the water supply, mining reduces the flow of water in irrigation canals.

Gold mining is primarily undertaken on Indigenous lands. In his seminal book *Slow Violence and the Environmentalism of the Poor*, Rob Nixon establishes a relationship between environmental violence and displacement from what he calls the "vernacular landscape." This landscape refers to a place "shaped by the affective, historically textured maps that communities have devised over generations, maps replete with names and routes, maps alive to significant ecological and surface geological features."[7] Furthermore, these landscapes are integral to community socioecological dynamics. The official landscape of the extractive state is oblivious to these maps and instead scrutinizes "the land in a bureaucratic, externalizing, and extraction-driven manner that is often pitilessly instrumental."[8] Martinez Alier points out that by violating land rights, mining companies, as well as other extractive industries, are "denying the right to life" of local peoples "whose relationship to land is central to their spiritual identity and survival."[9]

In Latin America, many Indigenous territories are located either in the mountains or its surrounding areas. One example is Ausangate. Peruvian anthropologist Marisol de la Cadena, in her much cited article "Indigenous Cosmopolitics in the Andes," refers to an episode that took place in December 2006, when "more than 1,000 peasants gathered in Cuzco's main square, the Plaza de Armas."[10] They had traveled from their villages located "at the foot of a mountain named Ausangate, well known in Cuzco as a powerful earth being, the source of life and death, of wealth and misery."[11] To attain positive results, local dwellers of the village cultivate and maintain a fulfilling relationship with the mountain and its environment, including surrounding mountains as well as minor or apparently less significant entities. This excursion to the Plaza de Armas was to join other demonstrators: a multitude of worshipers, both Catholic and of the Sanctuary of Coyllur Rit'I. More importantly, they were there to protest the potential concession of a mine in the Sinakara. They are known as "Qoyllur Rit'i (Star of Snow) or Qoyllurrit'i (Shining White Snow)," the largest pilgrimage center in southern Peru where tens of thousands of people flock every year.[12] The mountains have, to the Andean People, sacred attributes. Ausangate is the *apu*, which means in Quechua the lord and owner of the region. While they are part of Pachamama, the *apus*—those powerful mountain deities—"have personalities in their own right," they can be male or female, they are the custodians of eternal snow and ice, of the life-sustaining water, of wild and domesticated animals, and "they also watch over people's actions."[13] Similarly to Pachamama, they may penalize or grant requests.

Ausangate, the documentary also named after this mountain, came out in 2006, the same year of the episode to which Marisol de la Cadena referred in her article. Because of the overlap between its release and the demonstration (both happening simultaneously), the documentary does not dwell on the threat of the mountain's potential decapitation by a mining company, nor does it draw attention to any of the conflicts referred to by de la Cadena. The film suggests by way of a long establishing shot that Ausangte is a sacred region. The use of sound, predominantly music, overlapped with a woman explaining in Quechua what Ausangate means for her community, implies that this region represents a sanctuary for both the villagers and the Quechua people. The documentary is not explicitly environmental per se, or even political, but it acquires such a level of significance by presenting the daily customs of the people and the relationship they have established with the mountain, the *apu*, for generations. The communal lifestyle of the people bluntly contrasts with the individualist life of the modern city. For the villagers, those who seek a job in the urban spaces are moving away from their ancestors' values and therefore from Ausangate.

Marisol de la Cadena's argument, however, is not political but about politics. It is more about the interplay of conflicting powers within the society than about a space for the contestation of the very basis of power. In "Indigenous Cosmopolitics," she draws inspiration from recent political events in Peru—and to a lesser extent in Ecuador and Bolivia—where the Indigenous popular movement has introduced sentient entities (mountains, water, and soil—what Western epistemologies call "nature") into the public political arena to argue that indigeneity, as a historical formation, exceeds the notion of politics as usual, that is, an arena populated by rational human beings disputing the power to represent others vis-à-vis the state. According to de la Cadena, indigeneity's current political emergence challenges the separation of nature and culture that underpins the prevalent notion of politics and its consequent social contract. Therefore, current Indigenous movements propose a different political practice, plural not because of its enactment by bodies marked by gender, race, ethnicity, or sexuality (as multiculturalism would have it), but because they conjure up nonhumans as actors in the political arena. Ausangate and the sanctuary of Coyllur Rit'l are not the only "earth-beings" to have become public politically. Also in northern Peru, a coalition of peasants and environmentalists made Cerro Quilish a sacred mountain and enlisted it in the fight against Yanacocha, the largest gold mine in Latin America. Although, as de la Cadena remarks, not each "of the mining conflicts proliferating in Peru articulates the presence of earth-beings,"[14] these struggles were enough to lead former Peruvian President Alan García to describe sacred mountains as "an invention of 'old anticapitalist' communists of the nineteenth century who changed into protectionists in the twentieth century and have again changed into environmentalists in the twenty-first century."[15]

Latin American cultural representations have come to play a pivotal role in the call for integrating a plurality of forms of life that are not limited to the human. Three documentaries that came out between 2007 and 2010 address the problem of mining exploration and extractive politics in three different mountainous regions of Latin America. Each film operates as a critical tool that combines environmental justice claims, Indigenous and non-Indigenous activism, and modes of social and cultural resistance that range from struggle and street demonstrations, to blocking roads and placing pickets, to collective assemblies. I contend that these films set in motion what I call decapitation resistance. By this, I refer to a strategy based on the use of alternative knowledges that dispute and aim to reverse the epistemological mechanisms established by mining companies and extractive capital. Decapitation resistance implies an undisciplined knowledge, one that does not necessarily hark back to de la Cadena's ontological politics (for instance, by conjuring up exclusively the presence of earth beings). On the contrary, undisciplined knowledge challenges both hegemonic and homogenizing discourses by putting forward a heterogenous, hybrid episteme that binds together spaces and temporalities, modern and traditional customs, and material and digital risk assessments to generate collective action ("resistance"). Through the aesthetic production of documentary films, this episteme organizes a unique practice that brings together human-driven anthropogenic change, politics, and environmentalism. The documentaries analyzed here appeal to this form of undisciplined knowledge to contest the imposition of the official landscape. The ultimate goal of decapitation resistance is to preserve—and in some cases restore—the threatened vernacular landscape.

Cielo abierto (*Open Sky*) by Carlos Ruiz was released in 2007; *When Clouds Clear* by Danielle Bernstein and Anne Slick came out in 2008; and *Operación diablo* (*The Devil Operation*) by Stephanie Boyd in 2010. As Roberto Forns Broggi suggests, these films are examples of an ecocinema that operates as a collaborative initiative.[16] According to Belinda Smaill, this type of practice creates a reciprocal "social agenda among film-makers, technicians, and main actors," one that goes beyond empathy and generates a "recognition of the other in its specificity through a dissident gaze that arises from the civic capacity to question the base of the political state."[17]

Thematically, the three documentaries embody what an article from *The Economist* on February 6, 2016, referred to as "slicing off the mountain tops."[18] The figurative image used in the article corresponds exactly with a growing phenomenon where Andean mountains are at risk of being decapitated. The three documentaries address ongoing conflicts in Latin America since the 1990s, when Andean countries opened their economies to private investment through neoliberal policies and deregulation. As a result, there was a rise of extractive practices, through open pit mining, that involved slicing the tops off mountains or emptying lakes. Each documentary details a specific case study. *Operación diablo* focuses on the resistance of the people of Quilish in Cajamarca and the persecution that activists suffered in the hands of paramilitary groups hired by the company. *Operación diablo* introduces the problem of gold mining and the response by the inhabitants who live in the region, who take on an activist role comprising political resistance, radical protest, and collective meetings. Because of the immediate threat to their vernacular landscapes, they are forced to learn in greater detail about the perils of mining, a task they achieve by connecting with other communities. More precisely, their research is focused on the risks mining poses to their families and their environments. *Cielo abierto* takes place in La Rioja, Argentina, where a Canadian mining company, Barrick Gold Corporation, plans to explore the Famatina mountain in search of gold. The documentary features the local population of Famatina and Chilecito (both in the province of La Rioja, Argentina), who resist the establishment of open cut mining. Following the inhabitants of Famatina's surrounding areas, it draws attention to a growing political turmoil that ends with the expulsion of the company and the approval of the "Ley Provincial"—which forbids this type of mining—but ends up ignored by the local authorities. *When Clouds Clear* takes place in Junin, Ecuador, where a community of farmers who have been living in the mountains raising crops for many years have to confront the Canadian mining firm Ascendant Copper. The foreign company claims to own a large section of farmland that it intends to use to bring minerals to the surface.

The three documentaries illustrate the ongoing tensions between local residents and transnational corporations by foregrounding the complicity that local authorities established with foreign firms, whom, ironically, they assist in suppressing local dissents through force and violence. This takes the form of repressive crowd dispersal, or even more brutal actions, such as in *Operación diablo*, where the audience witnesses how a paramilitary squad hired by the company tortures and kills many locals. Yet this is not surprising. An article in *Nature Sustainability* indicated that between 2002 and 2017, 1,558 people in fifty countries were killed for defending their environments and lands.[19] Conflicts over natural resources are linked to different resources and/or sectors—for example, fossil fuels, minerals, timber, agriculture, aquaculture, and water, as well as access to land and/or bodies of water from which natural resources can be extracted. These conflicts, as a matter of fact, can be seen "as a continuation of colonial land

Figure 14.1. Close-up of a police officer during the repression of local villagers and activists. Stephanie Boyd, *Operación diablo*, 2010, video still.

Figure 14.2. Police ready themselves to violently repress protestors. Danielle Bernstein and Anne Slick, *When Clouds Clear*, 2008, video still.

and resource appropriation that established systems of dispossession and control."[20] From Chico Mendes in Brazil to Berta Cáceres in Honduras, environmental activists have been repeatedly murdered in Latin America. Other murdered activists include Vicente Cañas and Wilson Pinheiro, both in Brazil, for protecting the Amazon rainforest as well as Indigenous land; Jeanette Kawas in Honduras, for protecting the land from the construction of a dam and a palm plantation.

These documentaries play an important role in interrogating the contrasts that emerge from the "clash of the local and the global."[21] Decapitation resistance means to contest—or even reverse—the demonizing rhetoric used by the local media to describe the activists. This demonizing rhetoric depicts protesters as criminals, terrorists, *guerrilleros*, and/or antistate militants. Pacific marches that block the roads to the mine, like in *When Clouds Clear*, end with the police firing tear gas to brutally repress demonstrators. The two images featured here (see figures 14.1 and 14.2) provide a closer glimpse of the police force in two distinct situations. While figure 14.1 frames the covered police face through a tight close-up, figure 14.2 displays police presence by way of a medium shot of one officer, accompanied by three other officers in the background. What is striking about figure 14.1 is its enactment of perverse intimacy with state power and violence. The image doesn't display police violence per se, but the helmet, gas mask, and bulletproof vest suggest the disproportionate response by the police force to peaceful protesters. Significant too is the choice of a close-up that highlights the officer's eyes, which can be seen through the clear plastic of the mask. The intimacy of this shot perhaps serves as a way of communicating the search for an emotional clue hidden under the bulky suit. Figure 14.2 by contrast departs from such intimacy and leaves less room for ambiguity. The still captures the one-dimensional anger of the police officer, his hand pulling the gun, while the other three men look behind them to where the conflict will unfold. Farther in the distance, a local bystander can be seen. Examined together, the two images generate an effect of anger and frustration in the audience. Moreover, they illustrate the problematic tensions that define and organize a relentless conflict. Assembled side by side, they subvert the prevailing narrative that foreign corporations, mining companies and the local states orchestrate in tandem.

Together, the three documentaries index the similarity of tactics used by mining companies throughout different Latin American countries. Remarkably, the strategies employed by transnational corporations in three different countries—Argentina, Ecuador, and Perú—are almost identical. In all of them we observe the same mechanisms of bribery and/or intimidation. First, the representative intends to bribe the members of the community by offering textbooks and color markers to teachers and mothers, promising to build them a school. When bribery doesn't work, we watch the never-ending harassment and intimidation of the activists. It is important to emphasize that these protests are not propelled by anticapitalist or xenophobic motives; on the contrary, they are driven by the pursuit of the right to a healthful land in which to live. In a strict sense, the documentaries register the efforts of the local residents to organize, mobilize, and empower themselves and take charge of their own lives, communities, and environments.

The protests captured on-screen set in motion a process that James Holston, paraphrasing Henri Lefebvre, defines as not the right to the city, but the right to the land. While focused on "the dispossessed of global urbanization," Holston's call for an "insurgency" that arises when "we follow the development of struggles over daily life" emerges in similar "circumstances of degradation and peripheralness."[22] It is not my intention here to equate a rural environment with an urban one. However, from an environmental justice standpoint that argues for making "visible the disproportionate effects on poor and low-income communities" of the negative side effect of extractive capitalism, it is important to emphasize the common denominator of a community at risk of displacement and of losing the right to a meaningful and healthful life.[23] In different ways, both risk losing their vernacular place as a result of real estate development, gentrification, and the effects of global financial institutions, or of multinational extractive companies' operations. The "insurgent" notion of right underscores that these communities are entitled to claim and demand what belongs to them. Insurgent because they collide directly with those procedures carried out by transnational companies in complicity with the local authorities. Furthermore, they contend with—and resist—narratives of nation-states and social, economic, and cultural development that justify "decapitation."

A shot in *Cielo abierto* evinces these contradictions. The documentary displays an assembly that takes place between the local people of La Rioja and government representatives to discuss the potential effects of mining extraction in Famatina. Interestingly, the delegates are accompanied by "experts" who argue that mining will bring economic and cultural development to the town. This idea of development, not as much as a sustainable well-being and balance among thriving natural, human, and social beings, but as environmental degradation, is questioned by a villager attending the assembly. His response is definitive: he argues that the same mining company in the Argentine province of San Juan has destroyed the "camino del inca," one of the most valuable cultural references to the pre-Columbian era.

In the three documentaries, the local population becomes an agent of social transformation and a model of political resistance. These films embody the "Latin American practice of collective filmmaking" in their combination of the genre's two features identified by Sophia McClennen: "a commitment to making films with and for a marginalized community and a desire to alter mainstream commercial filmmaking practices."[24] The concept of the collective means, then, that the filmmakers intended to collaborate with the communities they were filming by soliciting their contributions, involvement, and participation, while simultaneously eluding as much as possible the imposition of their own ideas on their subjects. Through this practice of collaboration in which the process is connected in an organic manner to the final product, collective filmmaking is attentive to the dynamics of power. By doing so, they hope to evade social and economic power structures that are frequent in both Hollywood and auteur cinema.

There is an attempt to dissolve both fixed and ranked categories through the use of cinematic techniques that convey the filmmakers' position: from frequent sequences that show antimining families marching in protest, to the handheld camera moving inside the crowd, allowing it to take the demonstrators' perspective as they block the roads to the mine—such as in *When Clouds Clear*—where they are ultimately brutally repressed by the police. The use of montage and of still photos is another mechanism that mixes together characters, spaces and temporalities, as well as the use of documented footage from the media, which overlaps with the portrayed events. In *Indianizing Film*, Freya Schiwy analyzes similar strategies in documentaries such as Jorge Sanjinés and the Ukamau Group's *El coraje del pueblo* (*Courage of the People*) from 1971. This film was produced in close collaboration with the mining community of Siglo XX in the Bolivian Andes and recreates a history of Bolivia's largely Quechua and Aymara miners' objection to extractive capitalism and land exploitation.[25] It shows miner families marching in protest through a tactic that will reappear in *Cielo abierto*, *When Clouds Clear*, and *Operación diablo*: the handheld camera moving inside the multitude as the miners are massacred by soldiers. The on-site recording of the screams, shots, and overall confusion strengthens the documentary truth effect of the community reenactment. The use of long shots to capture the revolutionary collective and juxtapose it with close-ups of individualized police officers, company representatives, and government officials intensifies this contrast, and places films like *Courage of the People* as the forerunner of decapitation resistance visualizations.

All these documentaries make visible how local communities defend their right to inhabit a healthy and nontoxic land, without contaminated water and/or air, and where humans and nonhumans live in a state of communal reciprocity, respect, and equality. Very rarely in these visualizations are the earth beings described by Marisol de la Cadena introduced as political agents. On the contrary, they appeal to the notion of "buen vivir," a concept that connects ecological aspects derived from a lifestyle of Andean communities, based on a common experience that brings together humans and nonhumans. Eduardo Gudynas has developed this idea, underscoring that the concept of *buen vivir* is not traditional but new, and represents a particular way of relating to the Natural World, as well as an alternative perspective on developmentalism. In *Derechos de la naturaleza. Ética biocéntrica y políticas ambientales* Gudynas appeals to the need to assign intrinsic values to Nature in order to break away from an anthropocentric perspective that sees it objectively. By seeing Nature in a nonextrinsic way, and therefore subjectively, it is possible to assign rights to Nature and the nonhuman world.[26]

Jorge Marcone has recently described how environmental documentaries frequently neglect to portray the "more-than-human ontologies and temporalities associated with indigenous politics in Latin America."[27] They usually focus on local resistance to national and transnational interests, and on the exclusion of the Indigenous peoples for national decision making. So why is this the case? Unlike literature, environmental documentaries focus less on the sacredness of a mountain, a river or earth beings, and more on environmental conflict itself. Furthermore, they don't directly address the environment from an ecological perspective. Instead, they tend to focus on the political and social conflicts that arise from the confrontation among different actors (transnational mining companies, local authorities, village dwellers). In doing so, these documentaries fail to introduce a gaze that critically interrogates the ecological relationship between humans and the more-than-human. By departing from an ontological perspective that pushes past the human, their vision remains limited to an anthropocentric position that unsuccessfully engages nonhuman agency, as George Handley and Elizabeth De Loughrey suggest. Such an approach would consider the ways in which ecology works outside of "the frames of human time and political interest."[28] They are, to use Stephen Rust, Salma Monani, and Sean Cubitt's term, "ecologically entangled" in that they present people's daily activism and the relationship they have established with the land for many generations.[29] However, as Rust, Monani and Cubitt remark, "media, society, and the environment are inextricably entangled together," both in the way "media texts represent the environment" and in the unavoidable manners that "media texts and systems are materially embedded in natural resource use and abuse."[30]

Decapitation resistance aims to make visible what is hardly noticeable or becomes unseen. With (lack of) visibility comes the question of scale: How can we grasp the immensity of these (potential) toxic genocides, most of which take place in remote areas? Or, as Nixon inquired, "what happens when we are unsighted, when what extends before us—in the space and time that we most deeply inhabit—remains invisible?"[31] The contribution of the documentaries examined here clearly speaks to a broader understanding of human interventions in environmental destruction. But they also—if we agree with Rust et al. that media consists of "physical devices of mediation"—permeate both human and nonhuman worlds by destabilizing "the idea of an absolute division between human society and our environment."[32]

The culturally constructed division between nature and culture emerged at the end of the seventeenth century with the establishment "of the highly specialized and disciplined methods of knowledge production categorized as 'science,'" which, in turn, were frequently used to allow colonial expansionism and, later on, neocolonial development schemes such as resource extraction, deforestation, the construction of highways, roads and dams, among many other projects that "displace human populations and exacerbate species collapse."[33] In the documentaries, mining exploration and extractive politics of potential decapitation are "framed," literally and symbolically, as the main threat in which the politics of mining stimulates environmental degradation not only of the vernacular landscape but also of the daily livelihood of local populations, thanks to acid mine drainage, water pollution and scarcity, forest dead zones, and all sort of diseases caused by mercury and cyanide exposure.

As the threat of potential extraction becomes more real, the local community recurs to alternative knowledges that map the complexity and tension between extractive capitalism, environmental change, and regional cultural identity. While demands for environmental justice have become central to these struggles (although generally ineffective in stopping these policies), *Cielo abierto*, *When Clouds Clear*, and *Operación diablo* consist of a first attempt to decolonize and reverse the Western modernity project that aimed to discipline oral and non-European cultures. As stated above, they do not offer an appreciation of multinatural worlds and of a "pluri-versal, rather than universal," understanding of the cosmos.[34] But even when these cultural products fail to stop the imposed violence of extractive capitalism, they succeed in displaying what Martinez Alier has termed "social metabolism" and "entropy." In other words, the flow of energy and materials that societies exchange with their environment, the "stocks and flows, recycling, wastes and emissions."[35]

To extract means to remove. Extraction can be described as "capitalism's fundamental logic of withdrawal," as Matthew Henry has recently noted. This ranges from "value, nutrients, energy, labor, time" as well as "people, lands, culture, lifeforms," and "the elements," without "corresponding deposit (except as externalities of nonvalue in the form of pollution, waste, climate change, illness, and death)."[36] Those externalities are the built-in residues of extractive politics and capital: devastated sites such as those emptied out, decapitated mountains, abandoned after having been fully unearthed—now rendered useless from a profitable standpoint—as well as the vulnerable communities, also unprofitable, exposed to a toxic genocide, obliterated by the continued embodiment of the expanding frontier of extractivism. As Henry notes, this is an expansion that is characterized by the "privatization and enclosure of the commons," displacement and deprivation, and an economy that goes regularly through periods of success followed by periods of failure.[37]

Martinez Alier suggests that in mining conflicts, as well as with oil, pipelines, and many other struggles—as we have all recently witnessed here in North America with the Standing Rock conflict in North Dakota—ethnic groups deploy "vocabularies of human rights, livelihood, territorial rights for minorities, federalism and environmentalism."[38] It could be that strategically it is preferable to inscribe their environmental claims within a longer history of progressive struggles. But it could also be that, as Martinez Alier has rightly demonstrated, when it comes to these legal battles, "the weaker part must quickly attempt to understand the aliens' system of justice."[39] We agree that there is no larger cultural difference in the world today than those between a CEO of a transnational corporation like Texaco or Freeport-McMoRan and tribal peoples in the Andes, or Africa, polluted by the water from oil extraction or by mine tailings dumped into rivers. The documentaries examined here point to the damages of both extractive capitalism and mining and the threat they pose to human and nonhuman rights and the local, vernacular landscape. While they do not provide agency to nonhuman beings, decapitation resistance provides a critical tool for questioning hegemonic practices of power as well as social, economic, and cultural exploitation. It offers a first venture toward the production of undisciplined knowledge, understood as a practice of contention and rebellion. It operates as a strategy of challenge but also of survival.

Notes

1. See Sunaura Taylor's presentation on "Disabled Ecologies: Living with Impaired Landscapes" at the Othering & Belonging Institute at UC Berkeley, March 5, 2019, https://belonging.berkeley.edu/video-sunaura-taylor-disabled-ecologies-living-impaired-landscapes.

2. Canadian photographer Edward Burtynsky has captured in detail the anthropogenic degradation of these majestic landscapes in deeply disturbing pictures.

3. A recent report describes a new wave of coal demand in the Asian market. See Somini Sengupta, Jacqueline Williams, and Aruna Chandrasekhar, "How One Billionaire Could Keep Three Countries Hooked on Coal for Decades," *The New York Times*, August 15, 2009.

4. Joan Martinez Alier, *The Environmentalism of the Poor. A Study of Ecological Conflicts and Valuation* (Cheltenham, UK: Edward Elgar, 2002), 100.

5. Ibid., 102.

6. Fabiana Li, *Unearthing Conflict: Corporate Mining, Activism, and Expertise in Peru* (Durham and London: Duke University Press), 91.

7. Rob Nixon, *Slow Violence and the Environmentalism of the Poor* (Cambridge: Harvard University Press, 2011), 17.

8. Ibid., 17.

9. Martinez Alier, 101.

10. "Cosmopolitics" should be understood following Isabelle Stengers's conceptualizations proposed in her essay "The Cosmopolitical Proposal," where the "term cosmopolitical refers to the unknown constituted by these multiple, divergent worlds and to the articulations of which they could eventually be capable." See Isabelle Stengers, "The Cosmopolitical Proposal," in *Making Things Public: Atmospheres of Democracy*, eds. Bruno Latour and Peter Weibel (Cambridge: MIT Press, 2005), 994–1003.

11. Marisol de la Cadena, "Indigenous Cosmopolitics in the Andes," *Cultural Anthropology* 25, no. 2 (2010): 338.

12. See Inge Bolin, *Rituals of Respect: The Secret of Survival in the High Peruvian Andes* (Austin: University of Texas Press, 2002), 153.

13. Ibid., 32.

14. de la Cadena, "Indigenous Cosmopolitics," 340.

15. Ibid.

16. Roberto Forns-Broggi, "Ecocinema and 'Good Life' in Latin America," in *Transnational Ecocinema: Film Culture in an Era of Ecological Transformation*, ed. Tommy Gustafsson and Pietari Kääpä (Chicago: University of Chicago Press, 2013), 89.

17. Belinda Smaill, *The Documentary: Politics, Emotion, Culture* (Basingstoke, UK: Palgrave Macmillan), 91–92.

18. See "Mining in Latin America. From Conflict to Co-operation," *The Economist*, February 6, 2016, https://www.economist.com/the-americas/2016/02/06/from-conflict-to-co-operation.

19. Nathalie Butt, Frances Lambrick, Mary Menton, and Anna Renwick, "The Supply Chain of Violence," *Nature Sustainability* 2, no. 8 (2019): 742–47.

20. Ibid.

21. Tommy Gustafsson and Pietari Kääpä, "Introduction," *Transnational Ecocinema: Film Culture in an Era of Ecological Transformation* (Chicago: University of Chicago Press, 2013), 19.

22. James Holston, "Insurgent Citizenship in an Era of Global Urban Peripheries," *City & Society* 21, no. 2 (2009): 247.

23. Giovanna Di Chiro, "Environmental Justice," in *Keywords for Environmental Studies*, ed. Joni Adamson, William A. Gleason, and David N. Pellow (New York: New York University Press, 2016), 105.

24. Sophia A. McClennen, *Globalization and Latin American Cinema: Towards a New Critical Paradigm* (Cham, Switzerland: Palgrave Macmillan, 2018), 199.

25. Freya Schiwy, *Indianizing Film: Decolonization, the Andes, and the Question of Technology* (New Brunswick: Rutgers University Press, 2009), 42.

26. See Eduardo Gudynas, *Derechos de la naturaleza ética biocéntrica y políticas ambientales* (Buenos Aires: Tinta Limón, 2015).

27. Jorge Marcone, "Filming the Emergence of Popular Environmentalism in Latin America Postcolonialism and Buen Vivir," in *Global Ecologies and the Environmental Humanities: Postcolonial Approaches*, ed. Elizabeth M. DeLoughrey, Jill Didur, and Anthony Carrigan (New York: Routledge, 2015), 208.

28. Elizabeth M. DeLoughrey and George B. Handley, *Postcolonial Ecologies: Literatures of the Environment* (New York: Oxford University Press, 2011), 8.

29. Stephen Rust, Salma Monani, and Sean Cubitt. *Ecomedia: Key Issues* (London: Routledge, 2016), 2.

30. Ibid., 2.

31. Nixon, *Slow Violence*, 15.

32. Rust, Monani, and Cubitt, *Ecomedia*, 3.

33. Joni Adamson and Salma Monani, "Cosmovisions, Ecocriticism, and Indigenous Studies," in *Ecocriticism and Indigenous Studies: Conversations from Earth to Cosmos*, ed. Salma Monani and Joni Adamson (New York: Routledge, 2017), 4.

34. Adamson and Monani, "Cosmovisions," 2.

35. Martinez Alier, *The Environmentalism of the Poor*, 100.

36. Matthew S. Henry, "Extractive Fictions and Postextraction. Futurisms Energy and Environmental Injustice in Appalachia," *Environmental Humanities* 11, no. 2 (2019): 402.

37. Ibid., 404.

38. Martinez Alier, *The Environmentalism of the Poor*, 105.

39. Ibid., 110.

40. I borrow the term from Arturo Escobar's *Designs for the Pluriverse: Radical Interdependence, Autonomy, and the Making of Worlds* (Durham: Duke University Press, 2018).

Works Cited

Adamson, Joni, William A. Gleason, and David N. Pellow. "Introduction." In *Keywords for Environmental Studies*, 1–5. New York: New York University Press.

Adamson, Joni, and Salma Monani. "Cosmovisions, Ecocriticism, and Indigenous Studies." In *Ecocriticism and Indigenous Studies: Conversations from Earth to Cosmos*, edited by Salma Monani and Joni Adamson, 1–22. New York: Routledge, 2017.

Bernstein, Danielle, and Anne Slick, dir. *When Clouds Clear*. 2008; USA: Clear Films/El Otro Lado Films/NetHead Films.

Boyd, Stephanie, dir. *Cuando la tierra llora: Operación Diablo*. 2010; Perú: Guarango.

Butt, Nathalie, Frances Lambrick, Mary Menton, and Anna Renwick. "The Supply Chain of Violence." *Nature Sustainability* 2, no. 8 (2019): 742–47.

De la Cadena, Marisol. "Indigenous Cosmopolitics in the Andes." *Cultural Anthropology* 25, no. 2 (2010): 334–70.

DeLoughrey, Elizabeth M., and George B. Handley. *Postcolonial Ecologies: Literatures of the Environment*. New York: Oxford University Press, 2011.

Di Chiro, Giovanna. "Environmental Justice." In *Keywords for Environmental Studies*, edited by Joni Adamson, William A. Gleason, and David N. Pellow, 100–5. New York: New York University Press, 2016.

Forns-Broggi, Roberto. "Ecocinema and 'Good Life' in Latin America." In *Transnational Ecocinema: Film Culture in an Era of Ecological Transformation*, edited by Tommy Gustafsson and Pietari Kääpä, 85–100. Chicago: University of Chicago Press, 2013, 2013.

Gudynas, Eduardo. *Derechos de la naturaleza ética biocéntrica y políticas ambientales*. Buenos Aires: Tinta Limón, 2015.

Gustafsson, Tommy, and Pietari Kääpä. "Introduction." In *Transnational Ecocinema: Film Culture in an Era of Ecological Transformation*, edited by Tommy Gustafsson and Pietari Kääpä, 2–20. Chicago: University of Chicago Press.

Henry, Matthew S. "Extractive Fictions and Postextraction. Futurisms Energy and Environmental Injustice in Appalachia." *Environmental Humanities* 11, no. 2 (November 2019): 402–26.

Holston, James. "Insurgent Citizenship in an Era of Global Urban Peripheries." *City & Society* 21, no. 2 (2009): 245–67.

Li, Fabiana. *Unearthing Conflict: Corporate Mining, Activism, and Expertise in Peru*. Durham: Duke University Press, 2015.

Marcone, Jorge. "Filming the Emergence of Popular Environmentalism in Latin America Postcolonialism and Buen Vivir." In *Global Ecologies and the Environmental Humanities: Postcolonial Approaches*, edited by Elizabeth M. DeLoughrey, Jill Didur, and Anthony Carrigan, 207–25. New York: Routledge, 2015.

Martinez Alier, Joan. *The Environmentalism of the Poor: A Study of Ecological Conflicts and Valuation*. Cheltenham, UK: Edward Elgar, 2002.

McClennen, Sophia A. *Globalization and Latin American Cinema: Towards a New Critical Paradigm*. Cham, Switzerland: Palgrave Macmillan, 2018.

"Mining in Latin America. From Conflict to Co-operation." *The Economist*, February 6, 2016. https://www.economist.com/the-americas/2016/02/06/from-conflict-to-co-operation.

Nixon, Rob. *Slow Violence and the Environmentalism of the Poor*. Cambridge: Harvard University Press, 2011.

Ruiz, Carlos, dir. *Cielo abierto*. 2007; Argentina: Rioxa Films.

Rust, Stephen, Salma Monani, and Sean Cubitt. *Ecomedia: Key Issues*. London: Routledge, 2016.

Schiwy, Freya. *Indianizing Film: Decolonization, The Andes, and The Question Of Technology*. New Brunswick, NJ: Rutgers University Press, 2009.

Smaill, Belinda. *The Documentary: Politics, Emotion, Culture*. Basingstoke, UK: Palgrave Macmillan, 2010.

Contributors

Iván Eusebio Aguirre Darancou is Assistant Professor of Spanish at the University of California Riverside.

Mark Anderson is Associate Professor of Spanish at the University of Georgia. He is the author of *Disaster Writing: The Cultural Politics of Catastrophe in Latin America* (University of Virginia Press, 2011) and coeditor of *Ecological Crisis and Cultural Representation in Latin America: Ecocritical Perspectives on Art, Film, and Literature* (Lexington, 2016).

Tomás Emilio Arce Mairena is a PhD candidate in Spanish at the University of Cincinnati.

Lisa Blackmore is Senior Lecturer in the School of Philosophy and Art History at the University of Essex. She is the author of *Spectacular Modernity: Dictatorship, Space and Visuality in Venezuela, 1948–1958* (University of Pittsburgh Press, 2017) and the codirector of the documentary *Después de Trujillo/After Trujillo* (2016).

Katherine Bundy is a PhD candidate in Hispanic Studies at McGill University.

Mauricio Espinoza is Assistant Professor of Spanish and Latin American Cultural Studies at the University of Cincinnati. He is the author of *Respiración de piedras* (Colección Lira Costarricense, 2016).

Carolyn Fornoff is Assistant Professor of Latin American culture at the University of Illinois at Urbana-Champaign. She is the coeditor of *Timescales:*

Thinking Across Ecological Temporalities (University of Minnesota Press, 2020).

Moira Fradinger is Associate Professor of Comparative Literature at Yale University. She is the author of *Binding Violence: Literary Visions of Political Origins* (Stanford University Press, 2010).

Gisela Heffes is Associate Professor of Latin American Literature and Culture at Rice University. She is the author of *Políticas de la destrucción/Poéticas de la preservación. Apuntes para una lectura (eco)crítica del medio ambiente en América Latina* (Beatriz Viterbo, 2013) and *Las ciudades imaginarias en la literatura latinoamericana* (Beatriz Viterbo, 2008); coeditor of *The Latin American Ecocultural Reader* (Northwestern University Press, 2020); and editor of *Poéticas de los (dis)locamientos* (Literal, 2012) and *Utopías urbanas. Geopolítica del deseo en América latina* (Iberoamericana Vervuert, 2013). She is also the author of numerous works of fiction.

Amanda Eaton McMenamin is Associate Professor of Spanish at Wilson College.

Julia M. Medina is Associate Professor of Spanish at the University of San Diego.

Juana New is a PhD candidate in Film Studies at the University of Iowa.

Fernando J. Rosenberg is Professor of Hispanic Studies and Comparative Literature at Brandeis University. He is the author of *After Human Rights: Literature, Visual Arts, and Film in Latin America, 1990–2010* (University of Pittsburgh, 2016) and *The Avant-Garde and Geopolitics in Latin America* (University of Pittsburgh, 2006).

Vinodh Venkatesh is Professor of Spanish at Virginia Tech. He is the author of *Capitán Latinoamérica: Superheroes in Cinema, Television, and Web Series* (State University of New York Press, 2020); *New Maricón Cinema: Outing Latin American Film* (University of Texas Press, 2016); and *The Body as Capital: Masculinities in Contemporary Latin American Fiction* (University of Arizona Press, 2015); and coeditor of *Horacio Castellanos Moya: El diablo en el espejo* (Albatros, 2016).

Patrícia Vieira is Senior Researcher at the Centre for Social Studies at the University of Coimbra; and Professor of Spanish and Portuguese at Georgetown University. She is the author of *States of Grace: Utopia in Brazilian Culture* (State University of New York Press, 2018); *Portuguese Film 1930–1960: The Staging of the New State Regime* (Bloomsbury, 2013); *Seeing Politics Otherwise: Vision in Latin American and Iberian Fiction* (University of Toronto Press, 2011); and *Cinema no Estado Novo: A Encenação do Regime* (Colibri, 2011); and the coeditor of numerous volumes, the most recent of which is *Portuguese Literature and the Environment* (Lexington, 2019).

Index

Note: page numbers followed by *f* refer to figures.

7:19: La hora del temblor (Grau), 13, 49, 57–62. *See also* Chimal, Alberto

abattoirs, 114–15. *See also* slaughterhouses
accumulation, 4, 14; capital, 181, 186–87, 247, 288 (*see also* capitalism)
activism, 10, 212–13, 337; animal rights, 223; *El canto de Bosawas* (Hoijman) and, 282, 290; environmental animation and, 140; human rights, 233; Indigenous, 239, 277n52, 306, 321, 322n2, 331
agency, 73, 142, 153, 158n14, 206, 271–72, 316; animation and, 139–41, 144–46, 150, 154; cultural, 295; geological, 13, 62; human, 14, 52, 144, 244, 256; Indigenous, 212, 225n18; individual, 192; loss of, 222; material, 237; of matter, 7 (*see also* new materialism); nonhuman, 13–14, 62, 139–40, 144, 146–47, 256, 337, 339; political, 207; posthuman, 140, 144, 147, 152; subaltern, 269; tectonic, 48
Allende, Salvador, 135n18, 233

ALMA project, 73, 76, 82
Alonso, Lisandro, 89–90, 92–94, 96, 99–101, 102n3, 104n25; characters of, 105n33; cinema of, 105n31, 106n47; experimental camera work and, 13. *See also La libertad* (Alonso); slow cinema
Álvarez, Santiago, 135nn18–19
Amad, Paula, 80–81
Amazon rainforest, 26, 40n4, 334
Amazon region, 12, 25, 27, 33–35, 41nn6–7, 42n31, 43n32; films about travel to, 28–31, 32, 35–37, 39–40; portrayals of Indigenous peoples in, 42n28; rubber trade in, 26, 30–31, 37–38, 40n2, 225n11
Amazon River, 26–27, 29, 40n3, 45n54
Amazon River basin, 27; cinema and, 25, 28, 31
Andermann, Jens, 7, 9, 95, 97, 104n27, 168–69, 171–72, 178n18
Anderson, Mark, 7, 15, 52
animality, 317, 321; intercorporeal, 307, 309–10, 315–16, 319
animals, 1–3, 25–26, 69, 123–24, 127, 268, 287–88, 296–97; in

349

animals *(continued)*
    Amazonian river movies, 29–33, 38–40; in animation, 146–47, 153; disassembly of, 116, 128; domesticated, 218–19, 329; in *Esteros* (Curotto), 172–74; human, 112, 114–17, 120–22, 126–27, 131–33, 316, 319; human rights and, 221; killing of, 120, 122; in Latin American history, 113; marine, 117; nonhuman, 13–14, 111–18, 120–22, 124, 126–27, 131–34, 135n16; oil pollution and, 217–19, 222; slaughter of, 14, 32, 115, 117, 128, 131, 133–34, 135n8, 287 *(see also* abattoirs; Eisenstein, Sergei: *Strike*; slaughterhouses); Wixárika/Wixáritari (Huichol) peoples and, 307–11, 313, 316–17, 319. See also humanimal assemblages; humanimals; zoos
animation, 150; aesthetics, 14, 139, 144–45, 147, 153, 156; environmental, 140, 144; Latin American, 143; techniques, 142, 145–46; web-produced, 141. *See also* animated films; *Bendito Machine* (Malis Álvarez); cartoons
animated films, 14, 139–40, 145–46
Anthropocene, the, 4, 50, 153, 198, 282, 288; cinema and, 7; natural disaster films and, 13; new testimonial gesture of, 298
anthropocentrism, 2, 8, 141, 239, 337; animated films and, 139–40, 145–46, 152–53; capitalism and, 112, 134; cinema and, 3–4; human rights and, 15; in left-wing cinema, 14; modern science and, 232; Nature and, 101; Nicaraguan Caribbean coast and, 281–82; nonhuman animals and, 132; slow violence and, 97; visibility and, 117
Appadurai, Arjun, 184–85, 189
aqueous, the, 14, 164, 170–71, 173–75, 177n13
Arendt, Hannah, 231, 246, 248nn5–6
Argentine cinema, 14, 92, 161, 168. *See also* direct cinema
Araujo, Diego, 163, 176
Araújo, J. G., 30, 42nn29–30
Atacama Desert, 73, 76, 234–36, 241, 243
Avatar (Cameron), 140, 240

Barbas-Rhoden, Laura, 7, 103n14, 260
belonging, 70, 84
Benacerraf, Margot, 113, 122, 124, 126; *Araya*, 113, 122–24
Bendito Machine (Malis Álvarez), 14, 139–44, 146–57
Benjamin, Walter, 241, 246–47
Berger, John, 115–16
Berger, Marco, 161, 176
bioecocrítica (Heffes), 90, 102
biosphere, 47, 62, 242, 282–83, 289, 298. *See also* Bosawás Biosphere (Nicaragua)
Blaser, Mario, 70, 281, 290
The Blood of Kouan Kouan (Avgeropolous), 15, 206, 209, 211–13, 215–17, 221, 223
Bodanzky, Jorge, 34, 36, 43n39. See also *Iracema: An Amazonian Love Affair* (Bodanzky and Senna); *Once Upon a Time Iracema* (Bodanzky and Senna)
Boetti, Ezequiel, 162–64
Bolshevik/Russian Revolution, 112, 135n20
Bosawás Biosphere (Nicaragua), 282, 289–91, 294, 296–98

Brazilian dictatorship, 33, 35–36, 41n6
Brazilian government, 27, 33–36, 41n6
Brazilian independence, 30, 40n29
Buñuel, Luis, 121–22; *Los olvidados*, 113, 121. See also humanism

Calderón, Felipe, 305, 318–19
El canto de Bosawas (Castro and Allgood), 16, 282, 289–98
capitalism, 5–6, 61, 127, 181–82, 193, 195; animals and, 115–16, 120–21, 132–33, 135n16; consumerist, 101; critiques of, 111–12, 114, 131; exploitation and, 14, 112, 123, 127, 134, 249n19; extractive, 274, 319, 335–36, 338; global, 182, 185–86, 192–93, 198–99; neocolonial, 236; neoliberal, 209; turbo-, 91, 94, 100; Western, 265; world, 235
Capitalocene, 5, 288, 293, 327
Caribbean Fantasy: Una historia del amor en el Río Ozama (Gómez Terrero), 15, 183, 190–95, 198, 201n33
Caribbean (region), 183, 257, 277n52; Central American films about, 275n15; ecocritical studies about, 275n12; economic development in, 185; landscapes of, 270; stereotypes of, 260–61; tourism in, 277n52. See also Central American Caribbean; Costa Rica: Caribbean coast of; Dominican Republic; Nicaraguan Caribbean
Caribbean Sea, 188, 190–91, 260, 265, 285, 288
El Caribe (Ramírez), 16, 255–56, 259, 261–62
cartography, 76, 79, 84; of desire, 168; elements of, 167; of toxicity, 219; of tropical Latin America, 78

cartoons, 145, 150, 157n2
Central American Caribbean, 16, 255–56, 258–60, 264–65, 273, 275n12
Central American film, 255, 259–60
Cepek, Michael, 212, 224n10
Chile, 78–79; Indigenous activism in, 239; Latin American animation and, 143; national imaginary of, 235; water and, 76. See also Allende, Salvador; Atacama Desert; Guzmán, Patricio; Malis Álvarez, Jossie; *The Pearl Button* (*El botón de nácar*) (Guzmán)
Chimal, Alberto, 49, 58
Cielo abierto (Ruiz), 16, 331–32, 335–36, 338
Cinema Novo/New Cinema (Brazil), 35, 43n43, 113, 124
city-image, 166, 168, 176
civil society, 48, 52, 262
climate: crisis, 3; events, 247; global, 96; patterns, 246; warming of, 235
climate change, 4, 6, 10, 15, 232, 339
coloniality, 5, 90, 92, 97, 101, 234, 270
colonization, 5, 140, 156, 247; Brazilian, 35; British, 266–67; European, 100; of nature, 240; of nonhumans, 148; Spanish, 285
Conley, Tom, 76, 78–79, 167
consumption, 42n25, 99, 142, 185, 198, 277n53; capitalist, 128, 195; cultural, 10; hyper-, 98, 100; hysterical, 91; jouissance, 241; mass, 286; of oil, 207; of peyote, 317; of turtle eggs, 301n26; of turtle meat, 16, 256, 264, 268, 271–72 (*see also* Miskitos); of violence, 117
Cortés, María Lourdes, 259, 261

Costa Rica, 285, 288, 299n11, 301n23; Afro-descendant/Black and Indigenous communities in, 257–58; Caribbean coast of, 255–56, 258, 262–63, 273, 275n26; film industry in, 259 (see also *Caribe* [Ramírez]); hegemonic regions of, 256–57; Limón province, 257, 261, 270, 275–76n26, 276n29; tourism in, 256, 261, 263, 269–70, 273–74; U.S. military operations in, 283. See also government: Costa Rican

Covid-19 pandemic, 223, 274

Crude: The Real Price of Oil (Berlinger), 15, 206, 208–11, 213, 215, 218, 224n9; Indigenous rights and, 221; toxicity and, 216, 223

cultural studies, 259; Latin American, 5, 7

da Cunha, Euclides, 27–28, 41n7

Curotto, Papu, 164, 170–75, 178n25. See also *Esteros* (Curotto)

death, 15, 62, 73, 131, 216, 235, 329, 339; animal, 111–12, 133, 217–18, 222; disaster genre and, 58; human, 111, 114–15, 117, 217, 222, 237; in *Los olvidados* (Buñuel), 121–22; in *Strike* (Eisenstein), 113, 118

decapitation, 17, 329, 335, 338–39; resistance, 17, 331, 334, 336, 338

decolonial: methodology, 8; option, 100–101

deforestation, 13, 34, 36, 95, 235, 293, 299n4, 302n37, 338

De la Cadena, Marisol, 6, 70, 212, 281, 290, 292, 329–31, 337.

De la Torre, Santos, 16, 307, 309–10, 313, 315f, 321, 322n4

DeLoughrey, Elizabeth, 19n25, 182, 235, 248n10, 250n35, 337

Depetris Chauvin, Irene, 19n25, 218

Derrumbe (Esta historia no se olvida) (Carrasco), 56, 60

desire, 14, 164, 169–70, 172–74, 177n8, 237; cartographies of, 168; same-sex, 176 (see also queer desire)

development, 5–6, 29, 124, 140, 143, 145, 154, 273, 335; agricultural, 95; alternate paradigms of, 199; capitalist, 5, 277n53; Dominican, 182–85, 190, 195–96, 198, 200n14; economic, 40n2, 185, 255–56, 260, 270; in Ecuador, 207; extractivist, 12; global, 142; human, 155, 283; hydraulic imaginary of, 192; hydraulic order and, 197; hydraulic power and, 181; industrial, 79, 222; intellectual, 103n14; lack of strategies for, 262; national, 92; neocolonial, 338; obsolete persons and, 197–98; social, 212; socioeconomic, 273; sustainable, 259, 263, 277n53; technological, 44n44, 47; transnational flows and, 193; unequal, 198

developmentalism, 181, 197–98, 337

direct cinema, 282, 285

disaster, 143, 246–47; aestheticization of, 59–60; anthropogenic, 205–206; in *Bendito Machines* (Malis Álvarez), 153–54; ecological, 211; entertainment and, 59; natural, 13, 48, 63, 64n14. See also Mexico City earthquake (1985)

disaster films, 12–13, 61, 63n6, 211

documentary (genre), 6, 12, 20n40, 34, 71, 83, 268, 282; borders with fiction, 74; ethical limits of, 117; left-wing visual politics and, 111; nonhuman animals and, 114; study of, 169

documentary cinema, 13, 70–71, 83, 282

documentary techniques, 34, 43n38
Dominican Republic, 257; cinema and, 14–15; development in, 182–85, 190, 195–96, 198, 200n14; nation-branding in, 182–84, 188–89, 191, 196, 198; poverty in, 14, 182, 187–88, 191–96; tourism and, 182, 185–87, 189–91, 196; visual culture in, 188
drug trafficking, 259, 282, 284, 289

Echevarría, Nicolás, 16, 307–17, 321–22, 323n6, 323n8; *Cabeza de vaca*, 324n26
ecocide, 211–12, 214, 299n7
ecocinema, 29–30, 33, 36, 39, 42nn24–25, 93, 223, 307; affect in, 105n31; as collaborative initiative, 331; *Eco de la montaña* (Echevarría) as, 314, 321; *La libertad* (Guzmán) as, 89–90, 94; Latin American, 9–11, 178n22
ecocritical studies, 145, 178n22, 250n32, 260, 275n12
ecocriticism, 2, 4, 103n14, 146, 157n2, 260
Eco de la montaña (Echevarría), 16, 307–22, 322n2, 323n13
ecology, 83, 90, 98, 101, 102n5, 337; of Bosawás Biosphere, 292; language of, 274; liquid, 182, 184, 218; plant, 75; political, 223, 281, 294; residual, 183, 191, 193, 196–97, 199; social, 213; of toxicity, 217
economic liberalization, 181, 184–86
ecotourism, 6, 256, 262, 273–74, 284
ecoviolences, 91, 93, 96, 101
Eisenstein, Sergei, 63n6, 118, 131, 147; *Desastre en Oaxaca*, 61, 63n6; shock value and, 120; *Strike*, 113, 118, 119f, 128

embodiment, 139; of colonial conquest, 150; extractivism and, 339; nature and, 97, 221; of vision, 8
The Embrace of the Serpent (Guerra), 30, 37–39, 42n28, 44n47
environmental degradation, 3–4, 11, 15, 70, 77–78, 90, 246; in *El Caribe* (Ramírez), 262, 273; development as, 335; politics of mining and, 338; slow violence of, 94–95
environmentalism, 90, 146, 259, 317, 331, 339; Euro-American, 223; Western, 83, 212
environmental issues, 9–10, 30, 42n25, 261, 307
environmental practices, 146, 240
equivocation, 223, 226n35
erotics, 14, 168–70, 173, 178n23
Escobar, Arturo, 6, 185, 342n40
Esteros (Curotto), 14, 161–76, 176–77n3
ethics: of care, 15; environmental, 83, 207; erotics and, 14, 169 (see also *Esteros* [Curotto]); first, 207, 217, 224n5 (*see also* Levinas, Emmanuel); humanimal, 318; liberal humanism and, 221; of New Maricón Cinema, 164; of preservation and regeneration of forms of life, 243; queer, 163; of urban neglect, 196; Wixárika, 308
evidence, 71, 83–84; geological, 73; Indigenous knowledge of the cosmos and, 82
extraction, 6, 8, 140, 153, 198, 242–43, 246–47, 282; capitalist, 151–52; critique of, 14; mining, 335; oil, 206–207, 211–13, 339; resource, 3, 5, 40, 47, 222–23, 234, 236, 313, 338; of tropical wood, 328
extractive zone, 183, 282, 288. *See also* Gómez-Barris, Macarena

extractivism, 70–71, 84, 124, 339; Amazonian, 33; capitalism and, 116

face-to-face encounter, 1, 214
Farmacopea (Santiago Muñoz), 13, 70–71, 73–78, 83–84
Farocki, Harun, 231–32, 236, 248n5
film festivals, 9–11, 92, 96, 209, 255, 300n16; animation and, 143–44, 157n12; mestizo audiences and, 310
film industry: Costa Rican, 259; in Latin America, 8, 143; Mexican, 54, 63n2
filmmaking, 7, 17; collective, 336; cost of, 10; documentary, 9, 285, 290; left-wing cinema and, 112; political, 233; process of, 77, 179n27; technologies of, 232
film studies, 4, 260
flow, 182–84; audiovisual, 190; control, 187–88; infrastructures of, 192, 195; power of, 197; transnational, 198
Fornoff, Carolyn, 13, 260, 299n2
Forns-Broggi, Roberto, 7, 100, 178n22, 223
found footage, 60, 114, 135n19, 309, 314
Fredriksson, Anthony, 220–21
freedom, 102, 133, 181, 234; civil, 239; of handheld cameras, 75; human, 240; of movement, 60; ontonoetic, 218; of religion, 212–13
Fuentes-León, Javier, 163, 176
Furtado, Jorge, 113, 132; *Ilha das flores*, 132–33
futurism, 141–43, 150

Garibotto, Verónica, 29, 34
gender, 4–5, 161–62, 176, 291, 330; difference, 164; violence, 36
geoepistemology, 70, 78–79

geography, 170, 174, 246; of the Americas, 71; Argentine cinema and, 161; Chile's national, 76, 79; Mexican, 316; natural, 167*f*, 168; of Nicaragua's Atlantic coast, 282; plant, 72, 80; of Tierra del Fuego, 81
geological, the, 47, 49. *See also* agency: geological; Mexico City earthquake (1985)
geosphere, 13, 47, 62
globalization, 181, 183–85, 189, 196, 211, 233, 248n10, 259, 262
Global North, 97; art-house cinema circuit in, 98; funders in, 10
Global South, 92; environmental collapse in, 4; filmmakers, 10
Goethe, Johann Wolfgang von, 79–80, 197
Gómez-Barris, Macarena, 8, 19n25, 70, 183, 265, 282–83, 286
Gómez Terrero, Johanné, 183, 190–92
González Pérez, José Miguel, 266–67
government: Argentinian, 73, 92; Brazilian, 27, 33–36, 41n6; Chilean, 73 (*see also* Allende, Salvador; Pinochet, Augusto); Costa Rican, 262–63, 276n26; Ecuadoran, 212, 220; funding for environmental film festivals, 11; Mexican, 48, 53–54, 56–57, 63n6, 305, 309, 314, 321 (see also *7:19: La hora del temblor* [Grau]; Mexico City earthquake [1985]; Oaxaca earthquake [1931]); Nicaraguan, 256, 258, 267–68, 272–73, 277n47, 283, 290, 294, 299n7, 300n19 (*see also* Sandinista Revolution)
Grau, Jorge Michel, 49, 57–59, 62. See also *7:19* (Grau)
Guatemala, 63n6, 256

Index

Guerra, Ciro, 37–38, 44n48, 44nn50–52. See also *The Embrace of the Serpent* (Guerra)
Guerrero, Francisco, 49, 51. See also *Trágico terremoto en México (Furia terrenal)* (Guerrero)
Guzmán, Patricio, 15, 73, 76–77, 79, 82–83, 232–41, 243–47, 248n8, 249n24, 250n34; *The Battle of Chile/La batalla de Chile*, 135n19, 233, 235; *The Cordillera of Dreams/La cordillera de los sueños*, 232, 234. See also *Nostalgia de la luz/Nostalgia for the Light* (Guzmán); *The Pearl Button* (*El botón de nacar*) (Guzmán); satellite images

Hageman, Andrew, 98, 100
hapticity, 90, 94, 96, 101, 164, 170–71
Haraway, Donna, 5, 8, 149, 317
Heffes, Gisela, 7, 16–17, 90, 260, 301n24
Heise, Ursula, 140, 145–47
La hora de los hornos (*The Hour*) (Solanas and Getino), 9, 113, 127–28, 129f
Huidobro, Vicente, 231, 242, 248n5
human activity, 4, 50, 255
humanimal assemblages, 111–14, 116–18, 124, 126–27, 130–33, 135n18; in *Araya* (Bencerraf), 122, 124; Buñuel's, 121
humanimals, 123, 126–27
humanism, 15, 112, 121–22, 126, 128, 143, 221, 223, 234, 284; narratives of, 14, 115, 117–18, 127, 130, 134
human rights, 15, 207, 211, 221–22, 237, 302n33, 339; discourse of, 219, 239–40; ethos, 234; judicial documentary and, 248n14; liberal, 212, 239; Pinochet regime abuses of, 232–33
Humboldt, Alexander von, 13, 26, 70–72, 75–77, 79–81, 83
hunting, 324n22; scenes, 32–33, 43n32, 287. See also shark hunting
hydraulic infrastructures, 184, 194, 199n6
hydraulic order, 15, 182–84, 190, 192–93, 196–99
hydraulic power, 182, 187

Illich, Ivan, 194, 198
illness, 214–19, 321, 339. See also toxicity
indigeneity, 12, 212, 288, 324n26, 330; in *Eco de la montaña* (Echevarría), 306, 315–16, 319, 321; in *The Embrace of the Serpent* (Guerra), 44n47
Indigenous communities, 38, 257–58, 269, 273, 321
Indigenous genocide, 5, 211–13, 238
Indigenous land, 302n37, 328, 334; rights, 84
Indigenous peoples, 6, 44n52, 213, 223, 225n18, 236, 256, 269–70, 277n42, 288, 309, 319, 321; cinematic depictions of, 42n28, 44nn47–48, 83, 272; colonial erasure of, 4; exclusion of, 337; genocide of, 50, 211; knowledge of the cosmos and, 82, 242–43; memory of, 238; misconceptions about, 208; modernity and, 240; South American, 44n53. See also Kawésqar people; Mayangna people; Miskitos; Native Amazonian; Selk'nam people; Wixárika/Wixáritari (Huichol) peoples; Yamana people
Indigenous rights, 211, 213, 250n34, 302n36; activists, 208; narratives, 221

Indio Maíz Biological Reserve, 273, 284, 299n7
Industrial Revolution, 111, 114
infrastructure, 235, 290; in the Dominican Republic, 182, 185, 187–88, 190, 192, 195–96; human, 154; hydraulic power and, 182, 184, 194, 199n6; in Mexico City, 50; national exhibition, 12; precarious, 28
interspecies: cohabitation, 111, 124, 131; communication, 317; dynamics, 287; politics of survival, 122; relations, 113, 120, 312
Iracema: An Amazonian Love Affair (Bodanzky and Senna), 30, 33–36, 43nn38–39, 43n41, 43–44nn43–44, 44n47. See also *Once Upon a Time Iracema* (Bodanzky and Senna)
Ivakhiv, Adrian, 7, 260

Kane, Adrian Taylor, 19n25, 260
Kawésqar people, 82–83, 236, 243–45, 250n40

labor, 55, 142, 234, 237, 259, 320, 339; human, 13; manual, 128, 190; organized, 54; precarious, 187; slave, 5; social, 206; volunteer, 11; women's, 54–55, 291
Latin American history: centering animals in, 113; slow violence and, 142
Latour, Bruno, 246, 301n31
Lefebvre, Martin, 29, 41n22, 104n27
Leff, Enrique, 5, 48
left-wing cinema, 111–12, 114, 116
Levinas, Emmanuel, 214, 224n5. See also ethics: first; face-to-face encounter
La libertad (Alonso), 7, 13, 89–102, 104n21, 104n25, 105n28, 105n30

Lih Wina (Torres), 7, 16, 255–56, 259, 264–69, 271–74, 276n29
Littín, Miguel, 283–84, 299n12
Lola (Navarro), 56, 62

MacDonald, Scott, 29–30, 42nn24–25, 91, 94. See also ecocinema
Malig, Emma, 76, 245
Malis Álvarez, Jossie, 14, 139–40, 143–44, 147, 150, 156. See also *Bendito Machine* (Malis Álvarez)
Marcone, Jorge, 7, 337
marginality, 92, 97, 182, 191–93
Martinez Alier, Joan, 213, 225, 227, 328–29, 339–41
Marx, Karl, 149, 239
materiality, 3, 62, 172, 221; of celluloid film, 76, 206; of encounter, 15, 206; of the filmic image, 214, 222; of media, 47; of oil, 205; of suffering, 216
Mayangna people, 289, 296–97, 302n42; Bosawás Biosphere and, 292, 294; musical practices of, 282, 291, 295
memory, 77, 238–40, 242; collective, 233; cultural, 57; genetic, 310, 313; of illness, 214, 216; social, 234, 236, 240; sources of, 73
mestizo nation, 309, 314, 319–20, 322
mestizos, 257, 267, 269, 277n42, 301n29
Menem, Carlos, 92–93, 100
Mexican cinema, 47, 52, 62
Mexican Revolution, 48, 57
Mexico City earthquake (1985), 13, 48–49, 62–63; commemoration of, 65n28; corruption and, 50, 56, 58, 61, 63; as human encounter with geology, 47–48; trauma of, 48, 50, 57–60. See also *7:19: La hora del*

temblor (Grau); *Lola* (Navarro); *No les pedimos un viaje a la luna* (De Lara); *Trágico terremoto en México (Furia terrenal)* (Guerrero)
Mexico City earthquake (2017), 49, 51, 60, 64n17
Mignolo, Walter, 6, 71, 92, 100–101
mining, 17, 48, 281, 338; in *Cielo abierto* (Ruiz), 335; companies, 306, 318, 328–29, 331–32, 334, 337; concessions, 277n42, 305–306; conflicts, 330, 339; in *Courage of the People* (Sajinés and Ukamau Group), 336; earthquakes and, 50; gold, 328, 332; industry, 235, 291, 306; in Latin America, 152
Miskitos, 256–57, 271, 277n47; British encounters with, 266, 276n36; consumption of turtle meat, 16, 256, 264, 268, 271–72; turtle fishing and, 264–66, 276n37; turtle-fishing ban and, 268, 272–73
modernity, 90, 95, 143, 151, 247; Amazonian travel films and, 29, 35, 44n44; capitalist, 116; colonialism and, 142; displaced, 286; the Dominican Republic and, 186; Indigenous peoples and, 213, 240, 312; late, 205; Latin American countries and, 28; in *La libertad* (Alonso) 97–100, 105n27, 105n30; national cinematic, 168; neoliberal, 90, 92; postcolonial, 232, 239; urban, 184, 194; Western, 92, 97, 112, 338. *See also* petromodernity
modernization, 37, 43n43, 212; the Amazon and, 208; in Argentina, 95; of transportation, 154
Monani, Salma, 30, 337
Morton, Timothy, 90, 97
Mosquitia, 258, 265

national identity, 70, 76, 189; criollo-mestizo, 259; mestizo, 307; Mexican, 323n13
nationalism, 15, 36, 292; *mestizo*, 313
Native Amazonian: communities, 44n47; cultures, 39, 42n28; populations, 38, 43n41, 208–209
natural disaster films, 13, 53, 63. *See also 7:19* (Grau)
natural disasters, 13, 48–49, 61, 64n17. *See also* Mexico City earthquake (1985)
natural resources, 78, 98; in the Central American Caribbean, 273; Chile's, 79; cinema and, 47; conflicts over, 332; exploitation of, 151, 318, 332; extraction of, 3, 222–23; media texts and systems and, 338
nature documentaries, 2, 210, 218
Negrin da Silva, Diana, 311–12
neoliberalism, 100–101, 143; slow violence of, 95, 98. *See also* economic liberalization
New Latin American Cinema, 113, 120–21, 131, 133, 169
New Maricón Cinema, 163–64, 165*f*, 168, 174, 178n22, 178n24
new materialism, 7–8, 145–46, 158n21, 207. *See also* object-oriented ontologies (OOO)
Nicaragua, 267–68, 271, 273, 276n41, 301n23; Atlantic coast of, 258, 281–84, 294, 298, 300n15 (*see also* Nicaraguan Caribbean); cattle industry in, 302n37; cinema of, 259; Contra War, 283, 299n11; deforestation in, 299n4; hegemonic regions of, 256–57, 266; Región Autónoma Costa Atlántica Norte (RAAN), 258, 264, 281–83, 301nn28–29; Región Autónoma Costa Atlántica Sur (RAAS), 258,

Nicaragua *(continued)*
  281–82, 284; U.S. support of, 276n41; Zelaya government, 267, 277n47
Nicaraguan Caribbean, 16, 255–56, 264–69, 271, 273, 276n41, 277n47; Black and Indigenous communities in, 267, 269, 271–72 (*see also* Miskitos)
Nichols, Bill, 71, 169, 221, 309
Nixon, Rob, 90–91, 328, 338
No les pedimos un viaje a la luna (De Lara), 49, 54–56, 59–60, 62
nonhuman, the, 146, 156, 232, 234, 241; animal, 14, 112–13, 116–18, 124, 127, 131; animation and, 14; in *Bendito Machine*, 149–50; cinema and, 1–2, 9, 13–14 (*see also* Tablada, José Juan); environment, 7; in Latin American cinema, 12, 17; other, 317; representations of, 8; world, 62–63, 98, 265, 337
Nostalgia de la luz/Nostalgia for the Light (Guzmán), 15, 232, 234–36, 240–43

Oaxaca earthquake (1931), 61, 63n6
object-oriented ontologies (OOO), 140, 145–48, 153, 156, 248n8
Offen, Karl, 265–66, 271
oil, 226n31; boom, 8; companies, 100, 208, 211–12, 217, 256, 262–63, 269–70; Ecuador and, 207–208, 210–11; executives, 153; exploration, 263, 269–70; extraction, 47, 206–207, 211–13, 339; fields, 187; industry, 211–13, 225n11; materiality of, 205; pollution, 208, 214, 217–20, 222; prices, 63n2; spills, 15, 151–52, 207–208, 210, 216–17, 220, 250n34; Venezuelan cinema and, 8, 19n31; viscosity of, 220–21. *See also* petromodernity; toxicity
Ojo del tiburón (Hoijman), 7, 16
Once Upon a Time Iracema (Bodanzky and Senna), 34, 36, 43n39
Operación diablo (Boyd), 16, 331–32, 333f, 336, 338
Ospina, Luis, 113, 131; *Cali de Película*, 131–32
otherness, 210, 215, 258, 260

Padilla, Ignacio, 48, 50, 57
Page, Joanna, 19n25, 100, 157n14
Partido Revolucionario Institucional (PRI), 48, 52, 56–57
The Pearl Button (*El botón de nácar*) (Guzmán), 13, 15, 70–71, 73, 76–77, 79–84, 232, 234, 236, 238, 242–45
pedagogy, 14; of action, 130; humanistic, 127; moral, 116; violence as, 118
Pereira dos Santos, Nelson, 126; *Vidas secas* (*Barren Lives*), 113, 124
Pérez, Jorge, 29, 34
petromodernity, 205–207, 211, 213
peyote, 308, 310–11, 314–15, 317, 324n22. *See also* Vilchez: Hernán: *Huicholes: los últimos guardianes del peyote*
Pinochet dictatorship, 232, 237
pluriverse (Blaser and de la Cadena), 6, 15, 44n53, 70, 281, 294–95, 297
pollution, 192; in *Bendito Machine* (Malis Álvarez), 140, 151–52; in the Dominican Republic, 14, 182, 198; in Ecuadoran Amazon, 206, 208, 211; farmland, 219; mining and, 328, 338–39; oil, 208, 214, 217–18,

222; sound and light, 19n29; water, 152, 217–18, 338
porosity, 15, 206–207, 215, 217, 220–23, 243
posthumanism, 2, 4–5, 7, 157n14; ethos of, 3; filmmaking, 17; *Kino-Eye* (Vertov) and, 113, 120
poverty, 10, 120–22, 130, 181; in the Caribbean region, 261; in Costa Rica, 275–79n26; in the Dominican Republic, 14, 182, 187–88, 191–96; in the Global South, 92; sustainable development and, 277n53
Puenzo, Lucía, 161, 178n24
Puerto Rico, 76–77, 190. See also *Farmacopea* (Santiago Muñoz)

queer desire, 14, 168, 175–76

Ramírez, Esteban, 255, 261, 296. See also *Caribe* (Ramírez)
Rice, Alexander Hamilton, 27, 31, 78
Ríos, Humberto, 113, 127–28, 131; *Faena*, 113, 127–28, 130
The River of Doubt, 43n32, 78
River Ozama, 15, 183, 188, 190–92, 195–96, 198, 200n14
road movies, 12–13, 28, 34, 40; Amazonian travel cinema and, 28–30; *Eco de la montaña* (Echevarría) as, 309
Rocha, Glauber, 123–26; *Deus e o diabo na terra do sol*, 113, 124, 125f
Roosevelt, Theodore, 43n32, 78
Ruffinelli, Jorge, 161, 163
Rust, Steven, 30, 337

Salgado Bautista, Diego Augusto, 319, 323n8
Salles, Walter, 34, 43n38
Sandinista Revolution, 256, 258, 267

Santiago Muñoz, Beatriz, 13, 73–74, 77, 83. See also *Farmacopea* (Santiago Muñoz)
Santos, Silvino, 30–31, 33, 37, 42n30; *In the Land of the Amazons*, 30–34, 43n33, 44n47
satellite images, 232, 242–43, 249n23
Schiwy, Freya, 223, 336
science fiction, 59, 142, 156
scientific knowledge, 71–72, 83, 263
sea turtles, 265; consumption of, 256, 264, 272–73 (*see also* turtle meat); preservation of, 271, 276n29
Selk'nam people, 82, 84, 236
sensory perception, 69–70, 72, 76, 81, 83
sexuality, 5, 161–62, 176, 178n23, 179n28, 330; awakening of, 171; queer, 167
shark hunting, 16, 284, 288–89
slaughter, 114, 117, 120, 127; animal, 14, 32, 115, 117, 131, 133–34, 287; cattle, 113, 118; images of, 128; pedagogy of, 14, 130, 133
slaughterhouses, 113, 115–18, 120, 126–28, 130–31, 135n8, 136n27
slavery, 5, 276n36
slow cinema, 12–13, 61, 90–95, 101. See also Alonso, Lisandro
slow violence (Nixon), 96–97, 101, 142, 224n2; environmental, 13, 90–91, 93–95, 246; of neoliberalism, 95, 98; toxicity and, 205. See also slow cinema
socialism, 121; democratic, 233
solidarity, 49, 52, 57, 59, 62, 64n17; with Wixáritari peoples, 306
sovereignty, 216, 237, 240, 301n23; cultural, 256; Indigenous, 84; national, 267
spectatorship, 93, 169

Spivak, Gayatri, 232, 248n10
Stengers, Isabelle, 207, 223, 340n10
subalterns, 90–91, 97, 271–72, 297
submerged perspectives, 8–9, 183, 283.
    See also Gómez-Barris, Macarena
suffering, 60, 111, 215–16; animal,
    114, 117, 127–28, 134, 218; face of
    the other, 224n5; human, 214, 219
Swanstrom, Elizabeth, 140, 145–47,
    153
Swift (Gleyzer), 113, 127, 130

Tablada, José Juan, 1–2
Teja, Leonardo, 50, 57
testimonial narrative/*testimonio*, 16, 52,
    54, 221, 290, 297
testimony, 233–34, 297–98; spatial,
    185
Third Cinema, 113, 122, 126, 135n19
Tierra del Fuego, 80–81; Indigenous
    inhabitants of, 73, 76, 79, 83
Tire dié (Birri), 113, 122
Tlatelolco massacre, 48, 57
Torres, Dania, 255, 264–65, 271–72.
    See also *Lih Wina* (Torres)
toxicity, 15, 206–207, 213–17,
    219–23, 232, 246
toxic contamination, 217, 221
*Trágico terremoto en México (Furia
    terrenal)* (Guerrero), 49, 51–56,
    58–59, 62, 63n7
Trans-Amazonian Highway, 33–34, 36.
    See also *Iracema: An Amazonian Love
    Affair* (Bodanzky and Senna)
travelogues, 27, 30–31, 78
travel writing, 26, 39, 71, 83, 260,
    291
Trujillo, Rafael Leónidas, 195,
    199–200n14
Tuhiwai Smith, Linda, 291, 299n10
turtle fishing, 268, 272–73, 276n37
turtle meat, 16, 256, 264, 266, 268,
    271–73

Uexküll, Jakob, 69–70. See also sensory
    perception
underdevelopment, 43n43, 123–24,
    128
uninhabitants (Nixon), 91, 93, 97–101
United Nations, 305–306, 309, 319

Vertov, Dziga, 114, 118, 120–21, 131,
    135n21; *Kino-Eye*, 113, 118
Vilchez, Hernán, 305, 322n2, 323n6;
    *Huicholes: los últimos guardianes del
    peyote*, 305–307, 314, 317, 319,
    322n2, 322n6
violence, 59, 90–91, 94, 121; against
    animals, 115–17, 133–34; in *Barren
    Lives (Vidas secas)* (Pereira dos
    Santos), 124; in *Bendito Machines*
    (Malis Álvarez), 144, 154, 156;
    in Buñuel's films, 122; capitalist,
    14, 120, 133, 338; of collapsing
    buildings, 60; colonial, 239–40,
    274, 321; of COVID-19 pandemic,
    223; disabled ecologies and, 327;
    of dominant paradigms, 197–98;
    in ecocinema, 332; ecological, 13,
    33, 36, 96 (*see also* ecoviolences);
    of economic extractivism, 70;
    environmental, 328; in *Faena* (Ríos),
    127; founding, 232; in *The Hour
    (La hora de los hornos)* (Solanas and
    Getino), 128; hydraulic power and,
    187; lettered, 267; narco, 58, 259;
    of nonhuman animal suffering, 134;
    in *El ojo del tiburón* (Hoijman),
    287; self-, 98; settler, 236; spectacle
    of, 116, 134n7; state, 84, 285, 334;
    in *Swift* (Gleyzer), 127, 130; in
    testimonials, 297; toxicity and, 205.
    See also slow violence
viscosity, 15, 206, 215, 217, 222; of
    oil, 220–21
Viveiros de Castro, Eduardo, 6, 116,
    158n21. See also new materialism

Wavrin, Marquis of, 27, 31
Western Patagonia, 76, 81
When Clouds Clear (Bernstein and Slick), 16, 331–34, 336, 338
Willoquet-Maricondi, Paula, 30, 277n49, 314
Wirikuta, 305–309, 311–15, 317–22
Wixárika/Wixáritari (Huichol) peoples, 305–307, 309, 311–19, 321–22, 322–23n6; cosmology of, 16, 307–308, 310, 318–21. *See also* peyote; Vilchez: Hernán: *Huicholes: los últimos guardianes del peyote*
working class, 116, 135n16; consciousness of, 235
Xavier, Ismail, 35, 43n43

Yamana people, 82, 84
YouTube, 11–12, 51, 143
Yúdice, George, 257–58, 277n52

zoos, 1, 116, 134n7

www.ingramcontent.com/pod-product-compliance
Lightning Source LLC
Chambersburg PA
CBHW020219240426
43672CB00006B/361